A

Philip E. Lilienthal

BOOK 181 - 197
206-214

The Philip E. Lilienthal imprint
honors special books
in commemoration of a man whose work
at University of California Press from 1954 to 1979
was marked by dedication to young authors
and to high standards in the field of Asian Studies.
Friends, family, authors, and foundations have together
endowed the Lilienthal Fund, which enables UC Press
to publish under this imprint selected books
in a way that reflects the taste and judgment
of a great and beloved editor.

-222-227
234-251

276-281
318-324
328-335

Rediscovering America

TWENTIETH-CENTURY JAPAN:
THE EMERGENCE OF A WORLD POWER
Irwin Scheiner, Editor

Rediscovering America

Japanese Perspectives
on the American Century

EDITED BY

Peter Duus and Kenji Hasegawa

UNIVERSITY OF CALIFORNIA PRESS
Berkeley · Los Angeles · London

University of California Press, one of the most distinguished university presses in the United States, enriches
lives around the world by advancing scholarship in
the humanities, social sciences, and natural sciences.
Its activities are supported by the UC Press Foundation
and by philanthropic contributions from individuals
and institutions. For more information, visit
www.ucpress.edu.

University of California Press
Berkeley and Los Angeles, California

University of California Press, Ltd.
London, England

© 2011 by The Regents of the University of California

Library of Congress Cataloging-in-Publication Data

Rediscovering America : Japanese perspectives on
the American century / edited by Peter Duus and Kenji
Hasegawa.
    p.   cm.   — (Twentieth-century Japan ; 19)
   Includes bibliographical references.
   ISBN 978-0-520-26843-2 (cloth : alk. paper)
   ISBN 978-0-520-26845-6 (pbk. : alk. paper)
   1. United States—Foreign public opinion, Japanese.
2. United States—Civilization—20th century—Foreign
public opinion, Japanese. 3. Public opinion—Japan.
4. United States—Relations—Japan. 5. Japan—
Relations—United States. I. Duus, Peter.
II. Hasegawa, Kenji.
   E183.8.J3R37 2011
   327.7305209'04—dc22   2011004433

Manufactured in the United States of America

20 19 18 17 16 15 14 13 12 11
10 9 8 7 6 5 4 3 2 1

In keeping with a commitment to support environmentally
responsible and sustainable printing practices, UC Press
has printed this book on Rolland Enviro100, a 100%
post-consumer fiber paper that is FSC certified, deinked,
processed chlorine-free, and manufactured with renewable
biogas energy. It is acid-free and EcoLogo certified.

Contents

Illustrations

Acknowledgments

For assistance in the preparation of translations for this volume, we would like to thank Caroline Hirasawa and Aaron Skabelund. Our thanks also go to Columbia University Press for granting permission to use existing translations.

We are grateful to the following for permission to translate copyrighted material: Asahi Shinbunsha, Furusawa Yūko, Honda Katsuichi, Hyun Sunhye, Kagawa Tokuaki, Kita Hiroshi, Mutō Shunkō, Nakano Konjirō, Nihon Bungeika Kyōkai, Ōe Kenzaburō, Saeki Shōichi, Sakanishi Yūko, Sakano Tsunekazu, Satō Tadao, Shimomura Mitsuko, Yasuoka Shōtarō, Yomota Inuhiko, and Yoshida Ruiko.

And we would also like to thank the following for permission to use material for illustrations: Mizuno Ryōtarō, Nasu Miyo, and Yamada Shin.

And finally we are indebted to Robin Whitaker and Jacqueline Volin for their thoughtful and thorough editing of the volume manuscript.

Introduction

I.

Ever since the Frenchman Michel-Guillaume Crèvecoeur wrote his famous *Letters from an American Farmer* (1782), foreign visitors and sojourners in the United States have been alternately attracted and repelled, dazzled and distressed, inspired and irritated, awed and angered by their encounters with America. For Crèvecoeur, the country was full of promise. It welcomed all comers to its shores, and it offered them opportunities they could not find at home. "Here," he wrote, "individuals of all nations are melted into a new race of men, whose labours and posterity will one day cause great change in the world."[1] Unlike most visitors, Crèvecoeur chose to become part of that "new race" and spent much of his adult life on his farm in New York.

For other outsiders, however, America was a country rife with flaws and contradictions. Even if impressed by American freedom, openness, and energy, visitors were also appalled by American vulgarity, materialism, and racism. "What can be said about America, which simultaneously horrifies, delights, calls forth pity, and sets examples worthy of emulation, about a land which is rich, poor, talented and ungifted?" wrote two visitors from the Soviet Union in the 1930s. "It is interesting to observe this country, but one does not care to live in it."[2] Perhaps Crèvecoeur himself might have benefited from their perspective. When he returned to his farm in 1783 after a three-year absence in France, he found his house burned down, his wife dead, and his children living with strangers. If America was a land of promise, it was also a land of violence.

Most Japanese visitors to America in the twentieth century shared the deep ambivalence of the Soviet writers rather than the dewy admiration of Crèvecoeur. They veered between respect for America and repulsion from America, careening giddily from adulation to hostility, then back to adulation again. Some have argued that this reflects a much longer love-hate relationship with the West that reaches back to the mid-sixteenth century, when warring Japanese barons at first welcomed Jesuit missionaries, only to crucify them and their converts a generation later. Perhaps so. But swings between respect and repulsion, adulation and hostility have also characterized Japanese interactions with China.

In any case, the "love-hate" dichotomy hardly does justice to the complexity of modern Japanese perspectives on the United States. It over-simplifies their range, and it ignores the fact that positive and negative perspectives have often gone hand in hand. As one postwar Japanese observer noted, "Can someone who is close to us sometimes be our enemy and our conqueror, sometimes our lover and our teacher, and moreover our dominator too? If we assume that such a person can exist, then our feelings and our understanding about him would be extremely complicated. For the Japanese, the United States of America is a country just like such a person."[3] It became so only during the "American Century," when for better or for worse, the United States emerged as one of the world's hegemonic nations.

To the Japanese, America was a country difficult to fully understand because it was so different from their own. It was a country without a center, its people lacked a common ethnic heritage, its historical memory was short, and its geographical expanse was vast. Americans valued the present over the past, and they valued the future over the present. Over-flowing with self-confidence, they saw themselves as the best in the world in everything from natural scenery to technological ingenuity. "There is no country in the world more prone to thinking in a self-centered way than America," noted the politician and social critic Tsurumi Yūsuke.[4] It was a "land of exaggeration" where self-promotion was admired as a positive trait, not a defect to be corrected.

Japanese observers, of course, have exaggerated the United States in their own way. It is a commonplace that while Americans tend to look at Japan through the larger end of the telescope, making it seem smaller than it really is, the Japanese tend to look at America through the smaller end, making it seem bigger. Of course, when the Japanese felt themselves on the leading edge of history, as they did in the 1940s and the 1980s, they also looked through the larger end, making America appear smaller, poorer, and weaker. In either case, the distortions were substantial. For that reason, pendulum swings between overestimating and underestimating America are more useful to examine than swings between love and hate. What they reveal is not an enduring repertoire of attitudes toward America so much as an unstable menu of moods that reflected shifts in the power relations between the two countries.

II.

Until the turn of the twentieth century, Japanese impressions of America were fairly simple—and usually positive. To the earliest Japanese visitors, America and its people appeared exotic, confusing, or opaque. As a leader of the first diplomatic mission to the United States in 1860 wrote in his diary, "So strange is everything, their language, their appearance, / That I feel as if living in a dream-land."[5] But as Japanese began to travel abroad after the Meiji Restoration in search of "new knowledge" to build the country's wealth and strength, they had a clearer idea of what they wanted to know about America. In 1871–72 the Iwakura Mission, a delegation of the country's new leaders on a diplomatic tour around the world, spent its first nine months visiting San Francisco, Washington, New York, and Boston. As the mission's leader, Prince Iwakura Tomomi, told the American Congress, "We came for enlightenment and we gladly found it here."[6]

The United States at first served as a mentor, if not a model, for the Japanese as they sought to elevate themselves as a "civilized" country. American advisers helped Japan to build a new school system, develop its frontier on the northern island of Hokkaido, and carry on negotiations with other countries; the American banking system inspired the government's first attempt to build national financial institutions; the first generation of Japanese elementary-school children studied American school textbooks translated into Japanese; American missionary schools and colleges attracted bright and ambitious young men (and a few young women) seeking to absorb "new knowledge"; and America even provided new cultural heroes like Benjamin Franklin, a hardworking, practical-minded philosopher embodying the spirit of "self-help," which the Japanese had come to admire so much.

At the turn of the twentieth century, the image of the United States as mentor persisted, embraced by businessmen as trade between the two countries grew, but the intertwining of Japanese and American foreign policy in new ways produced a set of more complicated, and potentially more hostile, perspectives. Both countries were new nations on the march, both had become colonial powers in the Pacific, and both were stirred by a sense that it was their own mission to change the world. Inevitably Japanese politicians, journalists, scholars, and intellectuals came to view America as a strategic rival, and military and naval planners came to regard it as a potential combatant in the Pacific. Frictions also arose over legal and social discrimination toward Japanese immigrants in the United States, particularly on the West Coast. Naturally this confluence of issues nurtured an undercurrent of anti-American sentiment during the 1910s and 1920s, when paranoid alarmists on both sides of the Pacific wrote popular novels that imagined future conflicts between the two countries.

By the end of World War I, enormous changes in the United States that had resulted from its rapid industrial and technological development during the early twentieth century created another set of perspectives in Japan. America was not only a mentor, rival, and potential enemy; it was also an economic giant, a multiethnic immigrant society, and the cradle of a new urban popular culture—a jumble of perceptions hard to describe as either "love" or "hate." Many Japanese observers realized that America had become a huge and unpredictable country likely to have an impact on Japan in countless ways, and they sought to understand what kind of society it had. During the 1920s, Japanese visitors and observers began to construct ethnographies that attempted to define the essence of an "American spirit" or an "American national character." In doing so they became bystanders in dialogues the Americans were having among themselves about their own society and culture, and the Japanese often blended these dialogues with reflections about Japanese culture. Definitions of American "national character," however, could easily be reified into politically useful stereotypes.

To be sure, before World War II, America did not occupy a central place in the mind of the Japanese intelligentsia, who had looked mainly to Europe for intellectual and cultural inspiration since the Meiji period. It was in Europe, not in America, that they discovered elevated intellectual and artistic discourse. The debates of Europe's philosophers and literati fascinated Japanese academics in the 1920s, especially after Marxism erupted in Japanese universities, and during the 1930s, European political experiments—including fascism and national socialism—rather than the New Deal's attempts to salvage capitalism engaged their curiosity. Until the eve of war, intellectual journals and general-interest magazines paid scant attention to Americans, except to puzzle over what their intentions in Asia might be.

When war broke out in 1941, positive perspectives toward the United States were immediately supplanted by hostile and negative ones. While the word *love* overstates the intensity of respect that some prewar Japanese intellectuals felt toward America, *hate* hardly exaggerates the passionate intensity of wartime anti-American sentiment. The war in the Pacific, as John Dower has pointed out, was a "war without mercy." Like their American counterparts, the Japanese intelligentsia echoed official propaganda that viewed the enemy as a barbarous, cruel, inhuman, and bent on "world domination." They also heaped all the sins of Western imperialism on Americans, arguing that that they were no different from the European allies they were ardently defending, especially Britain and France.

While American intellectuals working for the wartime effort attempted, however ineptly, to undertake a serious analysis of the "Japanese national character" to understand their opponents, Japanese intellectuals cranked out virtual images of America, recycling stereotypes established in the 1920s to belittle its strengths and exaggerate its weaknesses. If the Americans tried to put Japan under a sociological microscope, the Japanese intelligentsia deployed self-referential comparisons with America to define Japan as "purer" than the enemy. Their dominant themes were that America had a material "civilization" *(bunmei)* but not a spiritual "culture" *(bunka)* and that, in the end, Japanese "spirit" would overcome American-style "modernity." A few intellectuals who had lived or studied in the United States attempted to provide a more nuanced (albeit critical) understanding of the Americans, but in the end their voices were drowned out by the roar of popular patriotism.[7]

Defeat in 1945 brought seven years of an American occupation intent on transforming Japan into a "peace-loving democracy." It was the first time in their recorded history that the Japanese experienced such direct and prolonged contact with a foreign people and its culture. The American presence was ubiquitous, and the Americans did their best to present a positive image of their country. Several hundred thousand American troops and their families living in a network of bases and housing areas across the country introduced the Japanese to the affluence of American material culture, and the media inundated the public with a flood of American popular culture, from uplifting articles in *Reader's Digest* to Hollywood movies that were uniformly upbeat and appreciative of the American way of life. In a sense, the Occupation created an "America-in-Japan" that became a central element in perceptions of Americans.

For some Japanese the Occupation was a liberating experience; for others it was a humiliating one. For most it was probably both. "To be occupied by foreign troops is, of course, an unbearable humiliation, but if that is our fate we must be patient," wrote one commentator in August 1945.[8] The best course, he suggested, was not to resist but to turn misfortune into an advantage, learning from Westerners in order to achieve parity with them, as the Japanese had done in the Meiji period. Many Japanese intellectuals and academics cooperated with the Occupation authorities in shaping and carrying out American reforms, and by the Occupation's end many had even begun to criticize the Americans for not carrying out even more sweeping changes. But none could deny the extraordinary impact of the American attempt to build a "New Japan."

Although the Japanese public welcomed the return of independence when the Occupation ended in 1952, America remained an unavoidable presence, not only in a cultural sense, but also in a physical one. As a condition of the return of full sovereignty, the Japanese government signed a mutual defense treaty with the United States, and American troops remained in Japan, ostensibly to protect the country from outside attack. While many Japanese were apprehensive about their country's strategic ties with the United States, American fashions, American fads, American pop music, American movies, and American brands continued to mesmerize the Japanese consumer, and public-opinion polls continued to rank the United States at or near the top of the list of "most respected/admired countries" in the world.

During the 1950s there was a burst of anti-American sentiment, particularly among intellectuals on the left, who were disappointed that the United States had chosen to turn Japan into a Cold War client state. In a sense, America had become a new kind of adversary that blocked Japan's emergence as a peaceful, nonaligned country. Intellectuals on the right, still smarting from the humiliation of defeat, turned a critical eye on the Occupation's assault on "traditional" institutions and values and launched a campaign to reverse many educational and cultural reforms promoted by the Americans. Oddly enough, many on the right also accepted the country's dependence on the United States for its defense, and most envied the economic strength and affluence that Americans enjoyed.

The generation that came of age during the postwar years was steeped in American influence. For them America was not an adversary but a country that, for better or worse, had transformed their lives, more often than not for the good. It was they who experienced most intensely a new sense of freedom nurtured by the Americans. They were attracted not only by the openness of the Americans but also by the "dryness" (i.e., un-sentimentality) of American culture in contrast to the "wetness" (i.e., sentimentality) of their own. Americans seemed to take a "hard-boiled" approach to life that made sense to those growing up in a society littered with shattered wartime dreams and illusions. But above all, this generation was more intensely curious about the United States than any earlier generation had been, if only because they had lived in an "America-in-Japan" during their formative years.

From the 1950s onward a steady and growing number of Japanese visitors made their way across the Pacific to see the United States first-hand. At first only businessmen, government officials, and scholars and students on fellowships could afford to make the trip. They brought back accounts of a postwar America in the flush of cultural triumphalism, proudly living in the midst of the American Century. Not every Japanese traveler came home happy with his experience, and not every one came back pro-American, but on balance they all came back with fresh views of life in America that were more concrete and less homogeneous than prewar perceptions and more grounded in social reality.

Before World War II most Japanese visitors to the United States gravitated to the West Coast or the Northeast. Few if any visited the South or the Midwest. Nor did they have much contact with African Americans or Native Americans. The only minority group they paid much attention to was the Chinese immigrant community, fellow "Orientals" whose treatment they deplored but with whom they did not wish to be identified. Postwar visitors went everywhere, and for the first time their accounts of the country highlighted regional differences, class differences, and cultural diversities that had escaped notice before. The search for an American essence continued, but it proved as elusive as ever.

Unlike the placidly affluent society of the immediate postwar years, America was rent by deep divisions during the late 1960s and the 1970s. The country was polarized politically over the war in Vietnam; the deterioration of inner cities and racial tensions provoked urban riots; and social maladies like drug abuse and crime were on the rise. To make matter worse, economic stagflation lasted nearly a decade. As a consequence the national mood in the United States shifted from confident triumphalism to sober self-criticism—or what some called "a sense of malaise." By contrast, Japan during these decades was experiencing the exhilaration of an "economic miracle" that made it the second largest capitalist economy in the world. While the American economy was plunged into the doldrums, Japan's was riding the crest of the waves.

Flush with a new GNP nationalism buoyed by Japan's emergence as an economic superpower, many Japanese observers began to offer friendly advice to Americans on how to cure their economic maladies, if not their social ones. And they also began to argue that many of the traditional Japanese values that Americans had tried to suppress during the Occupation—social discipline, loyalty to the group, respect for authority, and the like—were precisely the values behind Japan's economic success. A new nonfiction genre *(Nihonjinron)* extolling the virtues of the Japanese "national character" began to fill the shelves of bookstores in the 1970s. Following the lead of self-critical American observers of Japan, some Japanese writers even speculated that that the American Century would be followed by a Japanese Century or that "Pax Americana" would be replaced by "Pax Nipponica."

Not everyone viewed American decline with schadenfreude. As we will see in chapter 7, one editorial writer lamented, "Watching the United States steadily lose its magnificence is like watching a former lover's beauty wither away. It makes me want to cover my eyes."[9] Even as America's power and affluence seemed to fade, many Japanese continued to recognize its strengths as well as its weaknesses, and the pendulum between overestimating and underestimating continued to swing. Sure enough, in the early 1990s, when a Japanese speculative investment bubble collapsed, plunging the Japanese economy into a "lost decade," a burst of technological innovation in the United States restored America's national self-confidence. This reversal of fortune, coming hard on the heels of Japan's own binge of triumphalism, probably widened the next arc of the pendulum. Many Japanese commentators began to express concern that Americans no longer seemed to pay much attention to Japan. One writer even whimsically argued that Japan should become America's "fifty-first state." (The only stumbling block, he suggested, was whether Japan would be allowed to retain its emperor.)

At the end of the American Century, the United States remained a country that the Japanese could not ignore, its principal, and unavoidable, partner in the outside world. As one commentator noted in 1998, "Talking about America may be the number two Japanese pastime. Why do they talk about America? Because America is the world's strongest nation and the twentieth century has been the American century. Because America has been the linchpin of Japan's security. Because America is Japan's biggest market."[10] It seemed unlikely that this state of affairs would change in the near future.

III.

Travelers in a foreign land often find that it offers a mirror that reflects their own image. In this respect Japanese visitors to America have been no different from European or Chinese visitors. Indeed, some have been quite aware that talking about an "other" means talking about oneself. "Self is revealed to us no more clearly than when we come in contact with other peoples and other countries," wrote Uchimura Kanzō in the 1890s. "Introspection begins when another world is presented to our view."[11] If talking about America has been the number-two pastime of the postwar Japanese, then talking about Japan has been their number-one pastime for much longer. Comparisons between Japan and America have sometimes been odious and sometimes flattering, but they always prompt self-reflection. As the novelist and social critic Oda Makoto once observed, thinking about America was synonymous with thinking about Japan.

European travelers, particularly in the nineteenth century, saw a glimpse of their own future in America, a new country with a new population, unencumbered by the weight of history, tradition, or custom. America was a historical experiment that disclosed hints of what was to come for the rest of the world. Few Japanese observers shared that perspective, however. They generally agreed that what made America so different from Japan was the shallowness of its past. To be sure, there were useful lessons to be learned from America, and the Japanese were receptive to absorbing them when seeking to change themselves, but in their selective appropriation of American culture, their perspectives were closer to those of Chinese visitors, who also recognized how distant American society was from their own.

The Japanese, however, were quick to recognize America's virtues. Many visitors, for example, were impressed by the American work ethic. As Katayama Sen pointed out, the United States was a society that respected hard work and rewarded it. And not only did the Americans work hard; they also worked efficiently, expending little energy on empty formalities, cups of tea, and extraneous small talk. Even the American housewife was praised as a model manager, deftly juggling her responsibilities as wife, mother, and community member. Needless to say, when American virtues appeared to be on the decline, Japanese observers were quick to point that out too. In the 1980s Japanese observers often attributed the American economic slowdown to the loss of the country's work ethic. One Japanese TV commercial showed an American assembly-line worker panting for breath as he tells another, "I guess we just can't keep up with the Japanese." A quick gulp of a Japanese health drink keeps them both going.

Nearly every American virtue identified by one observer could be seen as an American flaw by another. The Americans might be punctual, practical, and businesslike, but these traits reflected a lack of tact and emotional delicacy. The American habit of doing business unaccompanied by intricate exchanges of pleasantries was seen as a sign of insensitivity more than as one of efficiency, and the slogan "Time is money" was proof that Americans were obsessed with the pursuit of profit. The United States often appeared to be a society with scant appreciation for the elevated and the beautiful or for civilized behavior and discourse. "A majority of Americans measure things by tonnage, square footage, horsepower, and especially dollars," wrote Ashida Hitoshi in the 1920s. "Words like *beauty, proportion,* or *pleasure* are concepts that have little to do with them." As a result of their emotional and aesthetic poverty, it was often argued, Americans had made few contributions to philosophy, literature, and art. "[America] has neither philosophy nor art worth the name," grumbled Uchimura Kanzō. "It is no exaggeration to say that as a civilization, America minus money equals zero."[12]

Like Europeans travelers, the Japanese admired the pervasive freedom in America, but they often found its inhabitants crude, boorish, brash, and boastful. High-ranking Japanese shogunal officials, though befuddled by the intricate etiquette of using dishes and silverware, were upset by the unseemly informality of the American "barbarians" who did not appreciate the solemnity of official transactions. The image of the "vulgar American" was embraced by later generations too, amplified by American movies, by wartime propaganda, and by the behavior of American troops in postwar Japan. Underlying this image was a sense that America was a society with too few constraints, one in which liberty was pursued at the expense of civility and order, and violence often lurked just below the surface.

Japanese visitors impressed by the egalitarianism of American society were also much more likely than Europeans to comment on the contradiction between the American ideology of equality and the American practice of racial discrimination. Americans regarded Japanese as members of the "Oriental race." That made Japanese more susceptible to, and more sensitive about, racial discrimination than the Europeans were. Criticism of American racial attitudes intensified in response to legal and social discrimination against Japanese immigrants during the 1910s and 1920s, and it became even more intense during World War II, when the Americans seemed to regard the Japanese almost as another species and interned Japanese-Americans in relocation camps. Anger at crudely racist American propaganda prompted one repatriated foreign correspondent from New York to plead with his countrymen to intensify their hatred toward the American enemy.

While European travelers often pointed to the constant influx of immigrants as a source of America's vitality, Japanese visitors, coming from a relatively homogeneous society, were often ambivalent about the ethnic diversity of American society. America's multiethnic population was rarely regarded as one of its strengths. During World War II, for example, the lack of ethnic unity and integrity was seen as undercutting the "national spirit," and racial tension was thought to be seething behind a façade of national unity. Postwar visitors witnessed America's continuing struggle with racial discrimination, an issue they usually ignored at home. Many also attributed the decline in the American work ethic and the country's low levels of literacy to the existence of a large minority population. As one Japanese told an American reporter, "We suspect [life in a multiethnic society] might be reflected in the quality of your products, in the difficulty you have in managing things."[13]

Nowhere has the difference between America and Japan seemed greater than in the relations between men and women. Since the first diplomatic emissaries expressed shock at the uxorious behavior of American husbands, Japanese visitors have tended to see gender relations in America as balanced in favor of women. The notion that the United States was a "land of troublesome women" was particularly intense during the 1920s, when the model of the American flapper was feared as a threatening American import. To be sure, before the war American-style domesticity was often offered as a model for the Japanese middle-class family, and after the war the efficiency, sociality, and activism of American wives and mothers were held up as examples for the Japanese housewife to emulate. But Japanese men have tended to find American women bossy, imperious, self-centered, and inattentive to the needs of the stronger sex. One prewar visitor wondered why the equality of the sexes was so firmly implanted in America when the equality of the races was not.

On the whole, the Japanese have tended to discover differences from the Americans more easily than similarities to them. It is striking that many Japanese who have lived in the United States for a long period are happy to return home with a renewed appreciation of their own country. Certainly this is true of other foreign visitors to the United States, and it is certainly true of many Americans who travel abroad, but the process seems more intense for the Japanese. It is interesting to note, for example, that even during the war few Japanese anti-militarist political dissidents sought refuge in America, as thousands of anti-Nazi European refugees did. Nor has Japan ever suffered a "brain drain" like other developing countries, losing bright young people who have decided to settle in the United States after being sent abroad to study there.

Nagai Michio, one of the first postwar students sent abroad, observed that what stirs Japanese who travel to America is not the American landscape but memories of Japan and the Japanese. "All kinds of feelings burst forth—affection, respect, glorification, a sense of inferiority, idealization—that shape an image of Japan as they compare it with America. Figuratively speaking, when we travel to America, we carry the shadow of Japan on our backs."[14] It is this intense attachment to their own land that most sets the Japanese apart from other travelers to America. Going abroad prompts them to appreciate what they have at home.

IV.

For much of the American Century, Japanese writers have lamented the existence of a "perception gap" between the two countries. What this usually means is that Americans do not look at Japan the same way the Japanese do and therefore are urged to "understand" it. Less frequently, indeed rarely, it means that Japanese perceptions of the United States are distorted and must be adjusted to better reflect its actual condition. Of even greater concern to many Japanese, however, is an "attention gap"—a feeling that Americans do not pay as much attention to Japan as Japanese pay to America. Certainly this is true of the U.S. media coverage of Japan. One can seldom open a major Japanese daily or watch a TV news program without coming across something about the United States, but even a national American newspaper like the *New York Times*, heavily committed to coverage of international news, rarely puts Japan on its front page, and outside the business section it usually offers only feature stories about some peculiar aspect of Japanese society or culture. In a sense, the Japanese look at America through the living room window, while the Americans peek at Japan through a hole in the back fence.

This book is not intended to address the perception gap. That will always be with us, and it is not limited to American views of Japan. There are perception gaps with our immediate neighbors, Canada and Mexico, despite (or, more likely, because of) their heavy economic and social traffic with the United States. However, this book may be useful in closing the "attention gap" a bit, by reminding American readers how important it is recognize the way others view us. With America's diminished but still enormous impact on the outside world, it is imperative to recognize that many, if not most, people living outside the United States do not necessarily share American self-images, particularly in moments of crisis. Often this prompts righteous indignation. ("How can they say such things about the United States?!") But it ought to prompt a moment of reflection instead. ("Why are they saying such things?") In the end, even wildly distorted perceptions of the United States can provide insights into those who utter them—and into how to deal with them. American readers are bound to be pleased with some of the observers included in this book and irritated by others, but in the end they can learn from them all.

The choice of what to include in the volume was necessarily arbitrary. The book has its origins in translations made for an undergraduate course on U.S.-East Asian relations. Many selections were chosen for their "representativeness" of a particular viewpoint. Others were included because their authors were well-known or their observations were intrinsically interesting. The only consistent criterion for inclusion—occasionally violated—was that the authors should have lived in or at least visited the United States. It is doubtful that the collection contains every possible perspective of the United States during the American Century, but it tries to include as many as it can.

Not surprisingly many of the writers are academics or journalists. Some of them are public intellectuals that the Japanese call "critics" (hyōronka), once described as writers who try on new ideas just as models try on the latest fashions from Paris. But also included are novelists (including a Nobel Prize winner), businessmen, at least two future prime ministers, a couple of Buddhist priests, one baseball player, and two film critics. Their politics range from the extreme left to the extreme right, and their religious affiliations include Christianity as well as Buddhism. Most of the writers are men. The only voices nearly left unheard are those of women, an absence that reflects male dominance in Japan's cultural discourse, particularly before World War II. If not "representative" in any systematic way, at the very least these authors as a group offer a wide range of Japanese perspectives on America.

The last selection is an essay from a 1989 book titled "No" to ieru Nihon (A Japan That Can Say "No"). One theme of the book was that Japan should no longer kowtow to the American superpower, but another was that the American Century seemed to be coming to an end.

The Japanese public continued to admire, and even envy, America in a vague way, eagerly embracing its consumer products and consumer culture, from Colonel Sanders to M. C. Hammer, but the intelligentsia was overtaken by an America-bashing mood in the 1990s. American society, plagued by homelessness, gratuitous violence, and the spread of AIDS, still seemed to be faltering, perhaps even spinning out of control, and Americans were no longer building the better mousetraps that once brought the world to their door. At the same time, there was an undercurrent of resentment that America was not taking the new Japanese economic superpower as seriously as it should.

Nothing was more symbolic of this mood than the 1992 visit of then-president George H. W. Bush, who arrived in Japan with three automobile-company presidents in tow to attend the opening of the first Toys"R"Us superstore in the country and to urge the Japanese to buy more American cars. In a news broadcast of the state dinner, Japanese television viewers were treated to the spectacle of the American president, suffering from an upset stomach, sinking below the table as he vomited into the lap of the Japanese prime minister seated at his side. It was a moment that suggested how far America had declined and what a long-suffering role its Japanese ally was playing.

While it is difficult to reach any consensus on just how long the American Century lasted, it seems safe to say that for most Japanese intellectuals, the end came in the early 1990s. Not only were the two countries at odds more and more frequently over trade issues as well as Japan's contribution to global security, but a new superpower, the People's Republic of China, was also emerging across the Japan Sea. It was easy for many in Japan to conclude that the next "century" would be an Asian one. Indeed, there was a surge of interest in the creation of a new regional order, as Japan's relations with the United States seemed to be deteriorating. And that is why this book ends not in the millennial year but with the emergence of new and more complicated Japanese perspectives on the world at large.

CHAPTER I

Illusion and Disillusion

Of all the foreign powers the Japanese encountered in the nineteenth century, the United States seemed the most different from the rest. It was a country to be admired, not feared. American gunboats under Commodore Matthew Perry had persuaded the Tokugawa shogunate to establish diplomatic relations with Western countries, but the threat of French and British gunboats is what ultimately convinced them to open their ports to foreign trade and foreign residents. And during the final struggles that led to the overthrow of the shogunate, the Americans remained benignly neutral while the French and the British, competing for influence, backed opposing sides. "Americans, because they are from a new country, are gentle," wrote a young official on the first Japanese diplomatic mission to Washington in 1860. "High officials do not arbitrarily despise commoners, nor do they abuse their power. The nation is rich and the people are peaceful, finding themselves in a position of perfect security."[1] By contrast, the Europeans, especially the British, seemed not only arrogant and high-handed but also duplicitous and disdainful of the Japanese.

Even before educated Japanese had any direct contact with Americans, they idealized the United States as a political and moral utopia. Young Japanese samurai determined to replace the shogun's regime with a more virtuous, and therefore stronger (in their minds), government avidly read a history of the United States written in Chinese by an American missionary, E. C. Bridgman, and translated into Japanese in 1854. These would-be nation builders found the history of the American Revolution and the creation of the new nation a gripping and inspiring tale. George Washington, the virtuous general who selflessly refused to be crowned king after his victories, became a cultural hero. He reminded Confucian-educated readers of the legendary founders of the Chinese state, Yao and Shun, who also stood aside when their work was done, rather than founding dynasties. "In recent times," wrote Yokoi Shōnan, an advocate of radical reform, "only Washington of America has acted in the spirit of righteousness based on Heavenly rule."[2] Unacquainted with how the Americans were actually governed, Yokoi idealized America as a republic of virtue.

Only in the late 1860s and 1870s did Japanese intellectuals begin to grasp the nature of American politics. They were impressed that all the people participated in their own governance, that laws were determined by "public discussion," and that in America "liberty" (for which a new word had to be invented in Japanese) was the highest civic virtue. "The government keeps its word," wrote Fukuzawa Yukichi, one of the most influential thinkers of the Meiji era (1868–1912). "Since there is no tyrannical king, the land belongs entirely to the people."[3] Even before the Meiji Restoration, future government leaders such as Itō Hirobumi and Kido Kōin queried Joseph Iteco, a former castaway who had lived in the United States, about the American Constitution, and in its early days the Meiji government established a rudimentary representative assembly. But as they looked around the world, the Meiji leaders found more congenial political models in two powerful monarchical European states, Great Britain and the imperial Germany, whose historical experience and traditions seemed closer to Japan's than America's did.

The model of America as the "sacred land of liberty" remained strong among government opponents who called for the expansion of "liberty and popular rights." Indeed, a handful of radical critics of the Meiji government fled to San Francisco in the late 1880s to continue their struggle there. Disillusion with the American model, however, was common among Japanese visitors confronted by the gap between political ideals and political practice in the republic of virtue. The first Japanese recipient of a Harvard law degree concluded that the great strength of the republic was that every citizen was interested in what the government was doing, but he also understood its defects as well: debate on public affairs entailed partisan conflict and confrontation; constant turnover of officials created instability; cunning demagogues took advantage of a credulous public; politicians pursued private interest rather than public good; and legislators accepted bribes in return for favors. A republic, he

FIGURE 1. This is probably the first caricature of Americans in a comic magazine. On the left, two Americans—with big noses and deep-set eyes—ogle a Japanese couple through a telescope. The protective husband shields his wife, hiding under three layers of hats. The caption reads: "According to a strange story I read in a foreign newspaper, Japanese who live in America are very careful to protect their wives, and they are astonished at the equality between men and women." (*Nipponchi*, August 1874)

wrote, was like an "inexperienced youth [whose] strength is not yet as fully developed as that of her elder sister, monarchy."[4] It was easy to conclude that the American-style republican democracy provided no model for Japan as it tried to develop its own national strength.

The religiosity of the Americans also impressed Japanese observers at first. Christianity "enters their blood with their mother's milk," noted the report of the Iwakura Mission. In every town and village, no matter how small, a Christian "temple" was to be found; Christian priests were learned men who taught believers to follow the good; and no matter how bizarre the Bible's teachings might seem to the Japanese, Americans earnestly embraced their faith with a passion far deeper than the perfunctory devotions of Buddhist and Shinto believers in Japan. It seemed clear that the firm moral code of American Protestantism provided the country's spiritual backbone and that it contributed to the enormous progress the country had made since its founding. American missionaries and even American advisers carried a similar message, preaching the gospel of civilization along with the gospel of Christianity. William S. Clark, an American educator hired to start an agricultural school in Hokkaido, mixed lessons on Christian ethics with his science lectures, and by the end of his brief stay all his students had asked to be baptized.

Indeed, it was American missionaries and teachers, rather than American merchants, who had the greatest impact on the first generation of Japan's new intelligentsia. Ambitious young men, often with few personal or social resources, flocked to the treaty ports and to newly founded mission schools to master English, the language that provided the opportunity to "rise in the world." With the collapse of traditional moral and social certainties, many also turned to Christianity for the moral guidance that Confucian education or the samurai ethical code had once provided. In sheer numerical terms Protestantism did not make much headway in Japan. By 1889 there were only thirty-one thousand converts in a population of forty million. But many Christians belonged to the new intellectual elite, especially in the fields of science, education, and journalism.

By the end of the nineteenth century, admiration for American Christianity had faded. For one thing, many Japanese Christians no longer felt the need for the ministrations of foreign missionaries, who often wielded financial support from American churches and missionary societies to dominate the local Christian communities. After a long dispute with his American benefactors, Niishima Jō, who founded an English-language school (later Dōshisha University) in Kyoto to "nurture those who might serve as conscience to the state," decided to refuse their further help. And during the 1890s many Japanese Protestant sects tried to become less dependent on their American counterparts.

Equally significant was the disillusion experienced by eager young Japanese converts who discovered American society to be quite different from what they had anticipated. Uchimura Kanzō, one of William S. Clark's students, arrived in California in 1884 expecting to find "templed hills, and rocks that rang with hymns and praises" but instead encountered pickpockets and profanity on the rude streets of San Francisco.[5] His admiration for America as "the hope of civilized nations" dwindled, and eventually he decided to create a purer "Japanese Christianity" that offered its own model to the world.

Inevitably many Japanese found that America betrayed their great expectations, but the Americans' penchant to preach about their own virtues probably magnified the disappointment of the Japanese. It smacked of hypocrisy. Beyond this disillusion lay a deeper psychological trend: a re-

admiration fades [margin annotation]

action against the head-over-heels Westernization of the country during the 1870s and 1880s. Something had been lost in that process, it was feared, and the time had come to reassert Japan's own particular identity. The recovery of cultural self-confidence was confirmed by the country's success in building national wealth and power. After a handy victory over China in 1895 the Japanese elite no longer viewed Japan as a weak and vulnerable country, prey to foreign pressure and exploitation; they could now see a future in which Japan would take its place among the world's important military and diplomatic powers. It no longer needed either foreign advisers or foreign missionaries.

Interestingly, many Americans came to the same conclusion. They saw the Japanese as a progressive, hard-working, and go-getting people very different from their sluggish and backward-looking Asian neighbors. As one popular book title put it, the Japanese were the "Yankees of the Pacific." When Japan went to war with China, the American press was generally sympathetic to Japan, and so was American diplomatic policy. "Americans can not but wish them success," said a Philadelphia newspaper. "Nippon is indeed the day-star of the East."[6] Conversely no matter how disillusioned Japanese intellectuals were with American culture and American democracy, the United States retained its reputation as a benign and friendly power. Only as the world entered the American Century did disillusion give way to increasing friction and distrust.

SUGIYAMA SHIGERU,
"ON RELATIONS AMONG NATIONS" (1878)

This article, which appeared in the *Hōchi shinbun,* one of the leading newspapers during the Meiji period, offers a relatively benign image of the United States. It emphasizes the differences between America and the other Western powers but ends on a note of ambiguity.

... Japanese article on America vs. other western powers

Back in the days when we kept our country closed, turned foreigners away, and stayed to ourselves, our world was free of constraints or anxieties....
But when we ended the closed-country policy by opening our ports and allowing foreigners to come into the country, our dealings with the out-

Sugiyama Shigeru, "On Relations among Nations," source: *Hōchi shinbun,* February 16 and 18, 1878. In *Nihon kindai shisō taikei,* vol. 12, *Gaikōkan,* ed. Shiba Takuji et al. (Tokyo: Iwanami shoten, 1988), 118–120.

side world changed completely. All our national affairs have become entangled with those of foreign countries. The ambit of our anxieties has expanded dramatically, and we can no longer shut our eyes to the storms that roil the vast sea of human affairs. We cannot stay the rising and falling winds and waves of the age by dint of our own efforts. . . . Alas, as a result of opening the ports, our people have become burdened by numberless anxieties, unable to move either hand or foot freely.

Even when intercourse among nations is peaceful and tranquil, the possibility that one country might gobble up another never fades. Although some countries talk about concluding treaties, carrying on cordial relations, and living in peaceful harmony, the ambitions of wild beasts unfortunately remain deep in their hearts. As international intercourse changes, the way countries build their wealth and power differs greatly from ancient times. A country like ours, protected from international relations [gaikō] by its geography, cannot fully comprehend the changes that have taken place among the Powers. But we should be aware that since ancient times they have built themselves up even as they shared borders with other countries. Look at what has happened in ancient history. There has been only one way to build national wealth and power: chewing and swallowing up neighboring enemies and annexing their territories. [There follows a list of famous conquerors: Pyrrhus and Darius of Persia; Alexander the Great of Macedonia; Julius Caesar; Charlemagne; Tamerlane; Genghis Khan; Ferdinand and Isabella; Louis XIV; Charles XII; Frederick Barbarossa; Napoleon I.] . . .

All the Powers harbor ambitions to swallow up other people's lands in order to build their own wealth and power. That is always at the root of war fever. Look at the recent destruction of Poland! Look at the present fighting in Russia! Whatever reason a country may give for going to war is merely a veil to hide its violent and feral intentions. Ah, thrust as we are into the midst of this pack of wolves and tigers, I pray that we can escape harm. How difficult that will be! Among all the countries involved in international intercourse, only the American republic takes friendship with other countries as its goal, declines to beat down the small and weak with threats of force, and builds its wealth and power while respecting the rights of other countries.

If you listen to what the American people are proud of, this is what they tell us:

"The principal goals of our country are peace and friendship. We venture to say that we do not go to war over land. Nor do we injure the rights of other countries. We establish mutually friendly relations with other countries in order to pursue trade. We do not make secret agreements for political reasons. And when we desire another country's territory, we pay a proper price for it. We do not send our soldiers to invade it.

"Moreover, once we have paid for territory, we do not override the rights of the people who occupy it. This is an unchanging principle of our government. The territory we have acquired is eight times the size of the original thirteen colonies of the federal republic. In 1803 we bought land between the Mississippi River and the Pacific Coast from France for $25,000,000. We called the territory Louisiana. By buying it we avoided war with Napoleon. This was the first time that we annexed land by a purchase agreement.

"In 1811 [in fact, 1819] we bought Florida from Spain for $5,000,000. In 1845 we annexed Texas in accordance with the desire of its government, and we incurred a public debt of $10,000,000 to do so. The result was a war with Mexico. We occupied the territory after military victory, and the war ended in 1848. Mexico agreed to a treaty that ceded to us Texas, the cause of the war, and in addition gave us the territories that have now become California, Nevada, Utah, New Mexico, and the Colorado Territory. Under the treaty our government paid Mexico $15,000,000 and made $3,000,000 in loans. Never before in recorded history have territorial rights already won by military force been bought for a proper price. Moreover, in 1854 [1853, in fact] we bought land near Messhira [sic] and the Arizona region from Mexico for $10,000,000. And in 1868 [1867, in fact] we bought the territory of Alaska from Russia.

"We sent settlers into all these territories and expanded our national borders to a degree undreamed of. Sometimes this led to hostilities with England, but these were unavoidable conflicts, not acts of aggression planned in advance. If we had used force deliberately to take over territory, it would have been simple to bring the indigenous savages living there under control and take over their land. But our sole principle in acquiring territory is to buy land for an adequate sum without resorting to military force. This is the reason that our government spends several hundred thousand dollars year after year to deal with the Indian problem. Our government's principle of expanding our territory without relying on military force is based on Washington's farewell warning to our people. That is the foreign policy of our republic, no more, no less."

We believe what the Americans tell us. The only country in the world that has remained aloof from the world's conflicts and has developed its domain in isolation is the federal republic [of America]. We respect the fact that the Americans dislike war, that they insist on peace, and that

America buys land instead of invading for the territory

they do not rely on military force except to fight in self-defense. However, even the America that we so respect has not hesitated to use threat backed by military force in their intercourse with other countries. Do we not remember the threats that the American commodore Perry made to the Tokugawa government as he negotiated during the Ansei period? Can we really say that was in accord with proper moral principles? Certainly his actions did not spring from affection.

So America is no different from other strong countries. It goes without saying that all of them exercise some kind of power in their intercourse with other nations. As Woolsey put it in his book on international law,[7] the [Perry expedition] is a fine example of the use of force to establish amity. "It is difficult to find better proof that an enlightened people can force relations on an unenlightened people than the case of the Americans in Japan," he wrote. Alas, it is not only statesmen, but also those who see themselves as learned scholars, who attempt to deceive posterity by spouting such wild theories. In truth, can it be denied that wars are difficult to prevent, that treaties are not reliable, and that relations with foreign countries bring trouble? I believe that the greatest source of future difficulties for our country today will be matters related to intercourse with foreign countries.

SHIBA SHIRŌ, "STRANGE ENCOUNTERS WITH BEAUTIFUL WOMEN" (1885–1887)

Shiba Shirō (1852–1922), author of the political novel *Strange Encounters with Beautiful Women [Kajin no Kigū],* came from a domain that fought against the imperial army during the Meiji Restoration. Despite that handicap he pursued a highly successful political career. After graduating from a government academy that trained talented young men for government service, he went to America, where he attended a commercial school in San Francisco, then studied business economics in Philadelphia. After his return to Japan, he served briefly in the army that crushed the Satsuma Rebellion, then became a government civil official. In 1891 Shiba won a seat in the new national legislative assembly, to which he

Shiba Shirō, "Strange Encounters with Beautiful Women," source: Tōkai Sanshi, *Strange Encounters with Beautiful Women,* trans. Guohe Zheng, excerpted in *The Columbia Anthology of Modern Japanese Literature,* vol. 1, *From Restoration to Occupation,* ed. J. Thomas Rimer and Van C. Gessel, 30–45 (New York: Columbia University Press, 2005); portion of excerpt presented here is from 30–33.

was reelected eight times. Under the pen name Tōkai Sanshi (Oriental Wanderer), he wrote several political novels, a genre inspired by Benjamin Disraeli, the British prime minister, who had authored popular fictional works. In Japan the genre served as a medium for expressing an author's political views. Often set in foreign countries or ancient times, with an exotic cast of romantic or heroic characters, and written in a melodramatic and bombastic style, political novels were popular among the young. The following selection reflects the earliest images of America as a revolutionary republic that could serve as a model for other nations in the world, including those in Asia.

by Tokai sanshi

. . .

One day Tōkai Sanshi climbed Independence Hall in Philadelphia. Looking up, he could see the cracked Liberty Bell; looking down, he could read the Declaration of Independence. He reminisced about the noble character of the American people at the time when, raising the banner of righteousness, they had rid themselves of the tyrannical rule of the British king and eventually succeeded in becoming a people of independence and self-determination. Looking up, looking down, he was overcome with emotion. With a deep sigh, he leaned against a window and gazed outside. It happened that just then two young women appeared coming up the spiral staircase.

Veils of light green covered their faces, and their hats, with white feathers on top, conveyed a faint fragrance. Wearing short light silk blouses and graceful long skirts, they glowed with elegant beauty that was truly breathtaking.

Pointing at Carpenter Hall, they were heard saying to each other, "That is the place where, in 1774, statesmen from the thirteen states met for the first time and deliberated on the future of the country."

At the time, the tyrannical British king ignored the Constitution and imposed unbearably heavy taxes on the American people, whose freedom was denied. The American people wanted to speak of their misery, but there was no one who would listen to them; they wished to appeal, but there was nowhere to turn. The minds of the people were therefore upset, and an armed conflict was on the verge of erupting. Gravely concerned about the situation, well-known statesmen from the thirteen states met in this hall to find ways to spare the people this misery and to eliminate the cause for the imminent disaster. It is here that the indignant Patrick Henry delivered his powerful and stirring speech declaring: "The king of Britain must be executed, and a republic must be established." Carpenter Hall still stands today with no changes in its old appearance and, along with Independence Hall, is a historical attraction in Philadelphia.

Then, pointing at the faraway hills and rivers, the two women continued: "That hill is called Valley Forge, and that river is called the Delaware River. Oh—yes—Bunker Hill."

Bunker Hill is located about two and a half miles northeast of Boston. Of truly strategic importance, it faces Boston Bay [sic] to its left and joins a row of hills on its right. One day in 1775, patriotic American soldiers secretly occupied Bunker Hill to stop the advance of the British army. The next morning, the enemy launched a fierce attack from both land and sea. The American soldiers responded vigorously and repeatedly repulsed the enemy's attacks. However, as the battle continued, the tide turned against the Americans. The enemy received as many as three groups of reinforcements, but the American soldiers fighting on Bunker Hill ran out of ammunition and did not receive any reinforcements. Eventually, when General Joseph Warren was killed, the American resistance collapsed, and Bunker Hill fell to the enemy. Later generations built a monument on Bunker Hill in honor of the heroes who gave their lives in the Battle of Bunker Hill.

Sanshi visited Bunker Hill in the late spring of 1881. While reminiscing about the heroic battles fought in the American Revolution, Sanshi could not help but think about world affairs today. While doing so, he found emotions burning in himself, the emotions felt by Lu You, a patriotic poet of the Southern Song dynasty of China. Then he composed a *kanshi* reflecting his feelings:

> A lonely traveler up on top of Bunker Hill,
> How many springs and autumns have you seen, the monument
>   in honor of the heroes
> The heroes who fought to eliminate the tyranny under the banner
>   of righteousness
> And who swore to kill the wolves in revenge for the country?
> When horses were pastured on the southern slope of Mount Huashan,
> Triumphant songs reverberated throughout the thirteen states,
> Public opinion is highly respected here by the government,
> The ways of protecting national interests dictate its policies.
> Freedom is not valued in Eastern Seas,
> And patriots worry in vain about the motherland. . . .
> Thinking of Japan from a foreign land,
> The falling flowers only intensify my loneliness. . . .

After the Battle of Bunker Hill, the Declaration of Independence was drafted in this hall, and the fundamental principles of freedom were proclaimed to the entire world. At the time, the Americans, including those from far corners of the land, left their plows and gathered together. They took up arms and decided to fight for independence. Seamstresses cut their cloth to make banners; white-haired fathers brought food and drink for the soldiers; loving mothers, while shedding tears, sent their sons to the battle; chaste wives urged their husbands to report to their units lest they might be late. The Americans would not yield even when they were stabbed by shining bayonets or blown up by cannon fire. They would have no regrets even if they were wounded or died on the battlefields. Swearing they would rather die for the sake of freedom, the Continental army fought for seven years the British army of a million wolves and tigers. During these seven years, Boston was first to be lost to the enemy; then New York fell, and finally Philadelphia, the capital, also was occupied by the enemy. It was then that General George Washington, leading his weary soldiers, decided to retreat to Valley Forge and have his troops set up camp there. This was during a cold winter. Snow covered the ground for a thousand miles around, and ice blocked all the roads. With no reinforcements coming or food or supplies, the soldiers were pale and emaciated, and their morale was low. The generals talked over the matter and concluded: "Unless we start a battle to boost our morale, this righteous and loyal army of ours is bound to dissolve or disperse."

That night, unbeknownst to the British, the American troops left Valley Forge and crossed the Delaware River. They then launched a surprise attack on the arrogant British army and won a marvelous victory. Thereafter, the morale of the army of freedom rose once again. In this battle, however, the officers and soldiers of the American army were poorly equipped. They had no shoes to wear on their feet and no clothes to protect their bodies from the fury of winter. They marched in the snow barefoot. Their broken shins and feet were dripping with blood, turning red the miles and miles of snow on the ground. Many in the Continental army died of cold. Oh, as human beings, who would prefer death to life? But inspired by their patriotic enthusiasm, the American people were concerned only about the difficulties of their country and, in serving their country, put aside considerations for themselves.

It is only fitting that after turning the tide in their favor and singing songs of triumph, the Americans raised horses on the southern slope of Mount Huashan and cows in the Peach Tree Forest and started to build their own nation. Outside their borders, Americans resisted European expansionism against their neighbors by adhering to the common principle of confronting powerful aggressors and protecting the weak and the bullied. Within their country, they built schools, replaced swords with farm tools, promoted industry and trade, imposed taxes on agriculture and sericulture, and in this way built this country. It is a country that is rich and strong, a country where people can enjoy freedom and peace. As the saying goes, a song of triumph can change the color of the clouds, and the morale of soldiers can turn into the light of the sun and the moon.

At the end of their talk, the two women released a long sigh: "When can we see days of such peace and prosperity *in our own countries?*"

When Sanshi heard this, he could not help but feel perplexed. He wondered, "Why should fair ladies such as they are, living in the land of freedom and bathed in the radiant virtue of civilization, be so sorrowful? In ancient China, when the emperor of the Jin dynasty was forced to move to the south and established the East Jin dynasty, its Prime Minister Wang Dao once met some friends of his at Xinting Pavilion near the new capital of Nanjing. These friends, gazing at the unfamiliar landscape of the south, all shed tears of homesickness for their country in the north—these ladies sound just like them."

By then it was turning late. Weary birds had returned to the forests, and all the sightseers at Independence Hall had left. Tōkai Sanshi, too, walked out of the city gate and went home to west Philadelphia.

INOUE ENRYŌ, "RELIGION IN AMERICA" (1889)

Inoue Enryō (1858–1919), one of the most influential Buddhist philosophers and educators of the Meiji period, was the son of a Buddhist priest. After being ordained as a priest in his youth, he entered Tokyo Imperial University to study Western philosophy. In the late nineteenth century, Buddhism was under attack by Japanese critics who saw it as corrupt, complacent, and of alien origin. The religion also had to compete with the appeal of both Christianity and Western science to a new generation of educated Japanese. Renouncing his priesthood after graduating from the university, Inoue devoted his life to interpreting Buddhism in light of new philosophical ideas from the West. The author of more 120 books on religion, philosophy, education, and Buddhism, he is probably best known for his writings on popular superstitions, such as ghosts, monsters, and other mysterious phenomena, which won him the nickname "Dr. Spook" [Yōkai-sensei]. After he returned from a trip to the

Inoue Enryō, "Religion in America," source: Inoue Enryō, *Ōbei kakkoku seikyō Nikki*, part 1 (Tokyo: Tetsugaku shoin, 1889), 30–42.

United States and Europe, a friend encouraged him to publish his travel diary, which dealt with Western religious institutions and customs that most other travelers ignored. Inoue's perspective on America was ambivalent. While grudgingly impressed by the high moral standards of Americans, he was heartened by signs that institutional Christianity was in decline.

. . .

There are said to be about 500 temples (i.e., Christian churches) in New York City. Since the population of the city is 1,200,000, that means there is a temple for every 2,500 people. In Philadelphia, with a population of 847,000, there are about 500 temples, or about one for every 1,794 people. The total population of the America is 61,000,000. For all religious sects, large and small, there are 92,107 temples and 77,230 priests (i.e., ministers). That comes to 662 persons for every temple and 800 persons for every priest. . . .

Everywhere in towns and villages all over America, there are always temples, that is to say, Christian churches. Generally they are built on a standard architectural plan. At the front of the church is a tall tower with a cross at the top, so that you can see a church in the town from a long distance away. City churches stand side by side with shops and stores, and they are located in all parts of the town. They are never set aside in separate quarters, as Buddhist temples are in Tokyo and other cities back home.

Every temple has a chief priest, a minister who conducts prayers, gives sermons, and performs marriages and funerals and the like. From time to time he makes visits to parishioners' homes to inquire after their health and welfare. He visits them when they fall ill, and he supports them when they meet with some misfortune. It is a very busy life.

In America it is the custom to respect priests, especially in the countryside. Priests must be careful in their interactions with men and women and in their reception of strangers. They must be extremely obliging and polite in their language, in their conversations, in their social visits, and in their treatment of others. In other words, they must win people's affections with kindness and politeness. Their reputations suffer if they do not.

When people from another church or another country come to visit a church, it is the custom to treat them with extreme courtesy. And believers from different sects cooperate with one another in establishing philanthropic societies, relief associations, and the like. I must say that these are excellent practices. On the other hand, Protestants and Roman

Catholics regard each other with hostility. Public disputes between them are said to be frequent.

If a church has a well-known minister, it is the practice to buy him a life insurance policy with church funds so that he can serve until retirement. That is an interesting way of doing things. Famous ministers in America have annual incomes of more than $12,000 (about ¥15,000), and the most famous earn more than the annual salary of the president.

Ordinary Americans regard believers in religions other than Christianity as "heathens" [literally, *gaidō,* "those outside the Way"]. Not only do they ostracize them; they also think of them as human beings of a lower order. Why heathens are ostracized is a puzzle to me. It is the height of foolishness. Recently, however, scholars who do not believe in Christianity and who support Buddhism have begun to appear. But when one analyzes their infatuation [with Buddhism], their glib theories seem to be nothing more than the expression of a simpleminded feminine mindset.

When Christian zeal still coursed through their veins, the Americans' spirit was wrapped in religious fervor. As they struggled against thick and thin, against snow and ice, and against hunger and starvation, Americans built a civilization. Today, however, the heat of their religious fervor has dissipated. It remains only tepid and skin-deep. Attendance at church on Sunday has become a social gathering where men gaze at women decked out in beautiful newly made gowns. Is this the true face of Christianity? People usually point to America as a place where Christianity flourishes, but if the reality is as I have described it, then one can imagine what Christianity must be like in other places.

According to what I have heard, Christian priests in the United States are of the highest moral character but are not sincere in their religious beliefs. Two out of three have their private doubts, but outwardly they speak and act like strict men of religion. The public therefore regards men of religion as having high moral character and sincere religious beliefs. They also equate religion with morality, and they believe that men of religion are therefore men of morality—and vice versa. When they discover a few immoralists among men of religion, the public never ascribes their transgressions to religion. In Japan, on the other hand, when a man of religion does something immoral, we are in the habit of blaming his transgressions on the religion itself and equating the religion with the man. Westerners regard religion as national religion, while Japanese regard religion as individual religion.

My view is that a religion is a "Way" [*dō,* or *tao*], and not the private possession of an individual. The heart of an individual may change, but a "Way" never changes. If a man of religion acts immorally, he is no longer a man of religion; therefore one cannot blame his transgressions on his religion.

Although Christianity is said to flourish more in America [than anywhere else], Sunday church attendance has gradually declined in recent years. Newspaper reports offer the following reasons:

The first reason is that the recent advance in [scientific] knowledge has had an influence on public sentiment. Many have come to doubt the existence of God or an afterlife.

The second is that those who neither attend church nor attend worship services do not suffer any ill consequences as a result. Although ministers preach that God is omnipresent, He cannot protect his beloved children from misfortune. And even though ministers say that God is all-seeing and all-hearing, He cannot protect them from illness and suffering. In experiencing life's joys and sorrows, there is not the slightest difference between those who believe in God and those who do not.

The third reason is that those who attend church hear the same sort of sermon every Sunday. They realize that instead of sacrificing the one day a week when they are free from work, they could be taking a stroll outdoors, chatting happily with friends, and enjoying themselves in a relaxed and carefree way.

The fourth reason is that it has become the custom for churchgoers to compete by displaying their splendid clothes and beautiful faces. Women want to show off to the men, and men want to attract the affection of the ladies. Consequently, those who are poor, those who cannot afford beautiful clothes, those who are put off by this custom, and those who are too old to care about their appearance decide not to attend church.

The chief tactic of [Christian] missionaries is to attract women and small children to their "Way" through moral instruction. Once women embrace Christian ideas in their hearts, it is inevitable that they will pass them on to their children. And it is inevitable that when women and children are bathed in the waters of Christianity, men will be bathed by its spreading waves as well. The ideas that one acquires as a child have the power to control one as an adult. Those who enter the wellsprings of Christianity when young will be unable to keep their heads above its waters for the rest of their lives. Like green sprouts nourished by the spring sun, women and children are easily bent by the winds of religion. Since women are the most easily bent, the principal goal of the Christians is to indoctrinate them. This is the best of all possible ways to do so, because it yields the greatest results with the least effort.

reasons for decrease in church attendance

In America religion breathes in the air of absolute liberty. Americans are inoculated with the spirit of liberty at birth. When the Americans first came from England, the English government had established a national religion and made the king the head of the church. The people were not permitted freedom of religion. Some who opposed this principle called for freedom of religion and independence of churches. They departed from their ancestral homeland to cross the sea to America and settle in a barren wilderness as colonists. Their children and grandchildren propagated, they built towns and villages, and finally they came into conflict with the English. They declared their independence to the world. There is no doubt that religious grudges played an indirect role in bringing about the war for independence. The republic established after independence was achieved had its roots the Americans' long-standing spirit of religious freedom and independent churches.

It is only natural that those who embrace the idea of liberty propagate it in many ways. Historically, ever since the clash between the new [Protestant] religion and the old [Catholic] religion, when Luther opposed the authority of the Roman pope and called for religious liberty, the idea of liberty has had a political impact and brought about revolution in many countries. Even though religion and politics are of a different nature, since human ideas are consistent with one another, the spirit of political independence expresses itself in religion, and the idea of religious liberty extends to politics and to claims for political liberty. As a consequence, politics and religion generally share a common type of organization. Under a monarchical system, religion organizes itself in accordance with monarchical rule, and under a republican system religion organizes itself in accordance with republican rule.

The political system in the United States is a free republic, and the organization of each federal state is nearly independent. The organization of the country's religion is also free and independent. Each church is independent, and each church establishes its own rules. There is no main temple *[honzan]* controlling them, nor is there a chief priest *[kyōso]*. Religious federations, however, do hold annual conferences, and the representatives of each church meet to make decisions about the general affairs of the sect. The organization [of these federations] is no different from the political structure of the United States. That is why I say that religion in America breathes the air of complete liberty. It is suffused with the spirit of individual liberty.

If American religion comes to our country, however, it will eventually cause great political problems. Protestantism in Japan today comes mostly from America. Its [America's] religion is an exact facsimile of [its] political organization and is based on the principles of a free republic. Once such a religion becomes established in the public mind, by imperceptible degrees it will nurture and spread the idea of republican liberty and lead to demands for republican freedom. Even now we deplore such an outcome. . . .

In America friends often get together to go on excursions to the countryside called "picnics." They decide on a time, a day, and a place, then sell tickets to those interested in coming along. If the destination is the beach, on the appointed day they hire little rental boats and a marching band. [The picnickers] carry their own box lunches, and after sailing across to their destination, they tie up their boats. Men and women go off to enjoy the countryside as they wish, and in the evening they return home in their boats. Except for the cost of the rental boats and the marching band, all the money taken in from the sale of tickets is devoted to charitable purposes such as contributions to churches, hospitals, poorhouses, and the like.

Every Monday, American temples hold events called "sociables." Parishioners invite friends and acquaintances to the temple, where they introduce themselves to one another and converse over tea and cakes until they go home. In other words, these are small friendly social gatherings [konshinkai]. American temples are not simply places to preach religion; they serve as social gathering places as well.

One day in New York City I visited a park where I saw stone statues of heroes and scholars lining the footpaths. I was told that they were great teachers who had brought about the moral uplift of the population. When most people see the image of a hero, it arouses in them love and reverence and a desire to become heroes themselves. The same is true of those who see the images of scholars. It is my view that if we erect in our own parks such statues of great teachers who morally uplifted our own people, it would be a great boon to their education.

In America newspapers are sold here and there on the street, with no one watching. The buyer puts his money into a collection box and then takes a newspaper [from the rack]. No one steals any newspapers. In restaurants, customers order their meals, and when finished eating they tell the cashier at the entrance what they had to eat and then pay the appropriate amount. They do so naturally without any coercion. That is how honest the Americans are.

Of course, people [in America] are not naturally honest. [Their honesty] is the result of being molded over generations and over centuries by social circumstances. There is a widely accepted adage that "honesty is the best policy." This is a principle established after many generations of experience. The construction of houses in Western societies is sturdy and provides excellent protection, so the notion of theft has been erased gradually over a long period of time. And in commercial [transactions] one cannot recover one's reputation if one has lost the trust of others, so people naturally have come to understand the need to protect their integrity toward others. Repeated experience and admonitions are built up over time, and through transmission over many generations they become custom and common sense. They become engrained hereditarily. Eventually people naturally reject larceny and deception and become honest and simple.

However, this country is not entirely without theft. From what I have read in newspaper articles, there are gangs of bandits in the Rocky Mountains who stop railroad trains and rob passengers of their money and precious goods.

UCHIMURA KANZŌ, "FIRST IMPRESSIONS OF CHRISTENDOM" (1893)

Uchimura Kanzō (1861–1930), the son of a samurai, began learning English when he was eleven years old. In 1877 he was admitted to the Sapporo Agricultural College to study fishery science. Under the influence of his American teacher William S. Clark, he converted to Christianity, a religion he embraced with passion. After a brief marriage, he went to the United States to study at Amherst College, then at Hartford Theological Seminary. He arrived in the United States with an idealized vision of America as a "Christian society," but he was profoundly disappointed by the social reality that he encountered there. Deciding not pursue a career as a Christian minister, he returned to Japan in 1888 to become a teacher. Because of his rigid personality and his Puritanical devotion to principle, he was forced to leave the First Higher School, the preparatory school for entrance into Tokyo Imperial University, after he failed to show sufficient respect at a ceremony for the Imperial Rescript on

Uchimura Kanzō, "First Impressions of Christendom," source: Uchimura Kanzō, *How I Became a Christian,* in *The Complete Works,* vol. 1, ed. Taijirō Yamamoto and Yōichi Mutō (Tokyo: Kyobunkwan, 1971), 105–106, 108–112, 116–119.

Education. He took up a career as a writer and commentator, becoming a special columnist for the muckraking newspaper *Yorozu Chōhō*, but was forced to abandon his journalistic career because of his pacifist views at the time of the Russo-Japanese War. In his later years he devoted himself to biblical studies and promoted the development of a Protestant church independent of control by the American missionaries. Before his death, he asked that his tombstone be inscribed in both English and Japanese: "I love two J's and no third; one is Jesus, and the other is Japan." His intensely personal and confessional memoir, from which this excerpt comes, was written in English and intended for a foreign audience. While the book was never widely read in the United States, it found a ready audience in Japan.

. . .

That I looked upon Christendom and English-speaking peoples with peculiar reverence was not an altogether inexcusable weakness on my part. It was the same weakness that made the Great Frederick of Prussia a slavish adorer of everything that was French. . . . My idea of the Christian America was lofty, religious, Puritanic. I dreamed of its templed hills, and rocks that rang with hymns and praises. Hebraisms, I thought, to be the prevailing speech of the American commonalty, and cherub and cherubim, hallelujahs and amens, the common language of its streets.

I was often told upon a good testimony that money is all in all in America, and that it is *worshipped* there as the Almighty Dollar; that the race prejudice is so strong there that the yellow skin and almond-shaped eyes pass for objects of derision and dog-barking; etc., etc. But for me to credit such statements like these as anything near the truth was utterly impossible. The land of Patrick Henry and Abraham Lincoln, of Dorothea Dix and Stephen Girard—how *could* it be a land of mammon-worship and race-distinction! I thought I had different eyes to judge of the matter,— so strong was my confidence in what I had read and heard about the superiority of the Christian civilization over that of the Pagan. Indeed, the image of America as pictured upon my mind was that of a *Holy Land.*

At the day-break of Nov. 24, 1884, my enraptured eyes first caught the faint views of Christendom. Once more I descended to my steerage-cabin, and there I was upon my knees;—the moment was too serious for me to join with the popular excitement of the hour. As the low Coast Range came clearer to my views, the sense of my dreams being now realized overwhelmed me with gratitude, and tears trickled *rapidly* down my cheeks. Soon the Golden Gate was passed, and all the chimneys and mast-tops now presented to my vision appeared like so many church-spires pointing toward the sky. We landed,—the company of some twenty young men,—and were hackneyed to a hotel owned by an Irishman who was known to show special kindness to men of my nation. As my previous acquaintance with the Caucasian race had been mostly with missionaries, the idea stuck close to my mind; and so all the people whom I met in the street appeared to me like so many ministers fraught with high Christian purpose, and I could not but imagine myself as walking among the congregation of the First-born. It was only gradually, *very* gradually, that I unlearnt this childish notion. . . .

The report that money was the almighty power in America was corroborated by many of our actual experiences. Immediately after our arrival at San Francisco, our faith in "Christian civilization" was severely tested by a disaster that befell one of our numbers. He was *pickpocketed* of a purse that contained a five-dollar-gold piece! "Pick-pocket-ing in Christendom as in Pagandom," we cautioned to each other; and while in dismay and confusion we were consoling our robbed brother, an elderly lady, who afterward told us that she believed in the universal salvation of mankind, good as well as bad, took our misfortune heavily upon her heart, and warned us of further dangers, as pick-pocket-ing, burglary-ing, high-way-ing, and all other transgressions of the sinful humanity were not unknown in her land as well. We did only wish, however, that that crank who despoiled us of that precious five-dollar-piece would never go to heaven, but be really damned in everlasting hell-fire. . . .

One year after this, when I was again robbed of my new silk-umbrella on a Fall River steamer, whose superb ornamentation and exquisite music conveyed to me no idea whatever of the spirit of knavery that lurked underneath, and so did once more liberate my heathen innocence, I felt the misfortune so keenly, that only once in my life I prayed for the damnation of that execrable devil, who *could* steal a shelter from a homeless stranger at the time of his dire necessity. Even the Chinese civilization of forty centuries ago could boast of a state of society when nobody picked up things dropped on the street. But here upon Christian waters, in a floating palace, under the spell of the music of Handel and Mendelssohn, things were as unsafe as in a den of robbers.

Indeed, insecurity of things in Christendom is something to which we were wholly unaccustomed. Never have I seen more extensive use of *keys* than among these Christian people. We in our heathen homes have but very little recourse to keys. Our houses, most of them, are open to everybody. Cats come in and out at their own sweet pleasures, and men go to siesta in their beds with zephyrs blowing over their faces; and no apprehensions are felt of our servants or neighbors ever transgressing upon our possessions. But things are quite otherwise in Christendom. Not only are safes and trunks locked, but doors and windows of all descriptions, chests, drawers, ice-boxes, sugar-vases, all. The housewife goes about her business with a bundle of keys jingling at her side; and a bachelor coming home in evening has first to thrust his hand into his pocket to draw out a cluster of some twenty or thirty keys to find out one which will open to him his lonely cell. The house is locked from the front-door to the pin-box, as if the spirit of robbery pervaded every cubic-inch of the air. . . . Whether a civilization which requires cemented cellars and stone-cut vaults, watched over by bull-dogs and battalions of policemen, could be called Christian is seriously doubted by honest heathens.

In no other respect, however, did Christendom appear to me more like heathendom than in the strong race prejudice still existing among its people. After a "century of dishonor," the copper-colored children of the forest, from whom the land was wrested by many a cruel and inhuman means, are still looked upon by the commonalty as no better than buffaloes or Rocky Mountain sheep, to be trapped and hunted like wild beasts. As for ten millions of Hamites whom they originally imported from Africa, as they now import Devon bulls and Jersey cows, and just for the very same purpose, there was shown considerable sympathy and Christian brotherhood some thirty years ago; and beginning with John Brown, that righteous Saxon, 500,000 of the flower of the nation were to be butchered to atone for the iniquity of merchandizing upon God's images. And though they now have so condescended themselves as to ride in the same cars with the "darkies," they still keep up their Japhetic vanity by keeping themselves at respectable distances from the race which they bought with their own blood. Down in the state of Delaware, whither I was once taken by a friend of mine as his guest, I was astonished to find a separate portion of a town given up wholly to negroes. Upon telling my friend that this making a sharp racial distinction appeared to me very Pagan-like, his emphatic answer was that he would rather be a Pagan and live separate from "niggers," than be a Christian and live in the same quarters with them!

But strong and unchristian as their feeling is against the Indians and the Africans, the prejudice, the aversion, the repugnance, which they entertain against the children of Sina, are something which we in heathendom have never seen the like. The land which sends over missionaries to China, to convert her sons and daughters to Christianity from the nonsense of Confucius and the superstitions of Buddha,—the very same land abhors even the shadow of a Chinaman cast upon its soil. There never was seen such an anomaly upon the face of this earth. Is Christian mission a child's play, a chivalry more puerile than that engaged the wit of Cervantes, that it should be sent to a people so much disliked by the people who send it? . . .

I have cautiously kept back my nationality from my readers, (though by this time it must be pretty well known to them). But I must make this confession that I am not a Chinaman myself. Though I am never ashamed of my racial relationship to that most ancient of nations,—that nation that gave Mencius and Confucius to the world, and invented the mariner's compass and printing machines centuries before the Europeans even dreamed of them,—yet to receive in my person all the indignities and asperities with which the poor coolies from Canton are goaded by the American populace, required nothing less than Christian forbearance to keep my head and heart in right order. Here again, American Hebraisms, which are applied even in the nomenclatures of horses, are made use of in the designations of the Chinese. They are all called "John," and even the kind policemen of the city of New York call us by that name. "Pick up those Chinamen in," was the polite language of a Chicago coachman, to whom we paid the regular fare, and did nothing to hurt his vanity as a protégé of St. Patrick. A well-clad gentleman sharing the same seat with me in a car asked me to have my comb to brush his grizzly beard; and instead of a thank [you] which we in heathendom consider as appropriate upon such an occasion, he returned the comb saying, "Well John, where do you keep your laundry shop?" An intelligent-looking gentleman asked us when did we cut our cues: and when told that we never had cues, "Why," he said, "I thought all Chinamen have cues." That these very gentlemen, who seem to take peculiar delight in deriding our Mongolian origin, are themselves peculiarly sensitive as to their Saxon birthright, is well illustrated by the following little incident:

A group of young Japanese engineers went to examine the Brooklyn Bridge. When under the pier, the structure and tension of each of the suspending ropes were being discussed upon, a silk-hatted, spectacled, and decently dressed American gentleman approached them. "Well John," he intruded upon the Japanese scientists, "these things must look awful strange to you from China, ey!" One among the Japanese retorted the insulting question, and said, "So they must be to you from Ireland." The gentleman got angry and said, "No, indeed not. I am not an Irish." "And so we are not Chinese," was the gentle rejoinder. It was a good blow, and the silk-hatted sulked away. He did not like to be called an Irish.

Time fails me to speak of other unchristian features of Christendom. What about legalized lottery which can depend for its stability upon its millions in gold and silver, right in [the] face of simple morality clear even to the understanding of a child; of widespread gambling propensities, as witnessed in scenes of cock-fights, horse-race, and football matches, of pugilism, more inhuman than Spanish bull-fights; of lynching, fitted more for Hottentots than for the people of a free Republic; of rum-traffic, whose magnitude can find no parallel in the trade of the whole world; of demagogism in politics; of denominational jealousies in religion; of capitalists' tyranny and laborers' insolence; of millionaires' fooleries; of men's hypocritical love toward their wives; etc., etc., etc.? Is this the civilization we were taught by missionaries to accept as an evidence of the superiority of Christian Religion over other religions? With what shamefacedness did they declare unto us that the religion which made Europe and America must surely be the religion from on high? If it was Christianity that made the so-called Christendom of to-day, let Heaven's eternal curse rest upon it! Peace is the last thing we can find in Christendom. Turmoils, complexities, insane asylums, penitentiaries, poor-houses! . . .

One thing I shall never do in future: I shall never defend Christianity upon its being the religion of Europe and America. An "external evidence" of this nature is not only weak, but actually vicious in its general effects. The religion that can support an immortal soul must have surer and profounder bases than such a "show" of evidence to rest upon. Yet I once built my faith upon a straw like that.

KŌTOKU SHŪSUI, "LETTERS FROM SAN FRANCISCO" (1905–1906)

Kōtoku Shūsui (1871–1911), the son of a rural merchant, plunged into the anti-government "popular rights" movement as a teenager. After being expelled from Tokyo for his political activities in 1887, he returned to pursue a career as a radical journalist, working for the *Yorozu chōhō*. He soon developed a passionate interest in the social problems created by industrialization. In 1901 he joined with Abe Isoo, Katayama Sen, and others to establish the first socialist political party in Japan. Strongly opposed to the war with Russia, he resigned from the *Yorozu*, which supported it, and began writing for a weekly radical paper, the *Heimin shin-*

Kōtoku Shūsui, "Letters from San Francisco," source: Kōtoku Shūsui, *Kōtoku Shūsui zenshū*, vol. 6 (Tokyo: Meiji bunken, 1968), 19–43, 82–88.

bun. In 1904 he coauthored the first translation of Karl Marx's *The Communist Manifesto* and was imprisoned for five months in 1905 for violating the press code. When released from jail he traveled to California to contact Japanese radicals living there. His account of his stay, published in *Hikari,* another radical newspaper, is notable for its critique of America as an oppressive capitalist society. Kōtoku's experience in America, including witnessing the San Francisco earthquake of 1906, solidified his anarchist sentiments, which eventually led to his arrest and execution by the Japanese government in 1911 for an alleged plot against the life of the Meiji emperor.

. . .

12/15/1905

Dear compatriots in the homeland, I am in good health. Our enterprise is moving ahead slowly but steadily.

On December 9th I was invited to a banquet by reporters from two Japanese newspapers here, and on the 11th a social tea party attended by more than fifty people was held for me. Some guests were socialists and some were not, but all of them greeted me in a kindly fashion.

Members of the American Socialist Party also visited me frequently, sent me various kinds of newspapers and magazines, and invited me to all sorts of meetings. Last night I attended a small meeting of a branch of the San Francisco Socialist Party. It was a most pleasant and refined gathering. They treated this comrade from afar in a cheerful and kindly way, almost as they would treat one of their own countrymen. When foreign Socialists visit Japan, I hope the Japan Socialist Party will treat them the same way.

I have become a member of the San Francisco Socialist Party in order to study their methods and to facilitate cooperation with them. I also meet once a week with the [Socialists] at the Heiminsha.

The Heiminsha is suitable as a club, but people drop by so often that we rented a little room about two or three blocks away . . . in the house of Mrs. Fritz, a member of the Russian Revolutionary Party. Three times a day we go to the Heiminsha or to the YMCA.

Our room is about four to five mats in size. From the entrance a *shōji*-covered window overlooks the street outside; on the left wall above the stove hangs a big portrait of Mr. Kropotkin, and on the right wall is a portrait of Bakunin about the same size. There are also landscape paintings of deep mountains and broad plains. On shelves by the stove are many books by Gorky, Zola, and Kropotkin as well as many photographs. . . .

As I am writing this letter three men from the Industrial Workers of the World (all of them Socialists) have arrived. I will be going to their meeting, where I have been asked to give a speech. . . .

As yet I know nothing about the middle and upper classes in the United States. I know nothing about them at all. But they have been well studied and spoken about by those who have traveled in the West until now. I think that I want to try to have contact with the social and movements of the lower classes. [From the January 20, 1906, issue of *Hikari*]

1/27/1906

As I reported, meetings to commemorate Bloody Sunday were held with great success in every state and every city in the United States.[8] Great sympathy has been shown toward the Russian Revolutionary Party, and assistance has been sent to it. Most members of the Japan Socialist Party attended a similar meeting held in Oakland on January 21st. That evening more than four hundred men and women from Alameda, Berkeley, and other surrounding communities attended. Among them were thirty or forty Japanese.

The meeting began under bright electric lights with an angry chorus of "The Marseillaise." Four appointed speakers each spoke for about twenty minutes. Mr. Anthony, representative from the Industrial Workers of the World, lambasted unions that had adopted the principle of harmonious cooperation between labor and capital, and he insisted on the urgency of revolution. Next Mrs. Olive Johnson, speaking with fiery eloquence, began by talking about the [First] International, organized by Karl Marx [sic] and others, and proclaimed that the workers' revolution was international. The third speaker, Austin Lewis, from the Socialist Party (formerly the Social Democratic Party), attacked the tyranny of the Russian government with cool anger. At the end, representing my Japanese comrades, I spoke, saying that the revolution of our comrades in Russia marked the beginning of a worldwide revolution and that we intended to exert our utmost efforts to assist in carrying it out. Applause and cheers swept in unceasing waves over the entire audience during the speeches. When my speech was done, a dozen or more comrades immediately rushed up to the

podium and with cries of "Thank you, thank you" and asked to shake
my hand. Since most of them were refugees from Russia, this was a
great pleasure for me. . . .

Mr. Simon, editor of the *International Socialist Review,* sent a letter
from Chicago in which he wrote: "Dear Comrade, I cannot contain
my joy at hearing that you have arrived in the United States. Here at
least you will not be in danger of facing imprisonment. But at the same
time I know from a certain incident that not even the United States is
a place where authoritarian government is impossible."

The United States is not at all a paradise of freedom. If it is a paradise at all, it is a paradise only for the wealthy. At least it is a paradise
only when compared to Japan, Russia, China, or Korea. Day by day
revolutionary thought is gradually rising in the United States. The revolutions of the twentieth century will be economic revolutions. Anywhere there is a gap between the poor and the rich, the billowing waves
of revolution are bound to arrive. [From the March 5, 1906, issue of
Hikari]

2/29/1906

As you know, in the United States the [Socialists] are divided into two
factions, those calling themselves simply the Socialist Party and those
calling themselves the Socialist Workers Party. They are in conflict with
one another. Until now I had visited people from the Socialist Party
from time to time, but since I still knew nothing about the headquarters of the Socialist Workers Party, feeling a bit bored I set out from
the house to visit. It is located in a dirty back alley. . . . After climbing
up the stairs, to the right there was a hallway with a meeting room the
size of several dozen mats, and to the left there was a poolroom with
newspapers and magazines. I stumbled into the midst of several dozen
comrades reading and talking there. It was very much like the headquarters of the Socialist Party.

I met many friends of Mr. [Ben Lewis] Reitman [an American anar-
chist] who visited Japan last year, and they often talk of Japan. I asked
about the attitude of the Socialist Workers Party toward the Japanese
exclusion movement among the labor unions in San Francisco, but
everyone expressed sympathy toward the Japanese and was very much
against the exclusion movement. Since the members of the Socialist
Workers Party oppose American unions that favor "harmony between
capital and labor," in June last year they organized a new revolutionary labor union—the International Workers of the World, with its head-

quarters in Chicago. As its name indicates it is completely cosmopolitan with no trace of racial discrimination. If Japanese workers unite themselves and start a movement to cooperate with this organization, they would secure powerful support. But since a majority of the poor benighted Japanese workers know nothing about socialism, they know nothing about the existence of the international labor union movement. They know only about the [anti-Japanese] exclusionist faction, and they confuse that faction with the Socialists.

[Members of the Socialist Workers Party] asked me why it was that their Japanese comrades did not hold open-air street rallies every night. Naturally the Americans, the Germans, the Italians, and the Irish all do this a great deal. [I told them that] it was because open rallies were prohibited in their home country, Japan, and that they ignored the fact that in a free country like this, street speeches were easy to organize. From now on, they said that they would encourage the Japanese workers.

There was a portrait of Karl Marx at the Socialist Workers Party headquarters. I bought it and will send it to the Heiminsha Milk Hall in Tokyo. It is my gift, comrades, so please hang it in the meeting room. If you hang it on the podium whenever there is a speech meeting, I think it will look quite rousing and make a deep impression [on the audience]. [From the April 5, 1906, issue of *Hikari*]

3/22/1906

Within the American Socialist Party today two factions debate and struggle with one another over the movement's policies. One faction, which principally champions the public ownership of monopolies, attempts to use the ballot box as its weapon; the other faction raises the banner of pure socialist ideals.

The first faction takes the following position: We must work to advance the true interests of the working class bit by bit and step by step. It is not good to see only the ideals and to neglect actual problems immediately in front of us. Our German comrades occupy an advantageous position, and our comrades in England won during the recent election. Both adopted election platforms directly related to the interests of workers.

The other faction takes the following position: The so-called system of national or municipal ownership will not destroy the system of wage labor. The national government and even local self-government units simply represent the private capitalists. Socialism fundamentally demands destruction of the wage labor system. If one supports national or municipal ownership under the present system, then one is making concessions to the social meliorists and state socialism.

The struggle between these two factions will become more and more intense. Not only in the United States but also in all the European countries, there are conflicts between the idealists and the pragmatists, the revolutionaries and the reformists, the radicals and the moderates, those who insist on spreading principles and those who aim at winning elections. Our own Socialist Party needs to study these issues carefully. I personally pray that our own Japanese Socialist Party will not fight and split apart because of such differences.

However, if I were to pick one or the other, I would prefer the idealist, the revolutionary, and the radical. I do not like lukewarm socialism, sugar-coated socialism, or state socialism. [From the April 20, 1906, issue of *Hikari*]

4/14/1906

America is a country of democratic government [*minshu seiji*]. It is a country of liberty. But freedom of speech, freedom of assembly, and freedom of publishing are being whittled away day by day, month by month. Those who attempt heated opposition to the politics, religion, manners, or mores of the gentlemen's clique [i.e., the bourgeoisie] all suffer cruel persecution. Several days ago at a big meeting of the workers' movement in San Francisco, many comrades were beaten by the police and thrown into jail. It was a demonstration to protest the incarceration of officials of the Western Miners League in Colorado.

The police frequently interfere with the street speech rallies by the white [i.e., American] Socialist Party. Naturally they have no authority at all to prohibit these rallies. Nevertheless, using one excuse or another, they interfere with them. Needless to say, speaking or writing anything about atheism, anarchism, or the like is subject to extraordinary restrictions. This oppression and persecution of workers is no different from what goes on in Russia or Japan. Look at the scars on my shoulders! I got them when the police beat me.

Can there be liberty, can there be human rights anywhere a capitalist class or a landlord class exists? In such a place one can hear only "the caterwauling of a gang of villains." No doubt we have heard such [caterwauling] in Japan since the end of the Russo-Japanese War. That is why our own Japan qualifies as a civilized country and a great power. . . . Millionaires, banzai! [From the May 20, 1906, issue of *Hikari*]

4/21/1906

Urgent newspaper reports about the earthquake and fire surely must have alarmed you. Please rest assured that we are all safe.

Huge fires have spread ceaselessly for three days and three nights. Most of the city around Market Street, the most important section of San Francisco, has been reduced to ashes. The San Francisco office of the Heiminsha was caught in the midst of the flames and barely escaped destruction.

My temporary dwelling place is a room at the front of a three-story building on a hilly rise overlooking the city. With a telescope in hand I am fortunate to have a grand and spectacular view day and night. It [the fire] is truly grand and spectacular, with little historical precedent, comparable only to the signal fires of the barbarians or the sight of Nero's Rome in flames.

It is reported that 300,000 people have lost their houses and are living in open air. Throughout the rest of the city, foodstuffs have been commandeered by the government. Food cannot be bought by private persons. The citizens of the city are all staving off hunger through the relief efforts of the authorities. If it becomes more and more difficult to obtain food for the next few days, we plan to leave the city together and move over to Berkeley. . . .

White people are said to be intelligent, but their lack of pluck is no match for the nonchalance of us Orientals. When they [whites] encounter untimely misfortune they do not lose their heads or rush about in confusion. They simply wail, weep, and act bewildered. In extreme cases, many go mad, either because they lost all hope when their possessions were destroyed by fire or simply because they were overcome with fear.

At the moment there are neither electric lights nor gas throughout the city. Lighting lamps or stoves inside houses is completely forbidden. It is pitch dark at night. Martial law has been declared, and anyone using fire inside the house will be shot immediately by the troops. Numerous people have been killed by looters, robbers, and scavengers. Ah, fire! How comforting it is. There are no gods, no wealth, and no authority at all anywhere. The many grand and powerful churches, the lofty city hall building, the countless banks, and great wealth have all disappeared in a rain of embers.

Hunger and cold will come, and so will the loss of jobs. Thousands of poor people will suffer cruel hardship. But that will not be the fault of the fire; it will only be the fault of today's social organization. [From the May 20, 1906, issue of *Hikari*]

4/24/1906

I have found the recent holocaust in San Francisco a very useful experiment. . . . Since May 18th the whole city of San Francisco has been in a state of complete anarchist communism. Commerce has stopped completely; postal services, railroads, and steamers to neighboring areas are all free of charge; members of the relief committee distribute foodstuffs every day. The delivery of provisions, the care of the sick and the injured, the cleanup of the burned areas, and the building of refugee centers are all undertaken by able-bodied youths recruited compulsorily. Since there are no goods to buy even if you wish, money has become completely useless. All privately owned property has disappeared. Isn't that interesting? Even this ideal paradise will continue only for the next few weeks, however, and then it will return to the old capitalist system. How sad that is. [From the May 20, 1906, issue of *Hikari*]

CHAPTER 2

Students and Immigrants

[handwritten annotation: majority of Japanese visitors to the US were students]

Until the end of the twentieth century, Japanese visitors to the United States were few and far between. Only three thousand or so arrived before 1890, among them "undesirables" from the country's lower orders: entertainers, gamblers, acrobats, prostitutes, and pimps. The majority, however, were students. For centuries, the Japanese had seen the outside world as a threatening place. Under the shogunate, movement out of the country (or back in) had been forbidden. But even before the Meiji Restoration, travel abroad became an opportunity to acquire "new knowledge" from the outside world to strengthen the country. In 1866 two young samurai arrived at Rutgers College, determined to learn "how to build ships and how to make cannons" to defend the country against the Russians, and during the next two decades the Meiji government provided scholarships to promising young men—and a handful of young women— to study in foreign universities, then return to work for the new nation. Others, with grand ambitions but only scanty funds, went abroad in hopes of "rising in the world."

Learning abroad was one thing, but settling abroad was another. For the Japanese, permanent migration was a novel idea. To prevent "undesirables" from besmirching the country's reputation (and to protect Japanese from the unscrupulous exploitation suffered by Chinese coolies), the Japanese government prohibited manual laborers from going abroad. Instead it tried to encourage migration from the main islands to Hokkaido, the archipelago's northernmost island, which became a frontier zone not unlike America's. The first wave of officially approved external migration began only in the 1886, when the government struck a deal with Hawaiian sugar plantation owners, most of them Americans, to send over contract field-workers. Once their contracts expired, the workers were expected to return to Japan.

Only in the 1890s did the idea of out-migration stir public attention, as politicians and intellectuals argued that sending Japanese abroad to live was a way of anchoring Japan's status as a world power. In 1893 a group of scholars, officials, and politicians (including Shiba Shirō) founded the Colonization Society to promote peaceful expansion by the Japanese. "Overseas settlement," the organizers proclaimed, "is a vital aspect of the national policy, adopted at the Meiji Restoration, of elevating our spirit, broadening our vista, introducing new knowledge, and reforming people's minds."[1] While that was a tall order, most agreed that Japanese settlements abroad would not only promote trade and access to raw materials but also create a Japanese presence on the world stage, enabling the country to compete with Western powers. As one supporter of overseas colonization wrote in 1906, "If our people succeed in constructing new Japans everywhere [in Asia] and engage in vigorous activities throughout the Pacific, then our country's predominance over the Pacific will have been assured."[2] That was certainly the view of Yamagata Aritomo, the army chief of staff, who thought that Japanese settlements on the Asian continent would serve the country's strategic needs.

Those who wedded emigration to realpolitik in Asia were inspired by the example of Western colonialism, but those who promoted emigration to America saw it as an opportunity for individual success. During the early twentieth century, publishers began turning out guides and handbooks for would-be migrants. Indeed, these books were part and parcel of a larger publishing boom in guides of all kinds for the ambitious—for provincials seeking their fortunes in the city, students seeking entry into one of the country's new colleges or universities, and would-be functionaries trying to pass the civil service examinations. All of these guidebooks were filled with practical information about how much money to carry from home, how to find a place to live, and how to work part-time while studying. All were relentlessly upbeat about the future prospects of the young.

The most successful guidebook for going to America was written by Katayama Sen, a former student in the United States who knew how difficult it was to make one's way in a foreign land with limited resources and limited language skills. He left no doubt about the advantages of traveling to America. "At a time when North America's power is rapidly rising and its influence steadily spreading all over," he wrote in 1903, "it is extreme foolishness not to go there. . . . [It] is a stupid, uncivilized thing not to consider going to America."[3] Advocates of Japanese emigration to other parts of Asia as an instrument of peaceful national expansion expected that the migrants would be the educated sons of the new urban middle class or of well-to-do rural landowners, but by 1900 a majority of migrants who crossed the Pacific were recruited from farm families, often younger sons who were unable to inherit the family land and were looking for work as manual laborers.

After Hawaiian sugar plantation owners engineered a "revolution" that overthrew the Hawaiian monarchy, the islands were annexed to the United States in 1898. Unhappy with harsh work, dreary living conditions, and meager compensation on the sugar plantations, sixty thousand former plantation workers flooded into the West Coast area between 1899 and 1903. At first they took jobs as unskilled farm laborers or railroad construction workers, jobs once filled by Chinese immigrants who by now had been prohibited from entering the country. In the end, rather than returning to the homeland, most Japanese immigrants chose to stay in America, buying or renting land to farm or opening small shops and stores that catered to their fellow immigrants.

The industrious Japanese immigrants, like other immigrants before them, at first gravitated to closed communities, where neighbors spoke their language and offered mutual support. A Japantown grew up in San Francisco alongside the city's Chinatown, and similar communities appeared in Seattle and Los Angeles. This new wave of "Orientals" provoked the anxious gaze of white Americans, even first- or second-generation immigrants, who distrusted the Japanese as cunning, clannish, and aggressive. Like Chinese immigrants, they did not seem interested in changing their eating habits, language, or religion. Equally disturbing, the Japanese worked harder, were less demanding, and led simpler lives than white Americans. That posed an economic threat to white workers, who feared losing jobs to cheap Japanese labor, and to white farmers, who feared that Japanese farmers would bring down agricultural prices by overproducing or underselling.

The influx of Japanese excited other kinds of fear too. What made Japanese immigration more ominous than Chinese was Japan's emergence as a major military and diplomatic power. After defeating China handily in 1895, a modernized Japan demonstrated its formidable naval and military strength by winning a far more difficult war with Russia in 1905.

FIGURE 2. The anti-Japanese movement in America was a constant target of the popular humor magazine *Tokyo Puck* during the 1910s and 1920s. Here two grizzled American laborers, perhaps immigrants themselves, are literally cutting the ground from under a resolute Japanese immigrant clad in a suit that suggests he is a cut above his tormentors. The English caption reads: "The stupid American labourers would not allow the yellow people to tread on the same ground. But [President Theodore Roosevelt] and other wise statesmen would not permit this outrage." Roosevelt was widely admired in Japan, not only for supporting Japanese immigrants on the West Coast, but also for brokering a peace between Japan and Russia in 1905. (*Tokyo Puck*, January 20, 1909)

Some American commentators feared that the proud and clever Japanese would begin to migrate en masse, threatening to overwhelm, perhaps even dominate, the West Coast. An eminent Harvard professor, Archibald Cary Coolidge, expressed concern that the Japanese immigrants constituted "the vanguard of an army of hundreds of millions, who, far from retreating before the white man, thrive and multiply in competition with him."[4] As if to confirm these fears, by 1908 the number of Japanese in the United States had reached an all-time high of 103,000, or about two-thirds of the entire Japanese population who had migrated anywhere overseas.

The notion of a "Yellow Peril" conjured up images of a race war between the white and the yellow, reinforcing anxieties over the immigrant issue. In 1908 Homer Lea, a former Stanford student and skillful publicist who promoted himself as a supporter of the Chinese revolutionary movement, published *The Valor of Ignorance,* an alarmist pamphlet predicting that a future military clash between Japan and the United States would end with an overwhelming Japanese victory and a Japanese occupation of the West Coast. (Not surprisingly, the book was promptly translated and well received in Japan.) A rash of similar books followed, and the Hearst papers reported rumors of a Japanese plan to establish a colony in Baja California.

Anti-Japanese sentiment was strongest on the West Coast, where most of the immigrants settled. Often it expressed itself in violent ways with assaults on individual immigrants or in boycotts against Japanese businesses. But anti-Japanese sentiments were also codified in local and state laws that banned marriage between Asians and white Americans, excluded Japanese immigrant children from regular public schools, placed limits on the rights of immigrants to own land, and curbed the immigration of family members. The immigration issue became a source of conflict that roused populist outrage in both countries, but neither government was comfortable about dealing with the issue. The Japanese government, however, did its best to minimize friction in 1908 by accepting the so-called Gentlemen's Agreement, under which the Japanese government informally committed itself to limiting the migration of unskilled workers to America.

Many Japanese who lived in the United States realized that cultural differences made it difficult for Americans to understand them, and vice versa, so they urged forbearance, however difficult that might be, in the face of discrimination. But the influx of several million immigrants from southern and eastern Europe between 1880 and 1920 fanned a broader anti-immigrant nativist movement aimed at maintaining the "purity" of

American society. In 1924 the U.S. Congress passed a new immigration law that placed national quotas on all immigrants from European countries and brought an end to all immigration from Japan and the rest of Asia.

To the Japanese, including those who saw themselves as friendly to America, the passage of the bill was a moment of "national humiliation." An angry crowd gathered in front of the American embassy to burn the Stars and Stripes, and a nationalist group proposed a ban on American movies. The new immigration law confirmed a conclusion that had already been reached by many Japanese who had previously traveled within the United States: America was a deeply racist society dominated by a white supremacist mentality that belied the American ideology of liberty and equality. (Nonetheless, few Japanese boycotted Charlie Chaplin and Harold Lloyd comedies in protest against the new immigration law.)

KATAYAMA SEN,
"ADVICE ON GOING TO AMERICA" (1901)

Katayama Sen (1860–1933), an early socialist and trade union organizer, came from a broken family in Okayama Prefecture. After seeking his fortune in Tokyo, he departed for the United States, where he attended Grinnell College, in Iowa, then studied at Andover Theological Seminary, in Massachusetts, and Yale Divinity School. He was converted not only to Christianity but also to the "Social Gospel," a movement to reform society through the application of biblical principles. On his return to Japan in the 1890s after a decade abroad, he founded the first modern settlement house in Tokyo and helped to organize the first socialist party in Japan. His best-selling guidebook for immigrants to the United States, aimed at ambitious young men of modest means, reflected his own experiences. Although its style was heavily didactic, the book found a ready audience among young people at a time when opportunities for rapid advancement at home had begun to narrow. In 1914 Katayama returned to the United States to live as an expatriate in San Francisco, then in New York, where he plunged into American left-wing politics. At the end of World War I, he helped organize the American Communist Party, and in 1921 he traveled to Moscow, where the Bolsheviks gave him a hero's welcome. For the rest of his life he remained in the Soviet Union, serving as

Katayama Sen, "Advice on Going to America," source: Katayama Sen, *To-Bei annai* (Tokyo: Rōdōshinbunsha, 1901), 8–9, 25–29, 33, 37–44.

an expert on Japanese and Asian revolutionary movements. After his death in 1933 he was buried in the Kremlin wall alongside other Communist luminaries.

. . .

The question that most worries Japanese who want to go to the United States with little or no money is whether they will be able to support themselves and study once they get there. . . . A decision to cross the Pacific Ocean to find a job and acquire an education without a penny to one's name is indeed a formidable one. . . .

The United States of America is by far the freest country in the world. It is unrivaled in the world for its industrial development, its economic progress, and its academic achievements. What distinguishes America the most is the high value placed on labor. The saying that "labor is sacred" is put into practice in North America. Wages are the highest in the world, and laborers are accorded high status. It is not at all unusual for a laborer to study while he works.

If we Japanese go to America with sturdy bodies and a willingness to turn our hands to work, it will be not at all difficult to realize our dreams. Even if we meet obstacles, success is not at all impossible. We are certain to achieve it. . . .

When those who want to go to America, or those who have already arrived there, ask me whether they need to worry, my answer is: "If your determination is strong enough to cut through rock and stone, if your aspirations and goals are higher than the Rocky Mountains, if you have perseverance, enthusiasm, and willingness to make a strenuous effort without becoming discouraged, and if you are in good health, you have all the ingredients you need for success." It is natural to worry about the cost of the ship's fare or the money needed to get settled after arriving in America, but those with the qualifications I described will never have to face any problems. . . .

America is a civilized country, so there are many kinds of occupations and many opportunities. Americans are alert and energetic. Laborers, unlike those in Japan, work very industriously. The kinds of work a Japanese can do in America are quite limited. If we look at jobs Japanese hold [in America] today, they include "housework," cooking, waiting tables, laundering, logging, picking fruit, farming, railroad construction, and peddling. There are also Japanese who work as receptionists, errand boys, and "schoolboys" [i.e., part-time student domestic workers]. Not everyone can do all of these jobs well. If you do not choose work that fits your own individual talents or that will help achieve your goals, you will face difficult challenges.

There are two main types of work in America: outdoor work and domestic work. Naturally those who work outside must use their physical strength, and those who work indoors must be alert and use their heads. In other words, one must train oneself for each type of work. First, let me describe the different types of domestic work available.

At present, most opportunities to get a start are in "housework"—helping out with domestic chores. The word *housework* refers to the work of maidservants and errand boys. Let me explain what kind of work this is. You wake up early in the morning, start the fire in the stove, and clean up around the front entrance. In due time you will prepare your own food, but first you will simply help the cook. Then you will check the master's bedroom to see that he is awake and open the windows. After that you will clean each room in the house, starting in the parlor. When you have finished with these tasks you will help with breakfast, and afterward you will wash the pots and dishes and clean up the kitchen. Then you will wash the windows and perhaps dust the rooms until about ten o'clock.

After lunch, you may be asked to perform some special task; then you will usually have a two-hour break. You must help prepare the evening meal, and after dinner, as at breakfast time, you will take out the garbage, wash the dirty dishes, and clean the kitchen. After finishing your tasks, your duties for the day are done.

From this point on you are free to do whatever you want. If you want to study, you may study. You can choose to stay indoors at home or go out. Above all, you must guard against laziness and disobedience and diligently apply yourself to your responsibilities. If you are lazy, you will be severely reprimanded. On the other hand, if you are trustworthy and industrious, if you never disobey orders, if you work with alertness and with enthusiasm, your employer will trust you enough to let you have the precious key to his house. The fact that Westerners place such a high value on trust is a sure sign of how civilized they are.

To be sure, housework earns you very little money. The usual weekly wage is roughly five dollars. Those who try to earn eight or nine dollars a week cannot do so without a great deal of struggle. If you do "housework" or work as a domestic servant, you will not be able to buy fancy clothes. But the job is economical and convenient. Every week you will have to wash and iron the laundry.

Even though housework is not all that difficult, a lack of perseverance is the reason Japanese fail at it. If you observe how the Japanese work, you see that they rush about when doing the most arduous tasks, but they immediately become tired and take a rest. And when they do very easy tasks, they seem to find it difficult. A Chinaman is like an ox who thinks nothing of plodding along at a steady pace for a thousand miles. But the same cannot be said of the Japanese.

Nor would anyone describe housework as fun. For every three hundred and sixty days of the year nothing changes. Of course, during the week there is some variety of tasks: laundering, ironing, cleaning the bath, and scrubbing the lavatory. And every day of the week there is different food to prepare, but the following week it will be the same old dishes once again.

On Sundays you will not have much to do. You need only take care of meals. However, as I said before, you must never shirk your duties, and you must act discreetly at all times. And you must restrain yourself. For example, you must never ask someone to do your chores because you have to go out on other business.

As I said, every week resembles the one before, so even if you are gradually able to advance toward your long-term goal, such as earning thirty dollars a month, you will certainly still want to try some other kind of work. Few people doing housework actually achieve success. However, if you persevere and aim at achieving great things, "housework" is not like being a Japanese maidservant or a manservant who is at the mercy of someone's every beck and call. The duties expected of you will be clearly defined, and if performed diligently to the best of your ability, your work will go very easily. As you exert yourself, in time you will become skilled, build up experience, and become an accomplished worker. And gradually you will come to understand the language too.

Since you will be doing the laundry you will learn how to wash clothes. And eventually if you learn how to wash men's shirts, you might apprentice yourself to a laundry shop in the hope of someday starting your own laundry business, with just a little money. . . .

Once you have decided on the choice of an occupation there is one thing that you must be aware of in order to succeed at your job. In any work they do, the Japanese lack perseverance. You must fortify your spirit with perseverance at all times. Like an ox that can walk a thousand miles without minding the distance, you must exert yourself and steadily make your way forward with indomitable enthusiasm.

Focusing on personal economy is also of utmost importance. If you emphasize personal economy you will come to value your time. If you value your time, you will realize how important perseverance is. When I say a sense of perseverance will invariably lead to success, I am not encouraging false hopes.

If you emphasize perseverance and personal economy, you will realize how important it is to save money. Naturally people with no money find themselves in a sorry state. While you are working you must resolve to devote yourself to saving money. When it comes to savings you must be extremely wary of other people. It can be very dangerous to entrust money to anyone. You should think twice about asking anyone to deposit money in a post office savings account on your behalf. Your time is valuable, of course, but even if you have to lose a day's work, you should still go to the post office and deposit the money yourself.

For example, many railroad construction workers who were loath to travel many miles just to deposit their wages entrusted their savings to friends and found themselves cheated. Contrary to what you might expect, taking a day off is not the same as throwing your wages to the wind. You should even be wary of your own boss. Let me warn you again and again to keep your money on your person at all times and never let it out of your sight. Workers trying to earn money in the United States are not treated as human beings if they lose their money. Not only will they be treated as less than human beings, they will suffer cruelties worse than those inflicted on beasts. . . .

Let me turn now to those who want to go to the United States to study. Students fall into three broad categories. The first consists of those sent on government scholarships to master a particular skill. These so-called scholarship students are graduates of universities, often the top students, who go to America to master knowledge in a specific discipline.

The second category consists of children of wealthy provincial families and the sons of high-ranking government officials and rich merchants. There are many such students. Naturally since their families or relatives provide their funds, they tend to be well educated. Even those not so well educated at least have money. So I do not think it necessary to say much about such students.

The third category consists of those who go to study in the United States at their own expense and who struggle to work their way through school. This type of student gets travel money from parents, relatives, or friends, then finds suitable work after he arrives. Some pursue their academic studies, while others acquire a trade or craft. This type of student is the most common of the three. When I decided to write this guide for students going to America, I thought I should give these students advice, warn them what to expect, and try to make things go smoothly for them.

First, determination is the most important thing required of those who go to America. Students cannot succeed without determination. Second, it is important to pay attention to your physical health. No matter what enterprises or studies you intend to embark on, you will certainly face tremendous difficulties if you do not have a robust constitution. . . . A poor student can feed and clothe himself, but one who is physically weak can neither work nor study. The physically weak are truly the poorest students. If an unhealthy person, against reason, insists on going to America, he only goes to his death. No matter what your goals or how intensely you go about your business, you will not be able to make a living if you are not in good health. And if you cannot support yourself, no matter how much you may want to study, you will be able neither to study nor to achieve your aims. . . .

Now let me turn to the background you ought to have before going to America. People with considerable working experience are the most successful in America. Those who have worked since childhood—delivering milk, delivering newspapers, or working as shop apprentices—are the best qualified to seek their fortunes in the United States. The sons of well-to-do rural families who get money from home supposedly to study, but shun exercise and devote themselves to having fun after they come to Tokyo— whether to study or not—will certainly not be able to endure the difficulties of life in the United States.

On the other hand, those who have supported themselves in Japan and whose bodies have been tempered by hardship will be able to overcome all obstacles and ultimately achieve success. Those who know nothing of hardship, who have lived in tidy houses, who have worn fine patterned silks, who have never suffered extreme heat or cold, and who have tasted fine delicacies, will not be able to succeed at all. Those who have supported themselves and have worked their way through school have what it takes to succeed.

What sort of temperament is best suited to studying in the United States? The most important thing of all is to be simple and honest. Anywhere he goes, but especially in America, an honest person will always find work. Americans like people who are honest and fair-minded and who do not invite suspicion or doubt. . . . Americans also have a strong aversion to people who are not straightforward and who do not say what they think. They like those who are not hypocritical, who are direct, and who are alert. If you lack these qualities, you must cultivate them thoroughly in preparation for your journey to America.

As in Japan or anywhere else, even those rich in ability can end in failure, lose hope, ruin their bodies, and lose their determination. If they lack perseverance they will veer off in the wrong direction. On the other hand, if a person works industriously and studies during his spare time, he will be able to settle into student life easily. The reason that those who the more talented think are slow as oxen eventually achieve success is simply that they have perseverance. This quality, more than anything else, will enable you to work your way through school in the United States. The single word *perseverance* encompasses everything and is all that you will need. Even if you have a sound body and strong spirit, in the end you will never reach the promised land if you lack perseverance. . . . Empty in body and soul, you will be cast up on the shores of despair.

With perseverance you can meet the demands on your body, and with perseverance you can pursue the fulfillment of the hopes of your spirit. If you abandon perseverance, how can you achieve your aims in life? I know of no way that we can achieve our own goals if we abandon our perseverance. Even a person of genius who uses his gifts to reap rewards for a while will never be able to maintain his position for long and will never find contentment. Without perseverance his mind will become restless, his emotions will become confused, and inevitably he will sink into corruption. Perseverance is like the businessman's capital and the student's tuition. . . .

As I said earlier, in order to prepare yourself for ultimate success in the United States, honesty and simplicity in spirit are essential, but the best way to develop these is by nurturing a sense of religious piety and by embracing religious ideas. Since religion goes hand in hand with morality, those with religious piety realize the utmost importance of morality. Those who want to pursue various enterprises in Europe and the United States, especially those who want to work their way through school, should study religion to nourish their souls and find physical respite through religion. Just as it is natural for a bush warbler to perch on a plum flower, a person with strong morals will have no trouble making many acquaintances and winning their trust. You will be treated well if you are armed with a fulfilled spirit. Never forget that a beautiful person with beautiful ideals will get his just rewards.

In conclusion, I wish to encourage fellow Japanese who support themselves while studying. If you can endure the hardships of study in Japan, then you are also ready to go to America. You ought to do so for your own sake, for the sake of Japan, for the sake of society, and for the sake of mankind. Since Japan is still a small country, its society does not know how to treat ambitious students properly. If you want to study, you must go to the United States. If you embrace the ideals I have discussed, the road of learning will open up for you. . . . My friends, I can guarantee personally that there is no need to hesitate. If you have high ideals and a mind to study, you will find tremendous sympathy in America, even if you are poor and have no resources. Those who were born in a log cabin or who polished shoes for a living have become ministers of state. My student friends, go to America! Those who want to put yourselves through school, go to America! America has opened the way for all of you to pursue your studies. America shows its great sympathy for all. You need have no fear. You need never feel discouraged. Just heed the advice of this writer. Take what I have said as your ideal, keep your spirits high, and aim at achieving victory in the end!

NOGUCHI YONEJIRŌ, "MY LIFE IN CALIFORNIA" (1911)

Noguchi Yonejirō (1875–1947) came to the United States in the late 1890s after dropping out of Keiō University. Although he worked briefly as a "schoolboy" for middle-class families in California, his ambition was to become a poet—an English-language poet. He sought the acquaintance of the poet Joaquin Miller, a flamboyant character living in the Oakland, California, hills, and under Miller's guidance he began to compose his own work. His peculiar syntax and Japanesque imagery attracted the attention of the San Francisco literary community. Aiming to gain a wider reputation, he left the West Coast for New York City, where he wrote a popular English novelette about a young Japanese woman traveling abroad. While in the United States, he had a number of love affairs, including one that produced an illegitimate son, the sculptor Isamu Noguchi. After returning to Japan in 1904, he became a professor of English literature at Keiō University, and he continued to write poetry and essays in both English and Japanese.

. . .

The new life after death, I believed, began when I left Tokyo for California; the 3d of November, 1893, when my friends saw me off at Shimbashi Station. Indeed, it was the day when my Japan and Japanese life suddenly died. The people, however, congratulated me on my departure

Noguchi Yonejirō, "My Life in California," source: Yone Noguchi, "My Own Story of California Life," *The Taiyo*, vol. 17, no. 4 (March 1, 1911): 15–21.

as [a] birth. I felt most ambitious at the station when they wished me Godspeed; but my heart soon broke down when my eldest brother who came to Yokohama to bid me a final farewell left me alone on the *Belgic.* I cannot forget the pain of sadness of that moment even today. I stood by an iron rail on the deck, a boy only eighteen years old, alone, friendless, with less than a hundred dollars in my pocket. I immediately grew conscious of the fact that I had to face unknown America, a land of angels or devils, the darkness. . . .

The steamer duly reached San Francisco on a certain Sunday morning; we, I and a few fellow passengers, were taken to the Cosmopolitan Hotel whose shabby appearance looked then palace-like and most wonderful. And within it was not less handsome. The American room was the first thing for us; even the sheets and the soft pillow, quite unreliable for the head acquainted only with the hard wood, were a novelty. We put all the fruits we had bought (what splendid California fruits) in a white bowl under the washing table; when, we were told, to our utmost shame, that the bowl was for an unclean purpose, we at once thought that we were, indeed, in a country alien in custom, and had a thousand things to study. We acted even more barbarously at the dinner table; we took salt for sugar, and declared the cheese to be something rotten. We did not know which hand, left or right, had to hold knife; we used a tablespoon for sipping the coffee in which we did not know enough to drop a lump of sugar; we could not understand that those lumps were sugar.

I stepped alone out of the hotel into a street and crowd; what attracted my immediate attention which soon became admiration was the American women. "What lovely complexions, what delightful quick steps," I exclaimed. They were a perfect revelation of freedom and new beauty for my Japanese eye, having no relation whatever with any form of invention with which [I] was acquainted at home; it is not strange to say that I could not distinguish their ages old or young; they appeared equally young, beautiful, even divine, because . . . my discrimination lost its power at once. True, it took some months, though not one year, before I could venture to be critical toward their beauty; for some long time they only looked, all of them, [like] perfectly raised California poppies. I am happy to say that my first impression never betrayed me during my thirteen years of American life; not only in California but in any other place, they were my admiration and delight.

Now to return to the adventure of my first day in San Francisco. I again stepped out of the hotel after supper, and walked up and down, turned right and again left, till the night was growing late. When I felt quite doubtful about my way back to the hotel, I was standing before a certain show window (I believe it was on Market Street) the beauty of which doubtless surprised me; I was suddenly struck by a hard hand from behind, and found a large red-faced fellow, somewhat smiling in scorn, who, seeing my face, exclaimed, "Hello, Jap[!]" I was terribly indignant to be addressed in such a fashion; my indignation increased when he ran away after spitting on my face. I recalled my friend who said that I should have such a determination as if I was entering among enemies; I thrilled from fear with the uncertainty and even the darkness of my future. I could not find the way to my hotel, when I felt everything grow sad at once; in fact, nearly all the houses looked alike. Nobody seemed to understand my English . . . ; many of the people coldly passed by even when I tried to speak. I almost cried, when I found one Japanese fortunately; he, after hearing my trouble, exclaimed in laughter: "You are standing right before your hotel, my friend[!]"

My bed at the hotel was too soft; it even imitated, I fancied, the motion of the sea, the very thought of which made me sleepless. I sat alone on the shaky bed through the silence of midnight, thinking how should I begin my new life in this foreign country. In my heart of hearts, I even acknowledged my . . . mistake in coming to America.

I had one introductory letter to Mr. Den Sugawara of Aikoku Domei or "Patriot Union," a political league, whose principal aim was to put an end to the Government of the Satsuma and Choshu Clans . . . ; I called on him next evening at the back of O'Farrell St.; the house was wooden and dirty. I really wondered at the style of Japanese living in San Francisco; I cannot forget my first impression of the house where I made my call. It reminded me, I thought then, of something I had read about Russian anarchists; I confess that my feeling was gloomy. The narrow pathway led me to the house of two stories; the lamplight from within made the general aspect still worse. I climbed the steps which could not be wholly trusted; when I entered within, I smelled at once fishes and even Japanese sake. . . .

The league was then publishing a daily paper called the *Soko Shimbun* or the *San Francisco News*, for which I was engaged as a carrier; the paper had only a circulation of not over two hundred. I did not enter into any talk about payment; I soon discovered it was perfectly useless when we hardly knew how to get dinner every day. You can imagine how difficult it was for five or six people to make a living out of a circulation of two hundred; I believe it was Mr. Crocker's kindness (the house belonged to him) that we could stay there without regular payment of rent.

When he decided to put up new houses, he only begged us to move away, not saying anything about the payment. By turns, we used to get up and build a fire and prepare big pancakes, you understand, with no egg or milk, just with water. And a cupful of coffee was all for our breakfast. . . .

When I began to reflect on what I had come to America for, to ask myself how far my English had improved, and what American life I had seen, I regretted my mistake in associating with the Aikoku Domei, and put an advertisement as a "schoolboy" in the *Chronicle*, following the way of many other Japanese boys. What domestic work has that "schoolboy" to do? The work is slight since the wages are little. One dollar and a half a week. We have to leave our bed before six, and build a fire for breakfast. Don't throw in too much coal, mind you, your Mrs. Smith or Mrs. Brown will be displeased with you surely. She can hear every noise you make in the kitchen; she can see how lazy you are as clear as can be, no matter if she be busy with her hair upstairs. "Charley isn't that water boiling?" she will cry down. Charley! Your father didn't give the name to you, did he? A great pile of dirty dishes will welcome you from the sink, when you return from your school about four o' clock. Immediately a basketful of peas will be ready to be shelled. You must go without dessert, if you eat the strawberries too often while picking. Saturday was terror-day. We had to work all day, beginning with the bathroom. Your lady will let her finger go over the furniture when you finish. "See!" she will show you her finger marked with dust. Patience! What a mighty lesson for the youth! You must not forget to wash your stockings before you go to bed and hang them on a chair. How could we afford two pair of stockings in our schoolboy days?

What a farce we enacted in our first encounter with an American family! Even a stove was a mystery to us. One of my friends endeavoured to make a fire by burning the kindling in the oven. Another one was on the point of blowing out the gaslight. One fellow terrified the lady when he began to take off his shoes and even his trousers before scrubbing the floor. It is true, however fantastic it may sound. It was natural enough for him, since he regarded his American clothes as a huge luxury. Poor fellow! He was afraid he might spoil them. I rushed into my Madam's toilet room without knocking. The American woman took it good-naturedly as it happened. She pitied our ignorance, but without any touch of sarcasm. Japanese civilization, I dare say, was born in the American household in some well-to-do San Francisco family, rather than in Yale or Harvard.

The work of "schoolboy" which I took up with much enthusiasm served for some time as a delightful break in my American life; but its monotony soon became unbearable, I decided to go on foot to Palo Alto, as I thought, as in a Japanese proverb, "The children who live by the temple learn how to read a sutra," I might learn something there. I slipped out of my employer's house one early morning from the window, as I was afraid the lady would not let me go if I asked [for] my wages.

When I reached the University ground, it was near evening; I called at the house of Prof. G. where my friend was working while he attended the lecture courses. I was permitted to stay with him till I found some way to support myself; through the kindness of the wife of Prof. G. I got a job at Mrs. C's to work morning and evening, and by turns, I found a place at the Manzanita Hall (a sort of preparatory school for Stanford) where I was admitted to appear at the school for my service in cleaning the classrooms and waiting on tables for the student-boarders. There were less than twenty students then; the work was not heavy, but if I remember rightly, I received no payment. I do not remember now how long I stayed there, what knowledge I picked up in the classroom; one thing I remember is that I read Irving's *Sketchbook* there for the first time, in which the description of Westminster Abbey incited my sudden desire for England.

The general influence of Stanford, silent, not unkind, courteous, encouraging, that I felt from the buildings, the surrounding view with trees, even the group of students, was, I confess, far deeper than my first impression of Harvard, or even Oxford of England; after all, the library and lectures are not the main things. As I said, I worked without payment at the Manzanita Hall; I began to feel uncomfortable in [the] course of time with my heelless shoes and dirty coat. I decided to work at the Menlo Park Hotel, Menlo Park, as a dishwasher, till I could put myself in a respectable shape.

The work was not light; I had to rise every morning before four o' clock and my work never finished till ten o' clock at night. It was about the time when Japan declared war with China; what a delight it was to read the paper with the battle news in my spare time! My mind grew restless from a sudden burst of desire to see my friends at San Francisco, and talk over the war, if it were necessary, even to fight with them. I dismissed myself from the hotel and hurried back again to the *San Francisco News*. I thought I was quite rich as I had more than thirty dollars for my savings, while my compatriots at the office were in the same condition as before; I could not help feeling sorry for them, and then I bought a pair of shoes for A., a new shirt for B., and played a philanthropist for a short time. When I awoke from a few occasions of extravagance, I found myself again penniless as my friends; the paper needed somebody who could translate from the English papers; and I was asked to help it even for a short time. As I had no particularly bright job before me, I consented to stay; under any circumstances, I thought I must put my fingers into their former order, as they had become swollen from the dirty dishwater with much soda. Even in America it is not easy to earn money.

AOYAMA TETSUSHIRŌ, "HOME LIFE IN AMERICA" (1916)

In 1913 Aoyama Tetsushirō arrived at Stanford University to study entomology. Two years later ill health forced him to return to Japan, where he wrote an account of his experiences in America. His idyllic description presents family life in America as a model of domestic harmony and peace that many middle-class Japanese families had begun to aspire to, and his description of the middle-class housewife echoes the ideal of the married woman as "good wife and wise mother" [ryōsai kenbo] that flourished in prewar Japan. The bucolic America he describes, with its tranquil Sundays and peaceful isolation, however, was soon to be shaken by the entry of the country into World War I.

. . .

Customs and Manners in America

To introduce the customs and manners of the United States, I must first say something about American society. Unlike Japan or England, American society makes few distinctions among the upper, middle, and lower classes. This, I believe, is because America is a young country and a republic. I will try to outline the daily life of ordinary Americans, including, of course, farmers, manufacturers, and merchants as well as government officials and schoolteachers.

First, let me consider those engaged in commerce and industry. Unlike Japanese merchants and shopkeepers, very few people in America work or do business in their own homes. They travel to and from work at the firm or factory, just as our officials and schoolteachers do.

A woman of this class lives about the same as a middle-class house-

Aoyama Tetsushirō, "Home Life in America," source: Aoyama Tetsushirō, *Amerika miyage* (Tokyo: Esshinsha, 1916), 55–72, 79–82, 84–86.

wife in Japan. Her life centers on taking care of the house and the children, lending her husband a sympathetic ear, and serving as a gracious hostess. She sews, washes, and mends all the children's clothes and all ordinary clothes, except for fancy party wear. She also keeps extremely detailed records of the household budget. For example, if she decides to have a new dress made, she will try to pick a fashionable and pleasing design that is not too expensive. The American housewife has a special talent for planning everything in an economical way and a skill for making the most of her money. She never leaves the daily cooking entirely to the maid. She always helps season the food, and she serves tasty dishes made with inexpensive ingredients. The housewife herself takes responsibility for the recipes; she goes to the grocer to buy the things she needs in the kitchen; and she makes cakes, jam, and butter for everyday use.

Let's look at the housewife's daily schedule. She generally gets up at around 6:30 or 7:00 in the morning. As a rule she takes a cold shower every morning. The shower, taken without fail in all seasons, is the only means she has to keep fit. Breakfast, usually fairly simple, begins at eight. It usually consists of mashed potatoes, eggs, and steak, so it is easy to prepare quickly.

Before breakfast the family members gather in the dining room for religious devotions. With the father presiding, the family reads from the Bible and sings a hymn together. After breakfast, they will read the newspaper or chat for a while about the current news and other things. The children soon run off to school, and the father departs for work. The wife remains at home to take care of housework and do chores in the kitchen. Then, taking along the small children, she will visit the market to buy what she needs for the day. When she returns home, she mends torn clothes, knits stockings, or makes lace. From beginning to end, she is no different from a model Japanese housewife. The morning, when she devotes herself to housework, is the busiest time of day for her.

Lunch is at noon, but it is not much of a feast. The children come home from school, and the mother eats with them. Then she begins preparations for the evening meal—baking a cake or putting a roast in the oven. At about 3:00, after finishing her various chores, she will visit with friends or, if she stays at home, she will play hostess to them. Teatime comes at 4:00. Women get together to chat while sipping tea and nibbling on various treats. Dinner is at about 7:30. Even in less affluent homes it is customary for the family to change into evening dress for dinner. It is the very picture of happy domestic pleasures. The atmosphere is like heaven on earth. As the family members laugh and chatter away at the dinner table, openly and honestly, the cares of the day melt away. The mother talks about funny or unusual things that happened during the day, innocent harmless talk that heightens the gaiety at the table. If guests have been invited, the atmosphere is even livelier, and a feeling of warm intimacy develops between the hosts and their guests. Once dinner is over, the wife plays the piano or the violin while her husband and children sing or dance. The noise, and the accompanying merriment, is hard for us Japanese to imagine.

Daily life in farm families is basically the same, except that living in the countryside makes it special. A wide lawn planted with shrubs and flowers or a flowerbed spreads out in front of the house. Cows, horses, pigs, and sheep graze in the pasture, and geese swim in the stream. It looks like the Garden of Eden. The farm housewife works diligently too, making butter, cheese, and jam. American farmers believe firmly in God, and on Sunday they go to church as a family and listen intently to the minister's sermon.

Family

Americans place great importance on the family, and they regard the home as a sacred place. They avoid anything that might hinder harmony within the home. Because they have built a nation founded on the family as the focal point of society and because morality of individualism has developed naturally, Americans believe that the nation is made up of themselves [as individuals].

The head of the family—the husband—is responsible for matters outside the family, but he leaves responsibility for all household affairs to his wife. In sum, bringing up the children and taking care of family finances are all the duty of the wife. Even if she errs in educating the children, the husband will not scold his wife in front of them. If he were to scold her thoughtlessly, the children would lose respect for their mother, and they might even fall into the bad habit of disobeying her. Since parents bring them up this way, children fear their mother, who stays at home to educate them with firmness and kindness, far more than their father, who is away so often. Of course, the mother's success in raising her children largely depends on her ability and character. If she has neither, then no matter how much she uses her authority to tell them to do this or that, in the end the children will become rebellious, and they may even stop listening to her.

One more distinctive thing about American families is the affection between husband and wife. It is probably fair to say that this affection is deeper in America than in any other place in the world. Once I asked my American friend Mr. Ryan what was most precious to him. He answered that, with the exception of God, nothing in the world was as tender as the love he shared with his wife. This is certainly the result of a system of strict monogamy—one husband, one wife.

Child Training

The most important component in the education of children is the instruction they receive from their mother. Great emphasis is placed on family education in America. From the time the child is born, the mother establishes a systematic schedule of nursing every two hours. When I lived in Menlo Park, an artist couple lived next door. Their baby would often cry on and on, and it sometimes interrupted my study. One day I asked the wife why she let the baby cry like that. She told me that she fed the baby every two hours and put him in a stroller between feedings. If she did that, she said, then the baby would gradually get used to it and stop crying between feedings. When I heard this, I thought to myself that it was quite cruel. Surely no Japanese mother would do the same.

Since elderly parents do not usually live with their married children, American housewives can raise their children exactly as they wish. Even when grandparents do live with them, they do not interfere in raising the children, so there is no clash between new and old ideas about how children should be brought up. What is best for the child is what is done. Since the world is always changing, it is not surprising to find disagreements between the thinking of the older generation and the thinking of the mother, who has absorbed the latest knowledge of the day. If there were constant clashes between the grandparents and the housewife, it would be a calamity. The young mother would have no choice but to follow her mother-in-law's advice, and that would be unfortunate for the children. I think it is best that the grandparents have little to do with raising their grandchildren.

American Women

It is easy to imagine that American women are like the "new women" who strut about so arrogantly in Japan today, but in reality it is quite the opposite. For example, here in Japan it is customary for the wife of a university professor to have a couple of maids and a rickshaw man to help her. But over there, the life of a university professor is quite modest. The family may have only one maid, but most have none at all. A housewife with two children must still attend to the cooking and everything else. And these wives are generally university graduates.

The fact that American women have, on the whole, achieved a high level of education has several consequences for family life.

First, the nicest rooms in the house are the dining room and the kitchen. It is actually pleasant to be in these rooms. By contrast, in Japan, most dining rooms are dark and dreary. Then there is the cleanliness of the bathrooms. As I indicated elsewhere, some Japanese [visiting American homes] have mistaken the toilet as a place to wash their faces. As this suggests, household cleanliness is almost perfect.

Second, generally speaking, the exterior of houses is quite progressive. The tastes of well-educated women are naturally refined, and they do not take pride in homes ornamented expensively to impress other people. Rather they rely on elegant but inexpensive methods of beautifying their homes.

Third, well-educated women are active on the social scene and have no trouble conversing with men. Since women in the United States accompany their husbands to parties, their conversation is interesting and their tastes diverse. I was often invited to dinner parties and various other events, but never was I served a sumptuous and delightful meal. Instead, the hosts did their best to put their guests at ease with music and entertaining conversation.

Fourth, when educated women marry they are very supportive of and sympathetic to their husbands. Husbands can discuss anything with their wives. The relationship between husbands and wives is as tight as a sweater. . . .

Saturday and Sunday

There is no school on Saturday. In the morning young people, from elementary school pupils to university students, clean their rooms at home. Housewives and their maids use the morning to clean the cooking utensils, forks, knives, and stove.

A splendid-looking lawn and garden surround every home. The children cut the grass and weed the flower beds every Saturday morning. In the afternoon both students and youngsters go to play in the park or to watch games at the athletic field. Housewives stay at home to wash the children's socks, underwear, and other soiled clothing.

On Saturday evening every household prepares a hot bath to wash away the grime and fatigue. After the bath they reply to letters they have received during the week or write greetings to friends. Students living in boardinghouses report news of the week to their faraway parents and siblings. It is customary not to study on Saturday night but to retire early, then sleep late the following morning in order to rest their bodies.

Since Sunday is a day of rest, men shave, put on a new shirt and collar, and attend morning church services for spiritual comfort. In the afternoon, the whole family usually goes for a walk in a park or on the outskirts of town.

In contrast to Japan, almost all the stores, except for pharmacies, are closed on Sunday. Generally speaking, Americans work during fixed hours from morning to evening, attending to their business without taking time even for a smoke. If you visit someone in his study or office for a chat, he will ask you to leave and continue the conversation on Sunday. If you visit him at home on Sunday to talk about work, he will turn a deaf ear and tell you to save it for tomorrow at the office. There is a sharp distinction between these two places: the office is a place to work, and the home is a place to rest. You will never see someone, as you often do in Japan, leaning on his hoe while he has a quick smoke. This habit of hard work is not limited to a few people. It is true of everyone from farmers, factory workers, and merchants to government officials. Houseboys and maids also work hard during their fixed hours, but once their day is done, they amuse themselves by going to plays and the like. Their bosses have no grounds for complaint. If an employee works just a little more than normal working hours, he asks for additional overtime pay.

This leads me to the conclusion that America is a country that values time highly. It is not surprising that the proverb "Time is money" originated in America. Americans work at a full tilt six days a week, then spend the Sabbath relaxing and playing. As a result, they go about their work with great vigor and finish their tasks quickly. You rarely see individuals or groups loitering in idleness, as you do in Japan.

Since Americans are very conscious of saving time, they also have the admirable habit of being on time for appointments. Once I asked my friend Harris if he would like to come to my place sometime. "Thank you," he replied, then asked precisely when—to the minute—he should come. I've made a serious blunder, I thought to myself. I asked him to come the next Sunday at 2:00. In Japan you invite a friend over to your boardinghouse merely to be polite, but in America you must not say what you do not really mean. In any case, my friend arrived at the promised time—not even two minutes late. In America, it is also customary to send an invitation to tea or dinner on a card detailing the time and place, and the guest is expected to bring the card with him when he visits.

I once tried to meet Dr. Kellogg, the chair of the Entomology Department [at Stanford]. He agreed to meet with me for seven minutes. I thought if I did not conclude our conversation within that time, I would be guilty of a breach of conduct, so I constantly glanced at my watch as I completed my business with him. . . .

Soldiers

I often saw military recruiting posters in post offices, hotels, railway stations, and other places in America. These posters were illustrated with splendidly uniformed artillerymen firing cannons or sailors on shipboard. It is usually idlers who do not enjoy work that answer these advertisements. Unlike Japanese troops, not all American soldiers have the same physique. Some are large, and some are small, but no two are the same. Since military service is voluntary rather than compulsory, American soldiers are not as disciplined as those in the Japanese Imperial Army. While I was in the field gathering insect specimens one day, I saw some soldiers in training. They often ignored the commands of their superiors, and as they marched along they munched on oranges and pears stuffed into their knapsacks. When you go to a saloon, you always see soldiers guzzling beer. Their lack of discipline is extraordinary. Soldiers are allowed to handle firearms only while they are training, and they are not allowed to wear a sword when off duty or returning home. When they do go home for a visit, they usually change into civilian clothes. This shows just how low the reputation of American soldiers has sunk. Even if they return home in uniform, children and young don't bother to look at them. They think that *soldier* is simply a synonym for *drunken bum*.

Two or three years ago, there was a sudden rise in the anti-Japanese movement in the United States. . . . The Japanese all responded boastfully, saying that if Californians tried to chase the Japanese out they might soon find themselves living on the other side of the Rockies, and the rays of the Rising Sun would spread over California. The appearance of such statements in a few newspapers and the publication of General Homer Lea's famous *The Valor of Ignorance*, a book predicting war between Japan and the United States, had such a great impact on the military that many American soldiers were prompted to request release from service.

Even the wives of officers worried about the possibility of war with Japan. If war came, they feared they might lose their husbands. Rather than part with them through death on the battlefield, I am told, some officers' wives decided to ask their husbands for divorce while they were still alive. And as a result, many officers, preferring not to be cast aside by their wives, decided to quit the army and go into trade or business instead.

SASAKI SHIGETSU, "EXCLUDED JAPANESE AND EXCLUSIONIST AMERICANS" (1920)

Sasaki Shigetsu (1882–1945), a Buddhist priest, arrived in San Francisco in 1906 with a mission of Zen Buddhists sent to proselytize in America. When his Zen master returned to Japan four years later, Sasaki remained as an expatriate, leading a peripatetic life on the West Coast. A journalist as well as a poet, sculptor, and priest, he wrote articles and essays for publications in Japan. His reaction to discrimination against Japanese immigrants might seem to reflect a kind of Buddhist resignation that human society is imperfect and that one must transcend its imperfections. But it also reflected the disdain with which many educated and urbanized middle-class Japanese, including consular officials, regarded the majority of the immigrants to America, most of whom came from rural areas and had little schooling. On the other hand, his own experience with discrimination was testimony to the pain it brought, and his decision not to enlist in American military service during World War I testifies to the ambivalence he felt toward the "exclusionist" America. During the 1920s he lived a bohemian life in Greenwich Village, where he helped to found the first Zen institute.

. . .

When I visited Seattle in 1913, I witnessed the uproar over the pending California Land Bill. Dispatches from California ran on the front pages of the morning and evening editions of the Seattle newspaper in type as big as horse shoes.

All sorts of rumors spread. One claimed that a Japanese merchant ship had been bombarded outside Manila Harbor; another reported that the

Sasaki Shigetsu, "Excluded Japanese and Exclusionist Americans," source: Sasaki Shigetsu, "Haiseki sareru Nihonjin to haiseki suru Amerikajin," *Chūō kōron* (November 1920): 5–9, 11–14, 16–19.

Japanese fleet was cruising the open seas beyond San Francisco's Golden Gate. Japanese living in the countryside left their fields to travel to Seattle to get the news. I felt as though white people passing me on the street were sneering at me. I could not help feeling humiliated. . . .

Japanese residents in Seattle gathered in the Japanese Hall at the corner of Washington and Maynard streets in a neighborhood known as "Japanese Town." They met to discuss sending the president of the United States a resolution in support of their countrymen in far-off California as an expression of the sentiments of the Seattle Japanese community.

It was a rainy evening in late spring. The auditorium of the Japanese Hall, a large building on the heights overlooking Elliot Bay, held about 2,000 people. That evening it was packed with an audience listening to an elderly Japanese gentleman speaking from the rostrum. He was one of the pioneers who had lived [in America] since the days of the early Japanese settlers, and the story he told was a page from the history of Asians' humiliation by the Americans.

"Wealthy men like [Mark] Hopkins and [Leland] Stanford of San Francisco made Chinese laborers in California suffer miseries rivaling the misery of their own downfall. Forty years ago transcontinental railroads were in the midst of construction. Most of the track was laid by Chinese laborers. The Union Pacific line across the Sierra Nevada and the Santa Fe line across the Mojave Desert are monuments to the Chinese who gave their lives in building them.

"Chinese workers were paid twice a year. On the evening of payday, all sorts of pleasant fantasies filled them as they waited for their palms to be filled with heavy gold coins. A horse-drawn carriage carrying a box with their wages inched toward them along the long road as they lined up double file on the plain at the base of the foothills, watching the setting sun. They did not know that their accounts would be settled not with gold coins but with death. The next day newspapers reported that dynamite used for opening tunnels had exploded accidentally, killing many of the laborers.

"The millionaire Hopkins built a lavish mansion at the top of California Street in San Francisco. On the evening of its completion he held a party to celebrate. He climbed to a balcony with a view of Golden Gate Harbor to raise champagne in a toast to his guests, but suddenly he slipped and fell to his death. The story went round—no one knows where it started—that just before he fell the ghost of a Chinese laborer appeared before him.

"Then, there was the massacre of Chinese living in Seattle. As I recall, it happened in 1882, when Seattle was still a small fishing village. The Chinese had set their sights on the town early on. Spokane had already become a big city by then, so the Chinese left to cross the Yakima Plain and settle in Seattle. They turned their energies to developing the city, but the white people did not like that, so they used violence to chase the Chinese out.

"The Chinese said that they would leave Seattle if the banks returned the money they had deposited, but the banks would have gone bankrupt had they done so.

"White people got hold of a rundown steamship somewhere. At gunpoint they drove the Chinese laborers from their homes along with their tearful wives and babies and forced them to board the ship to be sent back to their homeland. Many Chinese were killed at the time, but the Chinese government was too weak even to protest the affair with a few careful words."

A young man then stepped up to the rostrum to tell of an incident that had happened in Olympia, a mountainous region across Puget Sound from Seattle.

"A Japanese farmer raising vegetables lived next door to a white farmer who kept a pig. One day the pig broke through the fence into the Japanese farmer's vegetable patch and ate the vegetables he had taken such pains to grow. The farmer was furious.

"When he went next door to complain, his neighbor showed no concern. What happened was the pig's fault, he said, and therefore he was not at all responsible. The fence, he continued, belonged not to him but to the Japanese farmer, and if it was so easy to break through, that was entirely the farmer's fault. Build a better fence, he said.

"The Japanese farmer returned home, and, grumbling all the while, he reinforced the fence with wire. Two or three days went by without incident. But then the pig burrowed under the fence and ate the farmer's costly crop of cauliflower. The Japanese beat the pig off his property.

"Now the white farmer became angry. The Japanese farmer was wrong to beat [the neighbor's] livestock just because the pig, owing to [the farmer's] carelessness, had gotten onto his property again. It was only natural that a pig would burrow underground to get at vegetables growing in plain sight, he said. 'If you want to protect your crops,' he shouted across the fence, 'then build a stone wall that keeps the vegetables hidden.' That enraged the Japanese farmer.

"One night the Japanese farmer found that the pig had gotten onto his property again and was snorting around his house. His patience exhausted, he caught the pig, killed it, then invited the other Japanese in the neighborhood to barbecue the pig and eat it.

"His white neighbor was astonished to hear this, but the Japanese farmer told him that if he paid for the pig, the neighbor had no cause for complaint.

"The white neighbor worried what might befall him if he lived with Japanese neighbors who ate his family pig without a by-your-leave. The frightened man took the case to the Olympic District Court, hoping a get a legal judgment against his Japanese neighbor.

"The judge concluded that anyone who would seize someone else's pig, kill it, and eat it without permission was either insane or as savage as a cannibal and that, as such, he could not be judged under the civilized standards of United States law. So the judge acquitted the Japanese of all charges."

After finishing his story, the young man left the rostrum with a sad smile on his lips. . . .

From a distance the exclusion of the Japanese in California may seem alarming, but the closer one comes to the situation, the less significant it becomes. Personally I do not remember ever being subject to any kind of exclusionism that I did not expect.

Of course, I never wanted to become an American citizen, so when I was told that Japanese could never be granted citizenship I was not particularly upset. Since I also had no intention of becoming a permanent resident in the United States, I was not bothered that I could not buy land. I never wanted to convert to Roman Catholicism, so I was not surprised when I was not allowed to attend a church. And since I never wanted to eat side by side with white people, I was not at all inconvenienced by restaurants that turned away Japanese customers.

For the moment, I think, it is a good thing for the Japanese that California prohibits marriages between the white and yellow races. I was somewhat disappointed to learn that the California Academy of Arts gave no scholarships to Japanese students, but I never wanted to study the arts in California anyway, so this did not bother me either. In other words, as I see it, the exclusion of Japanese was just what I expected, so no offense was given on either side.

The Japanese send all the money they earn back to the home country. They cut an unsightly figure, living in dilapidated houses, caring not a whit about their reputation. As the proverb goes, like travelers they have thrown away their sense of shame.

Some Japanese, though proud of having built great mansions [in Japan], do not care if their American houses have no curtains. Some of these old fellows, thrilled that their sons have graduated from middle school, do not speak enough English to buy a postage stamp. I have some degree of respect for Americans who want to exclude the Japanese, and I am grateful that the Americans are rather sensible. Moreover, as a Japanese, I think we must try to make amends by trying even harder. I think we have a duty to accept the exclusionist conduct of the Americans. Indeed, I want to be of some help in accepting our lot.

Trolleys stop at every street corner in San Francisco. When people want a ride, they raise their hands, and the trolleys stop for them. I have never seen a trolley stop for a Japanese, however. Whenever I wanted to ride the trolley, I always looked to see who was standing two or three blocks away. If I saw a white woman waiting, I would hurry over briskly and board the trolley in her wake.

One day my friend S, an exceedingly courteous man from the Tōhoku region, tried to board a trolley by following an elderly white woman, just as I always did. Since she was having trouble getting on board, S, who could not bear watching any longer, pushed her up from behind. The old woman was overjoyed to board the trolley finally, and she turned to say thanks. As the trolley began to move, S, who is a big fellow, supported her lightly with his arm to keep her from stumbling. When the old woman looked at S, her expression suddenly changed. "Y-, y-, you're a Jap! Ugh! Get your hands off of me!" The other white people riding the trolley looked at him with the same disgusted expressions.

Things like this often happen. In Sacramento a young girl on a bicycle caught her wheel in the sidewalk gutter and was about to fall when a Japanese passing by caught her in his arms reflexively. A policeman arrested the man for insulting the woman. In Pasco, Washington, a Japanese who kept a woman from throwing herself in front of a train landed in jail, and in Vancouver, Canada, one of our countrymen who rescued a woman who had fallen into the ocean was charged with a crime.

Trolleys run at high speeds in America, so it is dangerous to jump on or off. In San Francisco, however, the Japanese are good at it. They have no choice. I too was one who did so.

One day someone grabbed my hat just as I jumped off the trolley, and two or three blocks later he threw it into traffic. Before I could run to pick it up, a horse had trampled it. I thought that I endured more than my fair share of that kind of behavior, and subsequently I stopped jumping off trolleys but got off when white ladies did. As a result I was seldom able to get off where I wanted to.

As I walked along the streets children jeered, "Jap! Jap!" When I went shopping I always had to stand and wait at the end of the line. Newspapers always spoke badly about the Japanese. Indeed, in San Francisco, it is said, any newspaper that did not malign the Japanese would not sell.

Military processions from many countries, including Japanese marines carrying a Japanese naval flag, were on parade at the Portola Fair, a local festival. As I watched from bleachers set up along the street, my heart beat wildly when I saw the Rising Sun fluttering in the breeze, but the white people sitting around me exchanged derisive smiles. My eyes filled with tears. . . .

While living in New York City I went to register for the draft in Union Square in September 1918. It was the middle of the World War. The United States had mobilized the Second Army, and it was preparing to call up men for the Third Army. Army troops marched down streets decorated with the Stars and Stripes as the sound of trumpets echoed off the tall buildings. The populace was in a frenzy of enthusiasm. The young men were all in uniform, and the only people in civilian clothes were the elderly, women, children, and foreigners.

In Union Square, sailors on a model battleship demonstrated what shipboard life was like. As we looked at this war vessel sailing over waves of grass, we joked among ourselves about when I might depart for Europe. Nothing is as fascinating as watching people caught up in excitement as their country goes to war. They acted as if they had lost their minds.

As I waited for a notice from the local draft board after I had registered for the draft, my feelings changed completely. I shed many tears at the bravery of my young poet friend, Skip Canal [?], as he went off to the front. As I now think back on it, it is difficult for me to understand my feelings at the time. Since I had been living in America for more than ten years, I think I had affectionate feelings toward the country. Or perhaps I had a sense of responsibility toward an America that had nurtured me. But why was I moved to tears when a friend I did not know very well went off to the front?

It was about then that I began to show enthusiastic respect for the American flag. I smiled as I watched foreigners who had not registered for the draft get arrested, loaded onto freight wagons, and hauled off to jail. A week later my draft notice arrived from the local draft board. My friends were amazed that as a Japanese I had been called up, and they came to see me off. I presented myself to the board at the YMCA on West 23rd Street. It was evening. Inside, the large hall was decorated with the Stars and Stripes, and a picture of Columbia, the goddess of liberty, was posted on the wall. Overhead bulbs shed their light like flower petals. The men summoned were packed together. Among them were Negroes and Jews. One Italian, who did not speak any English, brought along his wife.

First, we were interviewed by a female clerk and then waited our turn for the formal swearing in. Every unmarried citizen was immediately inducted, and so were married men with families, even if they had property or wives earning a living. Even foreigners not yet naturalized as citizens took their oath in response to the draft summons. The crowd treated them with respect.

Then came my turn. I stood before the committee. "First, to ensure that you will utter no falsehoods, raise your right hand and swear." I raised my hand and swore. "Are you an American citizen?" "No," I answered. "Do you wish to become a citizen of the United States?" I felt a flicker of doubt in my heart. How many Japanese could answer "yes" to this question? Japanese are not permitted citizenship rights in the United States. If I were asked whether I wanted to become a citizen and answered that I did not, it would be tantamount to refusing assimilation into this country. The same question was put to Japanese on the West Coast. I wondered what kind of vow a Japanese could make in this situation. I stared at the silent figure of Columbia on the wall.

To become a citizen of the United States, one had to swear to take up arms against your native country if war broke out with America. Could I take such a vow? In my heart did I want to become a citizen of the United States? The image of the goddess Columbia seemed sad that I embraced patriotic feelings toward both countries.

The committee silently awaited my reply. "No," I answered. "Do you have any intention to join the American armed forces to fight America's enemies?" It was painful for me to answer. I had been living in the country and had been nurtured by it for thirteen years. And now, as every American citizen was being called up to make sacrifices for the country, I had to say that I would not join the army and fight. I felt so pitiful.

If I committed myself to joining the American army and crossing the Atlantic to fight, I would have to forsake the patriotism and love that I felt toward the country of my birth. It was possible for me to do this, but I could not help thinking that my flesh belonged to my native land. I had to answer "no."

"If you returned to your homeland, would you fight its enemies?" What a delicate question! How broad its implications! The enemy we faced at the moment was Germany and its allies, but I was being asked if I would return to my homeland and fight against the United States should war break out between the two countries. I did not want to become an American citizen, nor did I want to join the American army. Now I had to attest whether I would someday fight against America. It is inevitable, I thought to myself, that the Japanese must be excluded from the United States. "Yes," I answered.

I left the induction room crestfallen. As I exited through a corridor jammed with people, my eyes were downcast. Some of my friends joined the army then, and some received citizenship after triumphantly returning from the war. Other joined the army but declined citizenship. But none of my friends died in battle.

ANONYMOUS, "THE SOUL OF AMERICA" (1921)

This anonymous essay makes conventional binary comparisons between America and Japan. What makes the essay unusual is that it argues that discrimination against the Japanese immigrants was as much a matter of cultural difference as of racial prejudice. The author also suggests that there are shortcomings in the Japanese national character as well as in the American national character.

. . .

1.

Everything the Americans do is an expression of the "soul of America" *[Amerika damashii]*. It differs a great deal from our own "soul of Japan" *[Yamato damashii]*. Indeed, the two are so different that Americans and Japanese have difficulty understanding one another. It is only natural that what Americans do appears mysterious to the Japanese. In this essay I will try to compare the American soul with the Japanese soul. Others can resolve the problems that arise from the differences between them.

While the Japanese display a spirit of self-sacrifice toward those who employ them, the Americans do not. Americans are content to take responsibility for themselves alone. The spirit of loyalty inspires the Japanese to work hard for others, even if it means sacrificing themselves. The

"The Soul of America," source: anonymous, "Amerika damashii o rikai seyo," *Chūō kōron* (June 1921), 83–87.

Americans lack such a spirit. When it is to their mutual benefit, Americans work very hard, but since they are reluctant to make personal sacrifices, they follow only their own interests.

The Japanese tend to submit themselves whole-heartedly to a superior. In Japanese families, for example, there is the household head whom family members obey in harmony.

This is not the case with the Americans. An American believes that if the wind blows the right way, anyone can become president. In the American family the husband and wife are the central unit, and the home is equated with the married couple. When the children grow up, they marry and form a separate new unit. They do not continue to obey the household head, as members of the Japanese family do.

In Japan a school diploma is the most important thing in getting a job. Actual ability ranks only second. But in America, where real ability comes first, displaying one's diploma is frowned upon.

When the Japanese organize a group, they first draw up rules and regulations, then exclude those who do not agree with them. If some difficulty upsets these rules and regulations, then the group falls apart. Americans, on the other hand, place more weight on resolving the difficulties. They change the rules and regulations constantly. Indeed, when new members join the group, new rules and regulations are often added to accommodate them.

In American courtrooms juries treat criminals as human beings. Not so in Japan, where we believe that the law should not be distorted to help one person.

With all these differences it seems that Japanese and Americans will never get along. It is no wonder that Americans may not like us even though we do not dislike them.

2.

Japanese peasants who migrate to America to become farmers rise before sunrise and work until dusk falls. Only when it is too dark to see a hand in front of your face do they return home. They work even on Saturdays and Sundays. American farmers, however, work only during certain fixed hours. When it becomes late they stop whatever they are doing, even if they could finish by working overtime. . . . Japanese farmers work tirelessly, always with a future goal in mind, but white farmers, who try to enjoy life each and every day, avoid real backbreaking work.

Japanese shopkeepers always undersell the market in America. They try to capture all the customers for themselves, and often they end up broke. White shopkeepers, on the other hand, prefer to offer their best-selling goods at an average price and sell them off gradually.

Japanese craftsmen in America try to succeed by turning out more products than their competitors. White people never do this but work only as hard as the slowest of the group.

The Japanese who volunteered to fight with American troops at the front [in World War I] showed themselves to be fearless and aggressive during attack and were cut down like flies as a result. I am told that American soldiers advanced just fast enough not to be left behind by others, with everyone arriving at the enemy trenches at the same time.

When Japanese vegetable farmers go to market they scramble to get there first with their carts. The second to arrive then sells his vegetables below market price. The third sells at cost, the fourth at a loss, and the fifth practically gives them away. At markets run by white people, who are aware of the problems of doing business this way, farmers set a fixed price and sell their vegetables gradually. The Japanese farmers return home weighed down with boxes and grumble to each other that they were not able to sell much that day.

Japanese stores in America are not very large. I am not referring to big trading companies that come from Japan with huge amounts of capital. Rather I am talking about the many small Japanese retail shops. When they pool their capital to form partnerships, they soon break up, beset by internal troubles. These small businesses do not suffer any losses but fall apart simply because of emotional clashes. If you ask what causes them, it is the fact that everyone scrambles to get to the top.

It seems that there is something in the Japanese character that makes us strive to reach the top of the pyramid. By contrast, it is in the American character to keep moving along parallel tracks. If you think about it, it seems unlikely that Japanese and Americans will ever see eye to eye. It is no wonder that they try to exclude us from their country even though we do not try to keep them out of ours.

3.

In Japan a marriage is a union between a man and a woman entrusting their fate to Heaven. Everything is left in the hands of the deities [kami] at the Izumo Grand Shrine. The purpose of such a marriage goes beyond the creation of a bond between the married couple. It is a marriage whose goal is the prosperity of the household, and it is a marriage that attaches little importance to love between the husband and wife. That is why the Americans so dislike "picture bride marriages" [i.e., marriages arranged through the exchange of photographs between the engaged couple].

The main goal of American marriages is the love between the man and the woman. They sacrifice everything for love. A couple gets to know one another before marriage without relying on a third party as a go-between. They become engaged through direct negotiations with one another.

Is that why Japanese dislike American-style love marriages? In Japan love depends on the will of heaven. Our duty is to our . . . lord and our country. American love is love between two hearts. Even when Americans went to war, they said they were fighting to protect their beloved wives and children against enemy invasion; they did not say that they were fighting for [President] Wilson.

I once saw a picture of Abraham Lincoln shaking hands with a farmer who came in dirt-stained clothes to greet him at the train station. I also saw pictures of Lincoln sitting with a factory worker on the steps of a Pittsburgh factory. I was struck by Lincoln's bearing in these pictures. For the first time I began to understand American democracy in some vague way.

Since childhood we Japanese have looked at pictures of Kusunoki Masashige [a medieval warrior known as a paragon of loyalty to the emperor] parting with his son Masayuki at the Minato River. We have also heard the story of Takayama Hikokurō [another paragon of loyalty to the emperor] weeping as he bowed in respect toward the imperial palace. And more recently we have read about General Nogi Maresuke, who followed the Meiji emperor in death [by committing ritual suicide].

But can most Japanese understand why Lincoln was such a great man? And can most Americans understand our cherished sense of loyalty? Unless we come to a mutual meeting of minds, it will be difficult for us to get along with one another. It is no wonder that Americans might refuse to have anything to with us, even though we do not think it difficult to associate with them.

4.

I once saw President [Theodore] Roosevelt on a tour to San Francisco. Children climbed on rooftops to see him. They whistled and tossed their hats into the air. . . . The president greeted them with a broad grin as he waved back to them. The Japanese watching with me did not enjoy this spectacle. They commented how dignified the Japanese emperor was when he honored the people with a solemn imperial procession. The smiling face of the American president, they said with a laugh, lacked any nobility.

Just before President Wilson left New York for the Versailles Peace Conference, the children of the city sang a popular ditty that went: "Mr. Wilson going to France / Mr. Wilson going to chew *[chou]*."[5] When a Japanese asked me what this meant, I explained it to him. With a sour look, he complained that Americans were too "plebian *[heiminteki]*." If we do not understand democracy, we do not understand the Americans. If we do not understand the Americans, we will certainly quarrel with them and become the object of their hostility.

In sum, Japan is a country that serves the ideal of loyalty; the United States is a country that practices the reality of democracy. If Japanese immigrants overprize their ideal of loyalty, they are bound to find themselves in trouble.

SHIBUSAWA EIICHI, "ON THE ANTI-JAPANESE MOVEMENT IN AMERICA" (1924)

Shibusawa Eiichi (1840–1931), a leading businessman and philanthropist, enjoyed a meteoric rise from son of a small provincial farm family to doyen of the Japanese business world. As the founder of the Dai-Ichi Bank, he helped establish scores of modern companies and was involved in financing several hundred more. Known for his strong sense of civic duty, he was consulted by political leaders and often spoke out on public issues. After the Russo-Japanese War, he grew increasingly concerned about maintaining friendly relations with the United States, one of the country's largest trading partners. The treatment of Japanese immigrants to the United States, particularly in California, was a growing source of friction between the two countries. Under the Gentlemen's Agreement of 1908, Japan agreed not to issue any passports to skilled or unskilled workers going to the United States, and the United States agreed not object to issuing passports to workers already in the United States or to their wives and children. In effect, the agreement put a cap on further Japanese immigration, and it reduced mutual animosity in the short run. Discrimination continued, however, and so did Shibusawa's efforts to mitigate it. This essay, written in reaction to the passage of the 1924 immigration

Shibusawa Eiichi, "On the Anti-Japanese Movement in America," source: Shibusawa Eiichi, "Hōhaitaru sekaiteki hai-Nichi taisei," *Taiyō* (June 1924): 1–6.

FIGURE 3. *Tokyo Puck* was often critical of turn-of-the-century American expansionism in Asia and Latin America. In this cartoon a bloated Uncle Sam, wearing a royal crown on his head and a "Pan-Americanism" belt, feeds a copy of the Monroe Doctrine to the fire. The scene implies the hypocrisy of the Americans for doing what they warned the European powers not to do. (*Tokyo Puck,* October 20, 1906)

law that effectively stopped immigration from Japan and other Asian countries, expresses his frustration at the failure of both governments to resolve the issue.

. . .

A Patriotic Youth

The recent passage of an anti-Japanese bill by the United States Senate and Congress is a most regrettable development for those like me who have been concerned with the issue over the years. It is unlikely that there is any Japanese citizen who does not share this concern, so it would be utterly ridiculous for me to act as if it were a personal problem. Nevertheless, as I think about it, since I have been involved with this issue a rather long time and I have felt friendly to the United States since my youth, my lament is all the more profound.

I was educated in the Confucian classics, so I was well-trained in affairs of the nation. I was exactly fourteen years old when the American commodore Perry came to Uraga in his black ships. His arrival shattered the illusions of all Japanese. Every corner of the country was filled with lively discussion and dispute. Voices calling for abolition of the seclusion policy and destruction of American ships were heard everywhere. As a patriotic youth of fourteen I gnashed my teeth and clenched my fists in fury at the American ships.

At the time the heads of Confucian scholars were filled with anti-foreignism. Isolationism—that is to say, nationalism—swelled in my young patriotic heart. I was fond of reading a book called *Shin'ei kinseidan* [A Discussion of Modern China and Great Britain], about how the Chinese and the British started a war over the opium problem and how Great Britain took Hong Kong away from China. Our country was embroiled in a vigorous debate between those who supported the shogunate and those who wanted to overthrow it. Growing up in this atmosphere and absorbed by these issues, I swaggered about like a die-hard nationalist.

When I was about thirty years old, the shogunate ordered me to accompany the shogun's younger brother on a trip to France to study the conditions there and in the rest of Europe. I came to realize that the isolationist policies I had adhered to were utterly wrong and that Japan needed to establish amicable relations with foreign countries, develop commerce with the outside world, and import foreign institutions. My isolationist anti-foreign thought was transformed into a recognition of the importance of opening Japan and cultivating relations with other countries.

My Impressions of America

Eventually our nation adopted a policy of opening the country and maintaining foreign intercourse. Among the countries that Japan established diplomatic relations with, the one that impressed me most profoundly was the United States. The more I learned about its government and its customs, the more deeply it moved me. The United States was the first to show sincerity toward Japan about the Shimonoseki Incident (1863–64), the debate over the abolition of extraterritoriality, and other issues. As I began to sense more and more deeply the Americans' high regard for justice and humanitarianism and also their kindness, I realized the errors of my anti-Americanism and anti-foreignism. I was filled with ever stronger feelings of friendship toward the United States.

Since then friendship between Japan and America has grown year by year, and trade has increased steadily. Seventy or eighty percent of Japan's raw silk exports now go to the United States. Since American capitalists set high value on the Japanese willingness to work for low wages as well as on their reputation for efficiency, Japanese immigrants have settled in California and other Pacific coastal locations. Friendship between the two nations has thrived under these circumstances, but since 1903 or so dark clouds have begun to gather over this friendship. Events related to the Russo-Japanese War have brought on this extremely unfortunate development. . . .

During the Russo-Japanese War, no one dreamed that our nation could actually win victory over Russia. In the United States, people thought that Japan would surely lose, and no one was happy at the prospect of a Japanese victory. But contrary to all expectations, the Japanese, victorious in battle after battle, backed Russia into a corner, and President Roosevelt mediated peace between the warring countries. Since the peace settlement did not achieve the results that our people anticipated, they blamed this turn of events on the unkindness of the United States. Heady with victory, Japanese nationals living in or near California took their spite out on American citizens. This sparked an anti-Japanese movement in California, eventually leading to the discriminatory treatment of Japanese schoolchildren and occupational restrictions on Japanese nationals. Thus anti-Japanese sentiment took on increasingly concrete forms. It was about 1905, I think, that I decided that this critical problem could not remain a formal diplomatic issue and that it was necessary to pursue popular diplomacy. Thus I resolved to devote myself to the service of popular diplomacy.

The Main Three Causes of Anti-Japanese Sentiment

The issue of the exclusion of Japanese immigrants continued to grow steadily more clamorous. President [Theodore] Roosevelt seized the opportunity to conclude the Gentlemen's Agreement with Japan without establishing a formal treaty. Thus the immigration issue was settled with a temporary arrangement that did not fundamentally solve the immigration problem between Japan and the United States.

At the time, I was on friendly terms with Foreign Minister Marquis Komura. He discussed with me a plan to foster Japanese-American relations by having the Japanese Chamber of Commerce get in touch with the main chambers of commerce in the United States. Since I had already turned the presidency of the chamber over to Nakano Bu'ei, I no longer had a direct connection to that organization, but Nakano consulted me on various matters, and as a citizen committed to the resolution of the U.S.-Japan conflict, I was more than happy to comply with Foreign Minister Komura's request.

In 1907 we extended an invitation to representatives from the American chambers of commerce. The following year they invited us to the United States, where our activities had no small impact on improving diplomatic relations between the two countries.

The anti-Japanese problem in the United States has lasted until today, but for a man like me, who has taken this problem so personally, it is extremely regrettable that affairs have reached the current deplorable state. Although the roots of this problem, as I have already explained, are emotional, it seems that various other causes are at work too.

First, there is the notion that the Japanese character is not assimilable into the American nationality. In other words, people think that an unassimilated race living within a nation can destroy the harmony of that nation. Since colored peoples of different races or religions can never blend in, prohibiting the naturalization or immigration of such races is essential to ensuring the peace of the United States. This is the main argument put forth by the educated classes.

Second, there is working-class exclusionism that stems from economic causes. This problem did not exist as long as America was sparsely populated. The Japanese were welcomed because they were efficient and willing to work for low wages. However, the American labor force has increased along with the general population growth, and Japanese labor has become an issue for Caucasian workers. Cheap, efficient, industrious Japanese workers, many of them with special skills, like raising grapes, came to be in great demand. This threatened the livelihood of white laborers, so they strongly favored exclusion of the Japanese.

Third, in the United States citizenship is determined by place of birth, while in Japan it is determined by one's parents. This results in the problem of dual citizenship. According to American law, a child born in the United States is registered as American, but according to our country's law, that same child is registered as Japanese. Dual citizenship creates other problems. More often than not, the parents of such children do not understand English. Since they may someday return to Japan, they teach their children Japanese. Finally when Japanese gather together they invariably form "Japantowns," where they follow Japanese customs. This is also a cause of anti-Japanese exclusionism.

For these reasons, many Americans started movements to exclude the Japanese completely. Eventually a ban on Japanese landownership was enacted in 1913 and was further strengthened in 1920.

Doubting the Sincerity of the Authorities in Both Nations

In the past when the United States Supreme Court handed down its decision about persons who had no naturalization rights, I feared that it would set unfavorable precedents. I repeatedly warned the government about this. Moreover, I also warned that patching things over temporarily was unacceptable. Whenever the government responded to the actions of the California State Assembly and other outspokenly anti-Japanese policies in California, I said the consequences for our compatriots in America and for Japanese-American diplomatic relations would be of grave concern if it did not seek fundamental solutions. I thought that, as a countermeasure, if a high-level committee composed of members from both countries were formed with the understanding of the United States government, and that if a treaty or an agreement based on that committee's findings were reached, this would ensure easy resolution of this long-standing problem. I proposed this two or three times, but unfortunately the government did not take my advice. . . .

While the Japanese government looked on passively, the situation in the American Congress took a sudden turn for the worse. A rabidly anti-Japanese bill passed both the upper and lower houses of Congress, and U.S.-Japanese relations have become even gloomier. Until now we have been protected, however imperfectly, by the Gentlemen's Agreement concluded in President Roosevelt's time, but the United States Congress regarded this not as a treaty but simply as a private arrangement that they were not obliged to honor. Since our only hopes have been dashed, our concern has become unbearable. Even though it is now too late to complain, if our government had been sincerely dedicated to resolving this problem, preventing things from turning out as they did would not have been that difficult. I believe that my proposals to the government would not have been in vain.

The Last Remaining Problem

Our last recourse is to appeal to the true feelings of the American people and to bring back the sense of justice and humanity that they are losing.

Using the power of opinion of ordinary American citizens, we must make the American politicians reflect on the mistakes that they have made. I am not demanding this simply for the convenience or benefit of Japan. I am simply a person who hopes to resolve this issue by appealing to those with a sense of justice. . . .

According to the newspapers, American public opinion is severely critical of the exclusion law. That is as it should be. In the end, reason will triumph. I believe that virtue will be restored in the long run. A Confucian aphorism states, "Virtue is victorious in the end." This principle holds true, I believe, not only for Confucianism, but also for Christianity. The Americans, who are a Christian people, surely are not insensible to this obvious doctrine.

The recent attitude of the American Congress shows complete disregard for justice and humanity. Now is not the time to waste words about its mistakes. Justice will win. I have no doubt that the day will come when Americans will wake up to this injustice. I recall my memories of that upright fighter for humanity Townsend Harris. I miss his presence deeply.

CHAPTER 3

Modan America

The victory of America and its allies in World War I changed the way that many Japanese viewed the outside world. The war "to make the world safe for democracy" had toppled the autocratic regimes such as imperial Germany, which Meiji leaders had sought as models, and it had thrust the United States to the front of the world stage. America had become a cultural, economic, and diplomatic force that had to be reckoned with as never before. It was no accident that in 1918, the year the war ended, the first professorial chair in American studies was established at Tokyo Imperial University.

Naive notions of America as a republic of virtue had faded, but the political values associated with American democracy—individualism, equality, freedom, public debate, and fair play—still attracted intellectuals across a wide spectrum. Yoshino Sakuzō, the country's prominent advocate of political reform, noted that democracy was the trend of the time and urged Japan to embrace it. What he had in mind was closer to British-style parliamentary democracy than American-style republican democracy, but he believed that government "of the people" and "for the people" (if not "by the people") was possible in Japan. Others argued that democratic values were deeply embedded in American society, in everything from business to sports. Even a right-wing ideologue like Nagata Hidehiro, who railed against the hypocrisy of American freedom and equality, admired America as a country that allowed individuals to rise as far as their talent and character could take them.

Critical assessments of the American political system came mainly from left-wing intellectuals inspired by the revolution in Russia, who argued that the Bolsheviks were extending equality from the political realm to the social and economic. The emergence of democratic regimes in postwar Europe, they argued, had been inspired not by the American example but by the Russian revolution. By contrast, the United States was for them a "false democracy" dominated by "money politics" that worked to the advantage of only the capitalist class.

Larger transformations in American society attracted more attention in Japan than American democracy did. The United States was no longer the exclusive domain of the largely piously Protestant northern Europeans who had settled the country in the nineteenth century and earlier. An influx of immigrants from southern and eastern Europe had turned America into a bubbling pot of clashing cultures, values, and identities that made it increasingly difficult to define what an "American" really was. The country's complex diversity, so different from Japan's relative ethnic homogeneity, raised questions about its long-term stability and coherence. It also prompted attempts to define just what the essential American national character was really like.

Nor was America still the largely rural small-town society the Japanese had first encountered in the nineteenth century. By 1900 the United States had emerged as the world's largest industrial economy, accounting for nearly a quarter of the world's manufacturing output and surpassing Great Britain as the "workshop of the world." A wartime boom turned America into a creditor nation and doubled its GNP, which continued to grow in the 1920s at the average annual rate of 6 percent. By the late 1920s, many left-wing intellectuals feared that the United States would dominate the world through the sheer force of its enormous national wealth.

To those living in a small island country with limited raw materials, one obvious reason for America's economic success was its vast endowment of natural resources. To be sure, exploitation of these resources required the drive, energy, and hard work that reflected the traditional values embodied in the American "frontier spirit." This aspect of American success was easy for Japanese observers to understand. But also clear was that, in part, Americans owed their remarkable industrial growth to the mass-production system pioneered by Henry Ford, which turned out a flood of ever-cheaper consumer goods. Scientific management, technological innovation, assembly-line production, and aggressive advertising had produced a new American brand of capitalism.

FIGURE 4. On a trip around the world, Okamoto Ippei, the most popular cartoonist of the 1910s and 1920s, drew sketches of American life. On the right sits a tidy row of suburban bungalows, all the same size and sitting on identical plots. On the left is a cafeteria, a type of restaurant unique to America, where customers picked their meal directly according to their tastes and wallets. Both sketches suggest the uniformity as well as the efficiency of daily life in America. (Okamoto Ippei, *Ippei zenshū*, vol. 8 [Tokyo: Senshinsha, 1929])

Japanese Response

Many Japanese observers were impressed by the convenience and speed that American consumers enjoyed. Japanese economists and businessmen began to study Frederick Taylor's classic work on scientific management, with its emphasis on the rational use of human resources. Some commentators were also impressed that the pursuit of work efficiency even extended into the home. In the early 1920s, Japanese promoters of a new middle-class lifestyle—"a cultured lifestyle," they called it—were inspired by the example of American consumerism, and architects drew up plans for "culture houses" *[bunka jūtaku]* that resembled shingled bungalows in American suburbs.

Many Japanese observers, however, were deeply ambivalent about the impact of the new production system on the American national character. By the late 1920s, industrial success appeared to have transformed

[margin annotations: Americans' Materialistic; Japanese fans of new American culture (music, art...)]

the individual American into a cog in a vast, impersonal, productive machine, increasingly alienating him from an older and more authentic American spirit. While efficiency and its attendant sense of time produced material wealth, they also drained human relations of emotional warmth and a sense of community. The Americans, as Kiyosawa Kiyoshi pointed out, were always in a hurry and always competing with one another. The country's growing wealth made money the standard for judging everything, and the easy acquisition of consumer goods accelerated the spread of materialism.

The urban popular culture that emerged in America's large cities during the 1920s seemed to reflect the country's shifting value system. Jazz, flappers, speed, bell-bottom trousers, skyscrapers, movies, gangsters—all aspects of the *modan* ("modern")—were the flip side of an increasingly mechanized American "civilization." By the end of World War I, American movies, music, fashions, hairstyles, and dance steps had swept into Japan, especially into its political and cultural capital, Tokyo. Japanese audiences became passionate fans of Charlie Chaplin, Rudolph Valentino, and Clara Bow, and the establishment of a national radio network popularized tunes like "Desert Song" and "My Blue Heaven." Young couples could be seen dancing cheek-to-cheek in Tokyo dance halls, and leggy show girls strutted in Asakusa musical revues inspired by Broadway productions.

Many Japanese feared that urban hedonism engendered by the pursuit of material wealth threatened moral decay, not only in the United States, but also in Japan. A 1925 dictionary defined "Americanism [*Amerikanizumu*]" as "a sort of materialistic faith that exalts money, seeks to use money to solve all problems, demonstrates an unbridled preoccupation with convenience, and seeks to be the first in the world in every field. Americanism suggests vulgarity and shallowness of taste, with a preference for gaudiness everywhere."[1] The appearance of "modern boys" [*mobo*] and "modern girls" [*moga*] cruising the Ginza prompted fears that the fleeting world of American urban culture, with its superficial faddishness, eroticism, and loose morals, was undermining Japanese society. "In the midst of the frightful whirlwind of Americanism that is battering contemporary Japan like a thunderstorm or a typhoon," Ukita Kazutami lamented in 1930, "the distinctive culture of Japan, with its two-thousand-year history, is being steadily relegated to the past."[2] Conservative intellectuals deplored the moral decline and social subversion associated with Americanism, and those on the left suggested that its ephemeral frivolity was an opiate distracting the middle class from their

FIGURE 5. In these sketches Okamoto Ippei depicts contrasting scenes of urban life in America. On the right is a soda fountain, said to have become popular since the country became "dry" under Prohibition; on the left is a dance hall, where couples dancing cheek-to-cheek to jazz music are "twisting their bodies like screws." (Okamoto Ippei, *Ippei zenshū*, vol. 8 [Tokyo: Senshinsha, 1929])

economic plight as they faced a deepening economic depression in the late 1920s.

Few distinguished Japanese intellectuals or writers visited the United States, much less carefully studied its society and institutions. It is probably fair to observe, as the economist Tsuru Shigeto did, that "the generation of Japanese who were born after the turn of the century held an extremely superficial view of America which remained more or less unchanged until 1945."[3] That superficial view is nicely summarized by a passage in a 1930 short story about a pair of successful middle-aged writers, Kitagawa and Sunaga, pondering the difficulty of understanding the new age of Americanism:

> Of Russia and America, the two forces which had emerged to break through the impasse of European civilization, [Kitagawa] could understand Russia. But America? America where Beethoven, Wagner, and the rest had been junked and all reduced to jazz? America where they held ridiculous contests to see how long people could dance without rest . . . ? America which was so intent

on earning the title "best in the world," whether in swimming, or track, or anything else? America which seemed to derive not from a taste for ennui and decadence but rather from a surplus of energy and a robustness of a bouncing baby? America which had amassed and so proudly flaunted the better part of the world's wealth? America which had spread the cult of advertising throughout the world and destroyed all hope of traditional Japanese refinement? . . . No, for Kitagawa and Sunaga, their inability to recognize America was not a theoretical problem. It was simply a gut reaction.[4]

Such diffuse cultural anxiety about the spread of Americanism was to surge with new intensity at the end of the 1930s.

ASHIDA HITOSHI, "AMERICA ON THE RISE" (1925)

Ashida Hitoshi (1887–1959) entered the Foreign Ministry after graduating from Tokyo Imperial University in 1912. He rose steadily in the ranks, serving in Russia, France, Turkey, and elsewhere. He was also a prolific writer of books on international history and foreign affairs. After resigning from the ministry in 1932 to protest the Japanese army's occupation of Manchuria, he was elected to the House of Representatives, where he spoke out against military involvement in politics. He also served as president of the *Japan Times,* the major English-language newspaper in Japan, and taught at Keiō University. After the war he served briefly as prime minister in a coalition government with the Japan Socialist Party. In this essay Ashida summarizes his puzzlement about the American national character.

. . .

The character and customs of all peoples *[minzoku]* vary depending on their environment, climate, population, and resources. Ultimately history and tradition give rise to differences among them. America dominates a vast and limitless territory, and its climate ranges from the arctic to the tropical. Although its population is 110,000,000, it has cultivable land to spare as well as an inexhaustible treasure house of natural resources to provide the whole world. The Atlantic and Pacific oceans, moreover, serve as impregnable fortress walls to deter invasion by foreign enemies.

For this reason the vigor and drive of the American people have fo-

Ashida Hitoshi, "America on the Rise," source: Ashida Hitoshi, "America wa seichō shitsu-tsu ari," *Chūō kōron* (April 1925): 128–130, 133–134.

cused entirely on domestic consolidation of the country. Its frontier, stretching without limit, was ample enough to accommodate more and more people. As a result immigrants rushed there to establish themselves without facing competition and resistance.

In this New World, with its enormous resources and uninhibited individual energy, the biggest factor that determines progress is *time*. Those who start up businesses [in America] see limitless demand before them and feel that they must pursue their enterprises with the greatest possible ingenuity and the greatest possible speed. In the Old World, businessmen think first about consolidating the foundations of their enterprises, but ... in America, where every day brings some new change, things must be done tentatively and for the short term. . . .

In terms of history, America is almost too insignificant to take notice of. If America were excluded from world history before the twentieth century, its influence has been so negligible that its absence would hardly be noticed, except for Edison's invention of the electric light. The ruins of Greece and Rome are difficult to explore in a single day, not only because there are so many piles of stones to visit, but because their histories must be studied for months or years. Sightseeing in America is much simpler than in Greece. With a single glance you can see what there is to see at Niagara Falls and the Grand Canyon. Understanding the emotions and the psychology of the Americans, however, is quite different from sightseeing at Niagara Falls. It requires more time.

The American people are a collection of European immigrants, but they are adamant in insisting that they are American and not European. European culture and American culture differ in age by thousands of years. European history begins with Egypt and Rome, although the discovery of the steam engine and electricity transformed it in more recent times. American history, on the other hand, begins only with the invention of the steam engine by James Watt in 1769. Traditions and history predating that event have some meaning for Europeans, but for Americans they are useless relics from the past.

There is no question that as a country and as a society America is a single organic unit. It is also an awesome unified inorganic machine. Materialism has established its tyranny there, crushing all before it from the Atlantic to the Pacific, and the breadth of America's territory and the wealth of its resources have made materialistic thinking the mainstream and enriched those who conquered the land. Most Americans measure

Money = everything)

things by tonnage, square footage, horsepower, and especially dollars. Words like *beauty, proportion,* and *pleasure* are concepts that have little to do with them.

Everything in the Americans' world is evaluated in terms of money. Even human life is no exemption. Railroad companies and personal injury insurance companies buy lives for $1,000 or $2,000 every day. The power of the dollar and the drive to accumulate dollars have reduced human life to the level of material goods. The dollar is not only a standard for measuring the value of goods; it is also a standard for measuring human lives.

From a European perspective, Americans are like lumps of coal made of human flesh. To get the most efficiency out of these lumps, their labor must be organized into a fixed time period in a manner most convenient for the economy. Not only are Ford automobiles turned out in the millions; modern America manufactures Fordist psychology too. Henry Ford may think that he has created a new gospel of industrial prosperity, but he is simply a product of the age.

The English love sports, but the Americans are excited about games. When the English play games with Americans, they do not see the Americans as enemies. They understand that Americans lack sportsmanship. Americans often try to win by any means. They emphasize efficiency in sports and the mechanization of athletic contests.

The English see sports as play, before or after work, and the outcome of the game is simply its conclusion. The Americans, on the other hand, become engrossed in the game for the sake of the game. In the pursuit of victory, the game inevitably become a kind of "business." It is not play; it is work. The most egregious example is that all [American] professional baseball players move as though they have been stamped from one mold, just like a Ford automobile.

America has no capital city in the sense that Paris represents France to the world, and London rules the British Empire. Owing to geographical circumstances, the North, the South, the West, and New England differ in many ways, but in none is there a city that serves as a regional capital. Each state has its own local character, and every city in each state has its own coloring. The inhabitants of Detroit may lack good manners, but those in Washington are refined, and although the citizens of Philadelphia bubble with curiosity, those in New York are always self-centered and restless.

Despite a lack of tradition and history, local spirit has encouraged local conservatism. Politics in America today revolves around the expression of parochial hometown spirit. The American Congress does not act on the basis of the Democratic Party platform, nor does it follow the policy agenda of the Republican Party. Senators, governors, and party bosses all act on the basis of this hometown spirit.

everything is locally based

American newspapers are also local in character. There is no national newspaper in America. This presents an interesting contrast with English newspapers. London newspapers cover events all over the world, running excellent articles on everything from earthquakes in Kamchatka to floods in Pittsburgh. New York newspapers treat a murder in a Fifth Avenue drugstore as more important than an earthquake in Kamchatka.

The American political system has inhibited the development of newspapers. In England popular opinion has been faithfully reflected in politics since the establishment of parliamentary government. Parliament is representative of the public, and it can give political expression to their opinions. Parliamentary debates sway the government, and parliamentary debates can bring about the fall of a cabinet. Parliamentary debates are thus important events for the newspapers, and the speeches of politicians receive more coverage than sports.

comparing Am. to Europe

In the American Congress, however, debate is often useless and lacking in verve. Congressional debates are not the center of general public interest, so they have little news value. Human interest stories are emblazoned in big headlines, but there is little interest in congressional debates or world events. To satisfy public demand for unusual news events, newspapers have no choice but to look for some sensational news in police blotters or court trials.

America is huge. It is therefore a land of exaggeration. . . . In America it is extremely difficult to discern what is really going on. [Americans] single-mindedly promoted the League of Nations, prohibited smoking (in a few states), and banned alcohol consumption. Yet most Americans normally smoke, and they like to drink alcohol. Somehow a strange force carried them away. Once a fad begins in some corner of New York, its 6,000,000 inhabitants become completely bewitched by it, and the whole city comes under the sway of a few zealots. That is the way America works.

If someone in the French Assembly were to propose a law to ban all alcoholic beverages, the French people would surely denounce him, and if the French government were to attempt to enforce it, it could expect violent resistance. In America, Prohibition is not observed very strictly, but it will not be repealed easily either. Americans have abandoned their bars and rediscovered their homes. Instead of spending their money on alcohol, they buy automobiles. Prohibition has not only rescued morality in America; it has bolstered the economy as well.

Those who wish to understand America must understand the towers of Wall Street. It is not enough to point out that they are the tallest buildings in the world. One must look for something intellectual or spiritual in the stone and steel that these buildings are made of. They overflow with "American spirit" *[Amerika no tamashii]*. Embodied within them is some great ideal. These structures, put together like square blocks of lumber, are in no way inferior to the Forum in Rome or the Arc de Triomphe in Paris. At least Americans think so.

America's future is an unknown quantity. How will America change when its population grows four or five times as large, when it resources are fully developed to the farthest corner of the West, and when the winds of culture begin to blow? America is giving birth to its own peculiar civilization, but what form it will take leaves my head spinning in speculation. At the moment all that one can say with assurance is: "America is growing. And it will yet grow without limit."

MAIDA MINORU, "THE CHARACTERISTICS AND PECULIARITIES OF THE AMERICANS" (1925)

When Maida Minoru (1878–1948) turned sixteen, he left his local high school in Fukuoka to study in Tokyo. An essay he wrote for the *Kokumin shinbun* in 1895 drew the attention of the elder statesman Katsu Kaishū, who helped Maida travel to the United States. While working for a local Japanese-language newspaper in San Francisco, Maida wrote his first book on the English poet Byron. As a student at the University of Oregon, where he studied law, he washed dishes to support himself. In 1907 Maida returned to Japan to work for the Tokyo *Asahi shinbun*, reporting on foreign news. Eventually he became a professor of diplomatic history at Meiji University and a prolific writer on contemporary issues, publishing in influential opinion journals. One conclusion he drew from World War I was that the United States was on the rise and forg-

Maida Minoru, "The Characteristics and Peculiarities of the Americans," source: Maida Minoru, "Nijusseiki no nazo: Sekai no kyōji: Beikoku oyobi Beikokujin no kenkyū," *Chūō kōron* (April 1925): 112–126.

ing close bonds with Great Britain. He thought that good relations with America were necessary to preserve the Anglo-Japanese alliance, and he wrote positively (though not effusively) on the prospects of the League of Nations. Seldom polemical, Maida thought his role as a journalist was not to lead the masses but to provide them with information needed for better informed judgments.

. . .

Pos opinion

If you ask me what I think about America or Americans, the first thing I would say is that America is a place where an extraordinary natural environment has nurtured a spirit of struggle *[funtō kibun]* in the freest and most uninhibited way. Americans may lack the subdued and refined grace found among Old World Europeans. Indeed, they smack of vulgarity. But as a people they perennially embody the peerless freedom and vigor of a youth in the prime of life.

America is a place where many ethnic groups have gathered from all over the world. The country encompasses not only the East Coast, centering on its cultural capital, New York, as well as other densely populated cities inhabited by an economically comfortable class of people with a strong sense of propriety; it also includes the Midwest, with lesser cities like Chicago, as well as the wilder South and West. It is difficult to say that every place in America looks the same. But were I to point out characteristics shared by all Americans, I would offer the following. . . .

When I describe the American character, we must remember that as a result of [Americans'] strength the United States has become the richest country in the world. It occupies the No. 1 position or No. 2 position in the production of goods needed by the rest of the world. . . . With a foreign trade volume rising to ¥20 billion, America is neck and neck with England, three or four times the size of Germany, France, et cetera, and seven times the size of Japan. It boasts an enormous national wealth in the amount of ¥700 billion, compared with ¥260 billion for England, ¥80 billion for Germany, ¥70 billion for Italy, and ¥40 billion for our own Japan. . . .

Why has the United States enjoyed such material success? This success, I think, is not simply a harvest reaped through the unparalleled drive and vigor of the American people; it also offers evidence for understanding the so-called American way of doing things *[katsudōburi]*.

Looking back through its history, ever since Columbus's discovery of the American continent in the 15th century and the beginning of immigration in the 17th, those who crossed the sea from Europe have faced a life of struggle with the natural environment. It was different from life in Europe, which had developed as a result of the long historical endeavors of its inhabitants, who shared a strong sense of continuity with the past. In a sense it was the daunting but great good fortune [of those who came to America] to confront obstacles posed by nature as they pursued their destinies in the new land. Their vigorous struggles to overcome hardship were not of an ordinary kind. According to accounts of the settlers who arrived with John Smith in the early 17th century, fewer than 60 out of 500 survived. Their suffering was extreme. To endure, to persist, and to survive under such difficult circumstances, one had to be endowed with extraordinary spirit and enormous diligence. In accordance with the principle of the survival of the fittest, only the successful lived on to create American society. We must remember that their descendants, the Americans of today, have inherited their character.

There can be no doubt that as natural resources were gradually discovered and developed, these restless and feisty Americans were amply rewarded, perhaps out of proportion to their industry and effort. Why was this so? It was because the United States, with its 3,000,000 square miles of territory, was endowed with vast natural wealth. On the East Coast the Appalachian Mountains, stretching across Virginia, Pennsylvania, and New York, are rich in coal deposits, and the rivers that flow down these mountains are the source of water that supplies electricity to thousands of factories today. The mountainous regions in the West, including the Rocky Mountains, are richly endowed with mineral ores such as gold, silver, copper, and lead, and the plains area spreading between the Appalachians and the Rockies is exceedingly fertile. The Great Plains are blessed with the Mississippi, the Missouri, and many smaller rivers that are an ideal source of irrigation. . . .

The Americans, in possession of these sources of wealth and demonstrating exceptional endurance as they struggled against difficult obstacles of nature, reaped a bountiful harvest that perhaps exceeded the price they paid [both in money and in effort]. Of course, we should not belittle the value of their accomplishments for that reason. We must remember that it was with Heaven's blessing they received their unexpected reward. Their efforts ended with success, and they came to feel that their way was the wisest way of doing things. . . . As a result of all that nature endowed them with, the Americans understood the value of hard work, and the whole of American society embraces that spirit. . . .

What nourished the American spirit of hard work was the country's long westward expansion. As the population began to grow on the East

Coast, those who preferred freedom and loved adventure slowly moved ever westward to regions yet untouched by the hand of man, where it was easy to prosper. . . .

It goes without saying, the frontier was the most powerful force molding the American spirit of hard work. The Americans were not a large population huddled together on a narrow territory as the Europeans were. They were scattered over the mountains, the plains, the rivers, and lakes of their vast territory, living in regions where wild animals roamed. They looked after themselves, pursuing their own goals unrestrained by others. They knew that they could not succeed without a firm resolve not to depend on others but only on themselves. This attitude became deeply embedded in their souls. . . .

While this attitude is a peculiar characteristic of the Americans, we should recognize that people shaped by this way of life have many flaws. Their first shortcoming is that they lack refinement. For example, the English and the French, living in the Old World, where the sources of wealth are dwindling, where a large population is crowded into a narrow space, and where many nations share borders, have learned to exercise self-control, to defer to one another, and to sacrifice themselves for the sake of the community. For the most part, they are polite and reserved. By comparison, the Americans are rough, and they tend not to understand proper etiquette.

[handwritten margin notes: Flaws) / American are rough]

But Americans are not, as some say, wicked people; they are good people. They are simple-hearted, frank, and quite likable. But they can also act like a terrifying mob. Take, for example, the persecution of the Japanese [immigrants]. Even if an Englishman does not like the Japanese, he would not hurl insults at them or assault them, but an American, if he detests someone, will immediately insult or pummel him. On the other hand, when talking things over leads to agreement, reconciliation [among Americans] is speedy.

Let me next suggest that extreme individualism is another characteristic of the Americans. Because they emphasize individual freedom so much and because they believe so blindly in the sanctity of property, they think of government as an instrument created for the interest of the individual. Without judging whether this is good or bad, there is no doubt that Americans tend to pursue their own individual ends and improve their own lives, even if it causes problems for others. This tendency is most conspicuous among businessmen, but it is true of politicians as well. Where does this come from? Its origins are no doubt to be found in the

[handwritten margin note: individualism]

English idea of individual freedom. From the beginning this has been the political philosophy in America. The notion of "Anglo-Saxon liberty" and the ideas of the English philosopher John Locke are deeply embedded in the Americans.

From the American point of view, government is no more than an instrument created by individuals for the sake of mutual convenience to maintain social peace and to provide a stable environment to carry on their own endeavors. That is why they think that the scope and authority of the government must be restricted to extremely narrow confines and that it must not interfere more than necessary in the affairs of the individual. This idea is expressed in the constitution of every state. It is presented in the many scholarly works as the so-called theory of innate human rights. . . . That is to say, all human beings are naturally free and independent, and thus they possess rights that can under no circumstances be taken away from them by others. Among these rights are the right to protect their life, liberty, and happiness, the right to protect their property and possessions, and the right to pursue their well-being. . . .

From childhood, ordinary Americans read the Declaration of Independence, writings of George Washington, and similar works that reflect the spirit of the nation's founding. These ideas are deeply etched into the minds of even the uneducated or the ignorant. As a result it is natural for Americans to assume that it is appropriate to elevate the individual. The self-centered American spirit of hard work I discussed above fits neatly with this kind of individualism.

I should add, of course, that the individualism of the Americans is not the kind of egoism [*rikōshugi*] or self-love that comes to the minds of some Japanese, nor is it the same as the egoism of the so-called miserly Jews or Chinese. The egoism of the Americans is the freedom to work and to move on as one pleases. The pursuit of money or the pursuit of wealth, we should remember, is only secondary. Americans, moreover, are relatively indifferent to the wealth they accumulate. For example, in recent years enormously wealthy men like Rockefeller, Carnegie, Eastman, and Duke have contributed astonishing amounts of money to various social and public charities. These men worked extremely hard; they often rode roughshod over others; and they had no qualms about sacrificing others as they forged ahead viciously. But without hesitation they donated their accumulated wealth to society. . . .

In any case, private enterprise based on individualism and boundless activity, rather than government, has brought about the astonishing development of America. One does not encounter the attitude of *kanson minpi* ["respect for officials, contempt for the people"] that one finds in some European countries. On the contrary, the idea that the government should be the servant of private enterprise prevails among the business class. A striking example is that to a remarkable extent the American diplomatic apparatus has become a tool of the capitalists. . . .

The United States is a materialistic country. It seems like a gathering place for money-grubbers with neither high ideals nor moral behavior. But in fairness I must also talk about those elements in America who embrace morality and ideals. Since the arrival of the first settlers, there have been two main currents in the United States. To oversimplify, those who represented the idea of material development in pursuit of wealth went to Virginia. By contrast, as everyone knows, those who expounded ideals, held strong religious beliefs, and pursued humanitarian ideals were the Puritans who sailed on the famous *Mayflower,* landed at Plymouth in 1620, and settled New England. As the years passed, the country flourished materially, but humanitarian ideals, centering principally in churches, universities, and other educational institutions, never lost their vitality. When America finally achieved independence, England was strong, but New England was weak. The New England moral view that what is good for the weak is disadvantageous to the strong led to the creation of a new government and stirred the new nation's people.

If we seek to understand how American idealism expresses itself today, I always find it interesting that when American foreign policy pursues self-interested goals or embarks on unjust actions in South America, many at home, invariably scholars and members of the educated class, raise their voices in courageous criticism. Even in situations where national diplomacy would not be criticized in other countries, critics in the United States hold to their views fearlessly. In a larger sense such critical voices may be weak, but to Americans they set a model of fair play. One cannot help but respect the existence of this minority of scholars and critics.

Although I am talking about a small group of exceptional luminaries, I intend no criticism of ordinary Americans. In situations where America's significant interests are not threatened, early on one always hears the call for what is right and what is just. There are many examples, not only in Mexico, but also in places distant from the United States, like China and Siberia, where so-called defenders of the just and supporters of the weak have been legion. In 1911 the United States expended funds to relieve famine in Russia, and it has generously invested several million dollars in relief projects in Armenia and other parts of the Middle

East. These relief efforts do not conflict with the Americans' larger interests but satisfy their humanitarian beliefs and ideals. In cases where their important interests are not at stake, this tendency of the Americans to take the side of morality and justice also creates opportunities for business organizations or conspiratorial groups to take advantage of the general public . . . and to pursue their own astonishingly hypocritical, sordid, and crafty goals.

Some will say that there are similar examples in any country. Certainly that is true, but I must respond that the level is higher in the United States.

I have tried to explain the American national character, but I should make some additional comments about racial prejudice. The Americans have gradually strayed from the spirit of human equality long urged by American men of religion. If we ask why, the reason probably is that the people of the United States, unlike those in our own Japan, do not belong to a single ethnic group. America includes many different groups, and its society has never become completely unified and integrated. Last year the population of the United States was estimated to be 110,000,000. If we break down the 105,000,000 figure in the 1920 census, there are 10,000,000 African blacks, 250,000 native Indians, 110,000 Japanese, and 60,000 Chinese. . . . Of the 94,000,000 whites, nearly one-third have foreign connections: 14,000,000 are whites born in foreign countries, and if we add the children of these foreign-born whites, the total comes to 36,000,000. Among them [i.e., foreign-born whites] are those of English origin, but the majority are of German, Italian, Russian, and Irish descent. Therefore, true Americans [i.e., native-born whites] account for little more than 50 percent of the population. The other 40 percent or so either belong to a different race or are foreign-born. Most of the latter, we should remember, speak a different language, worship a different religion, and observe different customs.

According to the laws of sociology, a society made up of different ethnic groups tends not to be tolerant; oppression and conflict are likely to occur. In a society where everyone shares the same racial lineage and where everyone shares the same literature, religion, and ideas, behavior toward others is exceptionally tolerant and free. Scholars argue that society is likely to become oppressive, friction is likely to arise, and politics is likely to become intolerant when ethnic groups with differing racial heritages, religions, and education gather together. . . . No one should be surprised that there is a trend toward racial discrimination in the United States or that this kind of thinking is spreading like a rash. . . .

To be sure, Americans have often pursued humanitarian policies of racial equality. The principal example is the Fourteenth Amendment of the U.S. Constitution. Since its enactment after the Civil War, which brought the abolition of slavery . . . , it has contributed much to racial equality. It provides that "no state shall make or enforce any law which shall abridge the privileges and immunities of citizens of the United States." In other words, it guarantees that no state can "deny to any person within its jurisdiction the equal protection of the law." The motive behind this legislation indirectly reflects the superb founding spirit of the country, but more directly it was the result of the Northern humanitarian movement against the enslavement of Negroes in the South that awakened the national conscience. It is a splendid law enjoyed in no other country in the world.

If one reads the constitutions of other advanced countries, one can find provisions to protect the rights of their "citizens" or their "people," but there is no other constitution that protects *human* rights. By using the word *person*, [the Fourteenth Amendment] includes foreigners as well as citizens. It protects the equal rights of foreigners, and it goes without saying that it applies to whites, to blacks, to Japanese and Chinese. At a stroke this amendment reveals the moral values of the American government to the rest of the world.

Unfortunately over the years the application of the amendment has proved inconsistent. The American courts have avoided giving full expression to the phrase "equal protection of the law." They have offered a strange interpretation of the word *equal*. "Equal protection" and "equal rights" do not mean the same thing. In other words, even though *A* and *B* are different, as long as they are relatively equal, that is fine. . . . In every part of the United States, blacks and Chinese have gone to separate schools from whites. . . . American pundits have justified this by saying that whites, blacks, and Chinese are equal but not the same under "protection under the law." . . . .

Gender Equality

What I find most ironic about the United States is that while racial discrimination flourishes in the United States, discrimination based on sex is extraordinarily limited. Among all the countries in the world, only in the United States is there complete expression of equal rights for men and women. In a few countries women have the right to vote. There are examples in France and Italy and . . . in many Central and South American countries. After the Great War women's rights have slowly expanded. In 1918 England adopted a law giving women the right to vote, and the

German constitution provided the same in 1919. But none of these countries accepted the right of women to vote as early as the United States did. Of course, a [national] constitutional amendment guaranteeing women the vote passed in 1920, but many states had already adopted such laws. . . .

In many civilized countries, even though women have been given the vote, discrimination between men and women flourishes as before. By contrast, the United States is steadily moving toward complete equality for men and women. Recently, there has been a view within the Republican Party that representation within the party should be shared 50–50 by men and women. The emergence of nondiscrimination with respect to sex in the United States, where racial discrimination is strong, cannot help seeming ironic. . . . A contradiction is a contradiction. When will the day come that Americans themselves become aware of the ironic contradiction between equal treatment based on sex but privileged treatment based on race? Unfortunately this is something we cannot know.

ABE ISOO,
"BASEBALL AND THE AMERICAN CHARACTER" (1925)

As a student at Dōshisha University, Abe Isoo (1865–1949) became a Christian convert. After a brief stint as a minister, he traveled to America to study at the Hartford Theological Seminary. Like Katayama Sen he was attracted to the idea of Christian socialism, and when he returned to Japan in 1895 he plunged into social reform movements. In 1901, together with Katayama and Kōtoku Shūsui, he organized Japan's first socialist party. After appointment as a professor at Waseda University in 1903, he continued his political activism. As a Christian and a socialist, he took a pacifist stand against the war with Russia, and he wrote extensively for both left-wing and mainstream magazines and newspapers. A strong supporter of the Japanese labor union movement in the 1910s and 1920s, he successfully ran for the House of Representatives after the establishment of universal manhood suffrage. At Waseda, Abe was an ardent promoter of tennis and baseball as character-building sports. The annual game between Waseda University and Keiō University, the best-known collegiate rivalry in Japan today, began with his help in 1903. His view of American baseball reflects greater familiarity with the collegiate

Abe Isoo, "Baseball and the American Character," source: Abe Isoo, "Yakyū ni arawareta Beikokujin kishitsu," *Chūō kōron* (April 1925): 150–156.

game than with the professional game—did Babe Ruth really abstain from alcohol and tobacco?—but this essay offers an unusual perspective on American politics.

. . .   *Baseball's influence on America & values*

As everyone knows, baseball is the most popular sport in the United States. Its extraordinary influence on the American character can be viewed from various angles, but before I discuss its spiritual influence, let me say a few obvious things about baseball itself.

When first introduced into Japan, both baseball and tennis were simply considered to be forms of physical exercise. In America, however, from early on these sports were treated not simply as physical exercise but partly as exercise and partly as entertainment. That was how society saw it, and so did schools.

To speak first about baseball simply as physical exercise, I would say that it is highly suitable for that purpose. Those who know little or nothing about baseball might think that the only ability required for baseball is bodily agility. Of course, moving with extreme agility is an important part of baseball, but if you think about how baseball is actually played, the most important skill is running. Indeed, running ability is fundamental to nearly all sports. In American professional baseball there are first-rank and second-rank teams. When we compare the two, there is almost no difference in the players' offensive and defensive skills. The only difference is foot speed. If a player does not excel at running, he does not qualify as a first-class player. Recently the Japanese have also come to recognize that foot speed is an essential requirement for athletes.

It is easy to understand, then, how useful baseball is as a form of exercise. As America became more deeply involved in the Great War in Europe, the country established a system of military training. Since American youths had always trained their bodies through sports like baseball and football, America was able to produce full-fledged soldiers in only five or six months. This was not unique to America. In England the connection between sports and military training has long been understood. In English public schools like Eton, Harrow, and Rugby, students vigorously engage in sports, and the English often point to the activities of public school students as one reason for the English victory at Waterloo.

The need for military training might disappear in Japan too if sports like baseball and football become more popular in the future. Athletics pursued for pleasure are far more effective in training the body than dull military drills. . . .

baseball as entertainment (& exercise)

If we look next at baseball as entertainment, we see that it provides that for both players and spectators. Leaving aside the players for the moment, baseball has gained wider and wider recognition among those who watch the game, and in recent years the same has happened in Japan too. . . .

America has magnificent professional baseball teams. There are, in fact, several hundred so-called professional teams organized into various leagues that play somewhere in the United States almost every day. Large cities have the top professional teams. At the moment there are sixteen of them, and there are second-rank and third-rank professional teams in smaller cities. . . .

The top American professional teams currently make an enormous amount of money. The athletes themselves often receive anywhere from several thousand to several tens of thousands of dollars a year. The huge sports arenas are equipped to hold anywhere from 30,000 to 60,000 spectators. Ten years ago one American magazine estimated that Americans spent more than $50 million a year to watch baseball games. Since then the figure has most likely doubled. In a country offering so many kinds of entertainment, baseball ranks fourth as target for disposable cash. Photography ranks first, theater second, and opera third. . . . It is clear from these numbers just how much Americans have thrown themselves into the game. Football games have become extremely popular on college campuses lately, but in terms of general attendance they cannot compare with baseball games.

Spiritual side of baseball

Now let me turn to baseball's spiritual side. Since baseball is a team activity, it has fostered a collective spirit in Americans. This collective spirit, one of the strengths of the American people, does not spring from baseball alone, but there is no doubt that baseball has nurtured it. Calling this spirit a "collective spirit," however, does not fully capture its significance. Missing is the spirit of obedience that makes team sports possible. The spirit of obedience is essential to team activities, and it is especially important in baseball.

There are two aspects to the spirit of obedience. The first has to do with training. Other sports require training, but it is of the utmost importance in baseball. . . . Since the athlete's ideal is to develop a magnificently healthy body, athletes train every day with the proper food, drink, and sleep. Various sports have become more popular in Japan recently, but regrettably many Japanese athletes lack a concept of training. Many drink and eat in excess. In America, however, athletes in all sports train their bodies under strict rules. Athletes in all university club sports eat their meals at a designated place. Their trainer chooses all their food, carefully measuring the quality and quantity. Just before the season and especially during the season, the athletes eat nothing but the food prescribed. . . .

During the regular playing season, professional athletes pledge to abstain from alcohol and tobacco. Certain professional teams even hire people to make sure that these rules are followed. The Bible quotes a precept of the ancient Greek Olympic games: "Victory demands restraint." In America this spirit is actually put into practice. Players submit to it without a word of complaint. . . .

The significance of democracy is not that everyone claims their rights or acts on their own selfish desires. Rather, it means that although people can act selfishly, they volunteer to control their selfishness. In baseball, players voluntarily submit to the orders of the team captain, and they must quit playing if they object. (This is how athletes differ from soldiers.) As long as an athlete is the member of a team, he has a duty to follow the orders of the captain absolutely, especially if the captain is elected by the players. This spirit is a noticeable feature of baseball, but it also pervades and dominates American life [in general].

The second aspect of the spirit of obedience has to do with the basic point of deferring to the orders of the captain. . . . Often a player who is performing poorly has to be replaced during the game. The pitcher, for example, is often replaced. The problem is that this practice is difficult for the Japanese character to accept. Players in Japan become extremely upset if they are removed midway through the game even though they are trying their best. Normally this is considered extremely disgraceful. If you look at the history of Japanese baseball, in the old days teams did not replace pitchers even when the team was losing. This became the custom only after they began to play with American teams. Substituting players is no problem nowadays, but many years ago when a Waseda University second baseman was taken out of a game for playing poorly, he was so offended that he quit the baseball club. Every athlete sometimes plays poorly and sometimes plays well, but there is no problem [with being taken out of a game] if the player realizes that he will get another chance in the line-up next time and that substitutions can work to the advantage of the whole team.

The Japanese have always placed too much importance on "position." When their new position differs from their old position, they are obsessed with whether they have been demoted or put into a position of inferiority. When someone who is lower in seniority rises to the position of chairman, then it is humiliating [for a more senior person] to work as a vice chairman. This does not bother Americans. When Woodrow Wilson became president, he named William Jennings Bryan, a three-time Democratic presidential candidate, to be his secretary of state. . . . It could be said that Bryan had seniority over Wilson, and in Japan it would be most unusual for a secretary of state to serve under a leader who had less seniority. . . .

Such changes in position are normal in baseball, but when a Japanese prime minister shuffles his cabinet, changes in position cause endless complaints. . . . If the Japanese were schooled in the spirit of baseball from the time they were children, even politicians' attitudes would change, and this spirit would be reflected in the national government.

To become a cabinet minister is the dream of all Japanese politicians. But once a politician has risen to this post he can no longer work at some lower position. It would be much better for a retired cabinet minister to take employment as a lawyer or a schoolteacher than to lead a life of idleness and leisure, but a politician who has served as minister cannot bring himself to work at any other job. He comes to think of being a cabinet minister as a profession in itself. To correct such an attitude requires a good deal of discipline, but relying on the spirit of baseball might be a way to do this.

So far I have been discussing the spirit of obedience in baseball. Now I would like to speak about the meaning of "fair play." Fair play is not limited to baseball; it is the true spirit behind all sports. The spirit of fair play emphasizes the idea that athletes compete on the basis of real ability. It rejects any other way of winning as mean-spirited. Americans display the spirit of fair play very well. They do not rely on organized cheering sections to win athletic contests. In our country, by contrast, cheering sections are thought to push one team to victory over another. Athletic competitions often appear to be competitions between cheering sections, and in extreme cases members of rival cheering sections may even come to blows. Some teams try to choose a sports field that works to their advantage, or they may demand a friendly umpire. As a result, athletic contests that ought to test ability become contests where victory is won by other means. This contradicts the spirit of fair play that is crucial to sports competitions. Athletes ought to reject the attitude that victory can be won by any means, no matter how ignoble.

In America the meaning of fair play places more importance on an athlete's attitude toward defeat than on his attitude toward victory. It is sufficient to have a graceful attitude in defeat. Blaming defeat on the cheering section or the umpire reveals a poor sportsmanship that violates the spirit of fair play. In America the defeated candidate in a presidential election always makes a congratulatory telephone call to the victor. Although this is just a convention, it still represents a commendable attitude. Tennis matches, even in Japan, end with having the opponents shake hands, and it is to be hoped that the practice of having team captains shake hands after a game will become customary in Japanese baseball.

In America companies choose and promote their employees solely on the basis of ability. They do not weigh a person's educational record or his personal connections. If the employee consistently works hard, the company will recognize this. In this way American society is overflowing with vitality, as everyone pushes himself to the limit. The American spirit of baseball reveals itself here too. Our society in Japan is also based on the principle of merit, and everyone takes pleasure in setting aside private concerns when they act, but we must also think about the enormous influence baseball has had on the American national character.

NOGUCHI YONEJIRŌ, "AMERICAN HIGH SOCIETY" (1925)

After returning to Japan in 1904, Noguchi Yonejirō established himself as a critic of and commentator on Anglo-American literature, and he wrote extensively in English on Japanese art and culture. When he returned to the United States and Europe on lecture tours, he was feted as a minor literary celebrity—the Japanese poet who wrote in English. In the late 1920s his writings became increasing nationalistic. Like many Japanese who traveled abroad, his experience intensified attachment to his own culture and nation. Indeed, when the war with America began in 1941, he celebrated the attack on Pearl Harbor with an ardently patriotic poem that mocked the defeat of the "Anglo-Saxon powers" on land and sea.

. . .

Americans have the bad habit of talking about themselves in an overly egotistical way, even when they have no need to do so. It is because of this bad habit that they always try to put themselves at center stage. To put it crudely, they are too "pushy." No other people in the world are as incapable of forgetting themselves as the Americans. No doubt they

Noguchi Yonejirō, "American High Society," source: Noguchi Yonejirō, "Amerikajin," in Noguchi Yonejirō, *Suwaru ningen no hyōron* (Tokyo: Kaizōsha, 1925), 27–32, 35–39, 41.

have an innocent side, but often they impress me as being crude. At first glance it may seem grand and even laudable to regard oneself as a model, but Americans needlessly strain their human energy to do so. Americans are not the only people who crave having their activities approved by others, but no other people have such a well-developed innate sense of self-promotion.

Let's take the example of a wealthy American. With great vigor he will hold forth about his wealth and how well he lives. He will advertise himself by the power of his money. When visitors come to his home, no matter who, he will invite them to five o'clock tea or to dinner with a hearty welcome. With a delighted expression he will introduce his new guests to the others. He will open his home and let everyone in freely, proudly showing off not only his gallery of paintings but also his pantry and even his bedroom. His businesslike way of being open-minded and asking to be judged for his true value is indeed manly. But one must also say that such tremendous conceit betrays a lack of human discipline.

It is said that it is not easy to gain entry into fashionable society in Europe. Indeed, although I have visited Europe many times and have even lived there, I have never been able to fathom the niceties of European society. By complete contrast, Americans explain themselves without being asked, so that even outsiders like us can easily grasp the state of their affairs.

Some time ago, I tried to explain American psychology by using Newport, Rhode Island, as a model of America's high society. . . . Newport is said to resemble Cannes, France. Like Rome and Florence, Cannes is cosmopolitan. But Newport, U.S.A., is thoroughly American.

Although I say that it is typically American, I do not mean to suggest that Newport represents America. It simply represents America's high society. When we speak of this society, we think of luxury and extravagance. Thoughtful people probably scoff at its hollowness and superficiality. Newport is a crystallized pile of great wealth where America's high society gathers to boast about the power of its riches. Even though it is not fundamentally representative of America, in Newport one can discover the strengths and weaknesses of the American people. . . .

As I have said, Newport is not a cosmopolitan place. When aristocratic or wealthy Europeans visit they are received with extreme hospitality but are not admitted into society. The Americans try to intimidate them by flaunting their wild extravagances, and they make fun of the Europeans behind their backs. Just by watching how the Americans ridicule them one can understand how immature and unrefined American culture is. And one can see such immature and unrefined behavior in Americans of all classes. . . .

America has no ancient history. Newport is a summer resort of recent vintage. When we look at the lower classes living by the seaside in two-story wooden homes, it is easy to imagine what Newport was like before it became a resort and residence for America's wealthy. Old Newport is a row of homemade cottages built of lumber brought down from the mountains and cut by colonial forebears. One is astonished at the great contrast between this lifestyle, which bespeaks the hardships of those days, and the present accumulation of great wealth. In America there is no middle ground between the poor and the rich. Scarcely thirty years have passed since wealthy people from the Pacific Coast first came to [Newport] to build their summer residences. Seeing how quickly this extraordinary summer resort has grown, one can understand how fully "go-ahead-ism" [*tosshinshugi,* a neologism meaning "pushiness" or "assertiveness"] has developed here. . . .

One need not be a psychologist to see that American society is as uncontrolled as a wild stallion. It is difficult to find words to express how free and unbridled the American psychology is. Americanism knows no moderation. Americans build buildings too high, their trains run too fast, their luxury homes are too extravagant, their newspapers have too many pages, and they spend their money too ostentatiously. Of course, I should not look just at American faults, but I cannot help feeling that excess is a shortcoming. Whatever its pros and cons, this kind of "go-ahead-ism" is to be found everywhere in America. . . .

Men do not have much weight in fashionable American society. This is quite different from European society. Most American men are involved in business, and very few are born into "high society." They do not inherit exclusive privileges from their forebears. Most are so-called *nouveaux riches* who made their fortunes in mining or in the railroads, and their humble origins mean that their mores, ideals, and tastes are conventional.

Recently, however, America has become Europeanized, and high society has become "snobbish." The elite compete to establish improbably ancient pedigrees; they boast about dubious ancestors; and they even form a special inner circle called the "Four Hundred." It goes without saying that their material fortunes rise and fall abruptly. Since many quickly lose their money and others move to Europe, the Four Hundred is constantly changing, but there are always recent arrivals to the class of the newly rich to fill its vacancies. . . .

In the past Oriental people, who regarded women as slaves, restricted women's activities. It is fair to say that this attitude had its origin in the passionate desire of men to possess exclusive rights over women. Consequently, love among the Orientals is mixed with deep carnal emotions like jealousy and envy. Among the Europeans the Latin race resembles the Orientals in matters of love.

The English, however, give their women freedom. The English climate, education, and religion calm the Englishman's temperament and cool his emotions to an appropriate degree. English men do not look at women from a purely emotional perspective. At the same time the education of women is well developed. To put it in plain words, a desire to monopolize the opposite sex is not very intense in England. In the United States women are granted even more freedom than in England. American women have an extremely robust sense of independence.

If we ask the reasons for the psychological development of American women, we must first look back at the formation of the United States. The American forefathers put enormous energy into building the country. They had to struggle not only with nature but also with the native people. They had to be active in politics as well as carry on commerce. One person had to do the work of ten. People then were content with a simple diet, drank coarse wine, and made their devotions to God. Since there was only one woman for every ten men, men showed respect for women and even worshipped them. The worship of women leaves no room for criticism of women based on sexual feelings.

Contemporary American men have inherited this psychological state. They regard women with an attitude that comes close to reverence, and they even consider it shameful to become enslaved to jealousy and envy. Since women are knowledgeable and well educated and demand equal rights with men, they are even encroaching on men's professions today.

Generally speaking, there is probably no other country where the relationship between men and women is as candid and pure as it is in America. Women of questionable morals are not permitted to intrude upon fashionable society controlled by women, and such women cannot openly associate in male society either. When men get together to talk in their clubs, their conversation hardly touches on women at all. Instead they talk about sports or entertainment or business. Naturally there are many Americans of dubious integrity, but compared to other countries, there are few cases of men who lead lives of dissipated debauchery. In America women attract men with their spiritual side and protect the purity of life. . . .

In France women are known for their skill at making small talk and keeping their conversation partners from being bored, but American women probably surpass them in having a "point of view." English women are taciturn, but American women are talkative. They are able to talk about many things. They are not profound, but they touch on all kinds of issues. It is natural that their education and their surroundings make them lively and that, as women from a country where "ladies are first," they never hesitate to assert themselves. They are certainly no less active than men, but they can be boring and tiresome too. From the perspective of an Oriental like myself, they are perfectly fine as friends, but I have many doubts about them as women.

SASAKI SHIGETSU,
"THE TROUBLESOME AMERICAN WOMAN" (1927)

Sasaki Shigeru took a Japanese bride in his youth, but they lived apart after she returned to Japan in 1916 to look after her mother-in-law. Sasaki, who moved to Greenwich Village, supported himself and his two younger children by writing about American life for Japanese magazines. In the 1920s he published six collections of essays, including the following comments on American women. Evidently he did not lack female companionship during his years in New York. One of his acquaintances reported, "All women talked freely and easily with him, as to a precocious youth." Shortly before his death in 1945 he divorced his Japanese wife and married one of his Zen students, the former wife of a Chicago lawyer.

. . .

"Tom! Get up and fetch me the paper and milk. And make coffee for me. You're a dear husband!"

He received these orders every morning, Tom says. What's more, his wife did not cook dinner. They would always eat a relaxed dinner at a restaurant agreed upon. Sometimes she did not show up, leaving him to chew on his spareribs by himself. Tom would always pay. He had to, because that was a way to maintain his dignity as a husband. Even after they returned home in the evening, he had to keep his mouth shut to maintain his dignity until morning. And the evenings when he did not want to maintain his dignity were fewer than there are winter days with thunderstorms.

Tom works for a printing company, and his wife was a department

Sasaki Shigetsu, "The Troublesome American Woman," source: Sasaki Shigetsu, *Jonan bunka no kuni kara* (Tokyo: Sōjinsha, 1927), 18–20.

store salesgirl. During their three years of marriage, his wife saved every penny of her earnings, but Tom was so poor that he had to borrow money from her every month. After their divorce, he was ordered to pay her $125.00 a month in alimony. Happily for him, this was less than what he had to spend on her as a husband. Tom now lives in a cheap rooming house on Third Avenue. With $125.00 deducted from his monthly pay, he spends the rest of his money on movies.

The following is Tom's story. He is not a sage, but we can learn some things from him. His story is a firsthand account of this nation's "troublesome woman culture."

"In Japan," Tom asked in a serious tone, "I hear that there is a union of home and workplace, allowing the husband and wife to watch each other as they do their work. Is this true?"

"That's unfortunately true," I answered. "The husband is forced to listen to his wife's complaints as he works, and the wife has to hear her husband's every utterance as she sews his clothes."

"That's great! So, the husband and wife know what each has been doing for the whole day, right?"

"That's right. When he hears his wife talking to someone in the kitchen, the husband stops working and comes in to check. When she hears him talking with someone in the shop, she comes running out with a knife," I said, widening my eyes ominously.

"That's scary," he laughed. "But it's a much better situation than in the West, where the wife calls his workplace a million times a day. Who knows how much we might save on the phone bill!"

"You lose time, though. When you are talking on the phone you keep the conversation short. But it's a pain in the neck when you are talking face to face. If you get into an argument with your wife during lunch break, you can forget about finishing that day's work," I countered, even though I wasn't speaking from experience.

Tom smiled and uttered an unlikely response: "That's sweet!"

Taken aback, I explained, "No, it's not. What's so sweet about feuding with your wife?"

"I know what you mean! That's what we do for the sake of love and of lovemaking!" he said, so thoroughly excited he was almost drooling. I understood what he meant. . . .

"OK then," I teased him, "if a man like you lived with a newlywed wife in a home-shop, I think your shop would immediately go bankrupt."

Tom grew serious. "It's no big deal if a shop goes bankrupt," he said. "That is nothing compared to the bankruptcy of a marriage. In the West, the husband and wife don't see each other's faces in daylight except on Sundays and sick days. Given her womanly feelings there may be times when a wife yearns to see her husband's face during the day. In that case the Japanese wife can do so freely, maybe with knife in hand, but in the West this is not possible. The American wife imagines her husband surrounded by beautiful, young, well-educated office girls, with the most beautiful stenographer sitting on his lap. She grows agitated and reaches for the telephone. But when a young lady picks up the phone and brusquely says he is not available, she cannot hear her dear husband's voice. She then begins to imagine that the young lady was breathing heavily, and she grows so agitated that she is practically ready to drag the iceman or the milkman or the policeman or any man who happens to be near into the house and shoot him with a pistol."

"I guess we do say that Western women have less self-control than Eastern women," I commented half-heartedly.

Tom went on to his next topic. "If women grow financially independent, it's natural that they will treat men like floor mats," he said. "If you give women jobs outside the home, they will inevitably grow independent. With their new freedom and equality, women will no longer need husbands. It won't matter who fathered her baby as long as it is her baby. With her new freedom, as long as her body is female, a woman can travel the world freely even without a penny to her name. That's the reason you don't see any woman beggars in New York. If things continue like this, the world is bound for chaos. Women are free to leave their men, but men who leave their women are forced by law to make monthly payments of $125.00. What nonsense! People talk about protecting the weak, but today's women are not weak. Women are scoring victory after victory by taking advantage of men's weaknesses. Since men are after women's love and women are after men's money, men are bound to lose. Love is infinite, but money is finite. Women have their weakness too. It is their penchant of peddling love for money. Leave women to their own devices, and they will naturally fall into this trap. So the way to protect women is to teach them morals, chastity, and the value of a legitimate child. If men are sincere in their desire to protect women, and women to protect men, they both should stop trying to grow independent through the power of money. . . .

"My wife wasn't working as salesgirl when we got married, so she was dependent on me. Once she took the job she made it clear that that her love was for sale too—and she began treating me like a nuisance. I don't know how many times I told her to quit, but she said that staying at home all day made her unbearably lonely. Instead, she said, she would earn a little money so that we could buy a car. Eventually I just gave up. Far from riding around in a car, she rode around on something else, and she ended up leaving me completely. It was my fault that I didn't sue for divorce on grounds of evidence. She sued me, I lost, and I have to pay her $125.00 a month in alimony until she gets remarried. Since she was working as a sales clerk, my alimony payment was less than it might have been, but some other guy is taking care of her food and rent, she's getting her wages as a salesgirl, and she's tucking away the alimony money I give her. She's so-called free-love incarnate. And I'm just a guy down on his luck. There are guys like me all over the place in America. They're swarming the streets of New York City. They're all a bunch of zombies revered in our 'troublesome woman culture.'"

After hearing Tom's story about his grueling, three-year-long, losing battle of love with his ex-wife, I tried to console him.

"These sorts of things happen not only in America," I said. "In my homeland of Japan, people are abandoning the ways of their ancestors. Men and women are turning away from a life centered on the family; everyone is independent, pursuing money or sex. Like New York the country is turning into a big Babylon or a big Yoshiwara [i.e., the main brothel district in Tokyo]. It's naturally the direct result of the liberation of women. But doing things this way may be a way to lead mankind to greater happiness. Maybe it's more fun to lead one's life in a big Babylon or a big Yoshiwara. All you need is money! No matter what kind of life a person leads, he lasts only fifty or sixty years. Philosophically speaking, Tom, there's no point in discussing your departed wife's chastity."

Such stories make us appreciate the stability of Japanese marriages. A Japanese woman conscientiously manages the family purse entrusted to her, and she does everything in her power to ensure that her husband eats good rice, even if it means eating tofu dregs herself. They give birth to two children a year. In the past they even sold their bodies if the husband grew poor.

Thus, if a Japanese man comes to America and makes the mistake of marrying an American woman, instant insanity awaits him. Japanese women are the best, he will say. That's debatable, but indeed, there probably is no other country in the world where women give birth to so many babies that they tip the house foundations, and where they increase the race so fast that they upset the foundations of the whole country. I'm no fervent flag-waver, but the Japanese people need to immigrate to places like Manchuria. Otherwise our island nation may soon capsize like a ship and sink to the bottom of the sea, just like the ancient continent of Mu. We'd better be careful. If we give birth to too many children, the weight of our population will sink the nation into the sea. Japan has been called the "land of the ship of heaven" since the age of the gods . . . , but just one layer below us is the "land of hell." . . .

If I were to make this kind of flippant remark in Japan, somebody would thrash me, but since I'm in America I can get away with criticizing Japan a little bit. A Japanese like me who comes to America and lives here for twenty years begins to see that Western culture is surprisingly dreary. Oil and electricity, elevated railroads, subways, skyscrapers, and such—the civilization of the big city destroys human morality and dignity, making people slaves to the power of money. Forget ancestors, native country, parents, husband and wife. *Loyalty* and *filial piety* disappear from the dictionary, love comes to mean sex, and chastity comes to mean who knows what?

When a little girl asks, "Grandma, what is chastity?" Grandma explains that back in the days when women relied on men for their livelihood, it was a falsehood they relied on to protect themselves. "Then, what is a chastity belt?" asks the child. Grandma answers, "If I remember correctly it was a rat repellant." Grandma was a careful girl who knew rats did not bring in money. I am talking about the future here, but even today in New York, if you talk about chastity in front of a woman, she will laugh at you as an old-fashioned loser.

I can say with certainty that the idea of love without money is no more than a long-gone dream for American women, from society ladies at the top to sweaty factory girls at the bottom. There may be a poet adored by society women who throws back his shoulders and proclaims that romance is still alive, but behind his back men will see him as a turncoat.

HIRABAYASHI HATSUNOSUKE, "MOTION PICTURES: THE AMERICANIZATION MACHINE" (1929)

Hirabayashi Hatsunosuke (1892–1931), a literary critic and essayist, was born the eldest son of a small landlord family. After graduating from Waseda University in 1917, he went to work as a journalist, translating foreign articles for a news agency. While writing cultural commentary,

Hirabayashi Hatsunosuke, "Motion Pictures: The Americanization Machine," source: Hirabayashi Hatsunosuke, "Amerikanizeshon no kikai toshite no eiga," *Kaizō* (February 1929): 69–71.

he became interested in Marxism and Marxist literary theory. In 1922, as an instructor in German at Waseda, he joined the newly organized but illegal Communist Party. During the late 1920s he became the principal theorist of the so-called proletarian literature movement. He was a pioneer of literary criticism based on dialectical materialism, and he wrote extensively on popular culture—movies, detective stories, and popular novels. In 1929 he wrote a famous essay emphasizing the equal importance of artistic and political values in literature. He died during a trip abroad in 1931.

. . .

Today American capital dominates perhaps sixty to eighty percent of the world motion picture market. Two years ago the British Parliament debated how to keep American motion pictures at bay. Recently Japan also attempted a boycott of American films, but it lasted only a short time. American capital backs the lion's share of the European movie industry, particularly that of southern Europe, and probably the Australian and South American movie industries as well.

As a form of entertainment, movies are the most likely to reach the masses and the most likely to have an impact on real life. From this perspective, the control of more than half the world's film by American capital means that the whole world is becoming Americanized. American movies do not always push an obviously American political point of view, but since moving pictures penetrate to the lowest reaches of the masses through the power of vision, their enormous propagandistic potential is unprecedented.

During the Great War in Europe the belligerent countries used movies as their most valuable weapon to propagandize the people of neutral countries. In Russia, where movies are used for the political education of workers, they are regarded as an important educational tool. In Japan, too, movies are used for everything from promoting temperance and frugality to preventing the spread of communism.

Since movies appeal directly to the eye and leave visual images in the mind, they are easily remembered, they can be replicated indefinitely, and they can be shown in many places at once. Hundreds of movie theaters can reach millions of people in a short period of time. For this reason audiences can be subjected to persuasion and propaganda without even realizing it. As a result American motion picture capital may come to dominate the world, just as American financial capital has. The other capitalist nations must not be caught unprepared. Indeed, in England and other countries, governments have promoted national film production in order to drive out American motion pictures. . . .

Motion pictures seem to have been introduced into Japan around 1900, and movie theaters called "electric houses" *[denkikan]* were established in 1903. (Incidentally the well-known journalist Fukuchi Gen'i-chirō coined the term *moving photographs [katsudō shashin]* to describe movies.) In any case, the history of moving pictures has spanned roughly thirty years.

During this short period, motion picture production has become one of the big industries in its birthplace, the United States, and motion picture capital currently totals many hundreds of millions of dollars. There are more than twenty thousand movie theaters in the United States. In a single bound motion pictures have become king of the business world. In a way Hollywood has become a borderless kingdom, and ultimately this has provoked international concern.

Japan has also become a vassal state of Hollywood. Even in the provinces, every movie theater shows at least one American film on its programs, and in our cities some theaters show only Western movies—usually from America. Many movie fans see nothing else. Publicity photos of Hollywood stars are displayed beside those of Japanese movie stars in every country shop. Picture postcards of geisha, such as we had in the Meiji period, have completely disappeared. Movies take up more and more space in magazines and newspapers, and more than ten movie magazines are being published.

From rural youths to urban schoolgirls, from company employees to middle-school language teachers, there is hardly anyone who does not know the names Ronald Coleman, Lillian Gish, Harold Lloyd, and Clara Bow. American movies have a tremendous power to penetrate society, and it is impossible to prevent them from influencing the lives of the Japanese people.

"Action" and "tempo" define the art of movie making. American-made action films and comedies provide typical examples. In Japan, action films have been transformed into so-called samurai [lit., "sword play"] movies. Many people believe that samurai films pander to reactionary nostalgic tastes, but I do not believe this is the whole story. Action and tempo—the lifeblood of screen art—are most readily adapted to Japanese sword-play. Japan's pathetically small-scale film industry cannot afford to use the automobiles, airplanes, guns, and bombs needed to express "action" and "tempo" in expensive large-scale action films. I think this is one of the reasons that the Japanese produce samurai movies instead.

There have also been a few recent attempts at comedy in Japan, but all are complete failures, since the Japanese are absolutely incapable of imitating this unique forte of the American film industry. This is clear when we remember that there is not a single Japanese film comedy star.

American action films and comedies have a dramatic effect on the lives of the Japanese people. Movies have influenced everything from the frocks of café waitresses to Boy Scout uniforms. Fashion trends like striped trousers, Harold Lloyd glasses, and bobbed hair can be traced straight to film. The most direct products of movies probably are the "modern girls" *[moga]* and "modern boys" *[mobo],* but one must add that cafés, drinking, and dancing are associated with movies too.

The influence of American moving pictures is not limited to such superficial matters. The mental life of the Japanese people is being Americanized by the hour. Although the Japanese are not—as one Westerner has said—a people not permitted to laugh, the long era of seclusion, a despotic government, and feudal morality have made the Japanese a people who take pride in concealing their emotions. Men who stoically suffer hardship are considered manly, and women who lower their eyes and speak little are considered modest. American movies are swiftly threatening to destroy these "beautiful customs" inherited from our ancestors.

As the number of windows in Japanese houses has increased, the facial expressions of Japanese have become more cheerful, and their bodily movements have become more nimble. (Of course from an American standpoint Japanese still seem extremely slow and phlegmatic.) And as more and more women walk along the Ginza [the "Fifth Avenue" of Tokyo] with a brisker stride and straighter posture, Japanese facial muscles move with more animation. I do not mean to be facetious, but I think that an anatomist could come up with interesting results if he were to compare the facial muscles of movie fans, particularly fans of comedies, with those who do not watch American movies. But by far the most remarkable psychological change in the Japanese that has resulted from the influence of movies is the bolder expressions of love professed between men and women.

In the past America spent money on sending missionaries to Japan and building churches there without much success. Today the movement to Americanize backward countries is succeeding smoothly, as it relies on laughter and rowdiness (while turning a profit) instead of sermons with sour faces. I do not know whether or not the American president has awarded medals to movie producers or movie stars, but from an American perspective they definitely deserve such recognition. In 1918

General Pershing's achievements at the French war front were worthy of recognition, but I mean it when I say that Charlie Chaplin has possibly had a stronger impact on the history of world culture.

We should leave the brouhaha over the Americanization of the Japanese to politicians who love to exploit national emergencies. Americanization in Japan began in 1853, and it is nothing to lose our heads over at this late date. If we truly regret the gradual fading of Japan's uniqueness under Westernization, we ought to abolish representative government, law courts, schools, newspapers, railroads, and telegraph lines before we start abolishing moving pictures.

What we see today is a process of Americanization rather than Westernization. This reflects the simple fact that the power of American capital has surpassed that of Europe. In a capitalist society the power of capital is almighty in both the material and mental spheres. We all shave our beards with American razors, ride in American taxis, watch American moving pictures, and even go to sleep in bedding made from American cotton. Wherever you go in the world today things are pretty much the same.

KIYOSAWA KIYOSHI,
"AMERICA, THE LAND OF SPEED" (1929)

At the urging of a Christian school teacher, the journalist and critic Kiyosawa Kiyoshi (1890–1945) arrived in America at the age of sixteen to continue his studies. Like readers of Katayama Sen's guidebook, he saw America as a promised land where a poor youth could earn enough to support himself as a "schoolboy" while attending classes. After studying briefly at Whitworth College, in Spokane, he began his journalistic career as a reporter for two Japanese-language newspapers, the Seattle *Jiji* and the San Francisco *Shinsekai*. Although his formal education was limited, he proved himself a perceptive commentator on the Japanese immigration issue, Japanese-American relations, and American culture. In 1920 he returned to Japan, where he worked for several leading daily newspapers, including the Tokyo *Asahi shinbun*. Forced to resign from the *Asahi* by right-wing political pressure, he continued his career as a freelance journalist with a reputation for liberal and cosmopolitan views. In the late 1930s he was a strong critic of the policies of the Japanese

Kiyosawa Kiyoshi, "America, the Land of Speed," source: Kiyosawa Kiyoshi, "Supīdo no kuni Amerika," *Chūō kōron* (November 1929): 203–212.

military, and he urged an internationalist foreign policy based on cooperation with the United States and Great Britain. During the war he kept a diary that was published posthumously in 1954, providing insightful analysis of wartime Japan.

. . .

The odds rarely favor American men when they compete against women, but, as might be expected in the homeland of competitive organizations and capitalism, sparks fly when they compete against their fellow males. Such competition, in fact, has come to center on the automobile. It is clear that today America has entered the "Age of the Automobile."

When I got off the boat at Seattle, I passed by a train station. (Even though Seattle is a city of 500,000 people, it boasts two train stations that are the size of Tokyo Station; the reason is that private companies run railroads.) On the roof of this station sat a huge advertising sign that proclaimed in red letters, "$3.00 to Portland. $2.00 to Vancouver."

As we drove to a nearby roadway Mr. Arima, current affairs reporter for North America, who greeted me at the pier, explained, "Passenger buses are making great headway these days. The railroads are bogging down in management difficulties. Competition for the railroads comes not from other railroad companies; it comes from the passenger buses."

"Take the long-distance train that goes to Tacoma," he went on. "It used to be as popular as the Japanese National Railway route between Tokyo and Yokohama. But with the development of the bus, it has gone bankrupt. Just look over there and see how often the bus comes by instead."

Large buses as solid as Tokyo trams passed by constantly. They connect to Vancouver in the north and to Los Angeles in the south. The two cities are the same distance apart as Hokkaido [the northernmost island in Japan] and Kagoshima [the southernmost prefecture], and the buses run several times a day. There are no sleeping bunks on the Pacific Coast buses, but they do have reclining seats that let you sleep comfortably. . . .

Although long-distance trains might survive, there is little hope for short-distance trains and railways. One cannot think about the traffic problem without taking into account the automobile. Three concrete-paved roads like the one between Tokyo and Yokohama connect Seattle, with its population of 450,000–460,000, to Tacoma, a city of 120,000–130,000, about fifty miles away. Another such concrete road will soon be built, I understand. The Americans do not begrudge spending money on highways at levels that are nearly extravagant. . . .

One European philosopher has lamented, "All Americans have become chauffeurs." What he meant is that all Americans seem to be driving automobiles and that their personalities are deteriorating into those of chauffeurs. In Seattle, a provincial town by American standards, there are 150,000 automobiles, or twice as many as in all of Japan. It is easy to imagine what the congestion is like. Even in modest households, a married couple and their children each have their own cars.

A college professor told me with a look of despair, "For example, let's take the supervision of girl students in college dormitories. It used to be that if you kept an eye on the yard or on the downtown section, you could fulfill your responsibility of taking care of girl students and could rest easy that everything was all right. But now the girls can get into an automobile and be anywhere in an hour or two. There is no way that you can keep track of them."

Since arriving in the United States, I have been asked to give talks here and there on current conditions in Japan. If the audience is fifty or sixty people, automobiles spread out around the meeting hall like a cortege for a Japanese cabinet minister's funeral. Many are farmers and workers with hands gnarled from years of work, who have traveled forty or fifty miles to come hear me.

Customs and morals seem to be changing in America to accommodate entry into the Age of the Automobile. To put it another way, with the arrival of the speed monster known as the automobile, manners and morals that survived until now are being smashed to pieces. For example, it has become the fashion for American men to go without hats, probably because hats are inconvenient when getting in and out of automobiles. Around Tokyo, automobile owners do not wear either hats or overcoats. The women's hats currently in style are shaped like upside-down rice bowls. No doubt they are more convenient for riding in automobiles. Older-style hats, with wide brims and long hatpins, would surely catch on the roof of the car like fish on a hook.

Anything that changes prevailing fashions can change prevailing morals as well. I am sure that I will have an opportunity to discuss this in future reports, but let me point out one new danger that has emerged in America: men and women riding together in automobiles.

"Hey, look out! That's a car with a young couple in it!" It has become normal for cars following such a vehicle to pass this on as a warning—like a danger signal. It is hard to tell where the automobile is going or where it will turn off the road. A car carrying a young man and a young woman zigzags along the road like a blind man dancing.

I guess that is the way it is with young men and women who do not care what others think. They race along the road, clinging to each other so tightly that there seems to be only one person behind the steering wheel. Indeed, it is no surprise that they often forget about the steering wheel entirely.

Some states and cities have issued regulations prohibiting drivers from placing their arms around a passenger's shoulder while driving. Since the passage of the Prohibition Amendment, the number of drunken drivers has dropped, but an equally dangerous phenomenon has appeared: young men and young women alone together in automobiles. Where is it that these cars are racing at such great speeds? When the young move far away from their families, the degree of danger increases. Since ancient times, love, like alcohol, has always been a demonic force.

The speed of the automobile symbolizes the rapidity of everything in America. A huge advertisement for airmail delivery sits on the side of the road, and on a slight rise a searchlight shines for passing planes. Several days after I arrived in Seattle, daily airmail flights began between Seattle and New York. Mail is delivered in New York within two days.

It is not just planes and automobiles that are fast. I think that Americans seem to have a different sense of time from the Japanese. They are much more sensitive to time.

When my ship docked in the United States, I decided to get a new glass face for my pocket watch. It had broken about two months before, but since I could not do without it I used the watch anyway without repairing it. I went to a watch shop the day I arrived in Seattle.

"Could you put a glass face on this watch," I asked.

"Just a minute," the storekeeper replied after inspecting the watch. I figured that he would tell me to come back in three or four days, for that is surely what I would have been told in Tokyo. But right in front of my eyes, the shopkeeper took out a box of glass faces and picked out a round one.

"I don't have one that matches your watch," he said. "Could you come back at around 2:00 this afternoon?"

Naturally I asked, "Today?" It was noon, and 2:00 was only two hours away. In Tokyo the job would have taken a week for one reason or another, but the shopkeeper got a glass face from a wholesaler and put it on my watch right on schedule.

The next day, when I went to a shoe store to have the soles of my shoes repaired, I reminded myself not to have high hopes. If I went to a shoe store in Tokyo and asked how soon my shoes could be repaired, they would keep telling me, "They will be ready soon"—even though they knew it would take three or four days. But having the example of the watch store before me, I thought to myself that an American shoe store could do my shoes in about a day.

I thought about getting a delivery boy to bring me my shoes that night—or perhaps asking a friend to pick them up. My trip was a long one, and that forced me to keep my possessions to a minimum. I had brought only one pair of shoes with me, so I was quite concerned about what to do about my worn-out soles.

I went to a shoe store in the white section of town. "I would like to replace the soles on these shoes," I said. "How long do you think it will take?" Of course, I expected a wait of about two or three hours.

"It will take about five minutes," the store clerk replied. After I took off my shoes, he started fixing them right away. Two or three minutes later, he was back. "All done. Please try them on." I could not believe it.

In Japan people say, "I'll be right with you"; in the United States they say, "I'll be with you in five minutes." And when you ask directions in Japan, people say, "It's just down the road"; in America, they say, "It's on the corner six blocks up." On all the major road intersections there are signs showing exactly how many miles it is to other major important locations. Time and speed: these are the strengths of America.

The Americans would probably say that prosperity is a matter of speed. They accomplish in two hours trivial tasks that usually take the Japanese a week. A ten-hour trip takes one hour; money circulates quickly; goods sell fast; and business discussions are wrapped up very quickly.

The Americans waste little manpower. Because they waste so little manpower, they manage to get things done with fewer people working; because they can finish things with fewer people, they can pay higher salaries; and because they pay higher salaries, the country is prosperous.

With some surprise Americans ask Orientals, who feel strong resistance to speed, "Can you have a mechanized civilization and prosperity in places where there is no speed?"

"How have things changed in America, the land of speed?"

This question came to mind as I recalled the years of my youth when I worked my way through school. When we were "schoolboys" we hated beating carpets more than any other chore. We would drape the carpet over a wire strung between two trees, then beat it with a wire carpet beater. The dust from the carpet would mingle with our sweat, turning us into human salt piles. But now people no longer need to do such dirty jobs, since they all have electric brooms that suck up the dust very easily.

"Housework is no longer a big chore, since no one would stand for doing such tedious work by hand," I was told by a woman who has worked in an American home for many years. "Instead of washing clothes inside the house, I take the clothes to the cleaners. The store charges a set price for every ten kilograms of wet clothing, and all I do at home is iron. I don't wash every dirty dish by hand but just flip a switch and the machine washes and dries them. Even middle-class households have refrigerators. Since the refrigerator will make ice for the ice water that Americans love to drink so much, there is no need to have large blocks of ice delivered to the house. In the past ten years American kitchens have been completely revolutionized."

The woman spoke with pride, as though it were all her own doing. With wages so high, only the wealthiest Americans can hire maids. Instead, the Americans produce one machine after another to replace them.

"Take the lid of that milk bottle," the woman said to me. "At first, it was just a round piece of paper pressed down on the top of the bottle. Next they added a small wire to hold it in place. Now they have a lid on the top like a hat. They are adding improvements to things almost every day. They have these clocks they don't wind at all. They automatically wind themselves as the pendulum swings. I hear that they're all the rage." The woman did not seem to tire at all as she talked about the mechanization of the American home.

"Everyone looks so young." As I stand here in Seattle, looking at these practical, energetic, and optimistic Americans, it strikes me that Americans do not seem to have aged at all in the ten years since I was last here. With no apparent effort, competition and individual enterprise have flourished.

As I walk around town, I see advertisements for local businesses posted on corner telephone poles. Charging private companies advertising space is a clever way for the city to make a profit. Everywhere I drive in Seattle I see extraordinarily large advertisements for the municipal electric power company. When I asked why, I was told that the company has to fight off fierce competition from private power companies. A gas leak started a small fire in the house of a friend. When this was reported in the newspaper the next day, a salesman from the municipal electric company came by. "See how dangerous gas can be," he said. "You might consider switching to electric power." He left after handing my friends an advertising leaflet.

In hotels, drug stores, and other places where people gather, there are machines that sell stamps. While I am impressed that the American authorities are so considerate, I am sure that this is the work of some private company. If you put in five cents for stamps, you get back only four cents worth. Twenty percent must go to the company or the store as profit. In Japan, if someone even thought about using postage stamps to make a profit, there would be cries of protest.

In hotel lobbies and other public gathering places, one can find great marble mailboxes. These boxes, however, are owned by advertising agencies that make a profit from leasing out advertising space in return for donating the boxes.

Everywhere you go there is competition. Town against town, individual against individual, industry against industry—you can feel all of them competing with one another. Competition brings needless sacrifices, but it also fosters individual initiative, invention, and improvement. Naturally there will always be some pitiful persons who fall by the wayside. But in America, where opportunities to work in new companies abound, people never lose the spirit that enables them to pull themselves up from the bottom of society just as easily as an athlete shrugs off defeat. Until the Great Plains can no longer be tilled or until material progress comes to an end, Americans are not likely to take much interest in socialism.

The tempo of the American people, however, is not always as fast as you might expect. The comic strips *Mutt and Jeff* and *Jiggs and Maggie,* which the Japanese became tired of in six months, have run in America continuously for some twenty years. They still hold people's interest as they always have. Crossword puzzles, which appeared in Japan for only a year, are still published in local newspapers and remain quite popular. It is the streets of the Ginza that are fast paced, not the streets of America.

Where do America's problems come from? They come from the fact that "all Americans have become chauffeurs." The strengths of a mechanized society are the strengths of America, and its weaknesses are the weaknesses of America too. In the years to come, America will be tested as it brings its fast-paced side and its slow-paced side together. . . .

CHAPTER 4

The American Enemy

Despite a rash of fictional accounts of future wars between Japan and the United States, diplomatic and economic relations between the two countries were relatively tranquil during the 1920s. Not only did Japan join the League of Nations as a charter member, but the Japanese government also cooperated with the Americans in establishing naval arms limitations in the Pacific and supported (albeit less enthusiastically) American diplomatic efforts to phase out the "unequal treaty system" in China. Economic ties between the two countries also expanded. The United States became Japan's largest customer (accounting for 40 percent of Japan's exports), and Japan became the main site for American investment in East Asia. Wall Street bankers such as Thomas Lamont, a senior partner of J. P. Morgan and Company, eagerly invested in Japanese colonial enterprises. To be sure, friction over the immigration question continued, but the Americans seemed willing to negotiate the issue by the late 1920s.

Japanese leaders were therefore shocked when the Hoover administration protested the Japanese military incursion into northeast China and the establishment of Manchukuo, a Japanese satellite state, in 1931–32. Since victory in the Russo-Japanese War, the Japanese had come to regard East Asia as a region of special strategic and economic interest to Japan, just as Latin America was to the United States. Indeed, journalists, politicians, and officials often referred to the country's policy in China as the "Asian Monroe Doctrine"—ironically enough, a phrase suggested by Theodore Roosevelt. The Japanese were upset that the Americans criticized Japan for doing in China what the Americans felt free to do south of their own border, and they wondered why the United States did not honor Japan's policy as Japan honored America's. Some suggested that it was another example of America's arrogance and its hypocrisy—its inclination to say one thing and do another.

During the 1930s an air of uncertainty swirled about American intentions in Asia. While the American government had spoken out against Japanese military activity in China, it had done very little to stop it. For all their high moral dudgeon, American leaders, struggling with social dislocations wrought by declining production and rising unemployment as the Depression deepened, were not inclined to involve the country in other people's disputes. Isolationism from the world's troubles enjoyed strong popular support, and during the mid-1930s Congress passed laws to maintain American neutrality in foreign conflicts. Even though American rhetoric escalated after full-scale war broke out between China and Japan in 1937, few Japanese thought the United States was likely to become involved in the struggle militarily.

Konoe Fumimaro, a future prime minister, returned from a 1934 visit to the United States with the impression that Americans knew very little about Japan and were not particularly interested in its China policies. Like many others, he concluded that since the United States had few interests in East Asia, the Americans could be persuaded to accept the legitimacy of Japan's actions. As the editor of a major Japanese newspaper wrote after a tour of the United States, "Americans are pragmatic and realistic. If Japan explains its position clearly, they will certainly understand it. . . . The Americans sympathize with the Chinese because China is the underdog. . . . But they are not anti-Japanese and they do not hate us."[1] The quest for "understanding" proved futile, and American hostility escalated in late 1940 when the Japanese government struck an alliance with the Axis powers, Nazi Germany and Fascist Italy, and moved troops into northern French Indochina.

Growing tension heightened Japanese interest in America. The number of books published about the United States and about its relations with Japan jumped in 1941, and general-interest magazines were filled with articles, symposia reports, and analyses of America. "There are many people wielding their writing brushes," observed one writer in *Kaizō* magazine, "but how many of these commentators are really qualified to talk about America?" Everyone seemed to be whistling in the dark, fearful about the depth of the crisis but optimistic about the prospects for victory. And all that Japanese politicians suggested, he added, was "to work

FIGURE 6. This cartoon history of America, embodied in the person of Merikan Gorō, a gangster with a mean-looking dog, suggests that American expansionist aggression provoked the outbreak of war. The six panels are read from top to bottom and right to left, as they are numbered: (1) Merikan Gorō drives his English master out of the North American continent; (2) with the resources he acquired as a result, he becomes a nouveau riche; (3) using his money power, he acquires more and more territory; (4) when he cannot use money, he shows his true violent character; (5) the gangster now extends his paws to the Orient; (6) will this upstart now reach out to seize Mt. Fuji too? The final question is answered at the top of the cartoon: "He has been aiming at Japan for more than 150 years. (*Hi no de,* November 1944)

together as one, surmounting all difficulties, and make sacrifices for the national destiny." Anyone pointing out the dangers of underestimating the Americans was drowned out by a rising jingoistic clamor.[2]

The final outbreak of war with the United States met with a wave of euphoria among the intelligentsia. Two days after the Pearl Harbor attack, the poet Murano Shirō exulted:

Look, now!
The citadel of evil is crumbling in the midst of the Pacific's seething waves.
Rise, descendants of the gods.
The time has come to attack and destroy the demons.[3]

The vehemence of the intellectuals' reaction to war with America reflected a sense that history was turning a page on the era of "white supremacy" or "Anglo-Saxon hegemony." As the literary critic Itō Sei summed it up, "From the age of thirteen, like most of the intellectual class, I studied English as a way of getting in touch with the world. The reason, of course, was that the English-speaking peoples possessed an unsurpassed culture, power, and wealth. In that sense, until today, they have been the conquerors of the world. . . . We belong to what they call 'the yellow race.' We are fighting to affirm the superiority of that race. Our fight is different from Germany's."[4] Even intellectuals on the left supported the war, which they hoped would liberate the colonized peoples of East and Southeast Asia from Western imperialism.

A recurrent theme during the war was that America was bent on "world domination"—which, of course, is exactly what the Americans were saying about Japan. The history of American expansion across the continent, once lauded as a triumph of the American "pioneer spirit," now became evidence of American ambition to gobble up other people's territory. In a 1943 pamphlet on the American national character, the distinguished philosopher Watsuji Tetsurō argued that its philosophical roots were to be found in the ideas of Thomas Hobbes and Francis Bacon. From the day they set foot on the American continent, settlers had to conquer both the "natives" and "nature" in order to survive. The Baconian side of the American character created the "mechanistic civilization" needed to conquer both, and its Hobbesian side justified the use of violence against American Indians, who were living in a "state of nature outside the social contract." Once the settlers overran the vast continent and annexed the Pacific coast, it was no surprise that Perry's fleet arrived in Japan and that the Americans annexed the Hawaiian Islands and the Philippine Islands.[5]

The government relied on the popular press to stir up hatred of the "Anglo-American beasts" [chiku Ei-Bei], a term roughly equivalent to the Americans' "dirty Japs," but the intelligentsia contributed to the war effort by offering analyses of why the Americans would lose. Recycling earlier images of America into a pathology of its flaws and weaknesses, they argued that despite obvious disparities between American and Japanese economic strength, the American war machine was vulnerable.

First of all, the economic superiority of the United States was temporary, and once Japan acquired the resources it lacked at home from East and Southeast Asia, the economic balance would be evened. The Americans would find themselves fighting a stronger adversary than sheer statistics suggested. Second, American society, with its complex ethnic mix, was riddled with hidden fault lines that would weaken any concerted war effort. Not only were ethnic and racial differences strong, so were regional and local ones—particularly between the North and the South. It was difficult to imagine that the Americans would fight side by side when they found it difficult to live side by side. And finally, although the Americans touted the superiority of their democratic institutions, the people were in fact politically divided, disorderly, and unable to reach agreement on national goals, as the Japanese were able to, and their leader, President Roosevelt, was a self-interested politician more concerned with his own popularity than with the nation's interest.

The Americans' greatest flaws, in the eyes of Japanese intellectuals supporting the war, were their materialism, hedonism, and individualism. Great economic strength had given them material advantages, but it had weakened their spiritual character and impoverished them morally. Their fighting spirit would be stifled by their worship of money and easy pleasure; physically and spiritually they would be no match on the battlefield for the tougher Japanese. In the end Japanese spirit would triumph over American matter, and Japanese right would triumph over American might.

Probably no one expressed these ideas more succinctly than Watsuji at the conclusion of his analysis of the American national character:

> The Americans won [the American continent] using mechanical means against indigenous people who had none. But now they are facing an enemy even more adept than they are at using machinery, and for the first time they are meeting defeat. ... The American people are relying on "numbers" to protect themselves. They think that "quantity" will overcome the enemy. In pursuit of their "myth of civilization" the Americans will fight until they have exhausted all their power. What awaits them is *nervous breakdown* [original in English]. The true strength of a people lies in its moral spirit, not in its quantitative

FIGURE 7. The wartime government attempted to "purify" Japanese culture by ridding the daily language of foreign-loaned words—and by discouraging the study of English. In this cartoon, a schoolboy practices his English by speaking into a garbage box. His mother stands behind, ready to douse him with salt, a traditional mode of ritual purification. "Dirty things belong in dirty places," she says. "When you're done, I sprinkle salt on you."

power. Gamblers [like the Americans] who bet everything in a fit of impatience will be surprised when they lose.[6]

The distinguished philosopher was no more prescient than the country's military leaders, and his message was not much different from what army recruits were told during their basic military training.

KONOE FUMIMARO, "MY IMPRESSIONS OF WASHINGTON AND NEW YORK" (1934)

Konoe Fumimaro (1891–1945) was prime minister when war broke out with China in 1937 and also during the U.S.-Japan negotiations in 1941,

Konoe Fumimaro, "My Impressions of Washington and New York," source: Konoe Fumimaro, *Seidanroku* (Tokyo: Chikura shobo, 1937), 55–58, 59–62.

which eventually led to the Pacific War. Born into one of the oldest aristocratic families in Japan, he entered the House of Peers at the age of twenty-five. At the end of World War I he attended the Paris Peace Conference as a member of the Japanese delegation. In a famous essay he criticized the internationalism of Great Britain and the United States as a hypocritical justification for their domination of the world's territory and resources. By contrast he pointed to Japan as one of the "have-not" nations of the world. By 1934, when he traveled to the United States on a fact-finding tour, he was a staunch supporter of military means to establish Japan as the dominant power in East Asia, and he advocated the creation of "a national defense state" to mobilize the population and the economy in time of war. In 1940 as prime minister he called for the establishment of the Greater East Asia Co-Prosperity Sphere under Japanese leadership. Although he resigned from office shortly before war with the United States began, he continued to exercise political influence behind the scenes, urging the government to begin peace negotiations with the United States in 1945 to forestall domestic rebellion. He expected to play a key role in government after defeat, but in late 1945 he committed suicide after he learned that he was to be indicted as a war criminal.

. . .

My stay in Washington [in 1934] was quite brief. My schedule included so many lunches, dinners, and social gatherings that I had few opportunities to talk openly with individuals. Those whom I met informally were people who had some connection with Japan, so I cannot say whether their opinions were honest opinions reflecting all sides of America.

The overall atmosphere in the United States suggests that America does not think about the Far East as much as Japan thinks about America. Even within the government there appears to be too much concern about domestic issues to embark on a concrete solution of Far Eastern problems. In general people either take a "wait-and-see" attitude toward the Manchurian problem or favor tacit recognition. Some influential figures say that the Manchurian problem has already been solved in substance. In other words, what Japan does in Manchuria is a matter of no concern, as long as it does not infringe on the rights and interests of the United States. There is also even a very small group who claim that official recognition of Manchukuo [the Japanese-dominated client state in northeast China] is simply a matter of time. Some appear to believe that since recognition is merely a question of time, the best way to work toward peace is for [the United States] to offer it quickly.

We should be aware that it is a mistake to conclude that America will offer legal recognition of Manchukuo in the near future. While some influential figures in America believe that the problem has already been solved, there are others who caution that much will depend on the attitude Japan takes toward China. Some say frankly that America will not sit quietly by if Japan monopolizes economic advantages in China. However, I heard no one object in a positive way to Japan acting as a stabilizing force [in China]. Whether or not they will accept this as a principle, out of concern about the reaction of Latin American countries and the League of Nations they seem to hope they can avoid the issue as much as possible. Interest in the Far Eastern problem has been on the rise since the Manchurian Incident, and the thinking of a small group has been dominated by the view that the standard for judging or for resolving Far Eastern issues should not be determined on the basis of simple theories, as it has been in the past.

That is the apparent reason that America has changed its attitude for the moment. But we should not conclude that this is because America has genuinely recognized Japan's position. For example, Americans still see Japan's actions in Manchuria as the consequence of particular political circumstances, and they hold the view that Japan will face an economic stalemate in the future. It will probably take considerable time for them to understand that Japan has adopted a necessary national policy.

As I said in a speech at the outset of my visit, my conviction is that friendship between Japan and the United States is possible if Americans recognize that Japan is a "Japan in a period of renovation"; that is to say, it is a Japan that has adopted a starting point in its determination to work for the country's advancement in the world. Both President Roosevelt and Secretary of State Hull appear to express understanding and goodwill toward Japan and the Japanese. And they leave no doubt that they hope for friendly relations between Japan and the United States and for the security of China. . . . (6/14/1934)

During my tour of Boston and New York I had many opportunities to speak with influential figures in the academic, business, and intellectual worlds. I was able to hear much franker opinions expressed in a freer atmosphere than in Washington. What most attracts the attention of these influential men are political currents in Japan today.

Some of these influential men hold the view that the Japanese government is gradually coming under the control of the military and that the Japanese people have no trust in the military. They also expect the influence of the [civilian] political parties to be restored. To cite an extreme example, a few of them even believe that Japanese politics today is reminiscent of prewar [i.e., pre-1914] imperial Germany, and they warn that Japan should not become a second Germany.

In response to such views, I point out that the power of the military does not determine the direction of Japanese politics and that the Japanese military is not at all like the German military before World War I. My interlocutors appear to listen with surprise. They believe that postwar principles governing the maintenance of world peace remain in force today, and they implicitly suggest that Japan's actions in the Far East today are tantamount to a violation of those principles. They are sympathetic to Japan, which borders both Russia and China, but a few harbor fears that Japan, taking advantage of political and economic unrest among the [world] powers, may pursue a policy of positive aggression toward China. Others, though they disagree with this, say that Japan's Far Eastern policy lacks clarity.

As they look at the Far East from a Western perspective, those with whom I spoke are surprised at the extraordinary gap between their so-called principles of peace and Japan's claims. But they do not think it necessary to abandon their principles or efforts to interfere with Japan because there is such a gap. Some, however, seem to think it appropriate to cooperate with the League [of Nations] to put pressure on Japan. But under the present circumstances, when the weakness of the league has been exposed and the powers are reluctant to take a positive position, America has no reason to take the lead.

What is especially striking is that some doubt that the principles they embrace apply to the new situation in the Far East. I am happy to report that most are beginning to feel that it is necessary to reconsider the realities in the Far East rather than argue about principles. Even so, they have not abandoned arguing from principle. They respect principles at all costs. Consequently they warn that if Japan insists on adopting new principles, it is necessary [for Japan] to clarify these principles so that they can be fully understood. To the degree that [Japan's new principles] remain unclear, Americans have no choice but to regard their own existing principles as preferable, and they see no reason to conclude a peace treaty between Japan and the United States. It would be like putting a roof on top of an existing roof.

In other words, from the American point of view, if their principles are wrong, then it is Japan's responsibility to point that out and to establish new principles in their place. The powers are ready to take such principles under consideration. As for the Amau Statement,[7] these Americans say that the powers regard the provision of economic and technological aid to China as legal and rational, and they have difficulty in understanding why it should be criticized. In general, they say that the American people agree with the present economic policy of the Nanking government.

In response I point out to them that even though the powers' economic support [for the Nanking government] is motivated by economic reasons, anti-Japanese politicians in China today are using it for political purposes and that there is a fear that the results will differ entirely from the powers' expectations.

There is no consensus on the coming [naval] disarmament conference [in London]. Experts say that present [naval strength] ratios provide a sufficient guarantee of Japan's predominant position in the Far East, but in general they do not think that Japan's demands for change are completely unreasonable. Some foreign affairs experts suggest that if there are substantial differences among the demands of the various naval powers, we should take into account their national defense goals for future naval construction rather than rely futilely on the establishment of ratios or cling to the current treaty. As for the connection between naval disarmament and political issues, many do not agree that there is an inevitable connection between the two. Those who believe that there is a connection qualify that by pointing to the stability of the political situation. (7/1/1934)

KADA TETSUJI, "AMERICAN PERSPECTIVES ON JAPAN, AND VICE VERSA" (1941)

Kada Tetsuji (1895–1964), a prominent commentator on economic and political issues, graduated from Keiō University in 1919. After spending a few years as an instructor at Keiō, he went to England to study in 1923. On his return he was appointed professor at Keiō, and in 1937 he received a Ph.D. in economics. His academic career came to an abrupt end in 1945. During the postwar years he was active in the business world, serving as an adviser to large firms such as the Japan Mining Company.

. . .

Kada Tetsuji, "American Perspectives on Japan, and Vice Versa," source: Kada Tetsuji, "Amerika no Nihonkan to Nihon no Amerikakan," *Kaizō* (March 1941): 14–21.

The American perspective on East Asia is based on a sense of Asia's inferiority, no matter what country is involved. Americans look even at Japan from this perspective. To put it bluntly, the Japan that they see differs not one whit from their impressions at the time of the Perry expedition. Japan itself bears some responsibility for this. Japanese cultural propaganda has focused on a tourist's vision of Japan—Mt. Fuji, cherry blossoms, geisha, and flower arranging. After so many years this tired propaganda, aimed at promoting American sightseeing by presenting a feudal Japan, has fused with [Americans'] sense of racial superiority and prevented them from appreciating Japan's strength.

That does not mean that Japanese politics and economy are not studied in America. The study of Japan's diplomacy is flourishing, and in recent years so has the study of Japan's political and economic development. An excellent example is the ten volumes about Japan and East Asia published by the Institute of Pacific Relations. Academic books in America sell poorly, however, and consequently they have little impact on American public opinion. In any case, if these volumes are any indication, the American perspective on Japan generally minimizes Japan's real power. By contrast, the Japanese view of America exaggerates America's real power.

The [American] undervaluation of Japan's power rests principally on estimates of Japan's economic strength. A typical example is *When Japan Goes to War*, a book by two American Communists, Tanin and Yohan, who argue that the Japanese economy will collapse in short order. The basis of their assessment is the assumption that conditions at one fixed point in time will remain unchanged. They pay no attention to wartime changes such as Japan's adoption of a wartime [economic] system or its acquisition of territories with new resources. They simply conclude that current conditions will continue. That is the flaw not only of their static perspective but also of their optimistic view.

Japanese politics in particular are badly misunderstood in the United States. Americans hold democracy as their political ideal, and they elevate it above everything else. To be sure, a fascist movement has emerged recently in the United States, and it supports Germany's demands, but it has no political influence. The majority of Americans criticize Japan from the standpoint of American democracy. Needless to say, this is a fundamentally mistaken way of looking at things. The general view is that Japan moved into a fascist phase after the May 15th incident [a failed military coup in 1932]. . . . [Many recently published books] stress a trend toward militarism in Japan but insist that democracy is the best possible political system.

Americans do not try to understand what is going on in Japan or to learn anything new from Japan. On the contrary, they take the position that they are Japan's teachers. This is a blatant expression of the sense of racial superiority nourished by their historical development. It resembles the attitude of white Americans toward American Indians and Negroes....

America's real power is overestimated in Japan.... This is especially striking in the case of economic affairs. We must recognize that American economic power is enormous, and it would not be incorrect to say that will continue to be the case. But admitting America's economic strength is not the same as saying that Japan's economic strength is inconsequential. However, the majority view in Japan is based on a comparison of economic statistics to determine which of the two countries is superior.

It is clear that if one compares productive power, resource reserves, and productive efficiency, the United States, with its vast territory and its large population, enjoys a superior position. Moreover, Japan is dependent on the United States for its most important manufacturing raw materials. This situation tends to instill an inferiority complex in Japan.

This superficial view prevails among [Japanese] students of America. Generally speaking it is also characteristic of [Japanese] business leaders, who are fond of concrete statistics. But is this sense of Japanese economic inferiority based on fact? And must we think of it as a situation that cannot change?

I believe this perspective arises from an inadequate understanding of real conditions in America. The feeling of anxiety that Japan stands at a disadvantage with respect to the United States ignores the significant geographical fact that the two countries are separated by 5,000 miles of the Pacific Ocean.

Sufficient understanding of the real situation in the United States has been hidden in the shadow of American statistics. American economic strength is immense, but the real issue is whether that great economic power can be properly deployed in the event of war.

First, there is a political problem. American democracy rests on two things: individualism and federalism. These put the national state at a double disadvantage. One is the opposition of the individual to state control, and the other is the conflict of interests between the federal government and the state governments. Even after the outbreak of World War II in Europe, the industrial regions and the agricultural regions [in the United States] have been unable to coordinate either politically or economically.

In American democracy, during a time of war or war preparation, there is a tendency for the unlimited expansion of presidential power to subvert its fundamental character. It was to the diplomatic advantage of the United States to take over the British bases from Newfoundland to the Caribbean in return for the loan of fifty outmoded destroyers to the British, but the president had to carry that out by his own dictatorial decision without the consent of the Senate. How long, one wonders, can American democracy continue under such circumstances? Who can guarantee that this trend will not cause political upheavals?

Second, there is the problem of the racial situation. Without going into a detailed discussion, there is a mixed racial structure in the United States. This is a difficulty for a country that has aggravated labor problems.

Third, there is a purely economic problem. Even with its vast resource base, the United States lacks important strategic materials such as rubber, tin, manganese, antimony, quinine, vegetable oil, hemp, and the like. These are all produced on the western side of the Pacific. One can imagine that when the waves are high [i.e., when war breaks out], America's supplies will be cut off.

In sum, the American perception of Japan and the Japanese perception of America do not reflect correctly the real power of the other. Because of its long tradition of seeing Japan as a developing country and because of its self-image as the number-one country in the world, America regards Japan as a small nation without much power. By contrast, because of insufficient analysis of its own actual circumstances, Japan overestimates America's power. One side overestimates; the other side underestimates. If America looks down on Japan, and Japan becomes too anxious about the American problem, Japan will be at a disadvantage. I believe that at this moment both Japanese intellectuals and the Japanese masses should reevaluate American power as well as our own and prepare for a crisis in the Pacific.

SAWADA KEN, "ON THE HISTORY OF AMERICAN IMPERIALISM" (1941)

After graduating from the Law Faculty of Tokyo University, Sawada Ken (1894–1969) went to work in the Tokyo city government. In a provoca-

Sawada Ken, "On the History of American Imperialism," source: Sawada Ken, "Amerika teikokushugishiron," in *Gendai Amerika no bunseki*, ed. Taiheiyō kyōkai (Tokyo: Seikatsu-sha, 1941), 111–134.

tive 1923 essay he boldly urged Japanese cities to "revolt" against the central state to achieve the power and autonomy they needed to flourish as cultural centers. The impact of this essay was magnified by the timing of its publication, which coincided with the Great Kantō Earthquake. During the 1920s Sawada, a proponent of "new liberalism," called for a gradualist approach to a socialist transformation, but his interests soon shifted away from urban and labor problems. In 1928 he published a best-selling biography of Mussolini aimed at a youth audience, and in 1934 he wrote a lively biography of Hitler that lauded the Third Reich as a heroically moral nation, not a vulgarly materialistic one. In 1938 he joined the Taiheiyō kyōkai, a think tank established by the liberal politician Tsurumi Yūsuke to advise the government on expansion in the Pacific. His passion was no longer the revolt of the city but rather the revolt of the heroic Japanese nation. His carefully argued case that the United States had always been an imperialist power echoed a widespread feeling among Japanese intellectuals that Americans were either self-contradictory or hypocritical in their condemnation of what they called Japan's imperialism.

. . .

1.

It is often said that American national policy underwent a great change in the year 1898. After the Spanish-American War, America, long secluded in its continental citadel, abandoned its isolationist attitude by acquiring the Philippines and plunged into the world of "imperialism," a world it neither understood nor had experienced.

No doubt this was a great change. But can such a sudden change occur so easily in any country's foreign policy? Can a people entirely lacking in the spirit of imperialism suddenly turn toward imperialism? Has any state that has traditionally eschewed imperialism ever made a 180-degree turn to become an imperialist state?

No country has been so imbued with the spirit of imperialism as America. The only reasons that America had not acquired overseas possessions in the Far East before 1898 were that its national strength was not yet developed sufficiently and that an opportune moment to expand had not yet arrived. The United States had always insisted that under the Monroe Doctrine it had the right to dominate and lead on both the North and South American continents. By acquiring the Philippines it simply expanded its sphere of influence to the Far East.

To put the matter succinctly, American imperialism, which once had looked toward the south, now spread westward.

2.

One of the important components of the spirit of imperialism is a pioneer spirit. From its beginning as a country, America has rested on a base laid by pioneers from across the Atlantic Ocean. These people, it cannot be denied, were warlike, and the independence of the United States was acquired by warfare. People with a pioneer instinct did not permit themselves to rest content with the idea of a "little America." The pioneer instinct would not let them sit idly by with arms folded as they confronted a vast undeveloped wilderness. Had this wilderness been the territory of another nation-state with powerful defenses, "aggression" into this wilderness could only have taken the form of war. But the Americans were able to expand westward without military aggression at first, because fortunately for them the land was occupied only by Indians with no organized state structure.

The peaceful but aggressive American movement westward began with the founding of the country. Even before the original thirteen states were fully developed, Americans, driven by the pioneer spirit, opened up the Allegheny Mountains with hunting guns on their shoulders and axes on their belts. Moving westward, they cut down forests as they went. In the name of humanity they slaughtered the Indians they encountered on their way, and they pacified indigenous peoples who submitted to their domination. The strong conquered, and the weak were steadily pushed aside. Expanding their power ever westward, by the end of the nineteenth century [actually the eighteenth] the Americans had already reached the banks of the Mississippi River.

[The author then describes the Louisiana Purchase, the annexation of Texas, and the acquisition of California and the Southwest after the Mexican War.]

Today if some other country were to wage a war like the Mexican War, the United States would probably brand it as "uncivilized aggression," and it would probably not hesitate to express willingness to intervene militarily.

In any case, the American territory, which now reaches from the Atlantic to the Pacific coast, has become the foundation of a great empire composed of the present forty-eight states. Perhaps this was simply the inevitable consequence of nation building. Nevertheless, we must remember that the American "spirit of imperialism" had already manifested itself palpably from the time the country was founded.

Just as Rome was not built in a day, neither did American imperialism suddenly emerge in the year 1898.

3.

The United States of America, founded as thirteen states on the Atlantic coast, raised the cry of "Westward ho" and accumulated more and more territory as it moved westward. It finally built a republic that reached the Pacific coast. But its diplomatic policy toward the European continent was extremely cautious. The Americans did not hesitate to take up arms boldly when the European powers tried to obstruct their grand enterprise of building a great republic—for example, during the War of 1812—but they always took care not to become involved in the conflicts among the powers on the European continent.

This earliest expression of this diplomatic policy is to be found George Washington's "Farewell Address." The first president warned his people not to "entangle [their] peace and prosperity in the toils of European ambition, rivalship, interest, humor, or caprice." This speech did not represent Washington's offhand personal remarks, nor was it an inflammatory utterance offered in the heat of conflict. It was a cautious statement that established the basis for American foreign policy adhered to in later years.

Of course, Washington was not a blind isolationist. Since the European powers still possessed territory on the American continent, there was great danger that Old World conflicts might spread to the New World, and there was fear that the ambitions of the European powers might lead to the seizure of new territory close to the United States. Washington gave special attention to this kind of conflict. America, he argued, must strengthen its military defenses, and in the event of such conflict, it should be able to decide to "choose peace or war, as [its] interest, guided by justice, shall counsel."

To turn his words around, this was equivalent to saying that Americans ought not become involved in European conflicts "until America's strength was sufficient." Or to pursue this logic further, once America had built up sufficient national strength, it would be fine to meddle even in territories outside the American continent. . . .

4.

What allowed the United States to expand the Monroe Doctrine, originally directed toward [South America], to the rest of the world was the
buildup of its national strength. Admiral Mahan's book *The Influence of
Sea Power on History* pointed the way toward this great change. . . . The
reason for the book's great influence on the history of the world of its time
was that the world powers were then moving in an imperialist direction.
Imperialist England galvanized by Disraeli, militarist Germany whose
foundations Bismarck had laid, and the New Japan victorious in the Sino-
Japanese War—all sought a theory for their expansionist policies.

Mahan's theory was based on a materialist view of history. His argument went as follows: By and large, the history of world sea power was
the history of a struggle to pursue the material profits of trade. Just as
there was a struggle for survival among individual human beings, so too
conflicts among nations were based on the instincts of self-preservation
and expansion. If necessary, the only way to resolve these conflicts was
by military force. For that reason, the nation-state had to sustain vast
military forces not only to protect its own rights and interests but also
to fight enemies to the death if necessary. The state had only two choices:
to expand or to be destroyed. And in order to expand the state had no
choice but to build a large navy. . . .

As I have said, Mahan's book had great influence on the world powers, but his theory also struck a sympathetic chord in the hearts of at
least three young men in the United States: Theodore Roosevelt, Henry
Cabot Lodge, and Albert Beveridge. Although not in the forefront of the
political world, by the time the Spanish-American War broke out they
had already formed a kind of "three-man alliance" that in reality, if not
in name, became a driving force behind the war.

As the assistant secretary of the navy, Roosevelt was in a particularly
strategic position to sway the McKinley administration. President McKinley, he thought, was a man "with the spine of a chocolate eclair." In September 1897, before the battleship *Maine* was blown up in Havana Harbor, Roosevelt wrote to Beveridge that in the event of war, the Asiatic
fleet should attack Manila and if possible occupy it. The following year
Lodge wrote Roosevelt a letter saying that there was no urgency to act
in regard to Cuba but that adequate naval and military forces should be
sent to the Philippines. Secretly the three men plotted to turn the Spanish-American War into an imperialist war.

. . . The great victory at Manila Bay in May 1898 changed American public opinion overnight and triggered fevered demands for Philippine territory. The American people had not changed direction suddenly, however. It was just that their long-repressed spirit of imperialism exploded suddenly.

Even the business world, which had been cool toward war, joined the demand for Philippine territory. Continuing hard times had beset the American economy. The country had often experienced depressions, but all of them had been surmounted through access to the country's remaining "free land." By opening up new territory, America had been able to achieve economic recovery. But now that free land had disappeared, the only way to restore America's prosperity was to play a more active role in the world. Economic imperialism held sway in the American business world, and businessmen demanded the acquisition of the Philippines as a base for securing markets in the Far East. This was imperialism, pure and simple.

The goal of American imperialism was to transform the Philippines into a second Hong Kong, making the islands into a citadel for the promotion of American power in the Far East, especially in China. America had been largely indifferent toward the Far East before the victory in Manila Bay. England frequently approached the Americans for joint support of an Open Door policy in China, but the Americans had refused to go along. In 1899, however, the year after the battle of Manila Bay, the famous Open Door Note was finally issued over the signature of Secretary of State John Hay. . . .

What American imperialism wanted was not preservation of China's territory but maintenance of an "open door" for trade. The Americans dreamed that the Chinese market would become huge, even surpassing trade with Europe someday. Having just acquired the Philippines, the United States was a complete newcomer to this promising market. Division of this market among those already established there would be a great disadvantage to those Americans who wanted to develop it, so they quickly expressed zealous support for the Open Door policy. Like two poles coming together, England, the oldest of the old comers in China, and America, the newest of the newcomers, found a common interest. Although Hay's Open Door Note was finally issued, the policy could not be realized without the preservation of China's territorial integrity. The initial goal was to use the preservation of territory as a way to maintain the Open Door policy, but ultimately further announcements, declarations, and diplomatic notes drew American imperialism into the trap of taking "responsibility" for the preservation of China's territorial integrity.

5.

The policy of dividing up China, it seems clear, was an imperialist policy. Those whose brains cannot apprehend reality argue that preserving the territorial integrity of China represented an anti-imperialist position. In reality, however, the fact that the interests of the English . . . and the Americans . . . were in accord makes clear that the partition of China's territory and the preservation of China's territory were simply different expressions of the same imperialism. The English insisted on the territorial integrity of China to maintain their existing influence in the Far East, and the Americans insisted on it to facilitate the penetration of their influence in the Far East. . . .

What then was the fate of the Open Door policy and the principle of China's territorial integrity that America insisted on? Despite frequent American pronouncements and protests, the actual situation steadily moved in the opposite direction. As a result of the Boxer Rebellion, the powers who occupied strategic positions in China gradually strengthened and expanded their spheres of influence. The Russian policy of advancing to the south moved most rapidly, eventually leading to the Russo-Japanese War. Although the United States initially displayed goodwill toward Japan as a country that could check Russia's southern advance, its attitude suddenly changed when Japan's victory became certain. Confronted with a Japan suddenly so powerful, the Americans were overcome by a feeling that while the tiger may have been fended off at the front door, the wolf had come in through the back.

American imperialism confronted the agony of disillusionment. The principles of the Open Door policy and the territorial integrity of China it had urged upon the world were not taken seriously by the other powers. Indeed, they were thoroughly trampled. Nothing resembling an international guarantee behind these principles was ever achieved. Moreover, the [American] economic penetration of China, the goal behind the Open Door policy, came to a halt as well. Not only did the Chinese economy fail to develop as rapidly as the Americans had dreamed, but America's own economic power had not yet matured to the point that the country could make any headway [into the Chinese market]. Nor could it assemble the capital that it ultimately needed to develop its economic interests in China. In the final analysis, the principles of the Open Door policy and the territorial integrity of China were not based on any hard statistics; they were backed only by hopes about the future.

The Philippines also became a source of painful disillusion. As the threat of Japan's national power grew day by day, these islands, far from becoming the foundation for a positive policy in the Far East as a second Hong Kong, were seen as a "hostage to fate." As relations between Japan and the United States worsened because of the immigration issue, and rumors spread of a coming Japanese-American war, the Philippines turned into a burden. In March 1907, when President Roosevelt ordered the American battle fleet to make a tour of the world, he deliberately had it visit Japan to demonstrate America's enormous strength. But in fact this kind of bluff had no chance of succeeding.

It is said that President Roosevelt, earlier the prime mover behind the annexation of the Philippines, remarked to the German ambassador that if he could find a way of doing so without losing face he would abandon the Philippines. And in a 1907 letter to Secretary of War William Howard Taft, he wrote, "The Philippines form our heel of Achilles. They are all that makes the present situation with Japan dangerous." . . . In any case, it was inevitable that American imperialism, based on territorial aggression and military impulses, should find itself confronting such cruel disillusion.

6.

[The author discusses "dollar diplomacy" and railroad building projects in China after 1905.]

7.

The Monroe Doctrine promised that in return for denying the [European] powers the right to intervene on the American continent, the United States would not interfere in European affairs. The only part of the world that mattered to Americans at the time was the European continent, so theoretically speaking there was no reason why America should not intervene on continents other than Europe, even though America still excluded outside intervention [in its own hemisphere].

Viewed from this theoretical perspective, as we have seen, the spirit of the Monroe Doctrine had already been violated in the Far East. However, the day finally came when the Monroe Doctrine was breached even in Europe, for whom the doctrine was clearly intended from the outset. This occurred when America participated in World War I.

It is not possible to explain the actions of the United States, which joined a war between other countries in the name of humanity or in the name of peace, even though the war was neither connected to America's own interests, nor [was America's participation] required by treaty obligations, unless we see [that participation] as the manifestation of an imperialistic spirit that sought to make the whole world conform to [America's] wishes. This spirit of world domination, however, was expressed most acutely at the [Paris] Peace Conference rather than during the war itself. At the Peace Conference the United States, backed by its enormously enhanced national power, took the attitude that it was the "ruler of the world." It forced the formation of the League of Nations on the other powers, who did not want it at all.

The League of Nations was intended to maintain the global status quo through collective security. In Europe the principle of collective security gradually went bankrupt as the situation there constantly changed. America, which for reasons of domestic politics did not join the league it had created itself, also proved tepid toward collective security in Europe. But it embarked on a policy of applying this principle solely in the Far East, as it did at the Washington Conference.

When the last war broke out, while the European powers plunged into conflict among themselves, the Far Eastern region became the arena of competition between Japanese and American influence. The United States adopted a policy of thwarting Japan's development at every chance. The most effective opposition to the Twenty-One Demands, for example, came not from the Chinese government but from the American ambassador Paul Reinsch. . . .

America checked Japan's actions at every turn. At the [Paris] Peace Conference it blatantly supported China and harassed Japan. Even though the other powers had made definite commitments to Japan, the United States blocked mandating the Pacific islands to Japan, and even though China and Japan had already signed a treaty [on the matter], the United States butted its nose into Japan's occupation of the Shantung Peninsula. At every opportunity the Americans took unreasonable actions to have their own way, but in nearly every case, they failed to prevent Japan from achieving its legitimate demands.

President Wilson's attempt to oppress Japan ended in failure, and so did the principle of forging global collective security through the League of Nations. The Washington Conference . . . , however, which sought to apply the same principles to the Far East, succeeded to some degree. No doubt what inflated the Americans with pride was bringing about the demise of the Anglo-Japanese Alliance, which they so despised. Indeed, America thought that the Anglo-Japanese Alliance was the basis for the expansion of Japanese influence in the Far East, and it sought to restrain Japan's activities and to facilitate its own development in the Far East through a collective security system that took [the alliance's] place.

8.

... There is no need to describe in detail here the attitude that the United States adopted at the time of the Manchurian Incident in 1931. We will simply recall that the United States, acting as though it were the ruler of the Far East, attempted to serve as an umpire between China and Japan. It talked about using all nonmilitary means or a collective economic embargo to force Japan to respect international treaties. Such a high-handed attitude is appropriate only when a country deals with conflicts among dependent territories within its own empire.

Since neither Japan nor Manchukuo nor China is a dependent territory of the American empire, all the American government's pronouncements and protests and proclamations had no effect at all. The United States appealed to the League of Nations, planned joint action with the English, and made threats to Germany, but the situation in the Far East, advancing with the force of a flood, was unaffected by all of America's frenzied dashing about. In the end the state of Manchukuo was established and formally recognized by Japan.

[Secretary of State] Stimson's principle of collective security, built on assumptions that had no foundations either in history or in fact, ended in pitiful failure.

9.

As we have discussed above, American imperialism underwent transformation many times, but as national strength grew, the sphere of its operation gradually widened. Its greatest success was the Monroe Doctrine, which was limited to North and South America, but in other places it always met with cruel failure and in the end could do nothing but retreat in despair.

The militaristic imperialism of Theodore Roosevelt fell into a trap. The Philippines, which were to be the base for the domination of the Far East, became a "hostage to fate," and in order to preserve the security of the Philippines it was necessary to make diplomatic concessions.

The imperialism of President Taft, based on the export of capital, was completely unable to advance the interests of American capital, and it also resulted in the weakening, not the strengthening, of the traditional American policy of preserving the territorial integrity of China.

And the deformed imperialism of Wilson, Harding, and Stimson, which attempted to dominate the Far East on the basis of the principle of collective security, not only failed to maintain the status quo, its immediate goal, but brought about a pointless emotional clash with Japan, needlessly stirring waves in the Pacific.

What was the cause of these failures? It was that these various American imperialisms were not based on realities rooted in history or tradition but rested solely on empty theories and fuzzy hopes for the future.

It appears that the diplomatic policies of President Franklin Roosevelt are somewhat more realistic than those of his predecessors. At the moment he formally holds fast to the nonrecognition of Manchukuo and to the principles of collective security with respect to the China incident, but in applying these policies he takes into account current realities. . . .

It appears, however, that the current world situation will not tolerate his opportunistic attitude much longer. Like it or not, the world is becoming more and more perilous. What we must take note of at the moment is that the Roosevelt cabinet has embarked on a policy of accelerated military preparation. If that means a return to the militaristic imperialism pursued by his distant relative Theodore Roosevelt, does it have any chance of succeeding? [President Roosevelt] will be fortunate if he does not follow in the footsteps of his predecessor.

Be that as it may, what we must bear in mind is that American imperialism, and the policy of intervention in the Far East based upon it, is not something that began yesterday. It has a long history stretching back to the founding of the country. We must face that fact squarely. We must bear in mind that in the near future America will not abandon its long tradition, and we must resolve to face it with determination.

MUNEO MATSUJI,
"AMERICA'S RACE PROBLEM" (1941)

After attending Dōshisha University, the journalist Muneo Matsuji (1897–1945) worked for the *Asahi shinbun* and then for the *Ryōtō Shinpō*, the first Japanese-language newspaper in Manchuria. In 1922–

Muneo Matsuji, "America's Race Problem," source: Muneo Matsuji, "America no minzoku mondai ni tsuite," in *Gendai Amerika no bunseki,* ed. Taiheiyō kyōkai (Tokyo: Seikatsusha, 1941), 207–218.

23 he attended the School of Journalism at the University of Missouri, where he studied under the prominent journalist Walter Williams. After returning to Japan, in 1925 Muneo wrote an introduction to the history and principles of American journalism. It was not until 1941 that he again wrote about America. He published essays about the racial discrimination that he had experienced during his stay in Missouri, and he promoted the idea of an international Jewish conspiracy—an odd but persistent element in wartime anti-Western ideology. In late 1943 Muneo was stationed in Japanese-occupied Indonesia as the *Asahi*'s Makassar bureau chief. He returned to Japan in May 1945 but died four months later.

. . .

What Is an American?

There is probably no country in the world more complicated than America. There are so many different kinds of Americans that it is hard to say just what an "American" is. Perhaps the only satisfactory definition is "a person who has United States citizenship," but that includes American Indians, Chinese, Russians, and second-generation Japanese, all of whom have citizenship. If you were to say to each of them, "You are an American," that would be off the mark. What a strange country!

From the beginning the "United States of America" was a gathering place for immigrants. This motley group of immigrants, unhappy at being ruled by England, complained right and left, then finally convened the Continental Congress, chose George Washington to lead them, and rose in rebellion. At times it looked as though the Americans might lose, but they stood their ground and finally won independence. Immigrants continued to flow in from European countries. The Americans, encroaching on Mexico, expanded their country's borders westward to the Pacific, building the America that we know today.

In the strictest sense, America was built by European immigrants, principally from England, who seized control of the American continent from its inhabitants, the American Indians. The Indians were not unified, lacked a state organization, and had no means to defend themselves collectively. Although skilled at riding through the hills and fields on horseback, they were armed only with bows, arrows, spears, and knives. Since they could not match the Europeans' firepower, they went down in defeat. Today some 350,000 American Indians cling to a pitiful existence on the eastern slope of the Rocky Mountains in the mountains, deserts, and valleys of states like Arizona and Colorado.

In addition to this already complex and heterogeneous population of European and mainly English immigrants, the Negroes were brought to America from Africa to meet a shortage of labor. As a result of Lincoln's emancipation movement and the Civil War that resulted from it, the slaves were freed and given citizenship. However, they still have not escaped oppression. American Negroes, who number 12 million, make up about ten percent of the American population. . . .

Looking at the United States from a racial perspective, one cannot help wondering what a real "American" is. Americans lack the purity of blood of a single race. America contradicts the spirit of "one race, one nation." It is a "nation made up of many races." The "United States of America" can be thought of not simply as the union of forty-eight states; it is also the union of forty-eight peoples in what one might call the "United Peoples of America."

Anglo-Saxons: The Most Powerful Group

Since the United States is such a strange sort of country, its leaders do their utmost to promote domestic national harmony, unity of public opinion, and a spirit of patriotism. They hustle about trying to "Americanize" different racial groups. They try to consolidate the national spirit under the Stars and Stripes; they stage flag ceremonies; and they promote flag worship. In the name of patriotism they urge the people to defend the fatherland. But just what does "fatherland" mean? To an immigrant from Germany it might mean supporting Nazi Germany, and to an Italian it might conjure up Fascist Italy. The problem of national consciousness in America is a delicate one. But there is no question that as a result of assimilation education, the second and third generations born in America think of the United States as their fatherland.

In the "United States (or Peoples) of America," this heterogeneous immigrant society, those of English ancestry, the Anglo-Saxons, have paramount influence. Seventy percent of all the white people in America and sixty percent of all American citizens are Anglo-Saxon. They constitute an absolute majority in the country, and at the same time they occupy an important position of leadership in the English-speaking world.

This situation has been the driving force behind America's present support for "Aid to Britain." Many of German and Italian ancestry oppose this policy, and the majority of the public do not relish the possibility of

American entry into the war in Europe. The reason that support for England has grown stronger and that America is rushing down the path toward war is that the Anglo-Saxons constitute the majority of the population. That makes it impossible for Americans simply to stand by, watching their elder brothers in England, teetering on the edge of survival, beg for American help. The United States cannot reject the ties of blood and friendship that the American Anglo-Saxons feel for Britain.

To achieve "American national unity" in whatever way they can, the Anglo-Saxon leaders have grossly exaggerated the threat of totalitarianism in their propaganda. They have spread the canard that if Britain falls the United States will be the next to face invasion. In other words, "defending England" has been proposed as the only way to stop totalitarian aggression against America. Anyone who opposes this point of view is accused of being a traitor. Appeals to patriotism have stirred up the entire country and pushed it toward support for aid to Britain and along the road to war.

When we see how skillfully this has been accomplished, it should not surprise us that the Anglo-Saxons control the world's resources. They are extremely clever. They have shown the world how they put "multiracial America" into a pot and bring it to a boil.

The Hidden Power of the Jews

One must not forget that behind the Anglo-Saxons lies the hidden power of the Jews. In fact, the Jews are actually in secret control of Wall Street capital as well as international capital. Anyone who has studied America cannot deny that the will of Wall Street influences Washington and plays a key role in determining American policy. . . .

Why are Jewish financial circles on Wall Street attempting to stir up the American citizenry and politicians to support England and enter the war? It is because they want revenge against Nazi Germany. Since the Nazis have come to power, they have systematically oppressed the German Jews and completely erased all their influence in Germany. Furthermore, with the rise of Germany's power, the Jews have been expelled from Italy, and so have the Jews and their business interests in other countries—first Austria, Czechoslovakia, and Poland, and then Denmark, Holland, Belgium, and France. But wealthy Jews fled to America like an avalanche. There they joined forces with American Jewish financiers to take revenge against Nazi Germany. If they were to be unable to sweep aside Germany's influence, then world Jewry would never again be able to sleep

without fear. To carry out their revenge, they plan to use the human resources of America's 130 million people and America's abundant natural
resources, first by sending aid to Britain, then by joining the war against
Germany.

Jewish enthusiasm persuaded the Anglo-Saxons in America to seek
vengeance against Germany, but the Jews also used it to rush to the aid
of their English brothers facing death and destruction. So it was that the
Anglo-Saxons and the Jews established a united front. The leaders of
Japan ought to be aware of this situation.

It is said that 5.12 million Jews lived in the United States in 1937, but
it is thought that the number has now risen to over 7 million. We do not
know the correct figure. According to a 1935 survey of religious beliefs,
there were approximately 3,000 local synagogues and 4 million believers in Judaism. After the Nazi persecution, the number of Jews who fled
from Europe was more than 2 million, so there must be at least 7 million Jews in the United States. . . .

Within the Roosevelt camp, Secretary of Treasury Morgenthau, a Jew,
is quite actively in favor of helping England, and there are many other
Jews in Roosevelt's inner circle—Supreme Court Justice Louis Brandeis,
the braintruster Sidney Hillman, Supreme Court Justice Felix Frankfurter,
and Jerome Fromm. Roosevelt himself is not an Anglo-Saxon. His ancestors came from Holland, but many Americans know that his great-
grandparents were of mixed Jewish ancestry. [In 1940] Roosevelt made
history by successfully winning an unprecedented third term. Even
though Wall Street [leaders] supported his opponent, Wendell Willkie,
they hedged their bets by making political contributions to Roosevelt too.
Perhaps [those on] Wall Street thought that in peacetime Willkie might
be more pliant to their demands, but in wartime it would be better to
use Roosevelt as their puppet to achieve revenge against Germany.

Through the machinations of a few Jewish financiers, the Anglo-
Saxons are now dedicated to aiding their English cousins, and world
domination by the Anglo-Saxons continues unchanged. But at the same
time, this situation suits the interests of English Jewish finance capitalists and international capitalists like the Rothschild family and Montague
Norman, the president of the Bank of England.

By means of this chicanery, 130 million Americans will be aroused and
led into war. The consequences will be immeasurable misery and misfortune for mankind. We must recognize that this is the true nature of
the conspiracy of the insatiable Jewish financiers sucking the blood of
mankind. . . .

We must recognize one thing about the war. To put it simply, it is not clear whether the domestic and international situation will turn out well for Japan. The reason is that somehow or other, in some murky and obscure way, we all have been drawn into the vortex of this international conspiracy. For example, manufacturing machinery is no longer coming into the country, and foreign trade is not developing as we anticipated, because the Jewish international capitalists on Wall Street—Kuhn, Loeb, and Company, the house of Morgan, and the house of Seligman—all decided to carry out a boycott against Japan after the Manchurian Incident. This turn of events is a reflection of this. They are all organically connected. Yet I wonder if the fine gentlemen of the Japan Industrial Club are aware of it.

Let me add one final comment. The Japanese immigrants and second-generation Japanese are part of America's racial problem. There are 130,000 of them living on the American mainland, largely in California, and 150,000 in Hawaii, making 280,000 all together. It is not difficult to imagine that our compatriots will find themselves in difficult straits if by some misfortune the rumble of cannon fire echoes across the Pacific. It behooves us to extend our sympathy to our unfortunate brethren in America.

MIYAKE DAISUKE,
"REMEMBERING AMERICAN BASEBALL" (1941)

As a student at Keiō University, Miyake Daisuke (1895–1978) was a star on the baseball team. In the 1930s he helped establish the Japanese Professional Baseball League, and he pushed for the professionalization of Japanese baseball on the American model. In 1936 he became the first general manager of the Giants and later managed the Hankyū Braves and the Nagoya Dragons. A prolific commentator on Japanese baseball, he published several books on the subject before and after the war.

· · ·

Given the current state of Japanese-American relations, some may find it strange to praise America, but in the sport of baseball America is a highly advanced country. I think that there is much that we can learn from it. The spiritual discipline of Americans committed to baseball, es-

Miyake Daisuke, "Remembering American Baseball," source: Miyake Daisuke, "Amerika yakyū kaisō," *Kaizō* (March 1941): 176–178.

pecially professional baseball players, provides us a model that requires no modification.

I have visited America many times to play baseball. I think that I must have played in American baseball games or watched American colleagues play hundreds of times. My memories about who hit home runs or who made fine plays are of little significance. What first comes to mind when I reflect on American baseball is the foundation it provides for solid spiritual education.

To put it another way, what players, fans, and others value in American baseball above skillful technique . . . is focusing on how a baseball player should be trained as a human being. In our country, where baseball is still in a period of transition, we must understand what baseball is before considering how baseball is done. Unless we do so, I fear that our teams may end as gangs of baseball hooligans or baseball bums.

"Attacking Aggressively, Fighting Bravely"

At the tournament held at the Meiji Shrine Stadium last fall, some described Japanese baseball technique as "attacking aggressively, fighting bravely [shingeki kantō]."

A year ago when I asked one of my sempai, just come back from working in New York for several years, what he thought of American baseball, he replied emphatically, "It's boring. They don't really play as if their lives depended on it. The proof of that is that games are finished in an hour or so. That's why it's not interesting." And when I visited a rural area in Japan recently, I asked a local what he thought of Japanese baseball. "It looks very interesting," he said, "but it ended so quickly that we were disappointed."

Back in the Meiji era, playgoers used to arrive at the theater at ten in the morning and stay until after midnight. People used to the customs of those days probably do not feel that they have been to the theater if the curtain rises at five in the evening and comes down at ten. In that sense, while it might seem strange to those who think that five hours in the theater is brief, the time required to do something has nothing to do with whether it is done in earnest or not.

There are thirty-two baseball leagues in the United States under the supervision of the American professional baseball organization. Two hundred fifty-six teams, with several thousand players, play in these leagues.

The organization publishes a handbook that regulates all aspects of the game—salaries, admission prices, schedules, and the like. While not published for the general public, copies are distributed to all the teams. The handbook describes in great detail the spirit that sustains America's national sport as well as how the game is managed, improved, and developed.

The first chapter of the book begins: "Play fair! Play hard! Play for the team!" It continues, "Even when playing a game in the remotest rural area, never forget that spirit! Remember that eight-year-old country kids will be watching as you play with that spirit, and they will realize what kind of a game baseball is. When they grow up, they will play baseball with a proper understanding of the game. That is how properly played baseball will be passed on to the next generation, and to the generation after that."

In America baseball is a profession, and because it is a profession it must have an audience. The only way that people will come to baseball games, says the handbook, is if "skilled players play proper baseball in earnest." The problem is how to develop the players' skills, how to make them play proper baseball, and how to make them play in earnest.

If asked about the biggest difference between American baseball and Japanese baseball, I would immediately answer that it lies in spiritual discipline. In other words, there is a difference in attitude toward the game of baseball itself. In America they not only have established rules for the game, but they are serious about putting them into practice.

Night Games

When I think about the most striking characteristic of American baseball, the night game pops into mind. Night games started about ten years ago. Before that there was a great deal of opposition to the idea, but now even the big leagues, who opposed it the most, allow twenty night games to be played during a season, and in the small leagues there are more night games than day games.

If you wonder why night games have become so popular, it is because baseball has become popular among women. Behind that is a very American kind of story. Men did not usually take their wives to day games, so women had objected to their going. But if the game is played at night, the husband can come home from work, eat dinner with his wife, and then both can go to the night game together.

At night games the lights go on at 8:00 P.M., and the game begins at 8:15 P.M. As a result women have become baseball fans, and the ballparks are flourishing more than ever before. If it were not for wartime restrictions on electric power, I think that night games might be good for Japan, though for different reasons.

MATSUSHITA MASATOSHI, "THE AMERICAN HOME FRONT" (1942)

As a child Matsushita Masatoshi (1901–86) was adopted by a childless uncle to carry on the family. The uncle had immigrated to America, so Matsushita never met his "American father." After entering Divinity School at Rikkyō University (St. Paul's), Matsushita later transferred to its Commerce Department, from which he graduated in 1922. His adoptive father died the same year, so he decided to use his inheritance to study in the United States, where he eventually earned a Ph.D. in political science at Columbia University. In 1929 he returned to Rikkyō University to teach. In 1940, he published *The American Right to Wage War*, and amid rising tensions with America his writings grew in nationalistic fervor and popularity. After the war, he assisted in the defense of the former prime minister Tōjō Hideki in the Tokyo War Crimes Tribunal. Matsushita himself was purged from public office in 1948 for his wartime writings but was later rehabilitated, becoming the president of Rikkyō University in 1955. He ran as a candidate for the mayor of Tokyo in 1967 and 1975 but was defeated both times. In the early 1970s, he established close ties with the Unification Church, serving on the board of its organizations and writing books about its Korean leader, Moon Sun Myung.

. . .

The hostilities waging in the Pacific have rudely awakened the United States to make all necessary preparations to meet the hazards of war. While the American people are steadily losing confidence in the Roosevelt administration because of successive defeats suffered by the armed forces of their country, Washington is finding it exceedingly difficult to check the rise of inflation.

On April 27 President Roosevelt sent a message to Congress outlining a plan to prevent wartime inflation. He said that the American people must lower their living standard to meet the unprecedented needs of war. On the following day he made a national radio broadcast to announce a seven-point plan to check inflation. . . .

Matsushita Masatoshi, "The American Home Front," source: Matsushita Masatoshi, "Beikoku kokumin 'seikatsu sekkei' no mujun," *Kaizō* (June 1942): 112–117.

President Roosevelt called these new wartime measures national economic planning. . . . Although this type of planning is urgently needed, it is problematic how much the American people will be able to readjust their mode of living, especially when they are rather inclined to maintain their usual standard of living as much as possible. To Americans, who have become accustomed to material life, it would not be easy to practice rigorous economy, in spite of the fact that they realize the urgency of becoming self-sacrificing to tide over the current emergency. On the other hand, [national economic planning] is nothing new or novel to Japan. Moreover, the Japanese people united as one have already reformed their standard of living to enable the government to prosecute the war until victory is finally achieved. . . .

It has to be recognized that the Americans are creative and energetic. The Pilgrim fathers came to the New World with a burning ambition to found a country of their own. They were Puritans in every way. But the subsequent development of America brought a lust for gold, and this caused the rise of individualistic capitalism. Hence, the creativity and energy of America have become more focused on the accumulation of wealth. This is why the American spirit is a quaint mixture of Puritanism and a hankering for wealth.

When the first settlers crossed the Atlantic on the *Mayflower* and landed on the American continent, they were full of energy and hope. They soon established a home for themselves. As a result of their pioneering activities, America rapidly developed into a land of opportunity. . . . Their untiring efforts to open up vast tracts of virgin land awaiting the hand of man to yield their riches brought the rapid development of various industries. But with the close of the nineteenth century, the outlook of Americans underwent a noticeable change. They became addicted to wealth seeking. As a result, from the outset of the twentieth century, they began to become devotees of Mammon. . . .

In order to pursue their policy of capitalist-imperialism, the Americans began to interfere in the economic life of other nations. It is no wonder that they propounded the policy of "Open Door and equal opportunity" in East Asia to solidify their capitalist intrusion into that part of the world as a fait accompli. Their desire to enrich themselves by exploiting the resources and wealth of other nations appears to be a fixed policy. Relying on their financial power and industrial expansion, they extended the sway of their capitalist-imperialism to Latin America, Europe, and East Asia. Because of their egoistic actions, war has broken out in the Pacific, and Germany is trying to eliminate their influence in Europe. Latin America today has been forced to become the economic granary of the United States, but the peoples of East Asia and most of the European nations refuse to submit to the domination of Washington and are united in shaping a new way of life for themselves. . . .

It is indeed strange that in this moment of crisis for the nation, the American masses have not yet fully realized that they should abandon their materialistic fetishism. They do not seem to ponder the fact that their ancestors founded the country by practicing the principle of "live and let live." In fact, the fundamental ideal of America, which envisages the utility of living in peace and harmony with other peoples, has been relegated to the backseat while the ideal of monetary materialism has spread nationwide. To the Americans, money has become everything, and as a result they have lost their spiritual power and vigor to maintain their traditional way of life. The United States has amassed wealth beyond the conception of other nations, yet it is finding it difficult to meet the exigencies of war. That shows that material potential or monetary power cannot stand and give battle to national power backed by solid national determination.

There seems no doubt that America's complacency will undermine its national strength. President Roosevelt has plunged the county into an unnecessary war in order to follow his own utopian principles and unworkable ideologies. The time is bound to come when the American masses will start to wonder why their country is waging a war in Europe and East Asia, far from the Western Hemisphere. They may also realize that there is no reason for America to block the return of normalcy to Europe and East Asia, especially when they are not in any way threatened by a change in the lives of people in those regions. But it is not possible to predict when the American people will come to view the situation in that light. They are still under the spell of materialistic fetishism.

NAKANO GORŌ, "THE WILL TO ANNIHILATE THE AMERICAN ENEMY" (1943)

When Nakano Gorō (1906–72) was a student of the Faculty of Law at Tokyo Imperial University in the 1920s, right-wing and left-wing student groups often clashed on campus. Nakano was among the majority of law students who remained aloof from the ideological struggles. After graduation, he joined the staff of the *Asahi shinbun,* as a correspondent first

Nakano Gorō, "The Will to Annihilate the American Enemy," source: Nakano Gorō, *Keishō* (Tokyo: Nippon shuppan haikyū kabushiki kaisha, 1943), 17–27.

in French Indochina and then in New York. In December 1941 Nakano planned to return home on what was rumored to be the last ship to Japan, but before it put into port at Los Angeles, Japanese naval forces attacked Pearl Harbor. In June 1942, after witnessing the initial outburst of anti-Japanese sentiment in the war's early days, he returned to Japan on a repatriation ship along with Ambassador Nomura Kichisaburō. Despite his cosmopolitan background, he enthusiastically supported the war effort. When the war ended, however, as a freelance journalist he published several books that took a positive view of American society, including his 1949 *Beikoku ni manabu* (Learning from America). He also wrote obsessively and translated works on the Pacific War, arguing that the attack on Pearl Harbor was a national disaster that destroyed the international reputation that Japan had built during the Meiji period.

. . .

The current great conflict fought between Japan and the United States is not only a fierce war of weapons, it is also an intense war of ideas. To fight to the end and ultimately win require both enormous combat power and a vigorous fighting spirit. To put it in a nutshell, we must unite all those on the war front and all those on the home front with a resolve to annihilate America that burns as intensely as a fireball.

To win this ferocious war, the people of our country, moved by feelings of every sort of enmity, whether malice, malediction, or disgust, must forge a powerful national will to fight to the end. . . .

The will to annihilate the enemy must be based on a spirit of hatred toward the enemy. The more we hate the enemy, the more our fighting spirit will grow. And the more our fighting spirit grows, the more our anger and indignation will grow. Hatred will well up from our feelings of anger and indignation. . . . That is the essence of hostility toward the enemy, and therein lies the wellspring of the people's fighting spirit against the American enemy.

In the year and a half since December 8, 1941, our fighting spirit has been ignited, but I wonder if the hatred and indignation of our 100 million people toward the enemy is strong enough. As a newspaper foreign correspondent who returned to his ancestral land by exchange ship after six months of internment in America, my frank impression is that the hatred and indignation of my 100 million compatriots toward the enemy nation and the enemy people are not strong enough. . . .

Why isn't our hatred and anger intense enough? I believe that one reason is the unique samurai spirit that neither reviles the enemy nor detests

鬼
畜
以
上

「ウェー、爆弾のジュウタンだの、病院船爆撃だのと、米英の奴等は、全く悪虐無道ひでえことをしやがる。」

FIGURE 8. While the wartime enemy was usually referred to as the "beastly English and Americans" *(kichiku Ei-Bei)*, cartoons usually did not depict them literally as such. But the father of this ogre family is horrified by their bestial behavior. "Jeez!" he says. "Carpet bombing! Attacks on hospital ships. These American and English guys are really doin' turrible stuff!" The caption suggests that they are worse than ogres. (*Manga,* October 1943)

the individual combatant. But another reason is that our people's racial feelings have not been ignited in response to the tactics and hostility of the American enemy 5,000 miles across the Pacific. In this fierce war, it is a pipe dream to say that one can hate the enemy country but not the enemy people. To hate the enemy country is to hate the enemy people, and the more we hate the enemy people the deeper our hatred of the enemy country becomes. Our people must be unyielding in their hatred of each and every individual enemy American. . . .

How can we raise a spirit of hostility to the highest level? I believe that we can do so by coming directly to grips with what is going on in the enemy country and by understanding their spirit of hostility. We must recognize the naked truth that the American people hate the Japanese people, look down on them, and treat them with cruelty, persecution, and rage, and we must remember what a heartless and relentless war we are engaged in. . . .

The enemy's counteroffensive against Japan is revealed most clearly in its inflammatory photographic propaganda. Almost with despicable glee, the American press magnate Henry Luce, publisher of *Life* magazine, the world's largest photographic weekly with a circulation of 4,000,000, together with his wife, Clare Booth Luce, a leader of an anti-Japanese, pro-

Chinese movement in America, have launched a hideous war of ideas in order to overthrow the Axis powers. Immediately after the outbreak of the war, for example, *Life* magazine, with the help of the Washington correspondent for the Chinese Central News Agency, ran a tawdry anti-Japanese article titled "How to Tell a Chinese from a Japanese." Its purpose was to protect Chinese "friends of America" living in New York and other large cities from being attacked, persecuted, or intimidated by Americans as the result of being mistaken for the Japanese "enemies of America." Using photographs that compared the faces and physiques of Chinese and Japanese, it cruelly contrasted the superiority of the former with the inferiority of the latter.

I was interned in a camp in Gloucester City, a godforsaken small town on the banks of the Delaware River across from the enemy city Philadelphia, when I saw the venomous article and photographs in *Life* magazine. It turned my stomach. I shook with rage when I understood what ugly and despicable methods the hateful enemy country had adopted in its anti-Japanese war of ideas. The tawdry but cleverly composed photographs were presented to the ignorant and simple-minded American masses as "what the Japanese are really like." They aroused and strengthened intense contempt and hatred toward the Japanese.

The aim of the American war of ideas is threefold: (1) to show that the Japanese are small and weak; (2) to show that the Japanese are bucktoothed and have bad eyesight; and (3) to show that the Japanese are bowlegged with flat faces.

The intent is to promote hostility toward the Japanese enemy by implanting and nurturing in the American people a despicable sense of the racial inferiority of the Japanese. The Roosevelt faction's strategy in the war of ideas is to arouse throughout the country a sense of hostility strong enough to overthrow the hated Japan by cultivating such a sense of racial inferiority.

Can there be anyone among the Japanese people who is not infuriated when he comes to understand the depth of the enemy people's hostility?

Since the war began with the utter destruction of Pearl Harbor, the United States, after a continuing series of defeats, has run amok in its effort to promote a fighting spirit of hatred toward both Japan and the Japanese. They have ramped up their persecution and oppression of 300,000 of our countrymen living there, and vengeance toward Japan has become the main goal of their mass propaganda.

For example, in April 1942 the United States Marine Corps launched a recruiting campaign throughout America. A recruiting pamphlet titled *A Hunting License for Japs,* which displayed the mean and crafty Yankee spirit, stirred anti-Japanese hatred among the simple-minded and naive American masses. The pamphlet was printed to look like a hunting license in full color with an official seal, and it was signed by R. Dening, the commander of the U.S. Marines. [An illustration of the pamphlet is attached.]

At the time I was interned in a hotel in the Virginia mountains along with Ambassador Nomura. When I saw a story in the *New York Times* about this extraordinarily outrageous "Japanese hunting license" pamphlet, I was so astonished, then so angered, that I ground my teeth with rage. Under the headline "Hunting License Published by the Marines," the newspaper report commented that the pamphlet ridiculed the Japanese as an inferior race little better than animals. . . .

We Japanese must think seriously about the true character of America's atrocious and arrogant hostility toward the enemy. Can anyone bear to hear of the cruel methods by which the enemy American army slaughtered our loyal and brave heroes in the recent bloody battle at Guadalcanal and then in the struggle to the death on Attu Island? Our blood boils in anger when we learn from the official battle reports of the Imperial High Command about the cruel violence wrought by demonic Americans crazed for blood. But if we clearly and coolly grasp the nature of enemy hostility toward us, we will finally understand the historical meaning of this great war between Japan and the United States, and we will recognize how deep the enemy's hostility is toward Japan.

The American enemy, doing its best to stir up an inherent sense of contempt and hatred toward Japan, looks down on the Japanese as an inferior race little better than animals, and it distributes to the ignorant and simple-minded American masses a propaganda pamphlet about "hunting Japs." Is there anyone who can call himself Japanese that does not feel anger and indignation at hearing this!

SAKANISHI SHIHO,
"WHY DO AMERICANS BREAK THE LAW?" (1944)

Sakanishi Shiho (1896–1976) first arrived in America in 1922. After graduating from Wheaton College, she completed a Ph.D. at the University of Michigan in 1929. She taught philosophy briefly at the University of

Sakanishi Shiho, "Why Do Americans Break the Law?" source: Taiheiyō kyōkai, ed., *Amerika kokuminsei no kenkyū* (Tokyo: Taiheiyō kyōkai, 1944), 37–42.

Virginia, then took a job in the Oriental Division of the Library of Congress in 1930. During the next decade she published several English-language books on Japanese poetry, landscape painting, calligraphy, and Kyōgen, and she edited a volume of Townshend Harris's unpublished letters. When the war broke out, she was interned, then repatriated to Japan, where she was employed as a contract worker for the Foreign Ministry, served on the editorial committee of the Japanese broadcasting system, and worked part-time at the Nihon gakujutsu shinkōkai. After the war she wrote widely on women's issues and international affairs. In this essay Sakanishi, clearly familiar with the cultural debates in the United States during the 1920s and 1930s, turned many American criticisms of American society into an analysis of American weaknesses.

. . .

During the days of the Puritans, America prided itself on its role of protecting the morality and ethics of the world and on its great contribution to the purification and improvement of society. Several years ago an American sociologist boasted, "In modern times the red light districts have completely disappeared from our cities. It's just what we expect of America." A French critic jeeringly replied, "No, they have not disappeared; they have simply moved to the backseats of automobiles." The moral problem raised by young men and women in automobiles is a painful one for older Americans. They usually evade it by grumbling about "young people these days . . . !" But that is like the ancient Hebrews who turned a goat loose in the wilderness in atonement for their sins. It is simply a way of covering up responsibility for their own transgressions. . . .

It is a fact that since the end of World War I American youths have come to harbor doubts about the ethics and morals embraced by the older generation. To put it another way, religion and public opinion no longer govern the lives of individuals as they once did. Other influences have emerged. These influences were not at all accidental but grew out of a response to a new environment. . . .

Mistrust and doubt about religion that had been smoldering for several centuries finally rose to the surface. Under the rigid scrutiny of science, the miracles the Bible described and the ethical standards it defined were swept away like an avalanche. Anthropology and sociology had the same impact. The family system and the relations between the sexes were no longer seen as rooted in the commandments and decrees of God, and human customs were seen as formed and developed in response to social and economic factors. There was no reason to think that ethical and moral principles would remain unchanged if social conditions changed. Even if one supposed that there was an eternal truth, one did not have to be bound by outdated restraints. The thinking of American youth today is best represented by the pragmatic philosophy of William James, who said that one should test what are called "truth" and "justice" to see if they exist. . . .

The "young people these days" that the older generation complains about lack neither religious sentiment nor a social conscience. Instead of relying on hard-and-fast (religious) rules, they try out things (scientifically) on the basis of their own experience. They give everything a try. If something succeeds, that is good, but if it fails, they change their minds. In an American society battered first by hard economic times, and then by war, young people are truly to be pitied. I think that as long as they find themselves constantly confronting poverty, inequity, and discord between the individual and society, they will not resign themselves to these irrational and unnecessary circumstances. They are struggling to establish new goals of their own. Of course that sometimes results in excesses, in mistakes, and in tragedies.

For a long time America has needed to reassess its ethical and moral problems. Absorbed in pursuit of a materialistic culture and content with the worn-out legacy inherited from their forebears, Americans are not ashamed of their hypocritical and self-deceiving lives. They boast that they are raising their living standard, but what they are raising is the lowest of the lowest of values—simply material pursuits. They are in a frightful state of spiritual decline. To conceal this hideous reality, they call making money through speculative investment "service"; they argue that the reason many people do not obey the law or take responsibility either as a nation or as individuals is that "America is still young"; and they interpret their mad pursuit of material culture as "improving living standards." People who criticize the misconduct of the young or their lack of principles do not seem to understand that they are looking at their own image reflected in a mirror. I don't think that we can blame contemporary young people for resisting—we should sympathize with them.

Since the outbreak of war there has been a frightful decline and a wave of crime among those slightly younger than "those young people"— minors from twelve to sixteen. According to a February 1943 issue of *Cosmopolitan* magazine, America is losing the war on the home front as well as on front lines. In the second half of last year, crime by minors rose 20%—and in the big cities by 100% or more. In Los Angeles a gang of twenty-nine boys and ten girls committed crimes like murder, robbery, blackmail, and kidnapping. In New York City five hundred girls between the ages of twelve and sixteen were arrested in city parks. Calling them-selves "victory girls," they hung out near places where soldiers gathered and offered themselves for service. Since 65% of all venereal diseases were due to these "victory girls," the city had to close public parks and set a curfew for minor girls this summer. Girls infected with venereal diseases are locked up jails and detention halls. The national government's public health authorities recently decided to open up thirty Depression-era youth camps to intern nine thousand of them immediately. *reasons for inc in*

This situation arose just a few months after the beginning of the war. *violence* The longer the war lasts, the worse the situation will become. One rea-son, as often pointed out even in peacetime, is the breakdown of family life. The family is no longer the smallest unit of society; it is an aggre-gate of self-centered individuals. The defense industry has hunted for workers, and the lower classes have prospered economically, but adults are busy pursuing their own pleasures, and they have no time to take care of their children. In many places schools have closed for lack of teach-ers, and even if [schools remain open], teachers do not have the time or the ardor to guide their students individually. The Department of Justice has argued that unless it is absolutely necessary for economic reasons mothers should not work in defense factories but instead should provide a good environment for their children at home. This policy does not ap-pear to have had much effect.

The increase in juvenile delinquency is due not only to the breakdown of the family but also to the massive movement of the population within the country. Workers, who take their families to the defense industry re-gions that springing up all over the country like mushrooms after a rain, have to live in their cars or in automobile trailers, where there are no fa-cilities for families, schools, or play. Children brought up in such an undis-ciplined and desolate atmosphere are not likely to turn out well. Gam-bling, drinking, black marketeering, and all sorts of other bad conditions prevail. Even more frightening is that delinquent boys and girls have no sense of conscience. They say that their misconduct is a service to the military men and boosts their morale. They say that murder is nothing compared to the massive murder perpetrated by their country. . . .

We do not know how the older generation reacts to all this, but to borrow the words of the prophet Isaiah, the parents eat sour grapes and their children's mouths pucker at the taste.

During the 1930s we often heard that Prohibition turned the Americans into a nation that did not obey the law. The historian James Trustlaw

Adams, however, has insisted that while it is true that Americans openly broke the Prohibition law and that the law strengthened their tendency to ignore laws in general, it is a boldfaced lie to say that Prohibition forced a bad habit on a nation that had always obeyed the law. Walter Lippmann has argued that disobeying the law is the one great peculiarity of the American national character and that Prohibition simply spread the tendency and made it commonplace. However, this tendency did not develop overnight; it had a long history.

It is usually said that the ancestors of the Americans came from England, a nation that has been more obedient to the law than any other in the world. As some Americans explain it, "Because the United States is a country of immigrants law-breaking is inevitable; it is foreigners who break the law; just look at the names of contemporary gangsters." According to the breakdown of Department of Justice statistics, the Orientals (the Japanese and the Chinese) commit the fewest crimes, followed by the northern Europeans. But the crime rate rises for the second and third generation. In other words, while there are many cases of foreigners who learned to break the law after arriving America, it was Americans who taught them how to.

During the colonial era the Americans developed the habit of judging for themselves which laws made in the mother country, three thousand miles across the Atlantic Ocean, should be obeyed and which should be ignored. That was natural, since there was no mechanism to enforce these laws after they were promulgated. Colonists not only broke unnecessary laws from the mother country; they violated colonial regulations as they pleased. For example, despite the fact that the sale of guns or alcohol to the native Indians was strictly prohibited for [the colonists'] own self-protection, they carried on this dangerous trade because it was profitable to do so. Even when at war with the French and the Indians during the 1750s, New England merchants sold weapons to the enemy at high prices. Naturally the war lasted longer as a result. John Hancock, a signer of the Declaration of Independence, avoided paying all but a few customs duties and kept smuggling alcohol. Disobeying the law became a kind of sport, and it was a matter of pride if one succeeded. . . . But it is also fair to say that crimes like murder and robbery did not occur at all among the pioneers, who were blessed materially and who lived a life of freedom on the wide frontier.

After the Revolutionary War, old customs persisted, even though the federal government now made the laws. During the colonial period, ignoring the law was not seen as criminal in the extreme sense, since the laws broken dealt with trade or relations with England. But as a result of the wartime economy, intellectual confusion, hard times, unrest, and class and racial conflict, a period of rampant violence [followed the Revolution]. The politics of democracy became the politics of violence. In 1786 farmers in Massachusetts led by Daniel Janes forced the closing of the courts and liberated imprisoned debtors from jail. Not knowing how far the violence would spread, the government sent a military force to put the rebellion down. . . . Endless conflicts followed—violence against immigrants who came to build railroads, intimidation of Catholics and Mormons, and troubles over the abolition of slavery. Abraham Lincoln lamented to Congress that law and order were being destroyed and that society was governed by ferociously violent emotions.

After the Civil War, order appeared to be restored on the surface, but the American's unprincipled behavior *[mudōgishugi]* continued as before. Newly promulgated constitutional amendments to protect the rights of Negroes were completely ignored. . . . When the Negroes, who until then were treated like beasts of burden, proclaimed their equality under the Constitution, racial prejudice buried deep in American society reared its head. Everywhere it produced an eruption of inbred brutality and shamelessly trampled the rights of the pitiful Negroes. . . . [Cruel treatment] was not limited to Negroes in the South. The phrase "lynch law" was first used in 1843 to describe the practice of punishing gamblers and thugs on the Mississippi River without recourse to the law. Later it came to mean murder committed in a fury by the masses contemptuous of tamer measures. The custom of not respecting laws meant that extremely illegal actions were considered to be "the people's justice." During the gold rush there were many lynchings in Nevada, Oregon, and California. There were fifty-two incidents in California in 1855. Even today every time a crime stirs up public sentiment, the police worry about lynchings and the government dispatches troops to stop them.

Thus it is that the Americans, from their arrival on the new continent until today, have ignored the law for political, economic, geographical, and racial reasons. Often there has been a lack of agreement between the lawmakers and the masses. The early Puritans believed that if their ideals were all made into law, then the people would respect and follow them. Sometimes they silenced those who voiced different views. It never occurred to them that in the end rashly proposing unenforceable laws would tarnish the idea of respect for the law. If it was acceptable for the people not to obey laws and regulations, there was no need to object to them.

Since no objections were raised, more and more laws were passed. As a result there is an enormous number of laws in America.

President Herbert Hoover, deploring the anarchy prevailing during his years in office, established the Wickersham Commission to investigate the problem. The commission reached the conclusion that laws ought to be obeyed, but if laws were unenforceable then everyone should work fairly and squarely to repeal them. The problem is not so simple. Many who have lived even a short time in America know that . . . every year at least several dozen books that appear in the book reviews are banned from sale in Boston. Should one break the law and order them from somewhere else? Or should one obey the law and not read them? In Tennessee not only is the teaching of evolution prohibited by law, but so are all books that make any reference to it. Should universities [in Tennessee] toss encyclopedias and scientific books out the window? Or should they let students use them secretly? This is a big problem. Many universities ban classics that are essential reading. Should the law be observed even though it means that the university will fail in its mission?

If you go for a ride in an automobile you have to be prepared for anything. Even if you obey all the regulations it is very dangerous to drive fast. There may be a 35 mph speed limit [in one state], but if you go to the next state it may be illegal to drive less than 35 mph. You will be stopped immediately by the highway police and charged with a speeding violation. It is no use to insist that you were maintaining the speed limit carefully. A tough highway patrolman hiding in the shadow of a huge roadside billboard comes after you in hot pursuit at a frightening speed just a few minutes after your car has passed. You have no hope at all of winning if, as President Hoover suggests, you dispute the arrest fairly and squarely in a court of law. You should just reach into your wallet and hand over a ten-dollar bill. (The fine for a speeding violation is ten dollars.)

It is not only citizens who fail to observe the law. According to the Fifteenth Amendment of the Constitution, Negroes possess the right to vote, but often they can not get close to the polling place. If President Hoover were living in the state of Mississippi, where the Negroes outnumber the white people, I wonder what he would do. There are only three choices: Do you resign yourself to rule by Negroes? Do you move to another state? Or do you ignore the Constitution and deny the rights of Negroes? According to the Fourth Amendment, the government cannot conduct unreasonable searches or seizures of people and goods. However, on December 7, 1941, even before declaration of war, the government, with complete disregard for the Constitution, rounded up tens of thousands of Japanese living in the United States.

Contradictions and deceit are built into the Constitution. In recent years intellectuals have complained that America is turning toward money politics, abandoning the founding ideal of the country and the basic principles of the Constitution. But there is a new way of looking at the Constitution. Some argue that its purpose is to protect property. It is really anti-democratic. In other words, at the time of the country's founding, affluent politicians feared the political power of the masses liberated by the Revolution. Choosing words intended to achieve a particular result, they held the rights of the people to the lowest level. . . . What seems exceedingly strange to us today is that since the beginning of this century the Constitution and the Declaration of Independence have been jumbled together in the heads of the Americans. The former was promulgated on July 4, 1776, and the latter was ratified twelve years later, in 1788. Americans believe that both [documents] support the basic principles of democratic government, but in fact the Declaration of Independence is based on French humanitarianism and proclaims a democracy based on liberty and equality, while the Constitution is a document written to protect the property of a minority on the basis of republican government. One is written for mankind; the other is written for property owners.

Given this background it is natural for Americans to ignore the law. Nowadays it has become their second nature. No matter how much those in power raise their voices in protest, halfway measures will have no effect. To borrow the words of the historian Adams, the only thing that can save America from this contradiction is a dictator who can compel obedience to the law with an iron rod.

ROUNDTABLE DISCUSSION: "GRASPING
THE REALITY OF THE AMERICAN ENEMY" (1944)

By the late summer of 1944 the war was coming closer to the Japanese home front. The American occupation of the island of Saipan put the home islands within reach of the B-29 long-range bombers. The urgency of the situation was evident to the participants in this roundtable discussion in *Hi no de,* a popular monthly magazine. While emphasizing the responsi-

Roundtable Discussion: "Grasping the Reality of the American Enemy," source: "Sekai no shinryakusha: Teki-Bei no jittai o tsukame," *Hi no de* (August 1944): 12–18.

bility of the United States for provoking the war, they also warned against underestimating the enemy's fighting spirit. Except for Edogawa Rampō, a famous mystery-story writer, all the participants were government officials or journalists familiar with the United States. Inagaki Kazuyoshi and Shimono Nobuyasu were officials of the government Information Bureau; Katō Masuo was assistant director of the Overseas Bureau of the Dōmei News Agency; and Kondō Shin'ichi was a Foreign Ministry official.

. . .

The Enemy's Grand Ambition to Annihilate Japan

Reporter: Thank you for taking time out of your busy schedules today. In light of the recent enemy bombing of northern Kyūshū and their forceful invasion of Saipan, the people need to face the gravity of the war situation. However the enemy intends to fight and whatever their lawless goals may be, this is a war that we absolutely cannot lose. . . .

Kondō: Ever since the beginning of the war, America has claimed to the world that the war is about the Atlantic Charter or that it is a war for survival, but these claims are a façade to mask their true ambitions. As the war has intensified in recent days, they have bared their hidden fangs.

This happened most clearly at the Cairo meeting of President Roosevelt, Generalissimo Chiang Kai-shek, and Prime Minister Churchill last November [1943]. Their Cairo Declaration states that they intend to reduce Japan to the status of the weak country it was before the arrival of Commodore Perry. For example, there are to be arms limitations to prevent Japan from possessing a single battleship, an army, or, of course, an air force, which has been so effective in the current conflict. Economically their intention is to deny to Japan any power in the world market. Japan, they think, ought to be content, as it was in the old days, with being an isolated and peaceful nation on a remote island, its people eating rice and wearing kimonos and living in the often-mentioned houses of bamboo and paper. No military factories will be allowed. Foreign trade will be heavily restricted. The formidable patriotism of the Japanese people evident on the battlefield is seen as the result of spiritual education, so it needs to be stamped out and conform to American wishes. The Americans believe that they will win as a result of their material superiority. Their plans for the postwar treatment of Japan are not mere fantasies or threats. They are real preparations.

Edogawa: Admiral Halsey, commander of the southwestern Pacific fleet, says that the Japanese are like apes and that they should be treated the same as apes. And since the Greater East Asian War began, the Japanese have been called "insects." Is there some basis for such language in prewar times?

Inagaki: It is clear from their behavior that the Americans regard the Japanese as the same as Negroes—as their servants.

Katō: Before the Russo-Japanese War, when Japan was still weak, American sentiment toward Japan was positive. But when Japan later grew more and more powerful, and especially as a result of the Manchurian Incident and the China Incident, the Americans began to feel threatened. Fundamentally they do not like small countries like Japan becoming strong and powerful.

When I was in America before the Greater East Asia War began, a taxi driver asked me about the tensions between Japan and America. I said to him, "It's obvious: America is not happy that Japan is becoming strong." He seemed convinced. "I see," he replied. "That's no good. Even a taxi driver like me can become a big businessman or somebody great if he tries hard. Stopping that is not the democratic way of doing things."

There was also a time when the Americans greatly admired the Japanese. After the Russo-Japanese War, American primary school textbooks even extolled the Japanese for their superior wisdom. There was a strong feeling of the need to understand the Japanese. The Orient held a mysterious allure for [Americans], and Japan was a country that epitomized Oriental wisdom. I heard that children were taught that they had to be mindful of countries like Japan.

During the past twenty years, however, there has been a general tendency in America toward anti-Japanese sentiment, but in my view as Japan grew stronger America adopted policies that held Japan to be a threat. As you know, when the Japanese advanced economically, the Americans could not sit by silently. They repeatedly exerted economic pressure on Japan. In this sense, the Greater East Asia War is a contest over power. In short, it is the result of an American desire to keep Japan weak.

Kondō: One reason for the American aversion toward the growth of a more powerful Japan is their conceited belief that Japan became a civilized nation thanks to their efforts. This does not fit the facts at all, but unfortunately, before the Manchurian Incident, even some Japanese agreed that it was the Americans who opened up Japan and that America was a kind of mentor for Japan. This idea comes straight out of the Americans' beautiful propaganda. We must recognize it as such, and we must make them change their condescending attitude.

Commodore Perry did not come bearing the gift of civilization to Japan. What he really aimed at was protecting American whaling ships and promoting trade with China. For him Japan was simply a supply base, a secondary goal. The reason why America stretched its claws toward East Asia was ambition and inflated self-esteem that dated from the time of the nation's founding. These gave rise to the egotistical notion that it is America's divine destiny to uplift the uncivilized peoples of the Orient. This is the root cause of the fundamental difference between our national character and that of the Americans.

Edogawa: I have heard that the so-called isolationists in America are only isolationist toward Europe and that they are aggressors toward Asia.

Kondō: That is correct.

Edogawa: If that is the case, it is something very important for us to keep in mind.

Presidents Change but Public Opinion Does Not

Inagaki: People have the mistaken impression that American isolationism is a policy of noninterference toward the Orient and therefore a good thing for Japan. In fact, isolationists are patriotic right-wingers who do not want America to become involved in European affairs. America fought the War of Independence to escape the conflicts of the Old World and to build the New World. The isolationists think it foolish for Americans to spill their blood by being drawn into Europe's troubles. However, they also think of the Orient as an extension of their West and therefore part of the New World. Their ideology is very aggressive. It is very dangerous for us to misunderstand this.

Kondō: During this war, too, it was the isolationists who argued for defeating Japan first. That supports what you have said.

Inagaki: Essentially the isolationists think only about America. It is foolish to spend American money, resources, or men for other nations. If we need to sacrifice, they say, then let us make sacrifices to develop our own country and to spread America's material civilization. With regard to the Far East, before the war they badly underestimated Japan, whom they argued that America could easily crush. Even when it became clear after the war began that Japan's economic and military might was stronger than imagined, they did not change their minds.

Under the Roosevelt administration they grumbled about whether or not to intervene in Europe. They had no intention of fighting against Japan. The nation now is united behind the goal of defeating Japan and turning it into an unarmed and peaceful isolated archipelago that they can freely control. No matter what happens in the [1944] election, American policy toward Japan will not change significantly. . . .

The Cairo Conference plan for the postwar treatment of Japan is a devious one. As someone who has lived in America, my sixth sense tells me that America will not be satisfied with such a soft proposal. I feel very certain that the American idea is to whip the Japanese until their will is broken. . . .

War as a Solution to America's Economic Problems

Inagaki: After the crash of 1929, it became clear that American capitalism could not keep going without lowering American living standards, so it was absolutely necessary for America to expand outward. Either through war or through diplomatic pressure, America needed to extend its economic hegemony over other regions.

Kondō: As Mr. Inagaki just said, the productive capacity of the American economy has outpaced consumption. Even if American people spend lavishly, they cannot absorb all the goods produced. Therefore it has become necessary to force every barefooted aborigine in the world to start wearing shoes or don Western-style clothes or learn how to use an electric refrigerator. Force the world to buy American brands. It doesn't matter if people do not want these things; force them to, even if they throw the stuff out later. Only then will the American economy function well. It is a very

selfish way of thinking. If other countries produce things that
aborigines want, that is a problem for [Americans], so they use
economic pressure to prevent it.

Inagaki: America claims that Pearl Harbor was the cause of the war,
but it is clear that before the war America built up its military strength
in East Asia to put pressure on Japan. . . .

Reporter: You must have been infuriated living over there in America
before the war. . . .

Inagaki: When they froze Japanese assets, Japanese people could
no longer withdraw or transfer funds without official permission.
Japanese-American trade came to a halt.

Kondō: There was significant pressure even before that. There was
the abrogation of the U.S.-Japan commercial treaty, then embargoes
on trade in aircraft parts, scrap iron, gasoline, and oil. The pressure
built up bit by bit.

Reporter: Did they think that Japan could not withstand such pressure?

Inagaki: I think the American government believed that Japan would
fight back when it could no longer withstand the pressure. However, they deceived the people into believing that economic pressure
would inevitably break Japan without resorting to war.

Reporter: Of course, some must also have wanted to subdue Japan
without going to war.

Inagaki: But by freezing economic assets they put a stranglehold on
Japan. Official permission was needed to conduct all trade. They
refused to sell the things Japan wanted.

Kondō: Ships stopped going there.

Inagaki: Even after the freezing of assets, Japan carried on negotiations to get official permission. The Japanese side did all it
could.

Edogawa: Japan was almost totally dependent on the American
enemy for war material. That fact alone shows that Japan had no
intention of starting a war. Taking advantage of this Japanese weakness, the Americans added one item after another to the embargo
list until there were more than three hundred items that Japan
needed. They thought that Japan would give in as they tightened the
noose. One can imagine the distress of the Japanese leadership just
before the outbreak of the Greater East Asia War.

Kondō: We should not forget that in addition to the economic sanctions, the Americans offered assistance to the Chinese government in Chongqing to strengthen their resistance against Japan. Even before the outbreak of the Japanese-American war, American soldiers were already training Chinese pilots and technicians in Chongqing. This proves that the Americans had abandoned neutrality in the China Incident and that Japan could wage war if it wanted to. . . .

Reporter: In retrospect, encouraging anti-Japanese resistance in China and encouraging a Sino-Japanese conflict . . . seems to have been just a big plot by the Anglo Americans, doesn't it?

Kondō: Sapping Japanese strength through the China Incident was a dream come true for America. Aside from making the Japanese give in, the Americans did not accept any resolution to the China Incident, where Japan had legitimate demands.

War without Peace Settlement:
Do Not Underestimate the Enemy's Will to Fight

Reporter: It was on November 26, 1941, that the Americans thrust on us an ultimatum that made all of our negotiations up to that point meaningless.

Kondō: What was the point of the negotiations? If America knew from the start that it would make those demands and destroy the negotiations, it would have been better not to negotiate at all. I think America simply wanted to buy time. That ultimatum ignored the blood and effort the Japanese people had expended since the China Incident and, going back even further, since the Sino-Japanese and Russo-Japanese War.

America always talks about the integrity of Chinese territory, the Open Door [policy], and equal opportunity. However, Vice President Wallace, who recently went to Chongqing, said before leaving that the Open Door is obsolete, and America must play the leading role the reconstruction of China. He has abandoned the long sacrosanct Open Door principle. This example shows the true intentions of the Americans. They mouth pretty words, but gradually the truth will come out.

Inagaki: Recently, I think, the real Chinese are starting to see clearly that they are being used as tools by the Anglo Americans to defeat Japan.

Reporter: Since the announcement of the Greater East Asia Declaration, the Chinese people must be beginning to understand the benevolence of Japan's treating China as a completely independent nation.

Inagaki: I think the Chinese people place great trust in us, since, unlike the Anglo Americans with their empty promises, we are taking specific measures. . . . But what the Japanese people need to remember above all is that the Greater East Asia War is not like previous wars where a third party appeared and negotiated a compromise peace. There can be no compromise. Win or lose, we must be very clear that this war will be fought to the very end.

Katō: People often say that the enemy has no war goals. To us it seems that the Americans have every kind of economic resource and can live comfortably in peace. Why do they need to venture out into the jungles of the Far East to fight? From our perspective they seem to have no righteous cause in pursuing this war. Even so we must not take them lightly.

The Americans are inherently brave. Their nation is still young, and the bravery and courage of the frontiersmen survive. People in the cities may be leading decadent lives, but people living in farm villages and in the provinces are as diligent as the Japanese. But they are also an extremely ferocious people. It is difficult to imagine any greater enemy for the Japanese.

Inagaki: Their lack of righteous war aims does not mean that they lack the will to fight. For example, wouldn't it be wrong to think that a thief is weak just because he has no moral goal? (Laughter) It seems to me there has been a tendency toward the wishful idea that since the enemy lacks war aims, they will stop fighting at some point or other. . . .

Reporter: I think you are right.

Shimono: On the other hand, some people think that since Japan is fighting a just war with a high purpose, victory is certain and that the enemy will certainly lose because it has no war aims. That may be so, but I think it leads to the facile feeling that we will win even without trying. It was the navy press chief Kurihara, I think, who said there is a difference between a belief in certain victory and a blind belief in certain victory. I think he is right.

Reporter: It is all right to believe in certain victory because this is a just war, but we must not grow overconfident as a result.

Shimono: The enemy's war aims may be like those of a thief, but the enemy is totally concentrated on the war.

Inagaki: You could even say that because they lack a moral war aim, their fighting spirit is even more brutal. It is true that the enemy faces internal frictions and that those living in the cities lead dissolute lives. But the Americans are a people who built a high level of material civilization in a century or so. It is dangerous to dismiss them completely just because they are soft on women or act like hooligans. . . .

Shimono: Recently the enemy's air force has begun attacking [the home islands] boldly with bomber planes.

Inagaki: They are extremely ferocious and daring. We must recognize the national character of these people, who just a century ago were traveling in covered wagons with their families and their guns, killing Indians and camping out as they advanced into the West. . . .

Win with the Spirit of Certain Victory
for One Hundred Million in Every Workplace

Edogawa: Speaking of underestimating the enemy, I understand it is not unusual to see Japanese in America ridiculed as monkeys in plays, movies, and puppet shows.

Kondō: Depicting the Japanese as inferior seems to be a policy for stimulating hatred toward Japanese. At the moment such depictions may inspire ridicule but not hatred. No matter how big a problem America has with Japan, the people will bear no real hatred toward the enemy unless they are made to understand what it means for America. So I hear that now there are fewer movies that simply inspire ridicule [toward the Japanese]. . . .

Edogawa: I agree. Hatred does not arise from ridicule. During the first Sino-Japanese War we referred to the Chinese as *chankoro* [Chinks], and during the Russo-Japanese War we called Russians *rosuke* [Russkies]. Some people worry that since we don't have a similar epithet for the enemy today, that means we are not stimulating hatred. I don't agree. Those epithets were used to ridicule.

Inagaki: You're right. I was in America for about six months after the outbreak of war. Before the war, cartoons depicted the Japanese as stupid-looking or dimwits. Once the war began, they were portrayed with hateful faces and armed with up-to-date weapons like huge machine guns or menacing fighter planes. (Laughter) Some cartoons even showed Japanese with fangs. (Laughter) In other words, [the message is that] the Japanese are beasts carrying civilized weapons. The Americans have adopted a propaganda policy, I think, that conveys the impression that we are an extremely dangerous people.

CHAPTER 5

The American Occupiers

On August 15, 1945, the emperor's radio announcement telling his subjects to "endure the unendurable"—defeat in the war with America—was met by feelings of anxiety and relief, humiliation and anticipation. Occupation by American forces was surely better than a bitter fight to the death on the soil of the homeland, but no one could be sure just how the American "beasts" would behave as conquerors. The central government cautioned local authorities to prepare for friction with the American troops, and it authorized the use of funds and materials to build "recreation facilities" (i.e., brothels, dance halls, and cabarets) to protect innocent Japanese women from molestation by American soldiers.[1]

Although American "civilization" had been dismissed as superficial and materialistic during the war, there was a sudden rush to learn more about the country once the war ended. *Mainichi shinbun*, a major national daily paper, quickly published a book of essays on the United States by Japanese familiar with the country, and a Japanese version of *Reader's Digest*, tellingly advertised as a "window to the world," went on sale in 1946. While critics later railed against its Cold War ideological agenda, the magazine immediately proved so popular that some bookstores only sold them bundled with other magazines. The magazine's unassuming style offered a readable alternative to the ponderous prose of Japan's high-brow journals.[2]

Learning the English language was another way of gaining a window to the world. Banned as the "enemy language" during the war, English returned to postwar Japanese society with a vengeance. The first postwar best seller was the hastily concocted *Nichi-Bei Kaiwa techō* (Japanese-English Conversation Manual), advising readers to greet the Occupation troops with phrases such as "Thank you, awfully!" It was modeled after manuals used by Japanese military in wartime Asia. As copies flew off the shelves, *Come Come English,* a radio program that premiered in February 1946, immediately won a large audience with its cheery conversation lessons and introductions to American culture by its American-educated host. Mastering English was not only a way to get acquainted with the Americans; it also opened opportunities to work for Occupation forces as they came flooding into the country.

The overwhelming gap in material affluence between the Americans and the Japanese had a powerful impact on their perceptions of the occupiers. One of the iconic images of occupied Japan is that of well-nourished American GIs and sailors congregating in PX shops overflowing with food and other consumer goods while hungry locals looked on. Most Japanese could only gaze longingly at PXs and Occupation housing off limits to them, but the comic strip *Blondie,* serialized in a major newspaper, provided Japanese readers with a peek into American home life. It presented an idealized picture of a warm and comfortable American family that reinforced a platonic envy of American affluence. The image of Dagwood making a late-night visit to a huge kitchen refrigerator to devour one of his supersized sandwiches, vividly read by hungry Japanese, was one of the factors contributing to the surge in consumption of household appliances in the 1950s and 1960s.[3]

Not everyone embraced American affluence. The novelist Ōe Kenzaburō, for example, was one of the children who had flocked around Occupation soldiers handing out chocolates. At first he refused the former enemy's gift, but in the end he could not resist. He remembers his capitulation, and the sating of hunger, as a profoundly humiliating experience.[4] Aversion to opportunists spouting broken English and fawning on the Americans was not uncommon either. The English conversation boom lost its momentum as the Occupation came to a close in the early 1950s, but even today advertisements for English conversation schools are ubiquitous in Japan's cities.

A facile embrace of America was not without its critics, but direct clashes between the occupying forces and the Japanese populace were remarkably few given the intensity of wartime animosity. Although rumors spread that the incoming American troops would loot and rape, many Japanese were pleasantly surprised by their civilized and friendly

FIGURE 9. The postwar fad for learning English is lampooned in this early postwar cartoon. In the final panel the husband reacts to the price of his wife's permanent wave: "Th-, th-, thirty yen? That's no joke, you know!" In Tokyo at the time, one could rent a small suburban apartment with a kitchen and washroom for about ¥50 a month. (*Manga,* January 1946)

manner. Nevertheless, assault and rape cases inevitably occurred. Occupation censors quashed direct reporting of these incidents, but newspapers either ignored them or ran articles with veiled references to attacks by "large people." There were also occasional acts of open resistance to the Occupation. One of the earliest major anti-American incidents was the Kamata Incident of April 1946, when a local vigilante group, angered by the Occupation's takeover of the nearby airport, attacked and injured two soldiers.

Such incidents multiplied as left-wing anti-Americanism grew during the later years of the Occupation. Initially, the Americans enacted sweeping reforms to promote the "demilitarization and democratization" of Japan. One beneficiary was the Japanese Communist Party, whose leaders were freed from prison by the American "army of liberation." The ebullient leaders, enjoying an unprecedented degree of legitimacy thanks to their record of wartime resistance, proclaimed that their "lovable" party would lead the country toward a peaceful revolution under the benevolent protection of the Occupation.

It soon became clear that this hope was a remote one, especially after General Douglas MacArthur, the commander of the Occupation forces, banned a general strike planned by the party and their left-wing allies in February 1947. Disillusion turned into hostility in 1950, when the Cominform publicly called on the Japanese Communist Party to renounce its "lovable" policy and commence an anti-American struggle. The conservative government and American Occupation became eager allies in the fight to root out the "Soviet-controlled" revolutionaries. The Communists, for their part, went underground and launched an ill-fated guerrilla campaign while issuing shrill denunciations of the alliance between the "traitorous" Japanese government and "American imperialism." A climactic clash between the militant left and the government came just days after the official end of the Occupation. On "Bloody May Day" in 1952 unruly demonstrators clashed with the police in front of the imperial palace and torched American vehicles nearby.

The intellectual community, heavily influenced by the popularity of Marxist ideas and contrite at failing to resist militarism, were alarmed by the crackdown on the extreme left and the increasingly cozy relationship between the conservatives and the Americans. They feared what was later called a "reverse course," a return to the bad old prewar days. As the country faced entry into a Cold War world, these concerns provoked an intense debate about the signing of a peace treaty. Many advocated a "comprehensive peace" that included the Soviet Union and the newly established People's Republic of China rather than a "separate peace" that included the United States and wartime allies other than these two Communist countries. In the end Prime Minister Yoshida Shigeru, under pressure from the United States, negotiated what he regarded as a lenient treaty that required Japan to accept responsibility for the war but did not penalize the country with economic or other restraints.

The Occupation formally ended on April 28, 1952, a date that most Japanese have forgotten today. While this may be an instance of collective amnesia, it would be more accurate to emphasize the anticlimactic nature of the Occupation's end. If people remember a date at all, it is probably one a year earlier, when General MacArthur, who symbolized the Occupation for the Japanese public, was driven through Tokyo to Haneda Airport for his return to the United States after being dismissed by President Truman. A crowd of two hundred thousand lined his route, carrying signs that were hand-made and often oddly composed in English, thanking him and wishing him well. It was a massive demonstration of gratitude to the benevolent authority figure who had presided over six years of change and reform.

While many Japanese felt grateful for the nonpunitive peace treaty signed with America, the national mood in 1952 was hardly festive. To the dismay of sake shops that had stocked up on "celebrate independence" bottles, the return of full sovereignty was accompanied by sober disillusionment and uncertainty. Many conservative leaders had begun to talk about "reversing" or "correcting" Occupation reforms, provoking public concerns about the future of Japan's "democracy and peace." A new war was being waged in Korea, the country's closest neighbor. American military bases remained in Japan, and so did tens of thousands of American troops. Many Japanese feared that the world might be on the verge of another global conflict, fought this time with atomic weapons, and that stability at home might be imperiled by a rise in Communist terrorist activity.

HOME MINISTRY,
"ILLEGAL BEHAVIOR BY AMERICAN SOLDIERS" (1945)

In the uncertain early days of the Occupation, the Japanese authorities worried about confrontations between the incoming American troops and

Home Ministry, "Illegal Behavior by American Soldiers," source: Naimushō hoankachō, "Beihei no fuhōi taisaku shiryō ni kansuru ken," in *Shiryō gendai Nihonshi*, vol. 2, *Haisenchokugo no seiji to shakai*, ed. Awaya Kentarō (Tokyo: Otsuki shoten, 1980), 313–317.

the Japanese civilian population. This document, issued to the police authorities in Tokyo, Osaka, and all the prefectures by the Security Section of the Home Ministry in early September 1945, expresses official apprehension about potential clashes. It also offers an interesting assessment of American national character quite different from wartime images.

. . .

As previously reported, although the occupation of the homeland by the American army until now is proceeding tranquilly without major friction, there is likely to be a breakdown of command and liaison between the General Headquarters of the Allied Forces and the military units under it as the landing of large forces continues. Orders of commanding officers are not always likely to reach the lower echelons, and illegal behavior, major and minor, is likely to occur locally because of the particular ethnic character and the victory psychology of the American soldiers. Even though the domestic population and domestic officials remain calm at present, we must realize that we cannot be optimistic about the impact that the gradual accumulation of various actions taken by the landing Occupation forces may have on public sentiment. Even if our side quickly and firmly protests all cases of illegal action to the General Headquarters of the Allied Forces, and their side generally responds with sincerity, these incidents may not always be resolved quickly at the lower echelons. It is expected that they will occur more and more often from now on.

Therefore at present we must do our utmost to anticipate and prevent such incidents, we must secure evidence of offenses as they occur and urge the [Allied authorities] to review them, and we must devise ways of minimizing the social impact that will arise from the occurrence of these offenses. We offer the following report on incidents that have occurred until now and suggest countermeasure as reference for your leadership and regulation.

I. Illegal Behavior by American Soldiers
   1. Rape and indecent behavior toward women and girls
      At present (September 2) there have been reports of two incidents involving three persons in civilian houses in Yokosuka (offenders are American marines) and two incidents involving two persons in Tateyama, Chiba Prefecture (offenders are American Eighth Army soldiers).
      a. These incidents occurred when groups of two or more soldiers, saying they were on postlanding reconnaissance,

carried out forcible inspections of both officials and civilians. The soldiers sought nearby women and girls to molest. In the case of the incident at Chiba, the reconnaissance soldiers in an automobile drove into a village near the landing site.

b. Incidents took place during the daytime when [the local] men were either away at work or off fishing. All cases of rape took place when women and girls were left at home inside the house. At first the soldiers used hand gestures to demand sex, and when they were refused they brandished their weapons. Recently some soldiers have offered what looks like paper money [i.e., military scrip] as payment [for sex].

c. Of the four incidents one was a gang rape, one was an attempted gang rape, one involved both a mother and a daughter. The age of the victims was around thirty years old.

d. There are examples of [American soldiers] mischievously touching the breasts, cheeks, and so forth of women staff workers in village offices and local post offices.

e. Under American military law, illegal acts like rape are punished severely and are strictly forbidden by commanders. For example, if two soldiers are involved in an incident, one usually keeps watch to hide what they are doing from their superior officers.

2. Illegal actions toward police officers

Illegal actions toward police officers have occurred frequently in Yokohama, Yokosuka, Tokyo, Tateyama, and other places.

a. Some incidents occurred because policemen were mistaken for Japanese soldiers or because the Americans feared they would be harmed by the policemen.

In Yokosuka, ten or more American marines disarmed four Japanese policemen and took them prisoner but released them after [the captives] explained they were policemen. In Tateyama, an American who saw a policeman running in the dark thought he was being attacked and wounded him with a rifle shot.

b. Some incidents result from a lack of communication between our government and the Allied General Headquarters about police equipment and uniforms.

In several places Americans have forced policemen at gunpoint to undergo body searches and to surrender their weapons. There have also been instances when the weapons were returned after a representative of the police explained who they were.

    c. Some incidents have resulted from so-called souvenir hunting. . . . American soldiers have forcefully taken weapons from policemen as well as other equipment like swords, wrist watches, and the like. In some cases they have seized Japanese swords, rifles, and small arms from local police stations.

3. Other illegal behavior

    a. There have been many cases where the Americans have stolen and ridden off in automobiles and other vehicles. The [Americans] have a deep interest in automobiles, three-wheel vehicles, etc. They drive off recklessly in police or official automobiles, stop other vehicles driving at high speeds, and threaten the occupants at gunpoint, regardless of whether they are officials or civilians.

    b. Stealing souvenirs. They take watches from Japanese pedestrians, they break into Japanese houses to steal various goods, and they buy goods on display or emblems from shops with tiny sums of American money or with surplus American army goods. . . .

    d. [There are] many cases of theft of food or foodstuffs. They take various foodstuffs from vehicles, loot alcoholic beverages from stores, and break into unoccupied houses to steal things.

    e. There have been few incidents involving the firing of weapons. With the exception of the incidents mentioned above, few of our citizens have been injured by rifle fire. We must recognize that the weapons are used as a psychological threat or out of contempt for our people.

II. Countermeasures

1. Firmly protest to [Allied authorities] to induce them to correct [illegal behavior] themselves.

    It is of the utmost necessity to act quickly whenever an incident occurs and to protest it firmly.

    a. Protests are being made to the Liaison Office in the Foreign Ministry.

    b. At the local level it is necessary to protest firmly and demand correction from the local [Allied] military commander immediately after an incident occurs.

c. Even in the American army, under military regulations rape is punishable by death, and souvenir hunting appears to be treated as looting under army regulations.

d. In order to protest effectively, it is necessary to identify the offender. That is, it is imperative to conduct an investigation and collect materials in order to confirm the content, the time, the place, and the names of the victims in the event as well as the name, appearance, rank, class, and other characteristics of the offenders.

2. Preventing rape and indecent behavior toward women and girls

a. It is expected that you will repeatedly and concretely forbid residents near the Occupation bases, especially women and girls, to take any actions that appear to trigger illegal actions by American soldiers or to conceal incidents from the authorities. It will be appropriate not to rely just on the press but to use public notice boards, word of mouth, and public meetings as well. In doing so caution should be taken to avoid disturbances.

Women and girls should absolutely not be permitted to walk alone or to go out at night.

When only women and girls remain at home, doors must be fastened tightly, or they must be made to evacuate to places where men are present. Even during daylight hours there is danger near American landing sites. . . .

You should direct people to organize local communal defense by using neighborhood groups and the like to cooperate in keeping watch. When an incident seems about to start, individuals should shout for help in a loud voice, and those nearby should assemble to prevent it.

If possible, appropriate ways to provide spiritual education for women and girls should be adopted. For example, they must be persuaded that in order to protect their chastity it is permissible as proper defense to resist as though determined to die and, if unable to stop [an assault], to cause harm to the perpetrator. In the event a crime occurs it should immediately be reported to the authorities. People should be instructed to preserve as much evidence of the crime as possible.

b. The number of policemen and police auxiliaries should be increased and organized into patrol units of two or more in the vicinity of Occupation bases. During reconnaissance by American soldiers, they [the patrol units] should patrol the village and deprive the soldiers of any opportunity to commit illegal acts.

(Thus far it appears that American soldiers do not commit crimes in places where [Japanese] men are present.)

c. The immediate establishment of comfort stations *[ianjo]* for American soldiers. When Occupation bases are established, comfort stations should immediately be built at appropriate locations in the vicinity. Although it appears that the Allied forces headquarters will not officially recognize comfort stations, building them is absolutely necessary as a means of self-defense. However, . . . as circumstances dictate it is important to devise and prepare as many temporary/mobile comfort stations as possible. . . .

3. Preventing illegal actions toward policemen

a. The Occupation forces should quickly be made to understand what the uniforms, the duties, the weaponry, etc., of the police look like. For that reason, immediately after the establishment of the Occupation, representatives of the police, either through liaison facilities or, if necessary, through direct contacts with American commanding officers, should request their understanding and strongly demand means of making sure lower echelons understand. . . .

c. When any sort of illegal action is made against policemen, act as carefully as possible to preserve evidence necessary for the investigation of the offender by presenting strong materials for protest.

4. Other matters

Since at present there is no effective method but to wait for the American army to adopt self-disciplinary measures for dealing with various illegal actions and mischievous behavior [by American soldiers] prompted by curiosity or by spur-of-the-moment impulse, it is necessary to work as hard as possible to instruct our countrymen to avoid any contact with American soldiers and to keep their valuables out of sight of the American soldiers. We also think that it might be effective to cooperate with the Occupation troops by attaching English signs to government and official vehicles.

FIGURE 10. A Japanese slang word for "stool pigeon" or "spy" or "double-crosser" is *inu* (dog). This early 1946 cartoon satirizes Japanese who fawned on the Occupation forces. The tail-wagging pack includes heavily rouged *panpan* dogs, slickly dressed business dogs, and a briefcase-carrying dog official. This cartoon captures the envy and contempt that many felt toward countrymen who profited from their connections with the Americans. Surprisingly, it was not censored by the Occupation authorities. (*Asahi gurafu,* January 5, 1946)

The American Temperament

The principal characteristics [of the Americans] are as follows:[5]

1. *Practical, businesslike.* They are realistic and manage things in a businesslike way. *(Business only)* As a result, on the other hand, they are emotionally insensitive, and they lack delicacy. Various forms of American culture (philosophy, literature, politics, economics, and science) demonstrate this.

2. They respect *straightforwardness.* They are frank and simple.

3. They prefer *speedy action.* They prefer what is fast (movies, airplanes, motorboats, automobile races, etc.).

4. *Self-conceited mind.* Their self-esteem and egotism are very strong. *("America First")*

5. *Adventurous spirit.* As a result of migrating to the American continent, their traditional spirit since the opening of the West is to have a taste for thrills.

6. *Punctuality.* They are punctilious (especially about time,

contracts, etc.). As their proverb *"Time is money"* demonstrates, they place extraordinary emphasis on being *"punctual to the minute."*

7. *Vulgarity.* They possess few refined feelings, and they act with brutality, for example, lynching.

The Attitudes Our Authorities Should Adopt

1. *Pride.* Basically always be aware of oneself as a representative of the Japanese people, and never lose pride as a citizen of a great power.

2. *Open-heartedness.* Deal with [the Americans] directly and frankly without prejudice, and adopt an attitude of simply listening directly to what they are asking.

3. *Kindly, cordial manner.* Adopt a friendly attitude as much as possible, and deal with [the Americans] politely. However, do not act obsequiously.

4. *Speedy management.* Take care of all matters promptly in a businesslike way.

KAGAWA TOYOHIKO,
"WHENCE THE AMERICAN SENSE OF MORALITY?" (1945)

After graduating from a missionary school, Kagawa Toyohiko (1888–1960), a prominent Christian evangelist and social reformer, spent two years at the Princeton Theological Seminary. On his return to Japan in 1917, concerned about signs of increasing social injustice and unrest, he moved into a slum section of Kobe, where he established a settlement house, organized a cooperative, and opened a church and Sunday school. His own version of the "Social Gospel" combined the Christian idea of love with a program of social meliorism. He gained a national reputation with the publication of two books based on his experience: *Hinmin no shinri kenkyū* (A Study of the Psychology of the Poor) and *Shisen o koete* (Beyond the Death Line), a novel about a young man, modeled on himself, who decides to work for the poor in the slums of Kobe. In the late 1920s he turned his attention to the rural poor, promoting the agricultural cooperative movement. On several trips to the United States, he be-

Kagawa Toyohiko, "Whence the American Sense of Morality?" source: Kagawa Toyohiko, "Beikokujin no dōgishin wa nani kara kita ka?" in *Beikoku to beikokujin* (Tokyo: Mainichi shinbunsha, 1945), 9–16.

came known as a "Japanese saint" because of his commitment to social improvement and his activities as an evangelist. At war's end, it was rumored that he might be appointed to an important official position, but he was passed over owing to wartime English-language radio propaganda broadcasts he had made to the United States. In this essay he provides a benign image of American society intended to counter wartime demonization of the American enemy.

. . .

The Good and Bad Sides of America

The well-known Baptist minister Dr. Harry Fosdick was jailed during the war for opposing the conflict with Japan and Germany. He was not alone. Sixteen hundred ministers and tens of thousands of ordinary people who opposed the war for religious reasons were also incarcerated. This would be unthinkable in Japan. Such dissenters would be ostracized as un-Japanese, but in Middle America no one found cause to question their existence. It was common sense. If there is one thing that Japan should learn from America, it is freedom of conscience untainted by modern capitalism or by the slavery system. After Lincoln's emancipation of the slaves in 1865 America's morals turned in a new and better direction. Before the colonialistic importation of immigrants to replace the slaves and before the onset of capitalistic patricianism, America's morality was a beacon to the world.

With the development of modern capitalism, however, things gradually deteriorated. The divorce rate rose, and so did the crime rate. Criminal gangs flourished as they never had before. Morality slackened drastically after the end of World War I, and the situation got further out of hand during the prolonged depression after 1931. Those who hastily criticize the United States for this decadent "Americanism," however, do not understand America. The good and true side of America resides in the small rural towns that embrace religious freedom. Those who live in these towns serve as a great reservoir of conscience largely unknown to the rest of the world. I call them "heavenly America," and all the rest I call "hellish America." "Heavenly America" is hard to see unless you look carefully. The Japanese could see only the "hellish America" during the war. . . . It would be a great loss for Japan there if we were to scorn the good side of America as well as its bad side. . . .

Prayer before Meals

It is a big mistake to misinterpret Americanism by thinking that self-centered liberalism reigns in America's homes. Religious households in America are not so different from the old samurai families of Japan. There is a fixed order and strict home training within the household. The housewife is a perfectly devoted spouse, and children see the family as a sacred sanctuary where they learn everything important. Girls are not allowed to go out by themselves at night, and boys are not allowed to freely associate with young girls. When young girls go out at night, chaperones always accompany then. When boys and girls socialize they do so with open doors in a manner that offends no one.

As one who understands America's strict home education, I shudder to see Japan's young act with supposedly "American-style" freedom. In America strict families read a few verses or a chapter of the Bible every morning without fail, and a parent always says a prayer before family meals. In the Midwest families belonging to religious groups all do so. As a consequence American families buy millions, even tens of millions, of religious books and calendars every year. Religious life in America centers on the home. Unlike Japan, formulaic religion is not forced upon people. Rather, Americans worship as a family on the basis of religious convictions they choose freely and voluntarily, and religious education starts at home at an early age.

Unlike Japan, where the sons of the wealthy and the aristocracy are pampered as they grow up, even the Rockefellers, one of the richest families in the world, said to be worth $85,000,000 a decade ago, made their sons work during summer vacations, shoveling coal in the boiler rooms of ships plying between San Francisco and Hawaii, to teach their sons respect for hard work. If their sons could not endure such extreme labor, they were seen as unfit to inherit the family wealth. To this day, America's finest families pursue home education that instills respect for labor. . . . Of course, as I mentioned earlier, as a result of growing capitalistic patricianism in America, such positive tendencies have faltered, and society has moved toward what we see in the Hollywood movies. Nevertheless, I cannot help but feel that it is in the Christian homes [of America] that [Japan's] samurai discipline has been preserved.

The story of Dr. Warfield, a professor at Princeton Theological School, . . . is a case in point. On the day of their marriage, his wife broke her back in a carriage accident. For the next fifty years her husband took care of his bedridden bride, providing her with nursing help and leading a celibate life at her side. Such a beautiful story would be nearly unthinkable in the Orient, but such things are not uncommon among America's wholesome families. It is there that we can see in the purest form the good side of America. I think it expresses the most beautiful aspect of "heavenly America."

Home Education We Should Learn From

I was surprised to see that in every well-established and respected American family I visited—for example, the descendants of the Jonathan Edwards clan that produced seven vice-presidents and dozens of university professors—a strict regimen of home education was being followed. It seems that home training forms the basis of America's disciplined social life. Even those who become bankers or executives of big companies take time to serve as principals or teachers in Sunday schools, and they play leading roles in religious organizations, using their business skills to evangelize their religion. One interesting aspect of America's home discipline is that spiritual discipline and business life are in perfect harmony with one another.

I do not know much about "hellish America," but we have nothing to learn from it. If we must learn from America, we should learn from "heavenly America." . . . What reveals the best side of America is its excellent family discipline, based not on paternalism [kazokushugi] but on mutual acceptance [yurushiai] rooted in religion, with the husband supporting his wife in her weaknesses and with the wife supporting the husband in his. Of course, since the end of World War I we have seen the emergence of promiscuity disguised under the name of "companionate marriage," and juvenile delinquency has been on the rise, but it would be a grave error for Japanese youths to confuse these temporary aberrations with the good side of the pure America and try to copy them. The excellence of the American family's discipline is hard to see on the surface of society, I think, but it is to be found in the religiously strict home education that is hidden from public view.

The Dissemination of Scientific Knowledge to Children

Because America is a young nation, great emphasis is placed on scientific education. Even the smallest cities have museums, and in every museum there are curators who offer formal lectures on the weekend. Elementary school and middle school students can hear their explanations of the museum displays. There are also [about 120] astronomical observatories accessible to children. On Friday and Saturday nights, these facilities are opened to local children and youth groups, with astronomy specialist staff offering hands-on instruction on the basics of astronomy. Books on the social education of children are readily available and sold at a reasonable price. The mailing cost for books is remarkably cheap, amounting to only about fifty cents to send ten books from New York to San Francisco. The cost of mailing books has been subsidized in order to provide support for social education in America. Universities also offer lectures open to the public, and they compete in supporting neighborhood settlement houses, where social work organizations have been started to spread scientific knowledge among the working class and the common people.

The spread of scientific knowledge among children is remarkable. For twenty years department stores have sold ready-to-assembly radio set kits to children, who can listen to whatever they wish on the sets they build. Children also gather discarded automobile parts and assemble them into makeshift soapbox cars. In the spring and fall children compete in racing contests for prizes awarded to the best. City and state governments encourage children to acquire a complete understanding of the internal combustion engine by the time they are eleven or twelve. Newspaper companies have joined in too, publishing cheap how-to books on the construction of internal combustion engines that can be found in any department store. Leading scientists write books on natural phenomena, animal and plant life, astronomy, and the like, which are sold in department stores, on street corners, and in train stations. . . .

Strict Social Education

Student self-government activities flourish in America. To promote democracy among teenagers, the schools encourage complete self-government among twelve- and thirteen-year-olds by allowing them to form clubs that democratically elect their own leaders and decide on their own rules. Without such training, democracy would not develop. The sorry state of Japan's neighborhood association meetings is due to the lack of such training. It is truly lamentable that because Japanese lack training in self-government, problems that America's children could solve in five minutes take two or three hours to resolve in Japan's village meetings. When I attended meetings in an American school, I was struck by how orderly they were. The students neatly divided the meeting into three parts: questions were raised in the first; opinions were stated in the second; and votes were taken in the third. The students took care of things with astonishing facility. . . .

The Logic of the Atomic Bomb's Creation

The atomic bomb, developed in the Arizona desert and dropped on Hiroshima and Nagasaki, hastened the end of the Greater East Asia War. It also made us realize how much Japan lagged behind in science as well. Physics, and especially nuclear physics, has made staggering advances in America. America has produced at least ten Nobel laureates each in the fields of nuclear physics and chemistry: Robert Millikan, who studied the electron; Ernest Lawrence, who split the atom in a cyclotron; Arthur Compton, who discovered cosmic rays; Clinton Davisson, who discovered that electrons are waves; Irving Langmuir, who provided a way to measure electrons; Harold Urey, who discovered heavy water; Carl Anderson, who discovered the positron; Linus Pauling, who measured the size of the atom; and others.

Many foreign nuclear physicists have also taken refuge in America: Albert Einstein, who was invited to Princeton University; the daughter of Madame Marie Curie, the discoverer of radium; Victor Hess, along with Compton, discovered cosmic rays and made other enormous contributions to nuclear physics as a professor at the University of Chicago. With such scientists working together the invention of the atomic bomb was an easy thing to accomplish. From what I learned in my own visits to the classrooms of the nuclear physicists, I predict that they will be able to make many other new discoveries as well. . . .

There are approximately five hundred universities in America. While each has its own character, they all devote a significant amount of funds in creating research labs. In the period leading up to the Greater East Asia War, the American government spent about 500 million dollars a year to assist research. There are forty-five research centers that spend several million dollars a year. In the future I think Japan has much to learn from this about scientific research.

ITŌ MICHIO,
"CULTURE AND THE ARTS IN AMERICA" (1945)

In his youth Itō Michio (1893–1961) aspired to become an opera singer, but he first appeared on the stage of the Imperial Theater in Tokyo as a dancer. After studying in Germany and performing in England, where he

Itō Michio, "Culture and the Arts in America," source: Itō Michio, "Beikoku no bunka to geijutsu," in *Beikoku to beikokujin* (Tokyo: Mainichi shinbunsha, 1945), 53–60.

became acquainted with the poet W. B. Yeats, Itō arrived in New York in 1916. Working from a studio in Carnegie Hall, he soon established himself as one of the leading dance teachers and choreographers in the United States. In the mid-1930s he spent a short time in Hollywood choreographing for movie stars such as Ginger Rogers. After the outbreak of war, he was repatriated to Japan in 1943, and during the American Occupation he served as the general director of the Ernie Pyle Theater. Like Kagawa Toyohiko and others who had long experience in the United States, he was sought out to explain America to the Japanese public. The following interview offers not only a grand historical interpretation of the origins of American culture but also practical advice on how to deal with the American occupiers.

. . .

The Differences between Eastern and Western Civilization

Interviewer: During the war, we here in Japan were blindered like workhorses, so we could see only a distorted America, and now we have awakened from all that. But we are still like babes as far as our understanding of America goes. . . .

Itō: Well, before I begin to describe American culture, let me first talk about the development of world culture and where it has come to today, or it will not be clear why American culture has progressed to its present state.

This is just a pet theory, but I think that six thousand years ago, when human civilization—the celebrated civilization of Egypt—was born on the shores of the Mediterranean Sea, it was a perfect balance between the spiritual and the material. What I mean by "a perfect balance" is that nature and humankind were in a relationship like mother and child.

Interviewer: Was this relationship a product of the geographical conditions of Egypt—the periodic flooding of the Nile River that assured the growth of the food plants needed to sustain human life?

Itō: Yes, and what is fascinating to examine is what has happened to the balance of human civilization since then. Human civilization that was born on the shores of the Mediterranean in Egypt split into two parts, one that moved eastward, and another that moved westward. Human civilization, or shall we say the human way of life that spread westward, was influenced by geography and climate to produce the way of life characteristic of Europe or a European-like civilization. The people who lived in the West could not maintain the balance, because they could not survive on the land without making a conscious effort to support themselves materially. As a result they emphasized material civilization. In contrast, the civilization that spread eastward arrived in India, a country blessed with a mild climate where one could survive even without wearing clothes. One did not need to produce food and store it for the winter months; food was within reach wherever one wanted. To these people, material existence was not a matter of conscious concern. As a result, they emphasized spiritual civilization.

American culture, of course, came from European culture. In fact, Americans often say, "America is a melting pot." In other words, older cultures that poured in from all over Europe were melted down in the American crucible to become American civilization.

What about Japan? It is the youngest country in Asia even though its history is twenty-six hundred years long, but I think that Japan is Asia's "melting pot." The ancient civilizations of Asia—India, China, Korea—have flowed into Japan and been melted down in the Japanese crucible to become Japanese civilization.

What I mean is that the human civilization that emerged on the shores of the Mediterranean Sea six thousand years ago has traveled around the globe in two directions to reach both shores of the Pacific Ocean. The civilization that went eastward arrived in Japan, and the civilization that went westward arrived in America.

Defining "Civilization" and "Culture"

Interviewer: I see. Looking at it that way, I definitely agree that American culture is the culmination of material civilization and that the spiritual level of Japanese culture is extremely high.

Itō: Exactly. Yes, it is necessary to distinguish between the meanings of the words *civilization* and *culture*. I define *civilization* as the way people can make their lives easier and *culture* as the way they can make their lives more beautiful. One look at American civilization and it is clear that their style of life is the most convenient. American houses adjust perfectly to the change of the seasons. For example, with one twist of the wrist you can produce ice water or steam heat. The Americans have radios and airplanes, and life is convenient—everything is in good order, and things go without a hitch.

But what about Japan? After being away from Japan for so long, I was really surprised when I went into a Japanese house. The facilities are so poor. In winter, the Japanese live huddled around a small *hibachi* and shiver as drafts leak in through the cracks. We really live in poor houses, don't we? But all humankind strives for beauty—consciously. The most admirable characteristic of the Japanese is the great emphasis they put on making their lives beautiful. . . . People who have achieved a convenient style of life will make the pursuit of beauty their next priority, but those who have attained beauty will strive to achieve a convenient life style. These two things are mutually complementary. And when a balance has been created between these two elements, then humankind will surely achieve an ideal existence for the first time.

The Life of Humankind to the Present

Interviewer: . . . It is true that America, as you have suggested, has been a pioneer in beginning the age of air power and that it will take a leading role in the coming age of internationalism.

Itō: That's right. As you well know, America is a perfect example of an international society. The only true natives in the United States are the American Indians. White Americans are simply immigrants who came from somewhere or other in Europe. That is why "international color" is much stronger in the United States than "national color." But this is not a situation the Americans created consciously. Various immigrant groups found themselves in circumstances where they had to live together, so a sense of community developed naturally. That is why Americans are so good at teamwork. That is something that the Japanese need to learn. Here in Japan all of our sports are individual sports, but over there team sports like baseball and football are popular. Americans are very good at doing things together, maintaining their own position while working with teammates on offense or defense. That is true not only for sports, but it is evident in war too.

Interviewer: So what you are saying is that all the different races who came from Europe were able to work together as a team, but geographically or organically all these racial groups were also able to maintain their own special positions.

Itō: This is certainly true geographically. The people living on the East Coast are of English descent; those in the Midwest, of German descent; and those in the West are Scandinavians, Russians, Spanish, and the like. There are also differences in the work people do. The vast majority of Americans in politics are of English descent, many Germans work in factories, and many Italians, Spanish, and Japanese work in agriculture.

I don't think that Americans first demanded freedom on the basis of some ideal. Rather, it was clear that governing so many different kinds of people would be difficult unless they were all given freedom.

But I do not think that Americans really understand democracy. As you know, America is both a republic and a democracy. Democracy came from Greece, where it was able to blossom because Greece was such a small country. But a large country like Rome could not be governed unless it were a republic. In America there are two political parties—the Republicans and the Democrats. But in fact the American political system is a republic. In such a large and extensive country, democracy is all but impossible.

No Time for the Arts

Interviewer: I have heard that the Jews have tremendous influence in the art world. . . .

Itō: That's true—in the world of the arts and in culture. Countries with art and culture and people with art and culture are those who have the time and energy to spare for it. Countries and people that have this leeway make a conscious effort to develop art and culture. The reason that American art remains fairly undeveloped is that until now the Americans have not had the time or energy to embrace the arts. They had to emigrate from Europe and settle the continent. They were occupied with securing their own lives and their foothold on the land. While they were doing so they did not have the time to give birth to true art.

Our experience in Japan demonstrates this too. During the war, with the demands for increasing production or whatever, even those who dreamed of art had neither the leeway to achieve it nor any time to make their dreams reality. This was just the same as in the United States.

It has been only recently that America began to produce true art. Until now, everything had just been borrowed or imported from Europe. It has only been very recently that the American masses have become aware of and shown respect for artistic concepts, taste, and cultural life.

Interviewer: So the reason was not that Americans did not have an artistic nature but that they simply did not have the time to develop it.

Itō: Right. Because the country and its citizens were both young. But both are finally becoming more mature.

Interviewer: You appear to be optimistic about the future. Do you expect that American art will blossom in the coming age of air power and internationalism?

Itō: Well, now we are talking about my special field. Dance, I think, is mechanical. It is an art form produced by a materialist civilization. So what will tomorrow's art be like? I think that when we have achieved a balance between the mechanical civilization of the West and the spiritual civilization of the East, a new human life, a new human culture, will be created, and from within it new forms of art will be born. I also believe that armed conflict will come to an end. Armed conflict is simply a war of destruction, and from now on we must begin to construct instead. I think that we will play a very important role in bringing about a balance between Western mechanical civilization and Eastern spiritual civilization. Among all the peoples of the world, I believe that we Japanese and the Americans are in the best position to achieve this balance. Just as much American art can be considered to be borrowed goods, the same is true for Japanese culture and Japanese art. We have borrowed from China, India, and so forth.

Interviewer: So you believe that the Japanese, like the Americans, are of mixed blood too?

Itō: Exactly. During the war I attempted to say this, but I was told not to. If you look at the faces of people riding on the subway in America, you can easily tell who is of German ancestry, or English, or Spanish. . . . And after I came back to Japan, I found that the faces of Japanese riding on trains have quite varied features. There is no doubt the Japanese are a mixture.

American Taste and American Art

Interviewer: We got off the topic, but I think that I'd like to return to our earlier conversation about the problem of American art. You have said that you think that American art is just beginning to be produced, but I'd like to hear about what kind of art you think will evolve in America in the future and what kind of art best fits the American character.

Itō: That's a tough question. When you talk about American art or American character, there are many social levels. It's just the same in Tokyo. There you will find people who enjoy *manzai* performances in Asakusa, those who enjoy *shimpa* plays, and others who like *kabuki* or Noh dramas. There are various different levels in America too, but generally the interest of most Americans is, first and foremost, work—working and getting rich. The ideal situation for Americans is to work and make money from morning until night. That is their hobby. They all enjoy making money.

Interviewer: If they work and make money, then they can think about the arts?

Itō: Right. There are fine people among the rich, who own Rembrandts and so forth . . .

Interviewer: Do they love the arts from the standpoint of "patrons"?

Itō: Well, perhaps it's better to say that they become truly immersed in art. This is something that the Japanese must learn from the Americans. Their lives have great breadth. They might have a particular specialty, but when it comes to their tastes and interests, they know what they want and what they want to know. They really are broad in outlook.

Interviewer: By comparison, the Japanese have such a narrow outlook. If a banker starts collecting *ukiyoe* woodblock prints, people treat him as if he were weird.

Itō: One finds the same thing among specialists who take the attitude that the less they know about things outside their field the better they are as specialists. "I'm a specialist," they say, "so I don't need to know anything else." That is another thing the Japanese must learn from the Americans—they are not afraid to say, "I don't know." That is a virtue. The Japanese, on the other hand, worry that they will look stupid if they don't know something, so they act as if they do. That is why they are never able to learn things that they do not know. If Americans do not know, then they frankly say, "I don't know. Teach me." They are very interested in what they don't know, and once they learn something new, they are grateful. They are very clear about what they know and what they do not know.

Interviewer: Very honest.

Itō: Yes, very honest, with no strange idiosyncrasies.

The War and Interest in Japan

Interviewer: What is the level of knowledge about the Japanese in America?

Itō: Before the war it was very poor. About all that the school geography textbooks taught was, "Japan's capital is Tokyo, and its principal products are silk and tea." The general level of knowledge about Japan was very low. A person would be considered an old Japan hand if he knew five words—*Fujiyama, geisha, harakiri, samurai,* and *sakura*. After the war broke out, studying about Japan actually became the fashion. Japanese-language schools were established. A *go* club opened on Fifth Avenue in New York, and the game became very popular.

Isn't this another thing that the Japanese need to learn from the Americans? Even though America was at war with Japan, it was in the American character to learn about the enemy but still recognize that some Japanese things were good. But in Japan people became quite emotional. They hated everything American, from haircuts to clothes, and they even gave up using English words. I got a big laugh when I heard about it, but apparently someone began to use the pages from his English-Japanese dictionary to roll cigarettes. Once the American Occupation forces arrived, the dictionary was valuable once again, but all he had left were the *X, Y,* and *Z* sections. The rest had gone up in smoke.

Communication Is Most Important

Interviewer: Often the Japanese make the mistake of thinking what they see in American movies is an accurate picture of what Americans are like.

Itō: I can remember when I returned to Japan during the 1920s or whenever it was that the Ginza was flourishing, I was quite surprised as I walked down the back streets of the Ginza and came upon places with dreadful names like "the Silver Slipper." In the United States a place with a name like "the Silver Slipper" would be as splendid as a palace, but here in Tokyo . . . I took a look inside but quickly fled back into the street. Inside it was like a costume party—there were Greta Garbos and Mary Pickfords. I should not have been the one to feel embarrassed, but I could not help doing so. And it was not only cabaret hostesses who acted like this. Fashionable middle-class women also strolled about wearing outlandish Western outfits. Everyone was suddenly wearing the same thing just because a certain Western movie star did, and they plastered on makeup as though they were on the stage or silver screen themselves. It was extraordinary! I was in Japan, but it was as though people were walking around in theatrical costumes.

Interviewer: From now on there will be other Americans besides the Occupation troops coming to Japan. We certainly don't want to have them see such embarrassing sights. Anyhow, we will have many opportunities to have contacts with the Americans. How do you recommend that we prepare for this?

Itō: Well, this is what I would like people to keep in mind. Up to this point, the newspapers have written that American soldiers do this or that, but what they do is perfectly natural, because they have lived in America where it is the custom to do such things. Obviously these customs are different from Japan's, so both sides may be surprised or feel bad about what the other does. But what I really want the Japanese to remember is that despite the prohibitions against speaking English during the war, if we don't learn English and begin to communicate our thoughts to the Americans and understand them, we will find ourselves in trouble.

I recently heard about an America soldier in Yokohama who rode off on a policeman's bike, leaving the policeman fuming with anger, but thirty minutes later he returned and thanked the policeman for letting him borrow the bike.

Interviewer: He must have said something when he took the bike . . .

Itō: Yes, he had. He had probably asked to borrow the bike to look at the bombed-out sections of town or something like that, but the policeman got very upset, because he did not understand what the soldier had said. While I was choreographing a dance at the Tōhō Theater, Japanese onlookers walked right in without a by-your-leave, but when Americans came in to watch, they took off their hats and crouched quietly to observe the rehearsal. One American came up to ask if he could take a look at the stage and asked if it would be all right to go up to the third floor to watch. When I said yes, he thanked me. But if I had not understood English when he asked me, I might have said nothing, and then he would have gone up anyway, and I might have thrown up my hands and grumbled about what he had done. The most urgent thing the Japanese must do now is to communicate their intentions to the Americans and clearly understand what the Americans are saying to them. If they don't, then they will have one unpleasant experience after another.

ASAHI SHINBUN EDITORIAL, "REMEMBERING GENERAL MacARTHUR" (1951)

On April 12, 1951, the front page of the *Asahi shinbun,* one of Japan's leading dailies carried a headline announcing that President Truman had relieved General Douglas MacArthur as commander of both the American forces in Korea and the American Occupation forces in Japan. When he departed for the United States five days later, crowds lined the streets as his limousine traveled from Tokyo to Haneda Airport. Another newspaper reported that the Japanese seemed to feel that they were being separated from a "beloved father." This editorial captures the shock and surprise of the Japanese public. Before and during the war, Japanese military leaders dominated civilian leaders—not vice versa.

. . .

In his capacity as commander-in-chief President Truman has relieved General MacArthur of all his duties. Since the end of the war, for nearly six years Japan has put all of its efforts into reconstruction under the guidance of General MacArthur, the supreme commander of the Allied powers. For the Japanese people, who thought that the signing of a peace treaty was not far off, this was shocking news indeed.

Why was General MacArthur, whom we deeply respected, dismissed so suddenly from his important positions as supreme commander of the

Asahi shinbun Editorial, "Remembering General MacArthur," source: *Asahi shinbun,* April 12, 1951.

United Nations forces and commander of American Far Eastern forces? President Truman said, "I have concluded that General MacArthur can no longer give his enthusiastic support to the policies of the United States and the United Nations. In keeping with the United States Constitution and my responsibilities as president under the United Nations, I have decided to carry out a change in the commander in the Far East." We do not wish to speculate about his reasons beyond that statement.

In any case, General MacArthur's dismissal as supreme commander for the Allied forces is now a fact. It is a fact that the Japanese people, who remain under occupation, can do nothing about. Since the end of the war we have lived with General MacArthur. For the Japanese people the highest leader of the Allied forces occupying Japan was General MacArthur, and we thought our relationship with the general would continue until the signing of a peace treaty. Whatever the reasons for his dismissal might be, the Japanese people regard General MacArthur's departure from his position as commander to be most regrettable.

At a time when the Japanese people faced an unprecedented defeat in war and when they were in a state of total collapse, it was General MacArthur who taught us about democracy and peace and who gently led the Japanese people down a brighter road. Like a parent delighted to watch his children grow, it was General MacArthur who happily watched the Japanese people, his enemies of yesterday, make their way on the road to democracy and who continued to encourage them on their way.

There is still room to question how far Japan has embraced democracy and how peaceful the Japanese people have become. We have not yet gone far enough. But it will be difficult to uproot the democracy and pacifism nurtured during General MacArthur's six years in Japan. For that we must express a large measure of gratitude, and not of pride, to both General MacArthur and the Allied nations.

In his announcement, President Truman said that he had relieved General MacArthur because he was unwilling to support the policies of the United Nations and the United States, but he made no criticism of MacArthur's Occupation policies. Regardless of his dismissal, General MacArthur will go down in history for the success of the Occupation's policies. President Truman also said, "General MacArthur's place in history as one of the greatest military commanders is firmly established." We too will probably never forget his great achievements. . . .

General MacArthur is about to leave. In the Far East, where the situation grows more complicated, many problems will remain, and their resolution will not be simple, but the foundations and the direction of the democracy that General MacArthur infused into the hearts of the Japanese will not change. With all our strength, we will continue to walk this road in the same direction that we have taken so far.

There is no better way to show our appreciation to General MacArthur, who led for six years from the end of the war until today, and this will also provide a bridge toward a peace that will bind us forever in friendship with the United States and with the Allied countries.

SYMPOSIUM: "WHAT WE HAVE GAINED FROM AMERICA, AND WHAT WE HAVE LOST" (1952)

In April 1952 the American Occupation ended, and Japan returned to full independence. That also meant the end of censorship by the American authorities. The monthly journal *Bungei shunjū* asked a random selection of Japanese academics, intellectuals, and businessmen what they thought the Japanese had gained from the Occupation and what they had lost. The responses revealed a wide range of reactions, from the positive to the hostile, and suggested that despite the radical changes brought about by the Americans, the future of their reforms was by no means certain. The responses also suggest that for many the American Occupation was a humiliating experience.

. . .

Hara Yasusaburō (president, Japan Chemical Company), "Offsetting Gains and Losses"

What Japan gained and lost from American Occupation policies offset each other in the following manner.

1. What Japan gained under the American Occupation
   a. Overall success in establishing democracy in the various facets of political, economic, and social life
   b. Individuals overcoming their traditional meaningless diffidence and now actively speaking their opinions and creating a social system with people's energy from below
   c. Revival of a stagnant labor movement, encouragement of workers' consciousness, and promotion of workers' rights

Symposium: "What We Have Gained from America, and What We Have Lost," source: "Amerika kara eta mono-ushinatta mono," *Bungei shunjū (Rinji zōkan)* (June 1952): 2–4, 6–11.

   d. Rise of original thinking and workplace schooling under the new educational system . . .

2. What Japan lost under the American Occupation

   a. Hurried democratization reforms that ignored Japan's traditions and customs and that were often hasty and unreasonable

   b. Disregard for traditions of the Japanese family system and overencouragement of individualism, which resulted in the spread of egotism and selfishness and the rise in conflicts between parent and child, husband and wife, and old and young

   c. Protection of workers' rights at a level so high above world standards that workers do not fully understand how the production they engage in contributes to the national economy and therefore stage walkouts and strikes that stress rights but ignore duties

   d. Implementation of a 6–3 educational system that ignored Japan's economic condition, instead of gradually introducing a 6–1 or 6–2 system appropriate for the country's fiscal base

   e. Release of Communists from prison [who were then] free to carry out their propaganda campaigns. As a result of their clever organizational leadership, their influence has spread among radical students and other young adults with the unfortunate result of a rise in indiscriminant acts of violence.

   f. Dissolution of *zaibatsu,* purging of business leaders, antimonopoly legislation, and coercive economic deconcentration on the basis of the hasty conclusion that *zaibatsu* played a leading role in conducting the war. Although not completely without reason, this weakened the Japanese economy to an inordinate degree and delayed its reconstruction.

Ikeda Kiyoshi (professor, Keiō University), "Judging Our Autonomy"

For better or worse I think the experience of having Occupation troops and their families live all over the country for seven long years, showing us their way of life, can be put on the "plus" side of the balance sheet. To be sure, there were upsides and downsides to their influence, but in general the ability to see how another people live was probably useful in rectifying our parochial island-nation mentality.

Of course, our ability to distinguish between the strengths and weaknesses [of the Americans] and to make wise choices about whether to incorporate or reject their ways will determine the ultimate success or failure of the Occupation for Japan. I can express my feelings only vaguely, but it seems that so far we have often lacked such wisdom. The recent trend toward a so-called reverse course seems to emphasize the negative rather than the positive aspects of the Occupation. On the one hand, we have yet to succeed in establishing a democratic political system or equal rights for men and women. On the other hand, we all know that the superficial imitation of American mores and customs is thriving in some quarters.

The Americans have also learned about Japanese life. We can think of this as a plus for both sides, since mutual understanding forms the basis for U.S.-Japan friendship.

It cannot be denied that there is a trend toward the loss of our autonomy in politics and other facets of life as a result of the Occupation. Rising voices call on us to recover our backbone and regain Japan's autonomy. Although this is undoubtedly important, it must be remembered that uncritical reversion to the past will not automatically lead to the establishment of our autonomy.

Nakaya Ken'ichi (assistant professor, Tokyo University), "The Limits of 'Freedom' "

What can America possibly give to another country but freedom? During the Occupation, it is true that America gave and taught us democracy. But we cannot forget that America also took freedom away from us. This is because the Occupation was carried out by the American military and not by America itself.

America gave us the new constitution with more freedoms than the Meiji constitution did, but come to think of it, the spirit of freedom embodied in this constitution is a common Anglo-Saxon idea [whose introduction] did not require MacArthur's intervention.

We must remember to distinguish clearly between MacArthur and the American military, on the one hand, . . . and the will of America as a whole, on the other. For example, the repression of public assembly and freedom of speech under the Occupation was a violation of human rights that does not happen anywhere in America. It goes without saying that such repression violates the spirit of the new constitution and what the Americans call democracy.

In American history, during the Reconstruction era after the Civil War, oppressive rule by a group of Northerners left a deep-rooted resentment in the South. Carpetbaggers from the North and the scalawags in the

South provoked people into acts of violent resistance. Oppressive rule by the American "carpetbaggers" controlling GHQ [i.e., the Occupation headquarters] and their Japanese "scalawag" followers will not be easily forgotten either. But we know that the vast majority of American people continue to defend freedom, and we hope that they will cooperate with us in winning it back.

Mutō Unjūrō (lawyer/ left-wing socialist), "Democracy and Chastity"

1. What we gained is democracy.

    Of the many things Japan gained from the American Occupation, I think the most important is democracy. Before the defeat in war Japan had extremely strong absolutist and feudal tendencies, not only politically, but also economically and socially. The pressure of a pyramidal structure with the sacred emperor at the top weighed heavily on Japanese people and stifled their lives. When the Americans arrived, they quickly dismantled this pyramid from the top and bottom, and the Japanese people were finally liberated from the long-standing absolutist and feudalistic forms. The American Occupation forces deserve much credit for this, but the reverse course during the last half of the Occupation was quite regrettable.

2. What we lost is the chastity of young women.

    There are also many things that Japan lost through the American Occupation. Taking a slightly odd point of view, I would like to mention the chastity of young women as one of them. Until the American forces arrived in Japan, there was no such word as *panpan* girl [streetwalker].

    Prostitution existed before, of course, but it is probably without precedent that so many women sell themselves so shamelessly. This is truly a national disgrace.

    It goes without saying that the socioeconomic circumstances that produced the *panpan* need to be rooted out, but in any case, I think that we must start by sweeping the *panpan* away from every corner of Japan for the sake of maintaining our appearance as an independent country.

    I do not necessarily oppose romantic and marital relationships based on free love, but I find it odd that after independence Japanese, especially young men, are not angered by the sight of the pretty young Japanese girls being bought—yes, bought—as toys by despicable foreigners [ketō].

Ishigaki Ayako (social critic), "Desert Mirage"

What Japan gained under the American Occupation:

· [Before the war] the Japanese people, knowing as little about the outside world as a frog in a well, were terribly self-righteous and dogmatic. The Occupation opened their eyes to what was going on in world trends, and they have striven to reach international levels in thought and culture. I think that their perspective has widened greatly. This is exemplified by the transformation of the "divine" emperor into an earthly human being. Another major accomplishment is the raising of the status of women to human standards.

What Japan lost under the American Occupation:

The Japanese people, men and women alike, lost their chastity. The horde of panpan girls overflowing the streets are not the only ones who did so. People lost their chastity by losing sight of what is pure and proper within their hearts They became fatalistic and careless, tossing aside their pride as Japanese. Even though we were misled during the war, at least we had a pure single-mindedness. Today that is gone. There is no joie de vivre, only deceptive cunning or hardened nihilism.

The American Occupation was supposed to promote freedom of speech . . . but this was like a mirage shimmering in the desert. It had no substance at all. The Americans talked about freedom of speech, but that freedom turned out to be an ugly mutilated monster.

Astonished by this the Japanese people stepped back and failed to say what they should say. And while this was happening, distinguished gentlemen in the government became quite adept indeed at tossing around grandiose words like trust and reconciliation.

We have become spineless and servile, bowing our heads to authority. We have lost our independent spirit.

Yoshimura Kimisaburō (movie director), "Gloomy Days"

Being a timid soul, I worry about being labeled a "Red" or a "fellow traveler" again, and it is difficult for me to answer, but I have decided to say what I think.

It is extremely regrettable that the recent peace treaty does not allow us to feel that Japan has achieved true independence or that the American military's occupation has ended. In my view, the Occupation continues today.

The Japanese people learned the value of freedom through occupation by the American military—the Allied forces if you prefer. Democracy too. Freedom of speech, freedom of assembly, freedom of association! Recall that Japanese Communist Party members [freed from prison by the Occupation forces] went to GHQ and shouted, "Long live General MacArthur!" We learned the preciousness of human life. We were able to reconstruct our devastated land and return to a decent standard of living. And how grateful we were for the tasteless cornmeal and wheat flour [distributed by the Occupation forces] that was a godsend for our starving selves.

We were fortunate to have been occupied by a civilized country like America, and the American soldiers acted like friendly and kind gentlemen.

However, things have been changing these past four or five years. The American soldiers are still friendly and kind gentlemen, but things once given to us are in danger of being taken away again. The peace constitution is in danger, and so are other democratic things.

Without question, it is the Japanese government that is trying so fiercely to impose such reactionary policies. But what "power" is allowing all this to happen?

The Occupation forces gave us "freedom," but now this "freedom" is about to be taken away. I am just an insignificant movie director, and I have no "power" whatsoever. I pass each gloomy day muttering complaints. I am one of 80 million pitiful "human resources."

Ukai Nobushige (professor, Tokyo University), "Return to Basic Principles"

1. What we gained is the basic principles of politics universal to all mankind. These have been written into the Constitution and gradually absorbed by the Japanese people. "All of the people shall be respected as individuals. Their right to life, liberty, and the pursuit of happiness shall . . . be the supreme consideration in legislation and in other governmental affairs" (Article 13). Even if a tyrant were to emerge, it would not be easy for him to take away these basic human rights repeatedly emphasized in the Constitution.

    The American Occupation gave us a constitution with idealistic provisions, such as the renunciation of arms. Simply as a matter of gratitude to America, I believe that we should not revise such provisions of the Constitution so easily. No matter what our opportunistic politicians say, the Japanese people should hold fast to this precious gift.

2. What we lost was little more than fleeting dreams from the past, but what we failed to gain was democratic discipline. Those in power simply mouthed the principles of the new democracy but left the people to their own devices and imposed restrictions on one thing after another.

The most troublesome matter is that now that the Occupation has ended, some [members of the Japanese establishment] are under the illusion that they can ape the Occupation authorities by exercising superconstitutional powers and restricting the people's freedom. It is now that the Japanese people are about to begin their training in autonomous democracy.

Our problem is that although the Occupation distributed the textbook for democracy, we did not go to school to study it but remained trapped in military barracks.

SATŌ TADAO, "WHAT IS AMERICA TO US?" (1967)

The film critic Satō Tadao (1930–) was a member of the so-called postwar generation that experienced war and then the American Occupation as they were growing up. Brought up in the "Old Japan," they witnessed the sudden birth of the "New Japan" after 1945. During the war Satō learned that he had failed the middle school entrance examination because he had not bowed his head when the principal recited poems by the Meiji emperor. A patriotic youth, he decided to demonstrate his manliness by entering a military academy for training as a pilot. After the war, he resumed his education at vocational school and night school. His image of America was decisively altered by American movies, and he discovered the misdeeds of the Japanese military through Japanese films like the 1947 *Senső to Heiwa* (War and Peace). As he titled one of his many books, "The movie theater was my school." Like many of his generation he feared he might be sent off to fight during the Korean War. A prolific movie critic from the early 1950s, Satō introduced the Japanese public to films from Asia and the rest of the world. He also commented on social and educational issues. In this autobiographical essay Satō expresses ambivalent feelings about the postwar American presence in Japan, probably shared with many other members of his generation. It is not hard to understand why he felt disillusioned about both the new and the old Japan.

Satō Tadao, "What Is America to Us?" source: Satō Tadao, "Wareware ni totte Amerika to wa nanika?" *Shisō no kagaku* (November 1967): 2–13.

· · ·

It is by no means pleasant for me to think about America. It remains difficult to judge how much I can free myself from old sentiments toward America—humiliation and revulsion, envy and jealousy. It would be deplorable for me to think about America only to be confronted with those sentiments.

When America reveals its grave moral flaws, such as its failure in the Vietnam War or the CIA's dark conspiracies, I condemn it indignantly in public. At the same time, I cannot completely deny that I also take a certain pleasure in seeing that America also has its shortcomings. The roots of this pleasure go back to the deep humiliation I felt during the Occupation when I heard General MacArthur characterize the Japanese people as fourteen [twelve]-year-olds. Granted Japanese people may be fourteen-year-olds, I thought, but are Americans arrogant enough to think of themselves as adults? Even now, my resentment persists.

In recent years, it is becoming increasingly common for me to think critically about America. While I believe that my critical thoughts are based on sound principles, sentiments unrelated to those principles may also play a role; this is an unpleasant thought. As an individual who tries to think internationally, I lamentably find myself a hopeless nationalist when my thoughts turn to America. . . .

Many of us believe in the old saying: "If you're looking for shade, find a big tree." By trusting in America's gargantuan strength, we have essentially accepted the idea that it is the best policy to live comfortable lives under its sphere of influence. Although I should cover my face in embarrassment as I say this, we have a tendency to consider those who are strong and who offer us profit not as our trading partners but rather as our masters. Shall we call this our "feudal nature"? During the war Japanese soldiers were difficult to take prisoner, but once captured they would blurt out military secrets even though international law stipulated this was not necessary. This may have been because the Japanese military did not educate soldiers about how to behave if captured. More fundamentally, however, I think it has to do with our subservience to authority. The Japanese government's actions during the postwar period make us aware of this unbearably shameful side of ourselves. This is not revulsion toward America per se but rather toward our own distorted image reflected in an American mirror.

As a young recruit I participated in the war against America, albeit almost as a sham, and then lived under the American Occupation during my impressionable late adolescence. My fear and loathing toward America stem from early childhood, but hostility is not the only sentiment I harbor toward America. American movies were constant companions during my late teenage years. There was even a period of several years when I watched practically every American movie released. Today, my main occupation is writing movie reviews, but my love for American movies is deeply ingrained in me. In that sense, I might say that America is a part of me. I have never been to America, and I do not have a single American friend, but America's existence occupies an extremely important place in my consciousness.

I was born in 1930. The war with China began when I started elementary school. Our teachers and the books we read and the radio broadcasts we heard told us the reason that China, which was so weak, did not surrender was that the Americans and the British supplied them with weapons. In *Shōnen kurabu* magazine, Hirata Shinsaku, an author of children's books, wrote articles about the army and stories about the navy in a future war with the United States. I read them avidly as a child. As a result, the war against America that started when I was in the fifth grade seemed very natural. I had no sense that its outbreak was unexpected.

At the time adults provided us with roughly the following view of the United States:

"America is the richest country in the world. Using power based on its surfeit of wealth, it is trying to dominate the world. Europe has colonized most of Asia, and its inhabitants live like slaves, but America is providing the economic support for this European villainy.

"American politics is dominated by a handful of rich millionaires. Its democracy is therefore a sham. America is a hedonistic country, and all Americans swagger about like loudmouthed drunkards. On top of all that, America is a land of gangsters, where gunfights break out constantly around Chicago. As all this makes clear, Americans are inherently brutal. However, we need not fear America. American soldiers, forced to fight for the ambitions of a handful of millionaires, are demoralized, and their bodies have been weakened by their trivial pursuit of pleasure. It is clear that they will be no match for the 'Yamato spirit' of the Japanese army."

It was therefore a great shock the first time that I saw an imported American movie after we lost the war. The Americans in the musical comedy *His Butler's Sister*, starring a grown-up Deanna Durbin, seemed to me so happy and satisfied. In itself that was a shock. When Deanna Durbin sauntered jauntily down the street in a wonderful big hat, people smiled and looked back at her. When she got on an elevator, men took off their hats and stared at her with admiring gazes. Everybody seemed genuinely happy. There was no doubt about that, given their lively rhythmic movements. If people were not really happy they would not move so rhythmically. But were Americans really so happy? How could it be that ordinary folk in the land of the "Anglo-American devils" were happy? If the Americans were inebriated by the pleasures of material civilization, weren't they not supposed to know true spiritual happiness? Weren't their spirits supposed to be savage, like the Chicago gangsters or the young woman [in a wartime American photograph] who decorated her desk with the skull of a Japanese soldier?

I was stunned in that movie theater. As I walked out into the street, I noticed that my steps felt unusually unsteady and dizzy, as if I had a bit too much to drink. As a result of what happened to me in that theater, I am now a movie critic. The poet Iijima Kōichi, who is the same age as I am, has also said that watching *His Butler's Sister* surprised him that Americans were humans like us. . . . Ours is the American-movie generation.

Having trained as an air force pilot recruit from the age of fourteen, I continued to believe for some time after the war ended that Japan had fought a just war. I thought that we had simply lost because we came up short in our ability to produce weapons. The first time I was forced to rethink this belief was when I learned Japanese soldiers, whom I thought could do no wrong, had behaved cruelly on the battlefront. The second time was when I discovered from movies that Americans are also happy in their own way.

The Occupation forces imported American movies both to educate the Japanese and to provide them entertainment. Movies depicting the darker side of American society were not shown. Artistic quality was a secondary concern. Only educationally useful films depicting Puritanical American traditions or wholesome recreational films were released. An example of a film that did both was *Going My Way,* starring Bing Crosby as a Catholic priest. The images of America so energetically disseminated were quite different from [earlier] images of America as a materialistic civilization, politics dominated by the rich, and gangsters on the streets. Starved both physically and spiritually, we accepted them as dazzling images of a virtual heaven on earth.

That said, I knew that the real America was not gentle and full of sympathy like the priest played by Bing Crosby. One day I can never forget is February 1, 1947. That was the day that a general strike planned by Japanese workers was canceled by MacArthur's orders. More than anything else, that incident drove home to me that America was not a friend of the Japanese people but rather our lord and master. With deep emotion I had embraced the idea that democracy meant popular sovereignty, but this incident forced me to realize that sovereignty really did not lie in our hands.

A democratic country composed of people who do not believe themselves sovereign: this, I believe, is the fate forced on Japan after it lost the war.

MacArthur, of course, was not a tyrant. At the end of the war, rumors spread about the horrible things the American Occupation forces would do. We thought of them as "Anglo-Americans devils." American soldiers were surprisingly gentle and friendly, however. The first officer to arrive in my town was at a loss when he couldn't find a public trash can to dispose of his cigarette stub. The word spread rapidly, and people were relieved to hear that the Americans were surprisingly civilized.

Once America occupied Japan, it thought of itself as Japan's teacher. It prompted the Japanese people to carry out many reforms, and it taught them many new ideas: democracy; liberalism; torturing prisoners is a crime; the emperor is not divine; Shinto must be separated from politics; labor unions must be aggressively organized; the status of women must be raised; romantic relationships are nothing to be ashamed of; a father yelling at his child is feudal; we must discuss things more. . . .

These new ways of thinking and these reforms, of a kind usually brought about only by revolutions, were launched with rapid-fire speed. I sometimes had to give a cry of admiration, and sometimes I simply stood paralyzed with astonishment. [When] I heard the emperor's declaration of humanity on the radio, I was so excited that I couldn't help accosting a bystander and discussing the news with him. For the entire day, I felt as though I had awakened from a powerful trance. Or when I went to work in an iron foundry, I thought of myself as a company employee, but after I attended a union-organizing rally one day I suddenly realized, "I am a worker." Until then I had thought of "workers" as manual laborers digging ditches or doing road work.

These were refreshingly new experiences. Day after day, a new world opened, and things once obscure appeared with clarity before my bewildered eyes. I was rapidly converted from a military youth into a democratic youth. . . .

Did we achieve sovereignty when the Occupation ended with the San Francisco Peace Treaty in 1951? In form, we certainly did. However, as felt reality, we certainly did not feel that we had become sovereign. The

American military remained in Japan as they had before, and so did American bases. Nor was Japanese sovereignty over Okinawa recognized. . . .

It is true that becoming America's ally was extremely profitable for a time. During the Korean War, Japan made money as a subcontractor for American military procurements. It felt good that our economy recovered and that we approached, even by a little bit, American-style living standards. The only reason Japan had to fear America was anxiety that its alliance with America might antagonize the Soviet Union and China. This anxiety was hypothetical, but the reality was that the American military remained just as it had during the Occupation. We had grown accustomed to accepting this accomplished fact as our fate. . . .

Since Japanese sovereignty exists only within bounds that satisfy America, Japan, it is thought, should try harder to keep America satisfied. The problem of Japan's national defense is something that Japanese people should think about independently, but we find ourselves in a situation where no distinction is made between thinking about the national defense of Japan and the national defense of the United States. Unlike the Americans, many Japanese do not view a Chinese invasion as a realistic threat. When we are told that we need to build a more solid national consensus on national defense because "China has developed nuclear weapons and the Americans consider them offensive weapons," a majority of Japanese find themselves perplexed.

Many Japanese recognize that the nuclear balance of power has prevented the outbreak of World War III. However, this balance is extremely unstable. The danger is not so much that the stronger party will attack the weaker, but rather the reverse—that weaker will stage an attack to prevent being overwhelmed by the stronger. Japan's recent experience of waging war against a clearly stronger America lends weight to this view. It is dangerous when one side in the balance of power is too strong. In the present conflict between America and China, America is clearly the stronger party. It follows then that Japan's cooperation with American military power has the dangerous effect of strengthening an already too-strong power. . . .

For today's Japanese, money making is no longer linked to building national wealth and strength. We are becoming a rich nation nonetheless. We accept this situation, but by no means do we derive deep satisfaction from it. In the past, we fought with the world's richest nation, America. At that time, we hated America's giant wealth. We called the Anglo-Americans "the haves," and appointed ourselves, together with

Germany and Italy, as the champions of "the have-nots." Defeat in the war taught us the stupidity of hating the prosperous, but that does not mean that suddenly we accepted the idea that prosperity was a value in itself. Prosperity is desirable, but at the same time, we cannot help feeling wary that it may be polluted by many poisons. . . .

When we think about what America is to us, one of the first images that comes to mind is "Americanism." The word is often a synonym for materialism, money worship, and frivolity. It also suggests standardization, mechanization, the temperamental tendency to respect functionality over nuance, the obsession with speed, and the rule of "ladies first." It is difficult to ascertain how much all this is specific to America and how much is a universal phenomenon accompanying society's modernization and urbanization.

Of all the American things introduced into Japan, there is a sharp division between those that take root easily and those that wither in Japan's spiritual climate. Mechanization of daily life, standardization, the love of speed, and the way we conduct romantic relationships fall into the former category; Puritanism, industry-based labor unions, and the free movement of labor according to skill fall into the latter. As daily life becomes more convenient and comfortable through learning new technologies or customs, we rapidly become more like America. . . .

According to Richard Hofstadter's *The Age of Reform,* what we were taught [during the war] about the epitome of American-ness was actually what Americans themselves historically considered a corruption of American values. From the 1890s to the 1930s, America changed rapidly from an agricultural to an industrial nation. The majority of Americans had been landed farmers, who were viewed as the embodiment of the nation's founding ideals of liberty and independence. Industrialization, however, lowered the status of farmers vis-à-vis city dwellers. Millionaires emerged in a society that had once prided itself on an even distribution of wealth. Impoverished European immigrants poured into the cities to meet the demands of industry and created ways of life foreign to traditional Puritan America. A handful of millionaires in the cities, sitting above these poor immigrants, built a base for money politics and corrupted traditional American spiritual virtues. This is why, it is said, independent farmers at the time strongly resented the city.

The images of spiritual impoverishment brought by material civilization and of the hedonism and violence of money politics were images embraced by American farmers of the time. When these images spread overseas, they became increasingly inflated. At the same moment, there were those in Japan who thought that Japan's best traditions were to be found in villages and regional cities and that big cities were nests of evil destroying those traditions. The evils of the big city were often identified as American. Big cities were materialistic and hedonistic, it was thought, and America was the head temple of materialism and hedonism. In some respects Japan's defeat by America in the war felt like the defeat of village values by urban ones.

I believe the reason for our remarkably smooth acceptance of the abolition of the traditional family system was not the demand for a new and different way of living. Rather, it was understood to be in essence a transition from an agricultural to an urban mindset. Indeed, the breakdown of villages had begun well before the defeat in war, and to the people swept out of villages and into cities as surplus population, the family system was just an empty formula.

However, although the family system was in reality breaking down, to the extent that its form persisted, it remained an ideal. We did not discard this ideal to replace it with a new one. Rather, since we were vaguely beginning to feel that the form was growing obsolete, we casually did away with it under American pressure. Thus we did not create a new ideal. Instead we substituted the old ideal for the image of the American family in the movies.

But here too, it is better to think of this not as American influence but rather as a problem that inevitably rises from the emergence of mass society.

CHAPTER 6

America Ascendant

[handwritten margin note: anti-american nationalism]

In the early 1950s liaisons between American GIs and *panpan* girls became a metaphor for the Occupation years. Occupation censors had stifled media commentary on the presence of the American military forces, but *panpan* girls clad in bright dresses and carrying handbags bought at the PX as they walked hand in hand with their American "boyfriends" were a constant reminder of the country's defeat and humiliation. Critics of the Japanese government's fawning cooperation with the occupiers, for example, railed against "*panpan* politics." The *panpan* themselves were the object of scorn and pity but also of respect and envy, for they had overturned a hierarchy in which American culture had been monopolized by the privileged few.

[handwritten margin note: American culture available to all?]

With the end of the Occupation, the *panpan* retreated from the city centers, partly as a result of a widespread desire to "sweep away" their obnoxious presence, but their physical disappearance was accompanied by their discursive proliferation. With the lifting of censorship, the *panpan* problem became a popular topic in the media. In 1953 *The Chastity of Japan*, a book based on "true" self-reported accounts of rape by Occupation soldiers, became a best seller. Written by a male author, it achieved a remarkable, albeit short-lived, success by linking the *panpan* to a national narrative of victimization.[1]

[handwritten margin note: panpans = victims of American GIs?]

The burst of *panpan* literature reflected a growing anti-American nationalism that accompanied protests against American bases soon after the Occupation's end. Unlike the Communist Party's strategy of orga-

FIGURE 11. In this bitter but wordless 1955 cartoon, a crippled Japanese veteran is confronted by a menacing-looking hirsute American with his Japanese girlfriend. The American is wearing an aloha shirt, a clothing style favored by the petty hoodlums *(chimpira)* who haunted the seamy entertainment sections around American bases, and the Japanese is wearing the white coat and hat required for disabled veterans licensed to beg on the streets of Tokyo. The title is "A Reunion of War Heroes." (*Manga sengoshi,* vol. 2 [Tokyo: Chikuma shobo, 1970])

nizing a Maoist-style guerrilla campaign in rural areas, anti-base protests were driven by local and indigenous concerns rather than by ideology. The protests were sparked by villagers' claims to their land rather than by futile calls for violent revolution.

In 1954 anti-American sentiment was also buoyed by the *Lucky Dragon* incident, in which a Japanese fishing vessel was irradiated by fallout from a U.S. hydrogen bomb test in the Marshall Islands. As crew members died of radioactive poisoning and fears of eating radioactive fish spread, a national anti-nuclear protest movement gathered force. The atomic bombings of Hiroshima and Nagasaki had attracted little national attention until then, partly because of Occupation censorship, partly because many Japanese regarded these catastrophes as "local" events. Some

Hiroshima and Nagasaki residents grumbled that it was only when Tokyo residents thought nuclear radiation might be contaminating their seafood that they suddenly became interested in the nuclear issue. In any event, a petition to ban A-bomb tests soon gathered thirty million signatures, and annual anti-nuclear rallies commemorating the atomic attacks gathered every August in Hiroshima.

For much of the 1950s, fear of "losing" Japan to neutrality or to the Communist camp loomed large in Washington. The explosion of protests against the revised U.S.-Japan Security Treaty in 1960 intensified American anxieties. The original treaty was signed with little fanfare, but in 1957 Prime Minister Kishi Nobusuke, a former wartime cabinet member who signed the declaration of war against America but luckily escaped trial as a war criminal, came into office determined to revise what he and his political allies regarded as a treaty not befitting an independent nation. He succeeded in persuading the Eisenhower administration to make the treaty more "equal," and to assure its passage he backed legislation to strengthen the police force in anticipation of domestic unrest.

Treaty revision was a complicated issue that did not seem directly relevant to people's everyday lives. Two events in May 1960 changed the situation. The first was the ominous capture of a U.S. pilot who had parachuted to earth in Soviet territory and the ensuing revelation that American U-2 spy planes, one of which had made a forced landing in Japan the previous year, had been flying missions in Soviet air space. The second and more decisively provocative incident was a snap vote in the Japanese Diet, when Kishi rammed through approval of the controversial revised treaty while protesting opposition party members were absent. This legislative coup was widely perceived as an attack on democratic procedures. It set in motion a wave of massive protests that lasted till the treaty's automatic ratification a month later. President Eisenhower's press secretary was mobbed at Haneda Airport, the president's trip to sign the revised treaty in Tokyo was canceled, and a woman university student was killed in the chaotic violence of a massive protest on the Diet grounds. While American media reported these incidents as anti-American outbursts engineered by Communist agitators, widely felt outrage toward Kishi's high-handed tactics, rather than Communist manipulation or anti-Americanism, had caused the protests to spread to a mass scale.

The massive anti-treaty protests in 1960 seemed to portend the breakdown of the U.S.-Japanese alliance, but this concern proved groundless.

FIGURE 12. The peace settlement negotiated in 1951 permitted
American military and naval bases to remain in Japan. This cartoon reflects the sentiments of many who were profoundly disappointed that the newly independent Japan did not adopt a
neutral position in the Cold War. It shows Prime Minister Yoshida
Shigeru as a policeman opening a cage labeled "Occupation" and
leading its occupants into another cage labeled "Peace Treaty/
Mutual Security Treaty." (*Manga sengoshi*, vol. 1 [Tokyo: Chikuma
shobō, 1970])

Ordinary Japanese rejected Kishi's tactics in ceremoniously inviting the
former occupiers back in, but chants of "Yankee, go home!" gained no trac-
tion. One young American observer, John D. Rockefeller IV, then a student in Japan, reported that as he watched demonstrators snake-dancing
through downtown Tokyo, they were always friendly toward him.[2] By
the early 1960s it was clear that the prospect of Japanese neutrality was
greatly exaggerated. On the contrary, reliance on the Mutual Security
Treaty became the foundation of Japanese defense policy.

One reason the treaty issue receded as a public issue was that economic ties between the two countries were growing. While anti-base demonstrations erupted in the countryside during the 1950s, a steady stream of Japanese businessmen was making its way to Haneda Airport for flights to the United States. One lesson of Japan's wartime experience was that it had been foolish to fight a country as economically and technologically advanced as the United States. As Kagawa Toyohiko noted, even children in America were encouraged to study science and to work with their own hands. Businessmen wanted to catch up with the backlog of foreign technology developed during the country's wartime isolation from America, and they were also eager to establish a foothold in the world's largest market. The government encouraged them to do so, providing foreign exchange and other incentives to promote exports to America and tie-ups with American firms.

Far from wanting to keep America at arm's length, Japanese business leaders once again embraced it as a model. During the 1950s business magazines were filled with articles on American management practices, and Japanese manufacturers became assiduous students of American quality-control techniques and advertising strategies. America also became a mecca for those seeking new technology. Morita Akio, one of the founders of the Sony Corporation, recalled his excitement on his first flight to America to secure licenses from Bell Laboratories to use transistors. "The place just overwhelmed me," he later wrote of his stay. "The economy was booming, and the country seemed to have everything."[3]

The American government did its best to promote pro-American sentiment. In the mid-1950s, for example, the State Department tried to discourage American automobile manufacturers from competing with domestic producers in the Japanese market. Under the Kennedy administration, efforts were made to restore what the new American ambassador Edwin O. Reischauer, a Japanese studies scholar, called the "broken dialogue" between the two nations.

The American government had offered scholarships for young Japanese to study at American universities since the later years of the Occupation, but in 1962 the two governments created a twenty-five-million-dollar fund to promote cultural and exchange activities between the two countries. Promising young Japanese scholars, writers, artists, and politicians were invited to make government-sponsored tours of the United States, and private American foundations launched cultural exchange campaigns of their own. A significant number of Japanese intellectuals traveled to America for the first time. Many wrote about their experiences in America from a critical perspective, but they did so in a con-

once Japan successful,
anti-American
sentiment is gone America Ascendant | 227

scious effort to relativize an America viewed with adulation and longing by the Japanese public.

The return of prosperity to Japan was equally important in damping anti-American sentiment. Prime Minister Ikeda Hayato, Kishi's successor, directed public attention away from the politically contentious security treaty by announcing a plan to double household income within ten years. Economic growth from the mid-1950s had already undermined left-wing claims that America intended to colonize and impoverish Japan. With the formation of the broad political consensus behind economic growth, America became an unobtrusive impetus and enabler of Japan's rise as an economic power.

As Japanese manufacturers flooded the domestic market with American-style consumer appliances—black-and-white TVs, washing machines, and refrigerators—it became more and more difficult to paint America as a threatening place. Electric regalia became the basis of the modern (American) legitimacy for postwar Japanese families. On their new black-and-white TV sets Japanese households watched idealized images of American life on programs such as *I Love Lucy* and *Laramie*, which reinforced a longing for things American acquired during the Occupation. The resurgence of prosperity relegated the image of America as occupier to oblivion and prompted a reembrace of the United States as a model of triumphant affluence. The new metaphor for "America in Japan" was not the *moga* or the *panpan* but the *shokugyō okusan* (the professional housewife) presiding over a democratic and efficient household.[4]

In the long run, the country's economic success story laid the foundation for a resurgence of national pride and national confidence that cast its relations with America in a new light. But the notion that Japan might become an economic rival or competitor of the United States did not emerge until the 1970s, when foreign pundits realized that Japan was on the verge of becoming an economic superpower.

American products in Japan

ISHIGAKI AYAKO, "THE AMERICAN HOUSEWIFE" (1951)

Ishigaki Ayako (1903–96), the daughter of an upper-middle-class family, first came to the United States in 1926 to visit a sister married to a Japanese diplomat. Attracted by New York's lively artistic and political

Ishigaki Ayako, "The American Housewife," source: Ishigaki Ayako, *Nijūgonenme no Nihon* (Tokyo: Chikuma Shobō, 1951), 43–52.

scene, she soon moved to the city, where she met and fell in love with Ishigaki Eitarō, a Japanese painter ten years her senior. A disciple of Katayama Sen, Eitarō helped organize the John Reed Club and eventually joined the American Communist Party. During the 1930s the couple took a leading role in protests against Japanese aggression in Manchuria and in organizing leftist anti-militarist groups. In 1937 Ayako moved to Los Angeles, where she became a reporter for a Japanese-language newspaper. Under the pseudonym Hara Matsui, she published *Restless Wave*, an English-language autobiography, in 1940. During the war she and her husband refused repatriation but were forced to register as enemy aliens. After the war they found themselves targeted by the American government because of their radical political affiliations. When the couple returned to Japan in 1951, Ayako pursued a career as a lecturer, writer, and journalist reporting on life in America. She was also a well-known feminist who urged Japanese women to throw off their dependence on men and argued that being a housewife should be recognized as a profession.

. . .

The American woman conjures up images of a liberated woman briskly and cheerfully walking through spring fields. Indeed, to the eyes of the doubly and triply repressed Japanese woman, whose fate is suffering, American women enjoy their freedom like flowers blooming in the spring sunshine. The reason is that they have benefited from the fruits of both political and social democracy. Let's take a look into their home lives to see how these abstract words gain meaning in women's real lives.

The first thing that prompts our envy is their efficient lifestyle. In big cities, everyone lives in apartment houses. Even in working-class households, hot water flows in kitchens and bathrooms with a simple twist of the faucet. Kitchens are bright and convenient, equipped with shiny white enamel-coated refrigerators. This is standard equipment in apartments, just as gas and water are in Japanese urban dwellings. This is a great boon to housewives. New apartments have communal washing machines in the basement. Insert a dime and your mountain of dirty laundry is quickly disposed of.

When it comes to house cleaning, American women do not use primitive tools like brooms and dusters, which just send dust back up into the air. They sweep their carpets with electric vacuum cleaners that suck up even invisible dust. These machines are a bit expensive, but they have become one of the necessities that newlyweds must buy. Americans may be frugal when it comes to buying lavish clothing, but they are not at all stingy about buying things that improve efficiency of home life.

In cold regions like New York, homes are equipped with steam heaters. Even if the cold temperature outside makes your hands and feet go numb, you can move about inside the home in a light dress, as if it were summer. It is a different world from Japanese houses, where winter forces one to abandon all activity and take refuge in the *kotatsu*.

There are countless examples of efficiency-oriented equipment in American homes. This is due to America's material affluence and its high living standards. . . . In the South, living standards are much lower, because the people's power has not been organized effectively there. Even in an affluent country like America, living standards will not rise if the people lack political consciousness. In every country, there are selfish profit-seekers who abuse their power if left unrestrained. Democracy is a system that restrains them and protects the welfare of the majority. However, the operation of this system requires the unceasing efforts of citizens. In the workplace, the worker asserts his rights and freedoms; in the home, the housewife devotes herself to improving daily life. When there is an excessive increase in meat prices, American housewives lower prices by conducting a boycott. This demonstrates the power of solidarity.

I think there are two reasons for the modernization of American home appliances. First, the cost of household help is high. Unlike Japanese families, American families cannot easily hire maids. Second, besides being housewives, many women work outside the home. The rationalization of home life thus became an urgent concern, and this, in turn, resulted in the lightening of the burden on housewives. It freed them to devote more time to improving women's status. Women's liberation is not simply a question of giving women the vote. In Japan, where women have not been respected as human beings, no one had any reason to care about making kitchens more convenient for them. Lavish amounts have been spent in Japan on decoration, but the modernization of the kitchen has been ignored.

Using the time freed from household chores, American housewives participate in socially useful activities. I will explain how one of my close friends spends a typical day.

[Before the war] I was concerned about the rising influence of the military in Japan, so I gave many lectures to American audiences in the belief that the only chance of rescuing my fellow Japanese from destruction was to overthrow the military leadership. At one of these meetings I met a woman who shared my sentiments. She subsequently organized many lectures for me. It was through such activities that we came to be close friends. This bright and warmly sincere woman lives in a suburban area about 25 miles from Boston. Whenever I travel there, I spend two or three nights in her colonial-style house surrounded by a wide lawn. We enjoy discussing political, social, and personal problems on the quiet porch into the night. She is a prototype of the socially active middle-class housewife who leads a wise and fulfilling life.

Her husband, a businessman, leaves the house early in the morning to drive to work in Boston. After her eleven-year-old and thirteen-year-old boys leave for school, she washes the dishes and cleans house for about an hour. On grocery days, she drives her own car into town six miles away. I once accompanied her, and I can tell you American grocery stores are ambitious establishments. Meats, vegetables, and canned goods line the shelves of the large stores. Shoppers can choose their purchases freely without bothering the salesclerks. . . . They pick up a metal-mesh cart at the entrance, push it through the store like a baby carriage, choose their purchases from the shelves, and stack them in the basket. Payment is made at the exit, where a salesclerk waits. This self-service system is an American method of increasing efficiency.

After returning from shopping, my friend browses through the day's newspaper. Soon noon arrives. When the children were small she had a housekeeper, but now she does all the housework by herself. Her family is affluent enough to afford two cars, but they do not spend needless money on a housekeeper. After a simple lunch, she usually has the afternoon to herself. Although she does not spend as much time ironing and sewing as Japanese housewives do, having two young boys means she has to mend clothes and do other similar chores that keep coming up. The wise housewife knows how to navigate these chores skillfully. The afternoon hours are precious time for self-cultivation. She busies herself with organizing lectures, participating in church and educational functions, and taking part in PTA activities. The evening meal is easy to make because the kitchen is so well equipped. When her husband returns from work it is time for an enjoyable family dinner.

One night after dinner, I went into the kitchen to help with the dishes. Her eleven-year-old boy insisted that wiping the dishes was his job and refused to let me help. The sight of a young boy in a middle-class household standing beside his mother and drying the dishes as she washes is unthinkable in Japan, where kitchen work is not thought suitable for boys.

All forms of work are respected. In my friend's house, everybody contributes to housework. The children make their own beds and clean their own rooms. The elder brother does not help in the kitchen, but it is his job to cut the lawn. In some homes, children are paid for their work. The children save this money to buy birthday and Christmas presents for their parents. In America even boys help with the housework so the mother is not left to do it all by herself. This custom nurtures a cooperative spirit of working together.

Everybody in my friend's family likes music. The mother and children all take piano lessons. The mother, being the most skilled, plays the piano for the enjoyment of the whole family after the dishes are cleared. Her hobbies and activities outside the home are enriching. The children do not just cuddle up to their mother; rather, they naturally grow to love and respect her as an individual. This in turn leads to a respectful attitude toward women in general. When her sons grow up and marry, they will become loving and understanding husbands.

The efficiency of home life has liberated American housewives . . . and provided them with free time. How that time is spent separates the wise and elegant women from the sullen and idle ones. . . . Some American women waste their time and energy on trivial pursuits. These women tend to be affluent and middle-aged. After their children grow up and marry, they go to bridge parties and matinees at luncheon clubs and theaters. Despite their ignorance about things they chatter endlessly on about this and that wherever they go. They are extremely self-centered.

America is a woman's world, it is often said. This is current in some respects. There are times when self-centered women . . . become despots over their husbands, just as Japanese husbands become despots over their wives.

The other day, I was invited to speak at an alumnae club meeting at a woman's university in New Jersey. . . . Two-thirds of the assembled ladies were affluent housewives. The meeting took place in a big mansion. . . . [The] husbands in attendance were reserved and reticent, seemingly overwhelmed by an atmosphere dominated by females. As I sipped coffee after my lecture, I accosted one of the men and asked him for his honest thoughts on the topic of "wives as seen by husbands."

"I can't talk aloud about such things," he answered, lowering his voice. Looking around at the other women busily engaged in conversation, he said, "One of these ladies here is a complacent, arrogant, and self-centered housewife. She thinks she knows everything."

As he spoke, a young lady with an intelligent look approached with cookies. The man stopped talking. It was her turn to give a woman's perspective. According to an article she had recently read in a woman's magazine, she said that American husbands wanted three things from their wives. Not only should they be good housewives; they also needed to be understanding and intelligent. According to the article, American wives tended to focus on the first, but they ignored the last two, leaving American husbands unsatisfied. I thought there was truth in this statement but was impressed by the respect men held for their wives.

Once the young lady left us, my male conversation partner remarked, "Well, I don't agree. I would be happy if American wives concentrated on being good housewives."

"Of course it is important for a woman to be an efficient housewife," I replied, "but if she lacks understanding and sympathy can you consider her a good wife?"

He thought for a moment, then took back his previous comment. "Yes, that's right. . . . I think American wives are overconfident. If their confidence is well-founded it's no problem. But it is a big problem when the wife doesn't understand human nature and has no interest whatsoever in how her husband feels."

It is true that some selfish wives abuse their husbands' deep affection and subject their families to their tyranny. With time and money to spare they devote their lives to play and waste. They lack the passion to enrich their human hearts, and they pretend to be wise by collecting flimsy bits of knowledge.

The old ruling class in Japan focused on such unwholesome American women to emphasize the decadence of a free society. It goes without saying that their intent was to prevent the liberation of Japanese women and keep them confined within feudal traditions. During the war they waged an energetic campaign against the corrupt nature of democracy. Those of us who lived in America and knew what it really was like were saddened and angered by the way such distorted information was being force-fed to our fellow Japanese back home.

The unhealthy type of American woman is . . . an unfortunate by-product of the leisure class. These women have nothing to do with human liberation, pioneer spirit, or truth-seeking American society. The good men and women of America reject them. Nobody associates the shallow and selfish woman with women's liberation. I think we have much to learn if we distinguish clearly between the good and bad points of the two types of American women I have described. Looking at American women as a whole, many of them lead enriched lives by effectively using the time saved through efficient housekeeping to engage in self-cultivation and to participate in social activities.

GOTŌ YONOSUKE, "THE DYNAMIC LOGIC OF AMERICAN CAPITALISM" (1956)

Gotō Yonosuke (1916–60) entered government service after he graduated from Tokyo University with a degree in electrical engineering in 1941. In late 1945, he joined with Ōkita Saburō, a former colleague in the Ministry of Transportation, in organizing a study group to plan for the postwar reconstruction of Japan. It met on August 16, the day after the emperor announced the end of the war. In the spring of 1946, the group completed a report, "Basic Problems for the Reconstruction of the Japanese Economy," which stressed the importance of technological innovation and trade. It became a blueprint for Japan's postwar economic policy. As the author of the government's economic White Paper from 1952 to 1958, Gotō became known as the "genius of the White Paper" for his ability to popularize technical economic issues through snappy catchphrases. The best known—"The postwar is over"—appeared in the 1956 White Paper, which called for a national economic mobilization to rejoin the ranks of the advanced industrial nations. After a year-long stay in the United States in 1955, Gotō published the book from which the following excerpt is taken. It overlapped significantly with the 1956 economic White Paper but included more explicit arguments and references to the American model.

. . .

The Faith of American Businessmen

Among American businessmen there is a growing conviction that the American economy will continue growing perpetually into the future. The proof of this is that they are competing to expand plant facilities. Business confidence is based on the fact that twice in the postwar period the American economy has endured drastic drops in military expenditures without suffering economic depression. The first drop came immediately after World War II . . . [and] the second came with the Korean War cease-fire. . . . Many world economists predicted the onset of a de-

Gotō Yonosuke, "The Dynamic Logic of American Capitalism," source: Gotō Yonosuke, *Amerika keizai han'ei no kōzō* (Tokyo: Chūō kōronsha, 1956), 229–253.

pression if military expenditures declined after World War II. However, a backlog of demand—an explosion of purchasing power for durable consumer goods that had been repressed during the war—filled the gap. After the Korean War rearmament ended, this backlog could no longer be relied upon. Nevertheless the American economy was able to minimize the economic downturn of 1954, and economic trends are now showing a strong upward curve. From this turn of events, American businessmen have learned the following two lessons: (1) the government can be counted on to take necessary measures to stem recession; (2) the current upward trend in the economy is due not to government measures but rather to the strength of free enterprise. . . .

The Debate over Business Cycles

In Japan, changes in the business cycle are determined by external factors, such as an increase or decrease in exports or the Korean War boom. In America, the basis for self-sustaining economic development lies in corporate investment, and corporate investment is influenced by businessmen's level of confidence in the economic future. This means that social psychological factors play an exceedingly important role in determining the business cycle in America. When we hear American officials say that the economic outlook is strong, before accepting that as what they really think, we must be aware that this is a psychological strategy for influencing the business cycle. Perhaps because of the government's psychological strategy or perhaps because of increased business confidence based on economic realities, America's big enterprises have been announcing plan after plan for long-term investment. . . .

In academic circles as well, people are debating the possibilities of eliminating business cycles by maintaining a constant level of investment. That means sustaining investment when the economy is in recession and not increasing it too much during a boom period. If this is possible, we must admit that the nature of capitalism has changed. . . . When I asked American economic policy makers about this possibility, their reply was: "No more 1929s. We can avoid a great depression. But we have yet to see whether or not we can avoid a 1938–39-scale economic recession."

Population Growth and the Expansion of the Market

It may seem strange to us Japanese that Americans talk about population increase as a driving force behind market expansion. In the lobby of the Department of Commerce in Washington, there is a sign like a huge automobile mileage meter that prominently displays the size of the current population, more than 160 million. Every twelve seconds, the last digit increases. In effect the Department of Commerce is tacitly saying, "Businessmen of America, behold. Every twelve seconds, the market expands. Produce more, sell more." In our country population increase is discouraged today. But in America it offers the most desirable and most reliable means to increase production. The American birth rate is rising, and the rate of natural increase exceeds that in Japan. In the past both Europe and America embraced the principle of having small families, (i.e., giving birth to and raising fewer babies), but recently they have shifted to the principle of having big families (i.e. the more babies born the better).

I spent the year of 1955 living in America with my family. My wife's first impression of Washington was that many women were walking the streets with their five-year-olds and three-year-olds, pushing a baby carriage with their newborn, and carrying another child in their pregnant wombs. . . .

The Technology War

It is often said that American capitalism means monopoly, but there is not one example of a big American corporation lazily extracting profits from a monopolistic position. To be sure, capital is highly concentrated in the American economy. US Steel, for example, produces as much steel as all the nations of Europe's Schuman Plan combined, and its Gary, Indiana, plant alone equals Japan's total production. Moreover, the manager of the Gary plant is a member of the company board. But that does not mean that US Steel controls the steel industry. It engages in intense competition with corporations like Bethlehem Steel and Republic Steel. In other words, even though capital is concentrated [in the steel industry], this does not lead to total monopoly. . . .

The "big three" of the huge American automobile industry are General Motors, Ford, and Chrysler. In 1954, Chrysler suffered major losses due to a bit of carelessness. Even General Motors, America's top corporation, would go under if it did not stay on its toes. That is how intense the competition is.

How do these automobile companies compete with each other? The answer is: through technological innovation. In countless ways, technology is contributing to the rejuvenation of American capitalism. Technological progress stimulates desire through the introduction of new products. One reason why sales of 1955 automobile models were so successful was the introduction of the two-tone model, with different colors on the roof and sides. Even though they did not understand what mechanical changes had been made in this model, the public immediately accepted this change as an innovation. When a family buys a new model, the housewife next door tells her husband, "Honey, our neighbor bought a new car. Let's get one too."

Most American households own a TV set. In big cities there are usually four or five channels. To eliminate the hassle of getting up and down in order to change channels, a new flashlight-like device now being marketed allows you simply to point it at the TV and change channels while sitting on the sofa. When the phone rings, the remote switch also allows you to watch the screen but turn off the sound if you don't want to be bothered by it, then turn it on again after you have finished the phone call. This is certainly an unnecessary innovation—one can simply get up and change channels by hand—but it is convenient. When a housewife sees the remote do its magic next door, she comes home and says, "Honey . . ." Television and other media like newspapers, magazines, and the radio are overflowing with commercials for such new products. The poor American husband is constantly fretting over how to keep his wife from watching these advertisements.

Corporations, for their part, constantly work at improving their plant and technology in order to send newfangled products into the market and expand their sales. Two examples that epitomize this trend are the peaceful usage of atomic energy and automation. On the one hand, technology stimulates demand and expands the consumer market; on the other, it promotes corporate investment and expands the investment market. It seems that in America the meaning of *consumption* is undergoing transformation. The idea of using a consumer product until it is physically worn out is being eclipsed by the idea of replacing it with something [altogether] new. "Obsolescence" of plant and equipment is accelerating too. Shortening the life of machinery alone has expanded the need for technological investment. The giant scale of corporations is a precondition for these investments in technology. Some argue that monopolies obstruct technological innovation, but I know of no other society in the world that is more enthusiastic about introducing new technologies than the American industrial world is. . . .

Agriculture and Economic Growth

Whenever I talk about the American economy, my friends tease me that I am overpraising America. "Of course, that's how you should feel if you got a fellowship to go to America," they say. But I have not closed my eyes to the dark side of the American economy. The weakest link in the American economy is agriculture. Agricultural production has increased 40% over the prewar period. This productive power helped relieve the postwar worldwide shortage of foodstuffs, but with the revival of world agricultural production American agricultural exports have declined since their peak in 1947. Income from agricultural production has also decreased 20% since then.

It might therefore seem that American agriculture is beyond salvation, but there is a new factor not well known in our country: the rapid decline in the number of people occupied in the agricultural sector. . . . The reason that this decline has taken place without government intervention is simply that the expanding nonagricultural secondary and tertiary sectors offer attractive employment opportunities to farmers. I believe the very fact of sustained growth of the American economy has proven a more effective agricultural policy than price support measures.

The same can be said about small firms. Wedged between big corporations and big labor, small firms appear to have no chance for survival. But in fact they do survive, because the continual growth of the American economy allows them to nibble at the leftovers of an expanding market.

Experts on agricultural and small firm problems say that things are fine as they are but that a cessation of economic growth would be catastrophic. American officials are thus very much concerned with the problem of maintaining economic growth. In America, there is not much debate over short-term market fluctuations. On the contrary, there is an active debate over long-term projections for what the American economy will look like in 1965 or 1975. I first thought this was a reflection of Americans' optimism toward current economic trends, but that was a misunderstanding. Their debate over growth rates is actually intimately linked to current economic trends. In other words, the debate over growth rates is actually a variation of the debate over the business cycle.

When Americans talk about economic stability they do not mean a static stability (i.e., this year will be the same as last year), but rather they talk about a dynamic stability based on a fixed growth rate. As President

Eisenhower has said in a speech, "In the American economy halting is the same as stumbling."

Learning from the American Economy

The American economy has continued sustained development driven by technological change. At the very least, it should not be seen as a stagnating economy. And one cannot simply dismiss it by saying that "the monster of economic maturity" dominates American society. Recently prominent Soviet economists have begun to recognize the shortcomings of Soviet academia's understanding of modern capitalism. The fact that America has steered clear of a depression despite two sharp drops in military spending in the post–World War II period has not only bolstered American businessmen's confidence; it has also encouraged the rethinking of the nature of capitalism in the Soviet Union. Haven't our country's progressive forces been dogmatic in their thinking about capitalism? Isn't looking at America through Soviet eyes as big a mistake as looking at the Soviet Union through American eyes? Now that a decade has elapsed since the end of the war, we must learn to view the world through Japanese eyes. When we do so, we will discover that the world is now on the verge of what can be considered the Second Industrial Revolution.

Atomic energy and electronics will change the world. Both are legacies of military technology. . . . In other words, today we are at the stage where World War II technology is seeping into industry. . . .

We are now standing in the midst of a technological revolution. Doesn't our nation lack an enterprising attitude toward this new environment? I understand the feelings of people opposed to atomic research. But when you introduce new things, there is bound to be friction. As a union leader I met in America told me, "When something new enters society . . . it necessarily encounters resistance from the old parts of the society. A society able to muster the flexibility to overcome this resistance will be able to develop. A society that caves in to this resistance and stops incorporating new things will perish. American society belongs to the former group. What about Japan?"

. . . If we do not overcome all difficulties of incorporating new technologies, building new industries, and making the effort to progress with the tide of technological revolution, ten or twenty years from now, Japan will find itself growing apart from the advanced nations. Developing nations will catch up to us, and we will become a nation indistinguishable from other Asian nations.

TSURU SHIGETO,
"AMERICA AFTER FOURTEEN YEARS" (1956)

Tsuru Shigeto (1912–2006), one of the most prominent and influential Japanese economists of his generation. After he was expelled from higher school in Nagoya for his involvement in leftist activities, his father sent him to America to study at Harvard College. After graduating in 1935, he continued with graduate study in the Economics Department in the company of Paul Sweezy, Paul Samuelson, and John Kenneth Galbraith. He also joined the John Reed Club, a Communist front organization. After receiving his Ph.D. in 1940, he continued as a lecturer at Harvard. When war broke out he was repatriated to Japan, where he became an economic adviser in the Foreign Ministry. During the Occupation, he served as an adviser to its Economic and Scientific Section, and he worked for the Economic Stabilization Board. As author of the first postwar economic White Paper in 1947, he called for the establishment of a social system based on the working class. In 1949 he joined the faculty of Hitotsubashi University and eventually rose to become its president. This reminiscence about his first postwar visit to America as a visiting professor at Harvard in 1955 captures not only his impressions about how much American material culture had changed during his absence but also his sense of how heavily postwar Japan had been Americanized.

. . .

I first came to America as a student in 1931 in the depth of the Depression, during the same month that Japan began its aggression in Manchuria. More than a decade later I returned to Japan in 1942 in the midst of World War II, and fourteen years after that and exactly twenty-five years since I first came to America, I arrived there once again. Having heard about America's rapid development during and after the war, I expected to see many new things but found not so much had changed. . . .

Come to think of it, when I left America the last time, there were neither television sets nor instant coffee like Nescafé. Nor did most households have appliances like so-called deep freezers. Undoubtedly many new things have been introduced into daily life, but even after being here two months I somehow do not feel like I am in America. When I mentioned this to my wife, I wondered why it was so. . . .

Tsuru Shigeto, "America after Fourteen Years," source: Tsuru Shigeto, "Jūyonenburi no Amerika," in *Tsuru Shigeto chosakushū*, vol. 12 (Tokyo: Kōdansha, 1976), 81–89.

They say that if you leave your hometown as a youth with a knapsack on your back, when you return fifteen years later, you will be struck by how it has changed "culturally," where new buildings have gone up, or how tall the trees have grown. While you remember the good old days, you also notice how much the old hometown has changed. My case is a bit different, however. Unlike the youth returning to his village thinking that it had stagnated, I had no particular unspoken expectations. My feelings on returning to my "second hometown" [Cambridge, Massachusetts] were such that I was unable to form any pat impressions about the America I was revisiting.

Postwar Japan has Americanized more than I had previously recognized, and I believe that left me without any impressions of freshness [in America]. Of course, one need not label [change in postwar Japan] as "Americanization." I have been able to travel abroad on many occasions, thanks to the spread of air travel, and it is clear that as a result of what economists call the "demonstration effect," the daily conveniences and kinds of recreation developed in America are spreading to the rest of the world as well. In the case of Japan, tens of thousands of [American] visitors came to the country under the Occupation, and American popular culture, lifestyles, and ways of thinking have been gradually imported as well. In effect hasn't Japan become like just another American state? (Here I'm not making an issue of administration or politics.) Flying from Tokyo to Boston or New York no longer seems to give one a sense of crossing national boundaries. It feels no different from flying from Hawaii to Los Angeles.

American military personnel and their families arriving in Japan do not feel they are stepping into a foreign country. There are radio stations broadcasting to Americans, American post offices that handle domestic mail, and "America villages" [where military dependents live]. Until recently, the Japanese Self-Defense Forces even used American military manuals.

Of course, things are not so convenient for those of us going in the other direction. Nevertheless, being in America made me realize firsthand the remarkable extent to which the general atmosphere in postwar Japan has become Americanized. It strikes me as symbolic that today Japanese people returning home from America have trouble finding suitable souvenirs. . . .

The lapse of fourteen years is great, nevertheless. . . . Statistics clearly show a remarkable increase of automobiles and their effects. Places like

automobiles in America

downtown New York, where cars had already reached the saturation point, have not changed much, but the changes in Cambridge, Massachusetts, have been dramatic. Devices for purchasing the right to park, called "parkometers," are ubiquitous, lining streets at car-length intervals. The lack of parking space has pushed residents further and further out into the suburbs, and it is now common for commuters to drive partway, park in a convenient lot, and then travel the rest of their commute on rail. The creation of the "Route 128" train station on the [outskirts of] Boston is a case in point. Express trains stop at the station, which is surrounded by a parking lot but nothing else. It is a bizarre sight to see hundreds of automobiles of all colors lined up there all day.

I hear that Volkswagens have suddenly become popular now that some families have begun to own more than one car. If one tries to buy a Volkswagen today, the wait is more than half a year. I think Japan may have a chance to enter the American market for compact vehicles, just as it has succeeded in becoming a competitor with Germany in cameras.

With the increase in automobiles, roads have improved. I imagined that New York's [Merritt Parkway] might extend all the way to Boston, but now there is a separate parallel express highway under construction. I was also surprised to find that a multilevel road two or three stories tall has been completed near Boston's already densely constructed [Haymarket] area. Buying the land and relocating the shops must have been in themselves very difficult. Compared to this, the construction in the Sukiya Bridge area in Tokyo appears to be mere child's play.

It seems that the number of automobiles will continue to increase well into the future. In recent years, however, an even more drastic increase can be seen in motorboats and other recreational water vehicles. . . . It is economic common sense that expenditures on durable consumer goods will rise as income rises, but I had not imagined that motorboats would become so widely owned. A friend tells me that most people can now afford their food, utility, and clothing expenses and that rising income is spent on homes and new kinds of durable consumer goods. Some consumer durables, such as automobiles, refrigerators, washing machines, and deep freezers, have become necessities.

Deep freezers, I think, did not even exist when I was in America before the war. The big ones are larger than a *nagamochi* [a traditional-style Japanese storage box], and the small ones hold about 2.5 cubic feet. The deep freezer is used for storing frozen foods and leftovers. A friend told me that his family did not need to buy beef for a year. They had bought a whole cow when beef prices were especially low and stored half of it in a deep freezer. The price of beef rose during that time, so they saved a lot of money.

A 2.5 cubic foot freezer costs about three hundred dollars. It would seem to most Japanese quite a luxury item. However, thanks to the spread of payment by monthly installments, less-affluent families are able to buy them. *Life* magazine reported on a poor Negro family living in Shady Grove, Alabama, who were ostracized for speaking out on racial discrimination and forced out of town. When they left, the one thing they took along was their deep freezer. To provide themselves with food they slaughtered their nineteen chickens, harvested their potatoes and corn, and put them all into their deep freezer. They had not completed monthly installment payments on the freezer, but relatives and friends lent them money to rescue them from their predicament.

Come to think of it, the monthly installment payment system has spread rapidly since the prewar period. The subject came up when I visited the famous historian Professor Arthur Schlesinger Sr. His wife complained about the unethical nature of this practice. She thought it was unethical to consume above one's present means by borrowing against future income. It is difficult for the older generation to accept. For an economist, the spread of this system is interesting, because it is a new factor that did not exist in the prewar period. The manufacturer has become a provider of credit and taken on the role of a bank. Firms like General Motors have established separate companies for this purpose. Instead of being deposited into bank accounts, the company's profits are diverted toward consumer credit, where they earn interest rates just as effectively. . . .

Compared to the prewar period, the number of Japanese in Cambridge and the number of Americans who know about Japan have risen substantially. Before the war, even if we include naval officers and diplomats sent abroad to study, I think there were not more than ten Japanese studying at Harvard. How many are there today? Apart from their families, I think there must be about fifty. Unlike the old days, many young scholars have brought along their spouses, creating an atmosphere of a Japanese student "colony." It is not really correct to call it a "colony." The students have made close personal ties with Americans in their specialties, and they have blended very well into the university environment. Young people are much more cosmopolitan than our generation was twenty years ago.

ODA MAKOTO,
"THE OTHER SIDE OF AMERICAN SOCIETY" (1961)

As a middle school student the novelist and social critic Oda Makoto (1931–2007) witnessed the August 14, 1945, fire bombing of Osaka. He saw people frantically run for their lives only to die in the flames. These scenes of death were a far cry from romanticized notions of dying for the nation propagated by the wartime state. Since the Osaka raid took place after the atomic bombings, the Soviet entry into the war against Japan, and the government's decision to surrender, the deaths seemed all the more meaningless. The Occupation's democratization reforms, especially the beginning of coeducation, when his school merged with a neighboring girl's school, also had an important impact on his life. Oda later remarked that these two formative experiences, "bombs and democracy," were what America meant to him. After graduating from Tokyo University, Oda Makoto traveled to the United States as a Fulbright scholar in 1958. "I just felt like seeing America. That is all there was to it," he later wrote. His seemingly unintellectual straightforwardness, together with his breezy, street-level, unromantic descriptions and stories, made his account of his travels abroad an immediate best seller. So was his 1962 novel, *Amerika,* about a Japanese facing racial discrimination in the United States. An outspoken critic of the political and social establishment, in the 1960s he organized Beheiren (Citizens' Federation for Peace in Vietnam), which spearheaded opposition to the Vietnam War in Japan.

. . .

The Gloomy Gay Bar: The Bottom of American Society [story of T & K, a gay couple]

T and K were "husband and wife." The two men were "homosexuals." When that became clear, the flustered newspaper reporter [who was visiting me] jumped up and fled the room.

Perhaps this is the reaction of a normal Japanese man. If that is so, my reaction would make me very abnormal. To avoid misunderstandings, I will clarify that I am not gay. I am what they call "straight" (this word refers to normal people who are not gay), and I prefer girls. My reaction to continue living with T and K . . . was the product of my abnormal curiosity. . . .

Oda Makoto, "The Other Side of American Society," source: Oda Makoto, *Nandemo mite yarō* (Tokyo: Kawade shobō shinsha, 1961), 34–51.

T and K's apartment had three rooms. The "husband and wife" slept in the master bedroom, and my room was across from the living room. It was a messy room, somewhere between a study and a den. In one corner was a folding bed, where I slept. . . .

Although T and K were "husband and wife," that does not mean that one of them acted and spoke effeminately, wore dresses, did the cooking, and worked at a sewing machine. Such couples do exist, but they are considered a special subgroup called "drags." There were two or three night clubs in New York that hired such people as "waitresses." One was the secret hangout of a certain Japanese executive during his business visits to New York. I remember later reading a surreal commentary he wrote on American life, marveling that the Americans really know how to enjoy life. "We need to learn from them," he said. Business executives are creatures able to think the most preposterous things. They are either too busy, or they have too much time on their hands.

"Drags" are abnormal in the gay world, but T and K were very normal in the sense that both looked like normal masculine men. Since they are gay, feminine tendencies must be lurking inside them somewhere, but they do not manifest themselves as they do with the "drags." I call them "husband and wife," but it is not as if one is husband and the other wife. I have come to know many gay "husband and wife" couples, and most of them are of the T and K type. In any case, it takes some getting use to. I even found myself shaking my head as I looked at these two gigantic men living together as "husband and wife."

When I told them that I was going to take a thorough look at the issue, T responded by taking me to a gay bar. "I bet these don't exist in Japan," he said. Like a nationalist who boasts of everything Japanese, I answered, "Of course they do. Tokyo has everything." But observing the dreary gloom of the place, I had second thoughts. Indeed, there might not be such places in Japan—the mecca of bars, cafés, and restaurants—or even in Europe.

At a gay bar in Greenwich Village the men were all standing, packed into a small basement bar. When I say "packed," I mean it literally. It was like the standing-room space in the back of a movie theater that has sold out its seats. Overcrowded and wreaking of toilet odors, it was a dirty and desolate place.

A not-so-nice-looking man standing at the door let us in. They call such men, who work at other bars too, "bouncers." Their job is to keep a lookout for the police and other unwelcome guests and to "bounce" them if they do arrive. Sometime after my first visit, I took a certain American author there. Thanks to his habit of dressing neatly like a conformist, he was mistaken for a policeman and was unceremoniously "bounced."

There was a strange atmosphere in the place. I mean that it was completely different from that in a Tokyo gay bar, an erotically grotesque space where effeminate men serve you sake. Such syrupy hedonism did not exist here. This place was as dry as a desert, prosaically businesslike, rough, and above all lonely.

As I stood there in a daze, T called me over to buy beer at the counter.

Bars in the West, especially bars in America, are places where you go to drink alcohol, nothing more. In exchange for your money, you have a glass shoved at you roughly. Of course there are no women to meet either. But even ordinary bars like this began to look very elegant when compared to the gay bar.

You pay a dollar. The bartender opens the beer bottle and hands it to you. That's it. No glass. Taken aback, I looked around and saw everybody drinking directly out of the bottles. (The scene was rather Freudian.) Drinking from bottles, talking loud and fast, men pushed their way through the room hunting for new partners. Feeling bored, I began to gulp down my beer. T stopped me with an exceedingly practical warning: "Hey, don't drink so fast. That's your minimum drink requirement." Sure enough, everybody seemed to be eternally nursing one precious beer bottle, whose contents must have turned lukewarm. This seemed to suggest even stronger Freudian connotations.

After my first experience, I went on an adventure tour, hopping through New York's gay bars. I don't know if it is true, but I heard that gay bars have formed a sort of union that pools funds to bribe the police not to raid them. Once the money runs out, however, a gay bar is raided right away, the owner and customers are arrested, and the place is closed down.

All the gay bars are essentially the same. They have dance floors where men dance cheek-to-cheek. This merely conjured the bleak and dreary image of male inmates dancing in the shadow of prison towers. . . .

In short, the gay bar seems to be a kind of social gathering place. No, it is too dirty and shabby to call it that. "Assembly hall" would be a better way to put it. Some come there not simply with the practical goal of finding a new partner; they just drift in, as if compelled by some more amorphous impulse. I think these men are in a perpetually unstable emotional state. By joining a group and escaping into it, they can finally achieve peace of mind.

At a gay bar in Greenwich Village, I befriended a Negro man. He was a strange person who hated jazz despite being black. He took up a position in the darkest corner of the dark bar and continually deposited nickels into the jukebox. He was not playing jazz records. I don't know if it is true of jukeboxes in Japan, but in America some clever jukeboxes have a blank record that plays soundlessly for three minutes. [My acquaintance] was paying for silence. Nickel after nickel, it was the same silent song. "That's stupid. You should just go home and sleep," I said irritably. He was an enormous man, like someone just come out of the jungle. This twentieth-century African chief confessed weakly, "When I'm not here with everybody, I get so anxious I can't sleep."

The Smell of America: The Lonely Runaways, the "Beats"

"If you're going to write about gay people, you definitely need to write about the beat generation," a woman beat poet told me.

One Sunday, she invited me to spend a quiet afternoon in the park. According to her there is only one "park" in New York—Washington Square Park, located in the middle of Greenwich Village. On Sunday afternoons, beat youths, who seem to have no better pastime than to gather in the broken fountain, play their guitars and dance like mad.

The woman poet's wish was to spend a "quiet afternoon," so I invited her away from the raucous performance to the surrounding benches under the trees. She was upset. "I am not like Japanese people," she said, "so places like this make me unbearably nervous." We went back to the raucous fountain area and spent our "quiet" afternoon there. She seemed happy.

"What is this, a Hottentot headhunting dance?" I sneered, but she just kept smiling.

I saw many gays among the beats at the fountain. I had met some of them at gay bars. When they spotted me, they gave out a curious shout, somewhere between "Yo!" and "Oh!"

Gays and beats are inextricably linked, in the sense that both are products of American modern society. To tell the truth, as I have been writing on and on about the gays, I suddenly realized something. Although gayness is a . . . sexual issue, I am really not talking about sex at all. The topic may seem obscene and grotesque, but I did not feel that way at all. It seemed more quotidian, more businesslike, more prosaic, dry, dull, and, above all, lonely. To put it more plainly, while I was describing gays, I was really writing about American society.

Wherever you go in America, you find supermarkets. For better or

Supermarkets in America (handwritten annotation)

worse, supermarkets are beginning to spread in Japan, so I probably don't need to explain this, but at a supermarket you take the items you want off the shelf, pile them into what looks like a baby stroller, and go the store's exit. A clerk calculates the total cost on a cash register, and then you pay. Many Americans go to the supermarket by car on weekends to buy food for the following week. Supermarkets are quite crowded on Saturday afternoons.

The A&P Company runs one chain of supermarkets. Since these A&P supermarkets can be found everywhere, they are typical of America. Wherever you go in America, they arrange the merchandise in exactly the same way. For example, if cans of soup are in the middle of the third shelf from the entrance at the A&P in Boston, they are in exactly the same place in a small country town near San Francisco. Once you are inside an A&P, you cannot tell whether you are on the East Coast or the West Coast or even whether you are in a good section of town or in the slums.

Of course, this is true not just of A&P stores. All supermarkets sell only canned goods and nicely wrapped frozen foods, so there is not much difference among them. When you open the door of any supermarket, whether in New York, Chicago, or in some town in the state of Omaha *[sic]*, the same smell will strike your nose. Well, that may be an exaggeration. The smell is not all that strong. Since the stores carry no fresh foods—even vegetables are kept in pretty wrapping—the nose is certainly not overwhelmed by a heavy odor, such as mackerel cooking on a grill. It is a very sanitary smell. It is a smell you could call harmless and useless. The smell of mackerel cooking whets some people's appetites, and it makes others nauseous, but the smell of a supermarket would never have that effect. It does not make one feel nauseous, nor does it make one feel hungry. It is like the smell in a Japanese pharmacy. And this smell, of course, is exactly the same on the West Coast as on the East Coast and in uptown or in slum supermarkets.

Indeed, this smell can be found not only in America. On my way home from America, I stopped in Teheran to stay with an American poet friend who was teaching English at the University of Teheran. One day I went with him to a PX-like store attached to the American Embassy. When we opened the door, that same familiar smell, that sanitary, harmless, useless smell, flowed into my nostrils.

"The smell of America," I said, and my friend nodded his head in agreement. In fact, I felt as though I were hallucinating—that I was in some small midwestern town, not in a small corner of the Middle East. In the store I found canned goods, frozen foods, American cigarettes, *Time* (a magazine read by most educated Americans), and *Life* (a magazine that can be found lying around almost any American home). And since Japanese goods are now enjoying a boom in America, the store even sold small bottles of bad-tasting sake (which the Americans pronounce as "saki").

If I were to translate this "smell of America" into high-flown language, then I would call it "conformism," a word that appears in any discussion of American society today. Everyone eats the same things, wears the same clothes, lives in the same kind of houses, thinks the same, talks with the same manners, and acts the same. This is certainly one of the biggest problems facing American society today.

To rid American supermarkets of the "smell of America," you would have to change all the items on the shelves. It would mean throwing out all the canned goods and the frozen foods and replacing them with fresh tomatoes or with fish still twitching on the counter. But that is probably impossible, given the way that society is arranged or, to put it more precisely, the way that our twentieth-century civilization is constructed. If that is the case, there are only two positions to take: we can adjust ourselves to the smell (that is, submit to conformism), or we can escape from the smell.

In the final analysis, beatniks and gays are perhaps fugitives from the smell of America. They dislike, detest, and ridicule conformism and a society that so overflows with it. But of course they do not have the strength either to destroy conformism or to change society in a fundamental way. On the contrary, there is nothing more conformist than their responses and reactions to conformism. They all laugh in the same hysterical way, and they all dance like cannibals in the same way. Everywhere you see the same goatees, sweaters, and slacks, and from every direction you hear the same sounds of jazz and bongo drums. They may be going wild, but they are all going wild in the same way—and to the same degree (but probably not to a degree that will actually either inflict damage on society or smash it up and turn it into something else). They form their own groups. If they remain isolated as individuals, the pressure of society will easily crush them, so unconsciously they flock together like schools of minnows, trying to confirm their own existence within these groups.

The beatniks probably suffer from infantile regression syndrome. The Great Depression is already a distant memory. It appears that American society today is tranquil and, more than anything else, affluent and that this situation will continue forever. Who are the beatniks? A bunch of brats raising cries of rebellion as they immerse themselves in the midst of "The Affluent Society" (the name of a best seller). No, let me put it more harshly. They are spoiled kids pretending to be adults, who bawl and throw tantrums in front of a grownup called "society."

The relationship between gays and beatniks is symbolic. Just as gays do not produce children, the beatniks do not actively contribute anything, whether good or bad, to American society. They could do so only if they had the ability to perceive what stands behind the smell of America. But the beatniks completely lack that ability—what is sometimes called a social perspective. This is true not only of the beatniks. Contemporary American intellectuals are even more lacking in this ability.

I don't feel like brushing the beatniks off as someone else's problem, however. When I say that the beatniks suffer from infantile regression syndrome, I am simply pointing out the enormity of what drove the beatniks to this point. To put it simply, I think that it is the smell of America. Once again, this is not just someone else's problem. Just consider the matter of supermarkets alone—several if not dozens of them have already sprung up in our own Tokyo.

What I felt in America, and what I have said over and over again since then, was not the overwhelming weight of Western culture. What I felt— at least what weighed on me—was the oppressiveness of twentieth-century civilization. What I felt more than anything else in America was that our twentieth-century civilization has reached an impasse—or to put it more bluntly, that it is desperately searching for a way to escape from a blind alley.

Perhaps that is the essence of what I call "the smell of America." Unfortunately no way out of the cul-de-sac has been found, and even worse, it appears that no way will ever be found. Whenever I looked at contemporary paintings or listened to music or watched ballet, I thought to myself that the American arts contained something that is more or less beatnik. And I felt that there was no way out. Art was desperately searching for something. The search had set its heart pounding, but in the end there was no way out. Trying harder only led deeper and deeper into a blind alley. It was trivialism—a preposterously enormous trivialism. There was perfection, to be sure, but viewed from a slightly different perspective, it was somehow an empty perfection.

I felt as though it was like a huge bonsai. If small-scale trivialism lies behind Japanese art, then American culture is the product of large-scale trivialism. Yet the two are strangely similar. Both take a force that tries to grow and expand naturally, then bend, twist, and force it into a strange shape. In other words, both cultures resemble bonsai. . . .

What I am talking about here has nothing to do with politics. When I use the phrase "our twentieth-century civilization," I am including the socialist countries as well. As long as the socialist countries move in the direction of a mechanized civilization based on automation and standardization, sooner or later they will find themselves in an exitless cavern; like the beatniks, they will confront the smell of America. But this is a problem not just for the socialist countries. It will also be a problem for the western European countries, for our own Japan, and someday for the Arab League countries, India, and the newly independent developing countries in Africa. That is what I mean when I say that the beatniks are not just someone else's problem. One can already see a manifestation of this problem outside the United States in the "angry young men" in England. However, in their case, the root of the problem lies in the English social structure itself, and unlike for the beatniks, it is not so directly tied up with . . . the smell of America. As for the so-called angry young men in Japan, I still do not have any idea of what they are so angry about.

The interesting thing about my beatnik friends is that most of them are from small towns in the countryside—Jack Kerouac, the founder of the beatniks, grew up in some rural town in New England—or from the suburbs near big cities, like Scarsdale, where T's mother lives. This is not accidental; it is inevitable.

If you live in New York and don't like supermarkets, for example, you can go to the slum area where T and K live, and an old vegetable peddler comes around with his pushcart. If you don't like bread wrapped in waxed paper, then you can go to the Italian section and buy fresh-baked bread. Or if you don't like Hollywood movies, you can go watch films like *Rashomon* that are intellectually and artistically high class. In short, in big cities like New York or Chicago, you can live without sensing the smell of America all that much.

But is that possible in a rural small town or in suburbia?

T's mother often invited me to Scarsdale. Whenever I went, she would always invite other guests for dinner. I would go shopping at the supermarket with her. We would return home in her shiny 1957 automobile, and her entire house would begin to radiate the smell of America. The dinner guests would start to arrive. They were always "conformists" who hated beatniks. (The Greenwich Village beatniks also appeared to detest the ladies and gentlemen of Scarsdale.) The topics of conversation would rarely depart from chitchat about articles in *Time* and *Life*, and after a while I could fairly well predict what they would say about this or that. It helped me improve my spoken English a good deal.

Then we would decide to go to a movie. We would go to what is called a drive-in movie theater, watching from inside the car as we sat a neat row of other shiny automobiles. Of course, the movie being shown was a Hollywood film, not *Rashomon.*

It takes only an hour to get from Scarsdale to New York, so it is not much of a problem to make the trip. If you get bored, you can always visit Chinatown or Greenwich Village, but if you live in some small midwestern town, that is not impossible. The problem is much more acute.

After living in America for a year, I went on a trip through the Midwest and the South. Following my principle of "seeing it all," I planned to take a look at any place, even rural towns, that was the least bit famous. I followed the plan assiduously.

Looking back on it now, I realize that this was an absurdly boring plan. Even before I was halfway through my trip, I already knew exactly what the next small city would look like.

I was traveling by bus, so the first thing that I would see was the bus station. Wherever I went, they were not the least bit different. In the center of the waiting room were large steel lockers, where you could leave your luggage, and to the left or right was a cafeteria. When you go to eat, you find spaghetti from a can and crunchy half-defrosted frozen veal cutlets. The food tasted the same and cost the same everywhere. Burping the same kind of burp, I would make my way out into the town. When I looked to the left, there was always a gentle slope leading up to the center of town. After a leisurely walk of four or five blocks to the top of the slope, I would come to the main street, where buses and trolley buses ran. To the right, there was always a Woolworth dime store and to the left a drug store having a big sale. Fed up with that, I would cross the main street and head down the hill in the opposite direction. When I got to the foot of the hill, there was always a park or a river. Feeling like a fool, I would look behind me, and there was an A&P supermarket, the smell of America—

It is not just the beatniks who want to escape; it was even a passing traveler like me. For fugitives from this kind of small town or from suburbia, the "smell of anti-America," however faint, in such international cities as New York, Chicago, and San Francisco, has an overpowering allure.

YASUOKA SHŌTARŌ,
"LIVING IN NASHVILLE" (1960–1961)

The author Yasuoka Shōtarō (1920–) led an unsettled life as a child. His father, an army veterinarian, transferred frequently from post to post. Growing up with few stable friendships, he did poorly in school, which he came to dislike. After failing to enter a university several times, he finally passed the Keiō entrance exam in 1941. When the government decided to conscript university students in 1943, Yasuoka was sent off to Manchuria, where he developed tuberculosis. He spent the early postwar years writing fiction under the influence of the so-called Aesthetic School. His career took off with his nomination for the 1951 Akutagawa Prize for a short story about a love affair between the protagonist and a housemaid working for an Occupation official. He soon became associated with a "new generation" of writers that included Kojima Nobuo and Endō Shūsaku. His fiction was notable for its attentiveness to the mundane details of everyday life. He usually viewed it from the vantage point of an underdog dedicated to exposing its hypocrisy, a stance he adopted in his journal recording a stay in Tennessee, sponsored by the Rockefeller Foundation during the early 1960s. In the passages below, he not only describes the social awkwardness that embarrassed many Japanese visitors to America but also offers his view of the complexity of the race issue in American society.

. . .

December 4, 1960

In Japan I had been told many times to beware of the dreaded American dinner party. Do not pick up your fork before the hostess starts eating; wait till the hostess finishes eating before putting down your fork; wipe your mouth with a napkin before drinking from your glass so that you do not leave a mark; do not remain silent but do not dominate the conversation; and so forth. Just thinking about these things weighed heavily on my mind, but in a town like this [Nashville, Tennessee] where you cannot even go for a drink outside the home, it is understandable that these events are a necessity.

Professor T., an economics professor with whom I had no direct connection, invited me to dinner, presumably out of sympathy as a

Yasuoka Shōtarō, "Living in Nashville," source: Yasuoka Shōtarō, *Amerika kanjō ryokō* (Tokyo: Iwanami shoten, 2000), 42–48, 84–92.

fellow Oriental. I must be grateful for this kindness. Still, I could not help dwelling on the fact that it was an Oriental and not an American who invited this newly arrived foreigner over to his house. Was this the result of racial discrimination? I know that it is pointless to think like this, but I cannot help it. I think that as long as the carnal scent of human blood endures, it is inevitable that human beings harbor prejudices toward one another. Prejudice may even involve "love." If true, this town, where prejudice manifests itself in a prototypical manner, will be an interesting place for me.

All this was mere speculation. Once I thought people might actually be viewing me with prejudice, I felt blinded and irritated. It was as though somebody had placed me in front of a thick wall, controlling my gaze via remote control. My irritation was compounded by the fact that I could not even tell whether this wall was simply a figment of my imagination. . . .

Gathered for dinner at Professor T.'s house were five or six international students from China. They were introduced to me as Mr. Lee, Mr. Ho, Mr. Wo, Mr. Ma, Mr. Another Ho. Unfortunately after the quick introduction I promptly forgot their names. I could not help feeling intimidated by the fact that some were Taiwanese military officers being trained by the American army. Professor K. and his wife, both second-generation Japanese Americans, were also guests. Professor T.'s wife was the only white person in the group.

As Professor T. prepared the dinner in the kitchen, Mrs. T. entertained us. This was a vexing situation. I understand this is not unusual in American homes, but with all the yellow faces around I could not help seeing her as the sole "Western woman." Of course, the conversation was all in English. In a display of welcome Mrs. T wore a Chinese-style silk dress on her overweight body. This too had an intimidating effect on me.

"Beautiful!"

"Wonderful!"

"Very sweet!"

Some of my fellow guests uttered these appreciative words with natural ease. All I could notice was that her white neck was turning red as the tight-fitting collar chafed it. I failed to summon a single polite phrase. Mrs. T. then excitedly put on a red gown decorated with gold and silver dragons, which she had specially ordered from Japan. Now it was my turn to say something. As I watched her prance around in her glittering gown, her image reminded me of a boxer stepping into

the ring. I could not rid my mind of this appalling image. I itched to
say something but could not and fell silent once again.

Once silent, there is no recovering. As conversational bullets flew
wildly across the room, I could not summon the courage to step into
the line of fire. The guide to party manners says that silence is the
worst offense, but there was really nothing I could do about it. All
I could do was endure my headache and wait for time to pass.

Finally it was time to eat. Professor T.'s dishes of wonton soup,
steamed dumplings, and fried rice were spread across the table. I re-
trieved a piece of wonton from the soup bowl with my stainless steel
spoon, slurped it into my mouth. Finally I succeeded in uttering my
first English phrase: "Very good."

"Dōmo arigatō," Professor T. responded jokingly in proper Japanese, allowing me to counter in turn with laughter. Speech and laughter
are such wonderful abilities, I found myself thinking, as if discovering
a profound truth. Then alcohol was served.

"Whiskey or beer?" Mrs. T. asked.

Overjoyed by my newly discovered voice, I answered, "I think American whiskey is not as good as Japanese whiskey, so I'll have beer. Some
say that Japanese beer is also the world's best, but I don't agree . . ."

What made me say such a thing? All I can say is that the table froze
in silence. Mrs. T., the bottle of whiskey motionless in her hand, directed
her cold gray gaze at me. She declared quietly, "I don't like Japanese
sake." Panic started to overcome me. On the one hand, I reprimanded
myself for being so rude a guest as to insult the drink offered to me.
On the other hand, I thought it was common knowledge that American
whiskey was not good. Why did Mrs. T. have to get angry at me for
this? I thought Americans liked honesty.

Things having come this far, it was best to relapse into silence. If
I get tossed out of the house, I thought to myself, I will not be able to
find my way home in the dark. But I was provoked when Mrs. K., the
Japanese American woman sitting next to me, pecked at her dumpling
with knife and fork and said in English, "I cannot bring myself to like
Japanese food. That raw fish on top of rice, what do you call it? Oh
yes, sushi. I can't stand that food."

"You grew up in America. Who are you to judge sushi?" I itched
to counter. But if I said that, a five-mile walk home in the dark
awaited me. With much effort, I succeeded in restraining my "patriotic" outburst.

Two hours later, after the party had ended, I found myself struck by an even stranger feeling. Mrs. K. began to talk with my wife in Japanese in the car ride back home.

"When I was little, I stayed with my grandmother in Japan. . . ."

She spoke with the accent of someone who had lived along the Inland Sea in Japan. If she came from that region, she must have eaten lots of fresh fish.

"When you speak about Japan with people over here, you have to be careful," she continued. "Even though Father and Mother are American, whenever something happens, it's Jap, Jap."

I didn't know what to say. Gazing outside at the smog-lined sky, I imagined Professor T. with sleeves rolled up, competently sifting flour and preparing his native land's cuisine. . . .

January 11, 1961

O., an international student, has a big red sign in on his bumper that reads 日本 ("Japan"). Why does he do such a thing? These Chinese characters are merely decorative and convey no meaning to Americans who cannot read them or understand them. But I cannot deny that I have tended to act like O. This derives from the constant feeling that I embody "Japan itself," while everything around me is non-"Japan." In this quiet town it is a rare for even a dog to bark at me, but if one does I find myself looking at an "American dog." . . .

As soon as some men arrive in a foreign country, they itch to visit its prostitutes. I think I now understand their feelings. No doubt it has to do with a sense of liberation, sexual desire, curiosity. But even more so it stems from a desire to conquer the other country's women with money. Of course, a separate question is: Does buying a woman assimilate you into the country a little bit, or does it make you more patriotic? I feel the same way whenever I encounter black people on the street. To put it bluntly, when I see them I have a sensation of relief that may be connected on some level with the psychology behind hiring prostitutes. Of course, a sense of superiority toward black people is shameful. It is merely the obverse of a sense of inferiority toward white people. But it is not that easy to detach oneself completely from such a sense of superiority (or inferiority).

In Japan I was told that racism in the South was directed toward people of African descent. The word *colored* referred not to nonwhite people in general but more specifically to the country's former slaves and their descendants. . . . However, I have come to see that this is not the case. Here in Nashville humans are classified by color. If you have a dark face you will be discriminated against regardless of whether or not you are of African descent. When Indian people go out, the men wear turbans and the women wear saris. If they do not, they will not be allowed into movie theaters and restaurants.

When two students from Indonesia, one relatively pale and the other relatively dark, went into a restaurant, the pale one got what he ordered, but the dark one was refused service. I hear the dark-skinned Indonesian is the future superintendent general of the police. "If this is how Americans are," he fumes, "I will throw all of them into the sea if they come to Indonesia."

Perhaps this racism can be excused as a peculiar regional custom. However, one cannot help but feel enraged to hear of a Korean student who was forced to quit his job as a server in the university cafeteria because students thought he was "dirty." In the South, cooking and serving food is a black occupation. It may be incomprehensible to us that people so discriminated against are allowed to cook and serve food, but it is the local custom. Perhaps it follows that refusing to eat food served by a "dirty" Korean of the yellow race is also mere "custom." If so, we cannot silently accept discrimination toward black people as somebody else's custom.

After I came here, I finally understood that the [black problem] is essentially a white people's problem. White people talk about the [black problem] as a matter of white conscience. This has nothing to do with black people themselves. The "black people" referred to in the [black problem] are already a part of the white people. We who are neither white nor black are not included, and, as a result, in a sense we feel inferior to black people. But once we try to empathize with black people as fellow colored people, this sense of inferiority turns into a sense of superiority.

I once heard a Japanese well-traveled in the South proclaim proudly, "I relieved myself in the black bathroom." His action was meaningless. It did not annoy white people, and it did not entail sympathy toward black people. All he achieved was to feel a fleeting sense of superiority and self-satisfaction from the act of urinating in a segregated bathroom. We do not feel at ease relieving ourselves in the white bathroom either. That is another problem, however. . . .

To be honest, my knowledge about the conflict between the North and South or why the conflict continues today is limited to what I have read in books. It is clear to me that this conflict is absurdly serious. For example, when people in this region talk about "the war," they refer to the Civil War rather than the two world wars. In universities, descendants of Southern soldiers receive a half-price discount on tuition. Churches have split into separate branches, like the Southern Baptist and Southern Methodist. Lincoln is the enemy, and General Lee's birthday is a holiday. The Republicans hold no seats in the state legislature, and elections are fought between Democratic candidates.

All this may seem strange in the face of the notion of American homogeneity. Come to think of it, the notion of homogeneity is a product of daily life based on mass-produced goods (homes, cars, furniture, clothes, food, etc.). But just because Americans eat the same canned food does not mean they all think alike. On the contrary, customs and laws vary widely among states and regions, and individual freedom is respected to the utmost everywhere. It was in such a context that Southerners asserted their right to own slaves and their right to secede from the nation if this right was denied. Northerners, on the other hand, saw this "freedom" as a threat to national unity. They sought to suppress the sedition of the Southerners. This was the cause of the Civil War, and these were the basic principles over which it was fought. In other words, the two sides fought over the meaning of "freedom," and the [black problem] was merely a by-product of their conflicting interpretations of the concept. (There may be a resemblance here to the relationship between the Greater East Asia War and the liberation of Southeast Asian nations. It is questionable to say that the Japanese military fought for the goal of liberating "Greater East Asia," but nevertheless these nations did become independent after the war.)

The black people in the South were also liberated from slavery, but this was the result not so much of the North's "ideals" winning over the South's "injustice." Rather, it was the result of wartime demand for human resources that forced both armies to free slaves. Whatever the motives, in the end the black people were liberated. This was doubly humiliating to the defeated South. Not only did the Southerners, defeated in war, lose slaves that had been their private property, but also the Northern army ousted city mayors, town mayors, local postmasters, and others and replaced them with black people. (This purge of Southern officials took place between 1865 and 1872, a period that lasted as long as the purge of Japanese officials by MacArthur's headquarters during the Occupation.) To chasten the Southerners, the Northern army deliberately put black people in positions of authority. This shows that the Northerners also viewed black people as "tools." . . .

The only thing we can say with certainty is that neither Northerners nor Southerners view black people as human beings like themselves. This reminds me of an eerie feeling I had when I visited the accounting section of my host foundation in New York. The office was high up on the fortieth or fiftieth floor, and all you could see from its big windows were clouds and skyscrapers. The impeccably clean and transparently bright office seemed to float in the air. After receiving funds for my travel and living expenses, the black manager shook my hand and wished me well.

His hand was neatly groomed with trimmed fingernails and smooth skin. As I looked around the room I was impressed by how neatly dressed everybody was. Suddenly it struck me that all the staff in the room were black. Dressed in immaculate suits and silent as an audience at a string quartet concert, they typed and examined documents with elegant movements. The silence. The perfect discipline. It made me think of objects on display in a glass case. Indeed, the entire office began to look like a display exhibiting "trust." It seemed to demonstrate silently to international students from all over the world: "See how we trust black people like this? We let them handle all the cash transactions."

Was I just imagining this? Perhaps I was. But I could not help being struck by how unnatural it was that not only all of the staff were black but that they were all dressed elegantly in a way that I had not seen anywhere outside this office. Do they represent the vanguard of black people achieving "first-class citizen" status? A first-class citizen can vote and join any school, church, or club. The ultimate goal of the civil rights movement is for all black people to become first-class citizens.

I cannot learn to like this term. If there is a first, there must be a second and third. (Where would I be categorized?) *First, second,* and *third* have a blunt and deterministic ring absent in words like *prince, marquis, viscount, count,* and *baron,* which signify aristocratic hierarchy. It may not be a bad thing for those in the lower strata of society to see their position clearly, and it may be a good thing to express their class position in clear language. And of course black people should strive to become "first-class citizens." But I am appalled that in the final analysis their goal of being "first" is nothing more than being "first-class white."

The discrimination between the "first" and those below them is based on whether an individual appears white or black. The more educated black people are, the more they tend to be overly sensitive to appearances. It reminds me of the Rokumeikan era in Japan [when elite Japanese men wore Western-style clothes and grew Western-style beards]. Driving a brand-new white Cadillac through the slums and wearing lavish furs and jewelry are actions of relatively less-educated black people, but these actions are a manifestation of a general weakness in black people: an obsession with appearances. . . .

In any case, because black people are hypersensitive to skin color, they sometimes act more haughtily toward poor whites or yellow people than the average white person does. In turn this is reflected in the sentiments of white people. Thus, the tendency to discriminate on the basis of color spreads and deepens everywhere.

I think this situation is probably what lay behind the white students' boycott of the Korean student waiter in the cafeteria.

ETŌ JUN, "AMERICA AS I SEE IT" (1963)

The literary critic and essayist Etō Jun (1933–99) was the son of a banker and the grandson of an admiral. Like many other patriotic youths of his generation, Etō had romantic dreams of dying on the battlefield. As rumors spread of an impending American invasion, Etō imagined that he would kill one American soldier before dying himself. He associated the end of World War II more with destruction and loss than with relief and liberation. Unlike the generation of intellectuals who dominated the early postwar scene, Etō was too young to experience a sense of liberation from an oppressive wartime regime, but his privileged family's affluent lifestyle was destroyed by postwar hyperinflation. After he graduated from Keiō University, his essays in the prominent literary journal *Mita Bungaku* established his reputation as a critic. His biography of Natsume Sōseki, a Meiji period writer who constantly wrestled with problems of cultural and personal identity, was widely acclaimed. During the 1950s Etō associated Marxism and progressive politics with the quest for a better order, but the mob violence of the 1960 anti-treaty demonstrations alienated him from both. In 1962 he went to Princeton University on a Rockefeller Foundation fellowship, and in his later years, he became a vocal neoconservative critic.

. . .

Etō Jun, "America as I See It," source: Etō Jun, "Watakushi no mita Amerika," *Asahi shinbun*, September 9–12, 1963.

While living in Princeton, New Jersey, since last September, the distance between me and "America" seems to be diminishing as fast as a taxi meter goes "click click." Without my realizing it, I have become less and less aware of being in "America." Recently the meter seems to have clicked again. The other day I went to talk with the head of the university library staff about the assignment of a study. As I was about to leave after our business was done, he smiled one of those unique outgoing American smiles and asked, "Mr. Etō, are you from California?" Without thinking I answered, "No, I'm from Japan, from Tokyo." It was only at that moment that I fully realized with a start that I really was in the United States. In my very bones I understood how overpowering this country is.

What I mean is that America has a tremendous latent power to assimilate outsiders. In the past "America" or "American" things never held any particular attraction for me. As a child I dreamt of going to Europe, a place that strongly appealed to me. I never felt that way about America. For better or worse, I never saw America as an object of affection. I had nothing more than a mild and rather prosaic love-hate relationship with the United States. I was acquainted with America as one is acquainted with fellow guests at a cocktail party; when the party ended I planned to go home promptly.

However, I realize that things are not that simple. It is not that my relationship with America had suddenly sweetened. I still felt that American food was bad and its opera insipid. The only thing that impressed me was Leontyne Price and George London in *Don Giovanni*. But quite apart from my aversion to America on grounds of personal taste, I came to understand that America's power to assimilate had begun to work on me without my knowing it.

Tourists aside, foreigners who live in this country for a short time eventually find themselves on the way to becoming Americans. This applies not only to resident aliens but even to legal American citizens who constantly find themselves required to become Americans. Is there any other country in the world that possesses the strange power that the United States, this huge colonial nation, does? The United States is a young country. Less than two centuries have passed since its founding, but the average age of American families is even younger. As I look at the Americans of my immediate acquaintance, I am astonished to see how many of them are members of the second generation, whose parents came from another country.

For example Professor J., an outstanding historian in the East Asian Department, is second-generation Dutch, and Assistant Professor V. is second-generation Italian. Mr. M., a federal government official who lives in the apartment next door, comes from a refugee family of Polish aristocrats. During World War II he joined the RAF to fight against Germany. All of these friends are newly minted Americans, who are in the process of becoming Americans, but neither they themselves nor anyone else doubt that they are Americans and no one calls them "second-generation." This being the way things are, it was perfectly reasonable for the head of the library staff to mistake me for a California-born scholar of Japanese origin.

That I felt inner resistance when he did so was entirely my own problem.

In concrete terms what does it mean to "become American"? To put it succinctly it means using English in one's daily life. Many readers might retort that this is perfectly natural, since America is an English-speaking country. Why shouldn't people use English there?

But let me compare this with our own Japan. Japan is a Japanese-speaking country, but we do not demand that resident aliens use the Japanese language. The difference becomes clear if we remember how much fuss Japanese journalists make about foreigners who speak Japanese, and it becomes clearer still when we examine that peculiar Japanese phenomenon, the "English-language boom."

In America no one asks if you are Japanese or French. It is a country that requires all residents from non-English-speaking countries to speak English. Since accepting a language also means accepting the cultural baggage that comes with it—a way of thinking, a value system, a lifestyle, and so forth—America requires that non-English-speaking people allowed into the country respect English-language culture, or, more precisely, Anglo-Saxon values. Driven to use English in their daily lives, foreigners find themselves on the road to becoming American before they realize it. And then they begin to notice that they are being placed in the American racial hierarchy that puts Anglo-Saxons at the top and blacks at the bottom. As the distance between me and America has shrunk, I found this has begun to happen with me too.

From the outside this "American-style" demand that everyone in this country speak English appears incredibly arrogant. In other words, it looks as though Americans consider all foreigners as "barbarians" who have come to its shores because of their adoration of the beautiful customs of the United States and their admiration for its ideals. Seen from the inside, however, insistence on using English can be thought of as necessary to govern an immigrant nation.

As I mentioned earlier, the difference between foreigners and Americans in the United States is a matter of degree. It is not the same as the difference between Japanese people and foreigners *[gaijin]*. In a sense, it is inevitable that foreigners in America are all treated as a reserve army of immigrants with the potential to become American citizens.

The role of the English language in unifying the country is more important than we imagine. How else could the country's political leaders govern the greatest colonial nation in history, a country that has grown over the past two hundred years, whose citizenry is composed of practically every race, that continues to accept new immigrants, and whose map spans a huge territory between two oceans? Could anything besides a common language unite the diverse peoples in this extensive territory and nurture their patriotic loyalty?

In economic terms the country is unified by the dollar, the common currency backed by its tremendous resources, but the dollar bill note is inscribed with the Latin phrase "E Pluribus Unum" ("From the many, one"). The English language simply serves the remarkable political function of realizing this dream. For people like the Japanese, born in a nation that developed naturally out of a single ethnic group, it is difficult to understand the tremendous political role that language can play.

For Japanese the problem of a national language is largely a cultural issue. However, in America, it is considered primarily a political issue. The Japanese language once played a political role in the [Japanese] colonial rule of Korea and Taiwan. In that instance the dominant ethnic group, whose mother tongue was Japanese, used language to control dominated ethnic minorities whose mother tongues were Korean and the Fukien dialect of Chinese. A similar example can be seen in the use of the French language in Algeria. In other words, language dominates through the force of number.

In contrast, however, Americans of Anglo-Saxon descent, the original English-speaking citizens, today make up no more than about twenty percent of the total population of 180 million people.

What is happening in America is not a matter of domination through number; it is domination through belief. It is a system of domination in which the other eighty percent of the population, made up of people from non-English-speaking countries, concede the superior position of Anglo-Saxon culture, discard their own culture, and accordingly accept the need to use English. They are controlled by their acceptance of English. From this it is evident that in America the English language plays a kind of creative political function.

Immigrants to America begin by mastering English, then make the utmost effort to turn themselves into full-fledged Anglo-Saxons. In American society immigrants who arrived earlier put social pressure on newcomers by taunting them and incessantly asking, "Have you really become American?" (What they mean is: to what extent have you become Anglo-Saxonized?)

Through this continual testing of patriotic loyalty, the United States has succeeded in achieving "From the many, one." Patriotic loyalty is the glue that holds American society together. In short, American society constantly coerces newcomers to imitate those already here. Since education is an organized way to encourage imitation, education is always compulsory. American society is an enormous classroom where honor students, "good American citizens," continually lash the whip at their lagging classmates. This dynamic relationship between the nation and the individual can be characterized as merciless. The only way to escape this mercilessness is to become a prize pupil oneself—and thus to "succeed" in every sense of the word.

What is the need for such compulsion? Needless to say, on the obverse side of the force of assimilation are other cultural forces working to divide the country. Individual states retain the power to secede from the Union. Latin, Jewish, and Negro lifestyles that diverge from the Anglo-Saxon lifestyle are deeply rooted. "Problem child" minority groups who make no effort to use English are scattered in unexpectedly large numbers throughout the country. Perhaps the mechanism that I have described is what holds America together against these centrifugal forces. Travelers to the United States ought to be aware of this mechanism, as they are of the Stars and Stripes unfurled all over the country every day.

The Anglo-Saxon "way of life" at the core of the American lifestyle is to be found not in the cities but in the countryside. It is to be found not among the wealthy or the working classes but among the middle class. And the political party that represents this lifestyle is not the Democratic Party but the Republican Party. . . .

In any case, this is the kind of place that America is. No matter how many superficial similarities they share, America is a built on fundamentally different cultural values from those of Japan. America is a country that scrubs the scent of luxury off even the most luxurious goods and puts them to practical use. In Japan, even practical goods, including such items as toasters and washing machines, are displayed as luxuries.

While we are on the subject of difference, American culture is also clearly distinct from European culture. I will go so far as to say that it is not "Western culture" at all—and even that it is so different that it requires a new category, "American culture." If we compare the Anglo-Saxon way of life at the core of the American lifestyle to the lifestyle of the English people, we can see that there is a greater difference between them than the difference between American English and British English. What is America so different? Perhaps it is the climate and geography of the new continent—and the vast spaces that spread across it. . . .

Such a huge space is not to be found either in Japan or in Europe. The endless impulse to conquer this space seems to have captured the hearts of the first colonial settlers to arrive in the seventeenth century. In his book *American Civilization,* the French cultural historian Bernard Faÿ observes that it was difficult for the English at home to understand the strange obsession of the settlers to push farther and farther into the interior of the country without trying to build cities on the coast and without regard for hardship and danger.

The Americans were the first people in history to conquer such a vast unsullied space. This instinct lives on in the simplicity of American citizens today. It is rare to find a people who move and who travel as readily as Americans. Every summer a scholar friend of mine drives with his entire family more than three thousand miles from Princeton to Seattle, taking turns with his wife at the wheel of their car. I have no doubt that he probably has more pleasant memories about dashing across the continent under his own steam than about the summer vacation itself.

The poet Charles Olson writes that America shows the faces of both Walt Whitman and Herman Melville, that is, the faces of democracy and expansionism. And it was this instinct—the inherent "American" expansionist instinct—that drove Commodore Perry to conquer the new space spreading westward across the Pacific Ocean and brought him to Uraga [Japan].

ETŌ JUN, "THE OLD FACE OF AMERICA" (1964)

If you were to ask any American you meet on the street for an impromptu definition of democracy, he would certainly reply, "The American way of life." But exactly what is the "American way of life"? Is it all that unique? Just how unlike anything else is it? What happened—and what did not—when this once exclusively indigenous idea was universalized and applied to postwar Japan? I would like to explore these questions.

Etō Jun, "The Old Face of America," source: Etō Jun, "Amerika no furui kao," *Asahi shinbun,* May 1–3, 1964.

As the phrase "American way of life" rolls off our tongue, the first things that come to mind are endless superhighways, New York skyscrapers, Hollywood romances, automobiles, Coca-Cola, and supermarkets—in sum, the many "new" and "big" things produced by a young nation proud of its unprecedentedly huge wealth and power. The image that most foreigners have of America has been formed by the achievements of its modern, colossal material culture.

It is a fact that most Americans are extremely naive. They prefer the *big* and the *new*. Nevertheless, Americans constantly find themselves annoyed at foreign images of a United States made up solely of the new and the big. In their eyes, these glittering new and big things are merely the by-products, not the roots, of the ethical values Americans believe in. What then are the roots? It goes without saying that they are the *old* and the *small*—the somber, the plain, and the down-to-earth.

Americans, I should add, are a match for the Japanese in their concern over how they appear in the eyes of foreigners. The Japanese also become angry that the typical foreign image of Japan consists of Mount Fuji, cherry blossoms, and geisha girls. To them these are symbols of an agricultural past, and they think that the symbols of modern Japanese culture ought to be the new "bullet train" that runs over two hundred kilometers per hour or the freeways built for the Olympics.

At first glance then, the values of the Japanese and the Americans seem to be the same, but in fact they point in quite opposite directions. In other words, the Japanese have a tendency to see value in their rupture with the past and exclusively in that rupture. Conversely, Americans locate value in continuity with an agricultural past. If we were to pursue this logic, we might arrive at the conclusion that for the Japanese, fundamental value lies in new material culture and technology, while for the Americans it can be found in old-fashioned ethics.

The Confucian scholar Arai Hakuseki [1657–1725] coined the phrase "Eastern morality; Western techniques (i.e., technology)." If Hakuseki were alive today, he would certainly be surprised to see that modern Japanese are more "American" than the Americans and that conversely modern Americans are more "Japanese" than the Japanese. Of course Hakuseki could not take into account Japan's experience of two severe historical ruptures: the Meiji Restoration and the loss of the Pacific War. Nor could he consider what a fatal blow "Western techniques," which he regarded so lightly, dealt to the very core of "Eastern morality."

For better or worse, American society did not experience this kind of historical rupture or the pressure of imported values. In the United States we can see the past alive and relatively intact. In that sense, we might even say that the United States, with only 180 years of history, is a far "older" country than Japan, which has experienced a rupture from its nearly two millennia of history.

As I have already said, the root of the American way of life, which places importance on the old and the small and which displays pronounced moralistic tendencies at its base, is represented in the life of the farmer. The American way of life is a composite of lifestyles and values that evolved out of American farm life. There is probably no better illustration of the rural origins of this way of life—that is to say, American-style democracy—than the American phrase "grassroots democracy."

American farming does not produce rice grown in irrigated paddies. In the North, farmers produce crops like corn, barley, and soybeans and, in the South, tobacco, cotton, vegetables, and fruit. The American farmer's way of life is completely different from that of the rice-cultivating Japanese farmer, who prizes the harmony of cooperative labor over the efforts of the individual.

Until the middle of the nineteenth century, the typical American was a man on his own. Determined to acquire his own piece of land, he had abandoned his European homeland to immigrate to the new continent. At first he worked in some coastal city, taking whatever opportunity presented itself to save up a little cash. Once he had money, he traveled west to the interior of the continent to buy a small plot of farmland—or land that he planned to cultivate.

Since he had come to the undeveloped new continent with a determination to succeed, the American must have been a man with a powerful will. Not only did success or failure depend upon his own labor; he had to be a man with an independent spirit, unwilling to depend much on others. Since he considered actions more important than talk, he was a man of few words. He was also frugal, intensely wary of outsiders, and the more he confronted adversity, the stronger his simple faith. He took pride in his own labor. Even though his holdings may have been modest, he was the king of his castle, and he believed that farming was a "sacred calling" that supported the existence of mankind.

When a few houses built by these independent immigrant farmers began to cluster around a humble church, small towns were created. Their association and life together in these towns is what is called "grassroots democracy." Many contemporary Americans over the age of sixty experienced the small-town upbringing that is at the core of the American way of life. For example, the wife of the chairman of the East Asian Studies Department at Princeton University spent her childhood in a small town in Oregon, where, she said, life was so hard that the nearest doctor was forty miles away.

Looked at from the inside, the colossal country that is the United States is composed of countless small towns built up by independent immigrant farmers. The character of the American middle class, which frequently seems so insufferable, derives from this historical background.

It is natural that independent farmers, who began with only a small amount of money, would be satisfied with their own lifestyle, would believe themselves to be pious and virtuous people, and would demonstrate a narrowness and a lack of interest in what happened beyond their own communities. It is also natural that those of immigrant origin would be sensitive to "equal opportunity" and suspicious of large companies or organizations that attempted to monopolize profits—or of anything that exceeded the scale of a man. They are kind to respectful visitors, but they do not try to hide their contempt and dislike for newcomers arriving late from other places. Of course they dislike foreign countries, because nowhere in Europe, Asia, or Africa are there independent immigrant farmers who share with them a similar history and similar values.

On the other hand the towering large cities that rise like "polluted" islands among the small towns extending to the horizon represent the way of life of the newly arrived outsiders. Major cities like Boston, New York, Philadelphia, Chicago, and Los Angeles are either port cities or modern industrial metropolises. They are symbols of America's *new* face. These cities were built by a continuous enormous influx of new immigrants over a period of roughly forty years from the last half of the nineteenth century into the beginning of this century. Unlike the older immigrants of either Anglo-Saxon or northern European Protestant origin, the new immigrants were either Catholics of Latin and Slavic descent or eastern European Jews.

These immigrants also came with a desire for their own land, but the land was already divided up among the older immigrants. The only opportunity remaining to them was to become workers. It was this group of new immigrants that supplied the cheap, abundant labor power that built America's industrial society. On the other side of the picture, these large metropolises were also the sites of big business, of labor bosses and labor unions who confronted big business, of corrupt politicians who allied with them, and of brawling saloons.

In the cities also lived pasty-faced intellectuals and "artists" and "writers" and "movie actors" who were connected with Europe, who lacked the simplicity of the grassroots communities, and who stood logic on its head. Those living the "true" American way of life peacefully in grassroots small towns secretly felt profound hostility, anxiety, and hatred toward all of this.

As long as things go well, these hostilities do not appear on the surface. However, once trouble arises, it explodes into anger directed against the extremely wealthy, the Catholic Church, labor bosses, intellectuals, communists, and foreign countries. One need only recall McCarthyism to see how vehement this fury can be.

Just recently an amusing incident occurred. A member of the Senate protested that Secretary of State Rusk should have confiscated Richard Burton's British passport, since his indecent public flirtations with Liz Taylor were corrupting the morals of decent young American men and women. The secretary laughed and said nothing, but this episode demonstrates that the roots of American anti-foreignism, anti-communism, and anti-intellectualism can be found in the mentality of the virtuous small-town farmer.

At any rate, I take the American way of life to be roughly this sort of thing.

Sociologists like David Riesman say that the American national character will change as American society changes. There will be a decrease in the rural "inner-directed" type of individualists and an increase in a "middle stratum" made up of salesmanlike "other-directed" types. That may well happen. However, as long as Americans believe the inner-directed model to be sincere and the other-directed model to be insincere, it is safe to say that America will continue to show its "old" face as it always has.

The American way of life is a double-edged sword. If this way of life has guided and nurtured American democracy to produce the results we see today, it has also brought with it a tendency toward arrogance, incurred the scorn of foreigners, and plunged reflective Americans into bewildered vexation. At any rate, it is a way of life unique to America or, to put it precisely, appropriate for no other country in the world.

If that is the case, when Japan received democracy from the United States, what exactly did it get? We got a political system based on a separation of powers with a cabinet responsible to the Diet and the abstract ideals of "freedom, equality, and fraternity."

Perhaps we also received the fruits of American-style "new" and "big" technology and material culture. But we never accepted the American way of life. This is because fortunately Japanese society was not a vacuum, and the Japanese were satisfied with a Japanese way of life. Despite the American Occupation's land reforms and legal changes, I think that Japan remains essentially the same.

Remarking on the achievements of the Meiji Restoration, the British historian George Samson once observed that even if Japan was Westernized in form, its coloring and its essence remained completely Japanese. Perhaps much the same thing is happening in postwar Japan. If, in one way or another, the postwar political system and human relationships are serving a real function in Japan, it is probably because elements inherent in the Japanese way of life are making this system and these values work. If this were not so, the results would be the complete opposite.

At any rate, in my opinion it is now time for the Japanese to take a good look at Japan's "old" character with eyes unclouded by ideology and without being blinded by the intensity of change in their surroundings.

ŌE KENZABURŌ,
"DEALING WITH PEARL HARBOR" (1967)

Ōe Kenzaburō (1935–), the 1994 recipient of the Nobel Prize for Literature, was born into a landowning family on the southwestern island of Shikoku. The war ended when he was ten years old. His father died in the war, and the family lost much of its property under the Occupation's land reform program. Ōe remembers feeling humiliated as child by accepting chocolates from an American G.I., but he was also strongly influenced by the democratic ideals in the new constitution drafted by the Americans, especially the ideal of freedom. He was also fond of reading stories such as *Tom Sawyer* and *Huckleberry Finn*. Although his mother implored him to stay in the village after his father died, he left for Tokyo in 1953 and entered Tokyo University the following year. While still a university student, Ōe gained literary acclaim for his fiction, winning the prestigious Akutagawa Prize in his senior year. A prolific author and a prominent public intellectual, he has been a vocal defender of Japan's postwar ideals of peace and democracy. Shortly after receiving the Nobel Prize he was criticized for declining an imperial medal for cultural achievement. Explaining his decision, Ōe recalled that his elementary school principal had beaten him severely when he failed to answer quickly

Ōe Kenzaburō, "Dealing with Pearl Harbor," source: Ōe Kenzaburō, "Pearl Harbor o mukatte," *Sekai* (September 1967): 188–196.

a question of what he would do if the emperor told him to die. His essay on remembering Pearl Harbor and Hiroshima was written after his first visit to the United States.

. . .

The young American literary scholar's wife, a slightly built woman who performed in modern dance, was a pure-hearted soul. With an angelic earnestness, she mulled things soberly, and she expressed her thoughts with an unadorned directness that seemed almost audacious. She was the most attractive kind of young American mother that I met in America, completely without malice toward anyone. As she walked along the beach with her daughter, both clad in bikinis, she reminded me of a doe and her fawn coming down to the water to drink. . . .

One day she said to me, "You know, the problem is the intensity of hatred. It's just like my husband, Peter, says. After Pearl Harbor, we all hated the Japanese. I doubt whether the hatred dissipated even after Hiroshima and Nagasaki. When you were a child during the war you hated America too, didn't you? What happened to that hatred after Hiroshima and Nagasaki?"

What happened to their hatred? What happened to our hatred? ("Americans will rape and kill and burn everybody with flamethrowers.") I couldn't help pondering these questions during my weekend on Nantucket Island. Shortly afterward I visited the author of *The Armed Society*. I was chatting pleasantly with him, criticizing the Johnson administration, when out of the blue, something cold and hard intruded on our conversation.

"Without Pearl Harbor," said this progressive American sociologist, "there would have been no Vietnam. The wariness that the Japanese implanted in us at Pearl Harbor is at the root of America's military intervention in Vietnam."

At that moment, my memory played a strange trick on me. Suddenly I realized that the children in Vietnam must be experiencing the fear that had seized me as a child—"Americans will rape and kill and burn everybody with flamethrowers"—and the hatred that it bred in me. But putting it that way is not quite right. After the defeat, something dissolved the powerful fear and hatred inside me; then the age of democracy arrived. Some will say this is too simple a story, but if there was a void inside me left by my former fear and hatred, what filled it was the sensation of democracy. Even when the Korean War began, I do not recall thinking that I shared with the children in Korea the words of fear and hatred that had earlier seized me as a child. ("Americans will rape and kill and burn everybody with flamethrowers.") As a university student, I often joined in demonstrations critical of the American Far East policy, but since my motives were based on logic I never joined in shouting [anti-American] slogans out of hatred.

I arrived in America as a Japanese who had completely overcome his wartime fear and hatred. One day, however, after giving a talk at Harvard about the impact of the atomic bomb experience on postwar thought in Japan, as I made my way through the dark campus toward my dormitory, I suddenly noticed a ghostly apparition awaiting me. I was accosted by two elderly American ladies. They appeared to be well-meaning, moderate people, but it became immediately clear that they had taken my talk as a personal attack.

"You said that you have high hopes for a new Japanese nationalism centered on the Hiroshima experience," said one of the ladies. "But how does that nationalism relate to America? What role will the emperor play? What is the place of Pearl Harbor?"

As I struggled for a response, wondering whether *nationalism* was the proper word, the other lady spoke up. "What does Pearl Harbor mean to your post-Hiroshima nationalism?"

I understood then that the ladies construed my talk as an expression of hatred by a person whose nation had been atom-bombed. Feeling under attack, they struck back with Pearl Harbor. If they saw in me anger stemming from the Hiroshima experience, they were seeing an apparition. From the beginning, with defeat as a turning point, I accepted the various postwar reforms, and I accepted all that happened in Hiroshima. My fear and hatred disappeared. It is true that during my visit to America I feared and hated the nuclear age, but these were feelings that I constructed of my own volition and logic after the war. The elderly ladies' tactic of striking back with the memory of Pearl Harbor was beside the point.

Nevertheless, I am still confronted with questions: What happened to our hatred? Why did Pearl Harbor disappear from my consciousness? With what new meanings will Pearl Harbor revive among the postwar generation? . . .

An editor from *Chūgoku shinbun*, exploring the meaning of the atomic attack on Hiroshima, recently made the following comment, presumably in response to a similar retaliatory charge: "The number of noncombatant civilians who died at Pearl Harbor was no more than a few dozen. I think of the problem of Hiroshima victims as a refugee problem."

A refugee problem. This situates Hiroshima close to Vietnam; it distances Hiroshima from Pearl Harbor. As a member of the so-called postwar generation, I myself feel obliged to deal with Pearl Harbor again. Taunts about the "democracy generation" do not upset me, but still I must ask what was democracy to me, what is it to me, and what will it continue to be? I must never lose sight of these questions. In pursuing them, I think that it will be useful to reflect on my fleeting memory of Pearl Harbor and the fear and hatred that it engendered.

I once wrote that the decision some of my classmates made to enter the National Defense Academy (Bōei Daigaku) represented the first instance of a fundamental parting of ways among the postwar generation.... Probably my cohort of high school students, born in 1934 and 1935, was the first recruited by the new institution. I recall hearing furtive and strangely heated talk about the new university while I was still in high school. Its emergence had a powerful dark impact on us. Teachers opposed it, at least on the surface, and those who applied to the academy must have had to muster courage to do so. It was not just one more university. I later wrote that National Defense Academy students shamed our generation. I meant that as a self-criticism for our collective failure to prevent our classmates from going there. I felt deceived and pained by their choice to enter a military school.

Why was the emergence of the academy such a dark and dismal shock to us? I think we need to think back first to the fundamental impact of defeat and the ensuing democratic education on my generation. Naturally this leads us to think about Pearl Harbor and about the wartime fear and hatred that filled our childish hearts.

Today we tend to understand the words *Pearl Harbor* as the Americans do, that is, in a passive sense. It brings to mind the picture of a peaceful life abruptly destroyed. But during the war Pearl Harbor obviously excited our young minds in the active voice. Our nine "military gods," stealthily attacking in their one-man submarines, had destroyed [the enemy], and they would destroy again! Nine seemed like an odd number, but we did not trouble ourselves about it. Military effectiveness was the only issue of interest to us; the sad consequences of the war, even the idea that one of the military gods might have been captured by the enemy, never crossed our minds.[5]

Throughout the war, Pearl Harbor was a glorious symbol of our military prowess. And the fears and hatreds of youngsters like me rested on the balance of military success.

The wartime experience of the Japanese children on the home islands was quite different from that of children in wartime Europe. Except for those living in Okinawa, Japanese children did not directly experience the cruelty of war. The war's impact was far more muted. The fear and hatred that Japanese children felt toward America were not deeply rooted in the horror of war. (An important exception is Okinawan children, who witnessed organized mass suicides. Surviving members of the post-war generation have been living side by side with nuclear armed bases [in Okinawa] for over twenty years now. They, who had experienced the horror of war most directly, are now being forced to endure life patiently in the shadow of the biggest horror of war.)

To be sure, during the war we had to fight our own fear ("Americans will rape and kill and burn everybody with flamethrowers"), and we did so by stirring up the flames of our hatred. But our fear and hatred belonged to the world of fantasy and imagination. The proof of this is that as children we were able to reverse our position by pretending "We will rape and kill and burn everybody with flamethrowers." . . . I don't think such role reversals were possible for Korean children during the Korean War or for children in today's Vietnam. For these children the horror of war is not part of an imaginary world. It is a very real problem that they faced in their everyday lives.

Then came defeat and the peace constitution with its democratic principles and renunciation of war. How did this affect us? For the first time we ceased to think about war in terms of military success. We chose instead to think first about war in terms of its horrors. This was our fundamental change of heart.

If we Japanese adopt this perspective, the issue of Pearl Harbor becomes of secondary importance. Greater war tragedies than Pearl Harbor struck both the American and the Japanese sides. Our fear and hatred are no longer directed at America but rather at war itself and the horrors it entails. For this reason, before so-called realists began their offensive, the pacifism of the Japanese people was based consistently not on a balance-of-power theory but rather on the power of imagination to sense the horrors of war. I see no reason to reject this thinking as unrealistic. Those who chose to enter the National Defense Academy, however, essentially chose to turn away from logic of war's tragedies and return to the logic of military effectiveness. They chose to reject the peace constitution's attempt to learn from the tragedies.of war, and they became experts on military effectiveness instead.

As a nation the Japanese people, who supported the peace constitution and recognized the horrors of war, especially as a result of the nuclear experience, are in a special position with respect to Hiroshima and Nagasaki. The idea that in thinking about the nuclear age we should focus on the horrors produced by the atomic bomb rather on the power of the bomb will gain influence abroad only if it is rooted deeply in the soil of Japan. It will never have an impact on the rest of the world as a universal concept if it is divorced from the existence of Japan and the Japanese people. We must not lose sight of this fact.

I often got the impression that even the most well-meaning citizens of America understand Pearl Harbor and Hiroshima/Nagasaki as events that offset each other. If we base our thinking on the human tragedies of war, most people will find it difficult to see any equivalence between Pearl Harbor and Hiroshima/Nagasaki. The balancing of Pearl Harbor against Hiroshima/Nagasaki is possible only if the logic of military effectiveness reigns supreme.

This problem is not confined to America. The dark fear that hit me as I watched late-night TV coverage of the Chinese nuclear test will stay with me for a long time. The exuberant expressions of the young Chinese researchers and workers as they watched the mushroom cloud rise in the desert seemed so beautiful and moving. . . . But as I saw them march out into the radioactive desert with only light protection immediately after the test, I could not help feeling apprehensive. The Chinese may now possess the proud knowledge of the power of their newly acquired nuclear weapon, but I have to doubt that they have any knowledge of the human tragedies that such a weapon can cause. Of course, they lack such knowledge. Even today, in this nuclear age, the only people who have real knowledge of the tragedies of nuclear weapons are to be found in the atomic bomb hospitals of Hiroshima and Nagasaki.

Thus, if we are to survive in this mad nuclear world, the people of postwar Japan must place the human tragedy of nuclear weapons at the center of their logic and refuse to bind themselves to the logic of the power of nuclear weapons. Some postwar Japanese, however, actively succumb to the logic of the power of nuclear weapons. Commenting on the recent Chinese H-bomb tests, Kōsaka Masataka wrote, "To put it in blunt terms, we should understand the Chinese H-bomb tests as the success of an extremely difficult and expensive scientific experiment. After all, the successful test does not have any military significance for the foreseeable future."

His words reflect a mentality strictly limited in its perspective to the power of nuclear weapons. Kōsaka must have experienced defeat as a youth and entered the postwar period well aware of the tragedies of war. Twenty-two years have elapsed since then. It is not a short period of time, but for some people it has been more than enough time to migrate from the logic of the tragedies of war to the logic of the power of military effectiveness.

I was able to spend a pleasant weekend with my friends on Nantucket. We swam in the rough waters, and we cycled to the other side of the island. I debated with my American literary scholar friend Peter about an essay he was trying to write, titled "Tough Guy Intellectual." It argued that the type of intellectual portrayed by the TV actor Ben Gazzara constituted a prototype of the contemporary American. I felt that the figure of the dead Kennedy was lurking in the shadow of this image. We also spent a lot of time throwing a plastic plate [i.e., Frisbee] on the beach. It is difficult to throw the plate, propelling it with centrifugal force, keeping its surface parallel to the ground. This plate-throwing game was last year's fad, but our friend Peter was still unable to give it up.

Whenever seabirds took flight, splashing the water beneath them, I kept remembering the vision of a crazed man pursuing Moby Dick to his death, and I frequently dropped the plate. Ahab screams, "Towards thee I roll, thou all-destroying but unconquering whale; to the last I grapple with thee; from hell's heart I stab at thee; for hate's sake I spit my last breath at thee. Sink all coffins and all hearses to one common pool! and since neither can be mine, let me then tow to pieces, while still chasing thee, though tied to thee, thou damned whale! Thus, I give up the spear!"

All perish, save Ishmael alone. "And I only am escaped alone to tell thee." But what for?

CHAPTER 7

America in Decline

While *han-Bei* (anti-American) sentiment and ambivalence toward the United States emerged during the early postwar years, particularly on the political left, a majority of the Japanese people continued to view America favorably, often in awed reverence. It was only with escalation of the Vietnam War in the 1960s and recurrent trade disputes during the 1970s and 1980s that the popular image of America tumbled to earth. By the 1990s, a new word was coined to summarize nonideological negative feelings toward America: *ken-Bei* (revulsion toward America).

During the Vietnam War the Japanese mass media coverage played a major role in spreading antiwar sentiment and diminishing America's image. Newspaper commentary on American policy was almost uniformly critical. The war was also the first one to be covered in the television age. Disconcerting images of dead bodies and burning houses intruded into family living rooms, reminding the Japanese of their wartime past. Many Japanese intellectuals suggested that Cold War America was going down the same path that militarist Japan had in the 1930s.

American bases in Japan were indispensable to staging of American military operations in Vietnam, just as they had been during the Korean War. Okinawa, dubbed "the keystone of the Pacific" by American officials, was especially critical for strategic air operations. Although the war's economic impact was not nearly as great as that of the Korean War boom, the Japanese economy profited handsomely from providing goods and services to American forces. Opposition to the two wars, however, took strikingly different forms. Unlike the Korean War, when a radical minority denounced an American conspiracy to "colonize" Japan, the Vietnam War stirred mass movements that opposed it, eschewing ideological anti-Americanism and criticizing Japanese complicity in the war. The principal antiwar organization, Beheiren (Citizens' Federation for Peace in Vietnam), pursued protest tactics like those of Western peace activists, who focused on grassroots activities such as letter writing and teach-ins. These new tactics were epitomized by scenes of young people chatting casually as they sipped *Beitei Kōra* (American imperialist cola) after their rallies were over.

In the fall of 1967 Beheiren emerged into the national limelight when four deserters from the aircraft carrier *Intrepid* requested help in reaching a third-country destination. After arranging their escape to Sweden, Beheiren members carried on similar operations until 1969. The U.S. Senate Armed Services Committee called Beheiren "the most active and effective" organization working with American deserters in the whole world.[1] To the relief of Washington and Tokyo officials, however, the staging of a second mass protest against the scheduled renewal of the U.S.-Japan Security Treaty in 1970, feared by some as possibly greater than the paralyzing protests of ten years earlier, fizzled despite continuing student turmoil on university campuses.

One of the organizers of Beheiren was the philosopher Tsurumi Shunsuke, who as a student at Harvard was arrested on charges of espionage shortly after Pearl Harbor. Though angered by the groundless arrest, he was relieved that he had not been tortured and had been provided with legal defense. After submitting a graduation thesis, written as he sat on the toilet seat in his prison cell, Tsurumi was repatriated to wartime Japan. He resented America but was grateful to it too. He later described his Beheiren activities as both a protest against America's Vietnam policy and an expression of gratitude toward the American people. Beheiren had its roots in Voiceless Voices, an organization that protested the 1960 treaty revision, but it mobilized the energy of a younger generation by recruiting members such as Oda Makoto, whose best-selling books on America had made him a celebrity and who soon became the charismatic symbol of Beheiren.

President Nixon and Prime Minister Satō, a fervent pro-American politician, shared a hostile view of antiwar protestors, but as the war wore on, there was increasing discord between their two governments. Nixon was under heavy pressure from American businessmen, particularly southern textile manufacturers, angered and hurt by the relentless influx

FIGURE 13. The defense policy of postwar Japan has relied on close military ties with the United States, sometimes characterized as a "nuclear umbrella." In this 1969 cartoon, Prime Minister Satō Eisaku sits safe and dry under an American intercontinental ballistic missile, counting his money. It suggests that the U.S.-Japan defense relationship made possible the country's rapid economic growth in the 1960s—or perhaps that the country had saved money by not building up its own military forces. (*Asahi geinō*, December 1, 1969)

of Japanese exports, to do something about Japanese competition. "The Japanese are still fighting the war," said his secretary of commerce Maurice Stans, "only now instead of a shooting war it is an economic war. Their immediate intention is to try to dominate the Pacific and then perhaps the world."[2] In August 1971, Nixon announced a decoupling of the dollar from gold, which boosted the value of the yen and made Japanese exports more expensive. It was the first shot fired in a trade conflict that lasted for the next two decades.

This "Nixon shock," unveiled on the anniversary of V-J Day, came in the wake of yet a greater shock the previous month, when the president announced that the United States had begun talks with China to normalize relations. Demand for opening trade relations with the PRC had been one of the major reasons why some Japanese opposed the "separate peace" of the 1951 San Francisco Peace Treaty. Having ignored such opposition while following the lead of American Cold War policy, the Japanese government was left looking foolish, and it quickly reacted by establishing diplomatic ties with the PRC. Strikingly, both of these pivotal shifts in American policy in 1971 were made without prior notice to the Japanese government. A meeting between President Nixon and Emperor Hirohito in Alaska shortly after these "shocks" did little to stem the souring of relations.

During the 1970s American complaints about Japanese trade practices gave the impression that America was in economic decline. This impression was reinforced by Japan's growing sense of familiarity with things American, which supplanted an earlier sense of akogare (yearning) for them. More and more middle-class Japanese traveled abroad and saw America with their own eyes during this decade. The number of Japanese going abroad surpassed a million in the early 1970s, then grew tenfold during the next twenty years. The United States, the most popular destination for the Japanese, accounted for roughly a third of all their overseas travel. Familiarity with America did not necessarily breed contempt, but it encouraged a sense of déjà vu.

The rapid diffusion of home appliances, the accelerating suburbanization, and the spread of a new middle-class life style in Japan also narrowed the material gap between the two countries. As rice paddies everywhere were turned into housing tracts, apartment complexes, and shopping centers, daily life in Japan came more and more to resemble daily life in America. The sprouting of countless suburban communities in formerly agrarian landscapes was an indigenized and amplified version of American-style housing tracts built for military personnel during the Occupation. The Japanese public also fell as deeply in love with the automobile as the Americans had a generation earlier. In 1970 demand for "my cars" (cars purchased by individuals) surpassed demand for business vehicles, and automobile ownership expanded rapidly.[3]

When McDonald's finally gained entry into Japan in 1971, a new wave of American-style consumerism washed across the Pacific. Thanks to the efforts of the Japanese executive Fujita Den, the golden arches that debuted in the fashionable district of Ginza in Tokyo, where the main street became a pedestrian mall on weekends, met with instant success. Fujita, a former interpreter for the American Occupation forces, jokingly championed a fast food diet by claiming, "If we eat hamburgers for a thousand years, we will become blond, and when we become blond—we can conquer the world." His comments echoed Japanese intellectuals a century earlier who had propounded the virtues of beef as a "civilized" food. Their writings had little effect on ordinary dietary habits. Fujita, however, had an impact on the Japanese "national body" in more substantial ways.

Although young Japanese devoured McDonald's hamburgers eagerly, Japanese consumers did not buy nearly enough American goods to balance surging Japanese trade surpluses. The result was a series of acrimonious trade disputes that grew in intensity and rancor during the 1980s. As Prime Minister Nakasone observed, high interest rates in America and a strong dollar gobbled up foreign trade and foreign capital like a "black hole absorbing stars." The Plaza Accord of 1985 sought to remedy the American trade deficit by a rapid devaluation of the dollar, but the measure had little effect on American imports from Japan. On the contrary, the sudden increase in the value of the yen led to rapid expansion of Japanese overseas investment, including the acquisition of trophy assets such as Rockefeller Center, the Pebble Beach golf course, and Columbia Pictures.

While alarmist American observers warned of a new Japanese invasion—and American cartoonists draped the Statue of Liberty in a Japanese kimono—exuberant Japanese writers touted the superiority of Japanese management and business practices. In 1979 a translation of *Japan as Number One,* an upbeat assessment of Japanese culture and society written by the American sociologist Ezra Vogel, became a runaway best seller. Growing national confidence even prompted the view that Japanese economic success was due to "Japanese values" or "Asian values." In any case, until the early 1990s, growing affluence confirmed a feeling that Japan was on the rise, at least in a relative sense, while America was continuing a long decline. Only with the sudden bursting of a speculative "economic bubble" in the 1990s did that view begin to shift.

Although the Japanese government pushed for a more active role for the Japanese military in its defense arrangements, there were growing doubts on both sides about the reliability of Japan's military ties with

FIGURE 14. The war in Vietnam created a heavy political and economic burden for the Johnson administration, and it aroused strong antiwar sentiments in Japan. On the top of a huge rock labeled "South Vietnam" a crowd of protestors carries a banner that reads, "American army, go home! Down with the government!" (Nasu Ryōsuke, *Manga seikatsu 50-nen* [Tokyo: Heibonsha, 1985])

the United States. In 1987 the national budget breached the previously sacred ceiling of 1 percent of the GNP on military spending. But when Iraqi forces attacked their neighboring Kuwait three years later, Americans found the Japanese response to calls for cooperation disappointingly slow and feeble. Some Japanese agreed, especially after the U.S. coalition's surprisingly quick victory over the Iraqi troops. Positive reappraisal of American military omnipotence after the 1990 Gulf War proved ephemeral, however, and so did the celebratory mood over Japan's economic triumph. What remained was the disconcerting feeling that America the cold warrior and Japan the economic warrior were facing a major transformation in their relationships with each other and with the wider world as the American Century drew to a close.

ODA MAKOTO,
"AMERICANS: BETWEEN WAR AND PEACE" (1965)

I.

An American friend (age 33) and I have often talked about how the Korean War was the most disturbing event to occur during the two decades since the end of World War II. But we disagree considerably as to its significance. Our disagreement stems from the different meanings that the Pacific War had for us. He believed that it was the war to end all wars. Of course I felt the same way, but what overwhelmed me was the fact that the defeat brought a complete change in Japanese values and brought a new Japan into being.

When the Korean War began my friend was shocked that warfare, which he thought had finally come to an end, was loose in the world again and that he might have to fight. Of course I felt the same way, but I considered it "someone else's war." At the time I was much more shocked by the establishment of the Police Reserve Force and by the communist purges in Japan.

An American reporter slightly older than I am was the member of a Civil Defense youth corps in New York during World War II. "It was quite an experience for a boy," he said.

I asked him if he had ever thought that Japan might win the war. "Never," he said quickly. "We were more concerned with Germany."

On December 8, 1941, the Japanese started marching toward their inevitable destiny. Many people thought, "It was bound to happen." We greeted war with excitement, anxiety, and resignation. The Americans considered Pearl Harbor just an unforeseen event. For us Pearl harbor was a fatal blow, but for them it was merely a mistake.

If Pearl Harbor was nothing more than a mistake, then it is possible to see Hiroshima in the same light. Some reasonable Americans realize that Hiroshima was an event of catastrophic significance. However, when asked about Hiroshima most Americans, including tourists visiting the city, invariably retort, "What about Pearl Harbor?" They do not see a qualitative difference between Pearl Harbor and Hiroshima. For us Hiroshima marks a historical beginning for mankind. For Americans, Hiroshima, like Pearl Harbor, is simply one of many events that occurred during the

Oda Makoto, "Americans: Between War and Peace," source: Oda Makoto, "Sensō to heiwa no aida Amerikajin," *Chūō kōron*, July 1965, 110–117.

Pacific War. I have often noticed this difference when I talk to ordinary Americans.

What about August 15, 1945? For us it was a fatal blow. It is well known that an extraordinary silence spread over the whole country for a few hours after midday. No doubt the Americans did not feel the same way. We Japanese still discuss August 15 passionately. Most Americans I have met say that they only vaguely recollect August 15, but—as a result of Pearl Harbor—they vividly remember December 8.[4]

One woman told me, "You see, we knew Japan would lose. It was only a matter of time." She was probably right. Hadn't America already converted its industrial base from military to civilian production a year before the war ended? . . .

2.

I have cited several examples to demonstrate the differences between Japanese and Americans. It is obvious that the depth of the scars left by the Pacific War is quite different in each country. Let us compare hard facts. While 1,200,000 Japanese soldiers were killed in the Pacific War, only 40,000 American soldiers were. Estimates vary, but the death toll in Hiroshima ranges from 80,000 to 240,000.

From this comparison we can probably conclude that the American concept of peace is different from our own. Our conception of peace, in all its diverse forms, is based on our past experience. The American conception of peace, however, is grounded in the universal principle that mankind needs peace. This principle reflects their confidence that America can change the world's destiny. In other words, Americans believe that America can guide the world in times of prosperity as well as in times of destruction.

Our way of thinking, rooted as it is in our past experience, does not look toward the outside world. Our slogan is "Japanese security comes first!" In the eyes of foreigners, this appears to be a self-serving but tacit understanding among the Japanese that has created a formidable domestic solidarity within Japan.

I believe it was Tanigawa Gan [a poet and social activist] who said that Japanese mothers and grandmothers participate in the peace movement to protect their children but have no intention of sacrificing those children in order to preserve peace. His words reveal not so much the contradictions within the peace movement as its intrinsic nature. It is not that the Japanese peace movement is completely indifferent to a conception of peace based on universal principles but that it recognizes the emptiness of such principles. Didn't our experience of the Pacific War teach us in the harshest possible way that all wars are fought "in order to maintain peace"? When we Japanese are told, "Take up arms to protect the peace!" or "Sacrifice your children!" we immediately reply, "Peace for whose sake?" or "Who is to make such decisions?"

Let me shift the discussion away from the physical to the psychological scars left by the war. Most Americans believe that the Pacific War was fought solely for the cause of justice. Americans fought—and died—to destroy fascism at its evil roots and to defend liberty. In doing so they protected their beloved families from aggression. In other words, there was no contradiction between the universal human principle of protecting freedom against fascism and the individual principle of protecting their families.

What about the Germans and the Japanese? They were not fighting for universal justice; they were fighting simply for individual justice. It was enough for them to protect their families against enemy aggression. But at the same time, that meant that they also protected Hitler. If they had fought against Hitler, wouldn't that have meant handing the fate of their families to the enemy? At this point we inevitably confront fundamental questions: "What is the homeland that we ought to protect?" "Who is the enemy that we ought to fight against?" "How should we define justice?"

The German playwright Hochhuth, who authored *Der Stellvertreter (The Deputy),* took a similar approach when he wrote about the way the pope treated the Jews under Nazi control. For the sake of a [just cause], making divine providence manifest in the world, the pope sacrificed the lives of Jews as though they were vermin. Consciously or unconsciously, more or less similar doubts are fundamental to Japanese postwar thought. As long as these doubts persist, there is little chance that the idea of taking up arms and sacrificing children "to preserve peace" will take hold in Japan.

Circumstances are far more complicated for the Japanese than for the Germans. Perhaps this is because of our position as an Asian people who suffered under years of Western pressure. Even though the principle was make-believe, the Pacific War was fought for the liberation of Asia, and it is undeniable that many Japanese participated in the war for the sake of that principle. Everyone talked about, and many believed in, establishing the Greater East Asia Co-Prosperity Sphere. In fact, judging from its consequences, the war hastened Asian liberation. (Liberation would have been possible without the Pacific War, I think, but it would have taken much longer.) Many Japanese still sincerely believe this, and this makes our conception of peace three times more complicated.

In other words, by protecting our loved ones from enemy aggression, did we contribute to the liberation of Asia? And didn't that mean defending the wartime military regime too? And supposing one had fought against the militarists, wouldn't the outcome have been quite different for the liberation of Asia or the protection of one's family?

Needless to say, apologists for the "Greater East Asia War" base their arguments on this dilemma and on the sincere feelings of many people. I have discussed apologist affirmations of the war with American journalists, as well as the dilemma and the sincere feelings behind it, but none of them had heard about any of this before. "I see," they would say. "So that is how things were. Now I understand the situation in Japan today." One was the editor-in-chief of a prominent newspaper who had come to Japan to work on a "special issue" on Japan. Naturally Americans, being Westerners, have never agonized over this kind of problem.

3.

Let me turn now to one obvious fact. Whether "to maintain peace" or for any other reason, the Japanese simply do not have the option of bearing arms. (Let us set aside the debate over the National Self-Defense Force for the time being.)

This fact has engendered the "idea of disarmament," and it distinguishes the psychology and behavior of the Japanese today from those of other people, especially Americans, who have the power to make decisions that affect the rest of the world. As might be expected, the idea of disarmament comes in all shapes and sizes. At one extreme we find people who feel powerless to have any real effect on the world and who passively believe that control over war or peace lies in the hands of others. At the other extreme are those who say that genuine peace cannot be achieved with weapons, that the idea of taking up arms "to maintain peace" always leads to war, and that peace will be impossible to sustain unless war is rejected in every sense. Such people take the positive position that real peace can be achieved only through creating a new way of thinking about peace that is independent of existing ideas. In the two decades since the end of the war, the Japanese have wavered between these two extremes.

What about the Americans? It is probably best to think about this by turning everything on its head. First of all, their concept of peace is based not on past individual experiences but on universal principles. (This clearly distinguishes them from Europeans.) Moreover their conception of peace does not admit any contradiction between universal justice and individual justice. Inattention to this contradiction is linked to their naive nationalism. Their conception of peace is also based on the realization that they have the power to move the world as they wish. It is backed by the power to do so. They possess a sense of "noblesse oblige"—a sense of self-confidence and a sense of responsibility for world peace.

When a conception of peace is based on universal principles instead of individual experiences, the role of religion, which supports such principles, becomes important. For example, the Quakers and the Reverend Martin Luther King have had a great influence on the peace movement. American society already had a system of fostering peace activism based on universal principles. It is a society that allows people to become "conscientious objectors" for religious reasons.

This is an important thing to consider in discussing the American conception of peace and the American peace movement. (There are currently about 5,000 COs [conscientious objectors] in the United States, and it is said that there were 15,000 during World War II.) One must claim religious reasons to become a conscientious objector. It is an advantage to be a Quaker, but other religions will do. There have been cases where Marxists who did not want to be shock troops for American imperialism became COs for "religious reasons."

If an FBI investigation results in the approval of an individual's right to be a conscientious objector, he is issued a certificate. When I asked a CO friend what the FBI's standards were, he told me that he had no idea. If a person without CO status refuses to serve in the army, he faces two years of prison. Currently twenty such people are imprisoned in United States jails.

By recognizing conscientious objectors, American society accords a permanent place to a conception of peace based on universal principles. Individual experiences change easily, but universal principles are eternal. Consequently, when universal principles are its focal point, a peace movement can grow under any circumstances, (even in the midst of war).

The American soldiers described in Kaikō Ken's *Vietnam War Chronicle* express their opinions and criticisms freely, but when battle begins, they quietly follow orders and plunge into the fighting with the cry, "Duty is duty." But we must remember that not all Americans feel that duty is duty. Some who are disturbed by the contradiction between universal justice and individual justice choose to become conscientious objectors. This is a fact that should not be overlooked. I believe that one of the keys to understanding American society and its people lies in the existence of a social framework that legally recognizes the presence of such conscientious objectors, even in wartime.

4.

A society that provides a system of domestic conscientious objection is indeed a superior one. Whenever I talk with Americans about our respective war experiences, they bring up the differences in our countries' social structures and their confidence in their own society. Even when we talk about the Japanese "special attack units" (kamikaze suicide squads) their reaction is the same.

Many quite different Americans say, "Kamikaze pilots were heroic, but we fought and survived under our own social system without using suicide squads." Under the American military code, a soldier can become a prisoner of war if he has fought to the best of his ability, and he can also resist unreasonable orders. Such a military code is shaped by their social structure.

When I talk about the war with Americans, at the end I always say, "You have been lucky—so far." When I talk about how deeply the war scarred the Japanese or about how we suffered the wartime contradictions mentioned above (of course we only became fully conscious of them after the war), I ask them what they would have done in our position: fight against America or fight against Tōjō? The first thing they usually say is that they have never thought about that. Then they say, "Our society has never experienced a hypothetical predicament like that, and it never will."

Here is one more fundamental difference between them and us. For us the end of the war brought profound changes in our social structure, but for them it had no such significance. A man whom I consider to be my mentor once told me that for the Americans the case was just the opposite [of ours]. To him American values had not changed in a fundamental way before, during, or after the war.

This difference is certainly one of the major obstacles to mutual understanding between Americans and Japanese. When I talk about this situation Americans usually respond, "Yes, how terrible the war must have been for you." Then, when I add that this is why the Japanese attach such special meaning to the two decades since the end of the war, they instantly agree, "Of course." But I wonder if they really understand or not. An easy way to explain to them the sudden transformation wrought by the surrender is to compare it to the Great Depression in the United States. That certainly was an event that altered many American social values.

The Americans are lucky in that they have never had to face fundamental challenges to their social structure or been forced to doubt it, even though they have constantly criticized certain aspects of it. . . . At the root of America's grassroots democracy is the claim, "We have always done things this way, and we have prospered as a result." Such an idea can lead to two other ideas. One is pride and confidence in the system, and the other is the conceited belief, "That is why we are right."

American pride and self-confidence probably act to countervail any force that tries to change their system or to root it out completely. My foremost impression when visiting American soldiers in Okinawa was not their material strength but their spiritual strength. Kaikō Ken probably felt the same way when he was in South Vietnam. Those willing to throw themselves into battle thinking that "Duty is duty" must have unshakable pride and confidence in their own system. But this pride and self-confidence can also quickly lead Americans to the conclusion, "That is why we are right." That gives rise to the peculiarly American habits of "forcing goodwill upon others" and "selling freedom by force." One extreme case of this is the war in South Vietnam.

"Grassroots democracy" is strong because it is based on real-life experience rather than on abstract intellectual understanding. But that strength itself is also a weakness. In other words, in the absence of fundamental doubts about the American system, indeed, in the fortunate inability to entertain such doubts, lie both its strengths and its weaknesses. What would happen if Americans found themselves in a situation where their system was fundamentally challenged? . . .

5.

Finally, a significant difference between Japanese and Americans is that for us the Pacific War was the last war (at least I hope so), while for the Americans it was not. They have experienced war or the threat of war many times since then. They faced the Korean War, a series of crises in Berlin, the Cuban Missile Crisis, South Vietnam, and the Dominican Republic. Just look at Okinawa. One cannot escape the feeling that the United States is preparing it as a supply depot both for South Vietnam and for a major war in the future. There are missiles and nuclear weapons. . . .

It is probably safe to say that many Americans see no qualitative difference between Pearl Harbor and Hiroshima. It follows that they may someday use nuclear weapons "to protect peace and freedom." It also follows, as their experience of the Pacific War (which they refer to as a "surprise attack") demonstrates, that America to the present day has turned its back toward Asia and looked only toward Europe (and indeed may still do so). And it also follows that their naive breed of nationalism, which has never encountered contradictions, is connected with all of this.

I once discussed nationalism with an American student who is both an ardent leader in the peace movement and a conscientious objector. "I am an internationalist," he said. "Nationalism is nonsense to me. I myself have never felt nationalistic while I was in a foreign country." "I am an internationalist of sorts too," I replied. "But would you still be broadminded enough to remain such an ebullient internationalist if their were foreign military bases in your country?" He looked at me a while without saying anything, then he shook his head and said, "I don't think so."

HONDA KATSUICHI,
"TRAVELING THROUGH THE DEEP SOUTH" (1970)

Honda Katsuichi (1932–), one of postwar Japan's leading journalists, is known for his adventurous spirit and his wide-ranging travels abroad. Even during his university days he twice came close to falling to his death while traveling in the Himalayas. After graduating from Chiba University he decided to become a journalist. The occupation seemed less constricting than any other. An admirer of the American journalist Edgar Snow, whose *Red Star over China* had a big impact on his generation of students, Honda shared a curiosity about people's everyday lives and a disdain for official knowledge. In 1963 Honda won acclaim for a series of reports on Canadian Eskimos that sought to counter "civilized" Japan's national bias against "primitive" peoples. After covering the American war in Vietnam, Honda went to China to report on wartime atrocities committed by the Japanese army in Nanking. As a reporter Honda consistently positioned himself on the side of the oppressed, the marginal-

Honda Katsuichi, "Traveling through the Deep South," source: Honda Katsuichi, *Amerika gasshūkoku* (Tokyo: Asahi shinbunsha, 1970), 97–106, 116–121.

ized, and the persecuted and conveyed their stories in simple and direct language. This perspective was reflected not only in his dispatches from Saigon and Hanoi during the Vietnam War but also in his reports on Harlem and the American South.

The footnotes Honda originally published with this selection as explanations for Japanese readers appear as numbered backnotes.

. . .

The Southern Scowl

[Shihō Mitsukazu and I] left Washington at the end of August. Luckily, the weather was unusually cool for several days. We stayed one night in Richmond, Virginia, the capital of the Southern Confederacy during the Civil War, then passed quickly through Greensboro, North Carolina, into South Carolina and headed for Atlanta, Georgia. Speeding along a three-lane highway, we rode through mile after mile of beautiful forest. The full-grown leaves, dyed a deep green, quietly awaited the onset of autumn. Every once in a while we caught a glimpse of unbelievably beautiful houses surrounded by broad lawns.

The Indians who once inhabited this entire bountiful continent have been pushed onto "reservations," where the land is almost worthless. They have been reduced to a pitiful minority group numbering about 600,000 that barely hangs on to survival. The call to take up arms under the banner of "Indian (Red) Power" is not widespread at the moment, however, so there has been no tragic bloodshed. When no one resists, problems are not likely to arise. But in the past there have been instances when Negro slaves who had escaped from their plantations joined with Indians to wreak fierce attacks on the armies of white men.

From Atlanta we drove to Birmingham, Alabama. We had now entered the region known as the "Deep South."[5] Within the United States, the Deep South has a bad reputation. It is known as the region where racial discrimination is strong and where the secret society the Ku Klux Klan (KKK), a ridiculous terrorist organization proclaiming the superiority of white people, especially the Anglo-Saxons, makes it home. Our destination was Mississippi, the state with the worst reputation in the Deep South, where prejudice is most severe and where the Negro population is the highest. Its record of horrors is appalling. My companion on this trip, 24-year-old Shihō Mitsukazu, was a senior majoring in sociology at Amherst College. Before this summer he had spent a year in Mississippi, living in the Negro community to study the Negro problem.

The first stop on my journey to the Deep South was a town where Shiho had made many friends. After reading frightening accounts about the Deep South and listening to Shiho's stories, I may have brought with me many preconceptions about the region. Once we entered Georgia, whenever we encountered white people in restaurants or hotels I had the feeling that they were looking at the two of us with strangely grim faces. Was this just something that I felt, or were they really so grim-looking? Since the passage of the Civil Rights Act,[6] the "Whites Only" or "Colored (Negro) Only" signs peculiar to the Deep South had almost completely disappeared from restaurants, buses, and the like. Even so, when we went into restaurants that had clearly once been for "Whites Only," we met with looks of disdain, unfriendly waitresses, ill-tempered whispers in low voices. Clearly their eyes did not look at us just with simple curiosity. Curious eyes, or hostile eyes? Only a fool would not be able to tell the difference. Once when we bought some fruit at a roadside stand, a man greeted us with a look that was clearly curious, not hostile. "Are you Japanese?" he asked. When we chatted with him, we learned that his wife was Japanese.

We hardly ever encountered such grim looks in New York, Washington, or Seattle. In any country, it is safe to say, the deeper you are out in the countryside, the more people are likely to look at you in a simple and naive way, but by the same token their prejudices are likely to be much deeper. The look that southerners gave us was no different. And their look is much grimmer in rural areas a little off the freeways than in a city like Atlanta. Even so, until we reached Birmingham I still could not escape feeling that I was imagining things. But at Birmingham we tried to stay at a motel. The neon sign out front read "Vacancy." When the 60-ish woman at the front desk took a look at us, she said, "We're full." The sign said there were rooms available, we protested, and there were almost no cars in the parking lot.

"They are all at a funeral," she replied coldly, looking at us with her "southern Scowl."[7]

Into the Deep South

There was another motel nearby the one that turned us away. They let us stay, and it was cheap, but it was in rather bad shape. When we drove from the motel office to our room, a car followed right after us, then made a U-turn and left.

"Those bastards are spying on us!" said Shihō-san.

I cannot say for certain whether or they were spying on us, but it was certainly possible. When we Japanese travel in the Deep South, we can categorize the attitude of white people as follows:

1. If we are accompanied by a white southerner or travel with an introduction by one, then we are welcomed more warmly and treated more kindly than in any other region.

2. If we go with a white northerner, the attitude depends on what kind of white person he is. If he is what is popularly called a "WASP,"[8] and if he appears to be a gentleman, then everything will be all right, but we will not be welcomed as warmly as in the previous situation.

3. If we are traveling with a white person who looks like a hippie or a student who looks like an antiwar activist, then we must be on guard. At best we will meet that "southern scowl"; at worst we might be killed.

4. When we travel only with other Japanese, if we clearly appear to be tourists, dress in good clothes (even if worn-looking), and adopt the attitude of innocent students, then we will not run into any problems, even in places far from the freeways or the usual tourists spots. (Even so in rural areas we might still encounter the "southern scowl.")

5. If we travel with other Japanese but don't appear to be tourists, wear poor-looking clothes, look suspicious, and have a Yankee license plate, then we can expect grim looks everywhere.

6. If we travel together with Negroes, the worst possible circumstance, then we must prepare ourselves for the possibility that we could be killed. It is much more dangerous for Negroes and non-Negroes to act together than for Negroes to act alone. And the danger is highest for non-Negroes who are Jewish.

On this trip the two of us fell into category 5. Shihō had a beard that made him look like General Nogi. (In fact, he is the grandson of the notorious General Araki.)[9] On top of this, he was very poorly dressed, and I was wearing some cool but sorry-looking trousers that I had bought in Saigon.

The reason that it was extremely dangerous to travel with Negroes was that you would be seen as an activist who had come to intrigue or spy in this paradise of discrimination, the Deep South. From around 1964, when the civil rights movement was flourishing and activist groups, with students at their core, came from the North to fight segregation, the danger became even more intense. The most fervent of the non-Negro activists were Jews. And it was Jews who were also the most fervent participants in movements opposing the Vietnam War and American bases in Okinawa.

Since journalists had to be on their guard nearly as much as activists, it was common knowledge that northern reporters could not cover stories freely in the South. Since state policemen were all on the "white side," they were even more dangerous than ordinary white citizens. It was not unusual for the police to be involved in the murder of activists, but culprits were rarely found guilty of these crimes. Only very few Japanese yet understand the actual state of lawlessness in the South.

When we got to our room, we discovered that the lock did not work. They had not given us a key at the motel office, but when we asked for one they made us pay a $1.00 security charge. They might as well have not given us a key at all. It was a nuisance, but we went to an outdoor movie theater with all our valuables still in the car.[10] They were showing Uncle Tom's Cabin, a movie version of Harriet Beecher Stowe's classic novel. Many in the audience were Negroes. Published just before the Civil War, the book had a tremendous impact on the issue of abolishing slavery. Nowadays the name "Uncle Tom" has become a synonym for "a Negro who plays up to whites." Among Negroes it is the strongest expression of contempt.

On our way back from the movie, we stopped by a former "Colored Only" bar. Naturally there were no white people there, just Negro men and women drinking beer and whiskey. Of course, two Orientals attracted their attention. Many looked at us with curiosity, but none with that dangerous look—the respectable "southern scowl." When we looked for place to sit down, we heard voices calling to us, "Come on over here."

The Mississippi Delta

Four days after leaving Washington we arrived in Jackson, Mississippi, the state capital. There we exchanged our rental car for one with a Jackson city number on its license plate. That evening we had dinner at a restaurant where dozens of Civil War pictures were hung on the walls.

There were portraits of famous Southern generals. At the counter small Confederate flags were on sale.[11] Throughout the South we saw cars with Confederate flag bumper stickers as well as motels with Confederate flags on poles. There were postcards with the Confederate flag on sale at airports. It is safe to say that wherever Confederate flags were most visible, segregationist sentiments were the most hysterical.

The next day we headed for Meyersville in Issaquena County, where Shiho had lived. The Mississippi Delta is not only the deepest of the Deep South; it can be said to be its "heart." For many Negroes it is the home where their heart is, but at the same time it is the heart of the South's discrimination. Issaquena County is one of the typical areas in the Delta region.

The endless cotton fields on both sides of the road were dotted with magnificent mansions that would turn the heads of bypassers in Japan. With their broad lawns and numerous rooms, there were even houses that reminded us of baronial castles in western Europe. All of these mansions, without exception, belonged to white people. And white people were also the owners of the vast plantations.

In stark contrast, scattered randomly here and there nearby these mansions, and at a distance from them too, stood wretched-looking houses that looked just a little better than the shacks thrown up in Japan immediately after the war. These were the houses where Negroes lived. And, of course, in their midst could be seen a wretched-looking church. It was the Negroes' church. Six years earlier a white man set off a bomb at a church in Birmingham, slaughtering four Negro girls attending Sunday school and injuring more than twenty others. It too was a Negroes' church.

At a glance it is clear that the churches attended by white are "temples" suited to their "mansions." Not only do many white ministers tacitly accept discrimination; some who belong to the Ku Klux Klan are devout preachers of segregation.

After arriving in Meyersville and until it got dark, we visited three or four families that Shiho had lived with. Since it was too much to ask for accommodation with them that night, we decided to stay at a motel in a nearby town. The town, not so nearby, in fact, was Greenville, about 70 kilometers to the north. Because we were low on gasoline, we stopped at a small gasoline stand and general store a few miles outside of Meyersville. It was possible that Shihō's face was known in town, so he stayed in the car while I went to ask for gas. The storekeeper, who pumped the gasoline and sold me some soft drinks, gave me that frightful "southern scowl." It seems that the whites already knew that we had visited a Negro community. . . .

After staying a night in Greenville, we went back to Meyersville once more. Negro homes do not have enough rooms for guests, but Mr. Robinson, a Negro with whom Shiho had become good friends, agreed to let us stay with his family. The Robinsons and their ten children lived in a house with only three rooms and a kitchen. Since there was also a woman living with the Robinsons to help around the house in return for room and board, there were thirteen of us altogether. The ten children included: the oldest daughter (17), the oldest son (15), the second son (14), the second daughter (11), the third son (10), the third daughter (8), the fourth son (7), the fourth daughter (6), the fifth son (5), and the fifth daughter (1). Three other children—two girls and a boy—had died as infants. Mrs. Robinson, who was 33 years old, had given birth to thirteen children since the age of 16.

The Robinsons' house was near the northern border of Issaquena County, about 20 kilometers directly north of the center of Meyersville. Scattered about nearby, about 100 meters apart from each other, were a dozen or more other houses, all occupied by Negroes.

The Ignored

After arranging to stay with the Robinsons, the two of us went to buy provisions for ourselves at a nearby market. To get to the nearest stores we had to go to Meyersville or to Rolling Fork in the next county, both more than 30 kilometers away by car. We set off in the car with Rosie, the oldest daughter, Louis, the oldest son, and a neighbor friend of Louis's as our guides.

The supermarket that Mrs. Robinson suggested to us was one on the outskirts of Rolling Fork. It catered to many Negro customers. Shihō told me that Mrs. Robinson had picked this store as safest for us to shop in, since what white people most disliked was the sight of Negroes and non-Negroes riding together in a car. As we got out of the car in the supermarket parking lot, two or three white men working on the roof of a house under construction nearby threw us hostile looks with that "southern scowl." Louis's friend remained to guard the car. Whites sometimes let the air out of Negroes' tires and in the worst case put sugar in their gasoline tanks. That is a special southern way to wreck an automobile engine. . . .

After dinner we played with the Robinsons' ten children under the porch lights. Just as Mrs. Robinson said, her family was "something like a little school," with the children noisily running about but all getting along with each other. They helped with the housework without complaint. Rosie, the oldest daughter, did most of the cooking, while Lorinna and Alberta, the second and third daughters took care of the laundry. Aside from looking after the baby, Mrs. Robinson was free to devote most of her time to the kindergarten where she worked. Mr. Robinson, like most Negroes in the area, worked as an agricultural day laborer and took on automobile repair jobs. On this day, he was off in Alabama to hear lectures on raising cattle.

The family went to bed around 10:00 P.M. One of the three rooms in the house was Mr. and Mrs. Robinson's bedroom, and another was the children's bedroom, but since it was impossible for all the children to sleep in one room, some slept in the parlor. Shihō and I slept in the parlor on a sofa with its back thrown down. Louis and Ronnie slept in their clothes on a patched-up rug on the floor beside us. Louis lay down clutching a shotgun, sleeping with its barrel pointed toward the door.

"If those white pigs come to attack," he told us, "I'll pull the trigger and nail them."

It was dangerous to sleep holding a loaded gun, I thought, but the next morning I found out that it was empty. It was old but still usable. It was not unusual for Negro families to arm themselves like this. It goes without saying that southern white households were equipped with the most and the best weapons. (Pistols and rifles are sold freely.) In the Deep South the number of firearms certainly exceeds the number of houses. The Negroes must always be prepared for the possibility that white people will shoot randomly at their houses in the middle of the night. The homes of people who campaign for Negro rights are especially targets. Families that allow non-Negroes like us to stay with them are probably much more likely to suffer "harassing attacks" than ordinary Negro families.[12] It was certainly no laughing matter that Louis slept holding a gun.

Negroes in the Deep South live with this chronic sense of fear, and that is not likely to change in the near future. When the state police, who are supposed to protect all ordinary citizens, are completely on the side of the white people, the Negroes have no alternative but self-protection. Sometimes even the National Guard are clearly arrayed against the Negroes.[13]

Alligators still live in semitropical Mississippi, and in late August the heat does not abate after the sun goes down. The sound of the ancient electric window fan rattled noisily through the quiet of sleep.

American-Style Poverty

One might think that a family owning a car, a refrigerator, and a television set was leading a tolerably comfortable life. At least one would not think that it was poor. The Robinson family, belonging to the rather average class in their neighborhood, owned all three.

Even so the Robinsons have not yet escaped from "poverty." I do not mean to say that since the standard of living in America is high their poverty is only relative. Paradoxically, one might even say that only in America could a family possess these three things and still be poor. Let me explain what I mean.

Not only was the rug that Louis and Ronnie slept on completely worn out; so were their clothes. There were holes in the knees and seats of their pants, and they did not fit at all. Since they did not have pajamas, they had to sleep in the same dusty clothes that they wore during the day. They looked not one bit different from refugees in Saigon [during the Vietnam civil war]. And the neighboring bedroom, where three of the children slept side by side, was just like the slums in Harlem.

Let's look around the house. What was there to see besides a sofa, a television set, and an electric fan? The only thing that catches the eye is a home encyclopedia, but the monthly installments for it still have not been paid. Even with so many children, there were hardly any toys. Nor was there a bath or running water. Water for cooking and laundry had to be brought from the kindergarten across the street. The main chore for the little children was carrying water home. They washed themselves in a washtub in place of a bathtub. When they woke in the morning, they washed their faces in a wash basin, but the children usually skipped it.

The toilet was in the vegetable garden about 20 meters behind the house. It is probably more primitive than anything you might find in the most remote rural areas of Japan. The tiny outhouse was built of scrap wood picked up here and there, and the toilet seat was a rough wooden board. The privy hole was crawling with maggots, and a swarm of flies took flight whenever the door was opened.

Everything was poor. Owing to reduced prices brought about by mass production, even poor people can wear nice clothes, but the Robinsons belonged to a social class where even that was out of reach. Those at such a poverty level are not an unusual minority. It is common knowledge that a large percentage of the American population—perhaps 40,000,000 to 50,000,000 peoples—live at this level.[14] Needless to say, the largest number are Negroes.

Why then do they have automobiles, refrigerators, and television sets? Let us suppose, for example, that the Robinsons want to go to the market. Whether you go to Rolling Fork, where we went shopping by car, or to downtown Meyersville, by foot it would be a 60-kilometer round trip, which would take from early in the morning until late at night. Even by bicycle it would take a half-day. It is simply not possible to live that way, so a car is more important for getting around than *geta* [wooden clogs] or shoes. You cannot live without an automobile. A refrigerator is just as much of a necessity. If you cannot keep the food that you have bought, then you would have to make a roundtrip to the store every day using expensive gasoline. And if you live in town, then you would have to go out to the farm everyday by car. The advantage of living on a farm is that you do not have to go shopping every day.[15]

The Robinsons' automobile is an old used car that often breaks down. Even though everyone owns a car, it is not at all unexpected for them to suddenly stop running. Breakdowns are inevitable, so neighboring families help out by giving each other rides when they go out. When you see a Negro's car running down the road in the Deep South, it usually carries two or three times the passengers one normally does. Since roads were built in America from the start, it is impossible to live without an automobile.

What about television sets? Perhaps the same thing happens as in Japan. Material poverty often gives rise to spiritual poverty. To use leisure time profitably, first, you must spend money, and second you must have a richly "cultivated" background. In families that lack both, nothing surpasses television for spending leisure time. In the United States used television sets are extremely inexpensive. At the Robinsons, the television set has poor reception, but it is left on until the end of the day. . . .

Our usual image of the "American housewife" is that of a woman who considers the husband more important than her children—and who sees herself as "wife" rather than as "mother." But housewives in Negro society are much more likely to think of themselves as mothers than as wives. It is from the ranks of such women that the most powerful supporters of the Negro movement continue to come. Compared with male activists, they may be less obtrusive but they are no less unwavering and resolute in their commitment.

Some point out that apart from economic and social factors, the strength of such Negro mothers was influenced by the system of slavery. During the days of slavery, husbands usually played only an incidental role within the family. Easily bought and sold, they were separated from their families. As a result only mothers raised many children. Their "role as mother" extended as well into the families of their white "masters," where they took care of white children too.

KIRISHIMA YŌKO, "THE LONELY AMERICAN" (1971)

Kirishima Yōko (1937–), the daughter of an affluent Tokyo family, grew up in Shanghai during the war. In the confusion of the early postwar years her family experienced rapid decline. After graduating from high school, Kirishima went to work for Bungei shunjūsha, a prominent publishing firm, at the age of twenty. In a romantic relationship with a much older retired American navy officer estranged from his wife, she gave birth to her first daughter secretly by taking a two-month sick leave from the company. When she tried to do the same with her second child the company turned her down, forcing her to resign and become a freelance writer. After her third child was born in 1967, she broke up with the father. After visiting Vietnam briefly as a war correspondent, Kirishima went to live in Los Angeles from 1968 to 1970. Her best-selling book, *The Lonely American (Sabishii Amerikajin)*, was based on her experiences there. In 1972 the book won the prestigious Ōya Sōichi nonfiction prize. When she returned to Japan, she was struck by how Americanized Japanese society had become during her absence. An outspoken unmarried mother of three who defied social norms by pursuing a career and taking many lovers, she soon became an influential voice in the nascent women's liberation movement. She has published more than forty books expressing her views about the role of women in Japanese society.

. . .

"Distinguished-looking executive seeks passionate big-breasted girl to accompany him to orgy party at exclusive members club. Must have few or no sexual inhibitions and live in western L.A."

"Muscular athlete, 42 years old, 6 ft, 160 lb, married engineer. Seeks similar male for sincere and cautious sex."

"Military employee stationed in Vietnam seeks beautiful white girl. Will provide air fare and a comfortable life with housekeeper." . . .

Would any newspaper in Japan consider posting such classified ads? Readers of underground papers in America are not at all surprised by

Kirishima Yōko, "The Lonely American," source: Kirishima Yōko, *Sabishii Amerikajin*. (Tokyo: Bungei shunjūsha, 1971), 5–7, 19–27, 36–37.

their raw frankness. Classified sections in these newspapers are full of them.

Despite their name "underground" these newspapers are not clandestine publications. They are sold at street-corner newsstands along with the *New York Times* and the *Los Angeles Times*. . . . The most substantial of the underground papers and those with the widest readership are the *Free Press* in Los Angeles and the *Berkeley Barb* in San Francisco. Both proudly acknowledge that they are anti-establishment, and they rail vocally against the Vietnam War, racial discrimination, and many other things. The "silent majority" sees them as an enemy.

While I rarely glance at their no-holds-barred articles, stuffed with insider terminology and self-righteous, avant-garde, left-wing prose, I love reading their classified ads. I am not the only one who does. Most of their readers do. In any case, they are very interesting. Nowhere else have I seen human desire displayed so blatantly, with such rawness and openness.

My curiosity mounted as I read one ad after another. I decided to try an experiment. I chose six safe-looking ads in the *Free Press* and sent off letters responding to them. . . . Perhaps because of my caution, the quality of those who answered was surprisingly high. What began as an experiment turned out to be a practical way of meeting new people. I made many valued friends this way.

Most Americans live regimented lives, never straying a step outside their company or family communities. Their circle of acquaintances is terribly narrow and shallow. Naturally everyone was astonished to see an unattached foreigner like me move into a new city only to be instantly surrounded by a variety of men. They wanted to know my secret. If I had told these good-natured and earnest people that I used a loathsome "bulletin board for sickos" in "Satan's newspaper," no doubt they would have been shocked and angered and ceased to be my friends. But when I introduced my newly found friends without saying how I met them, there was no problem at all. My old friends formed friendships with my new friends, and my circle of acquaintances kept expanding.

To tell you the truth, none of the friends I met through the *Free Press* ads could be categorized as anti-establishment. They were all outstanding and intelligent professionals: a corporate executive, a doctor, a reporter, an accountant, an aeronautical technician, a scholar, a lawyer, an architect. Their incomes ranged between fifteen and forty thousand dollars, and one or two were much richer. Ironically, all were conservative on political and economic issues, and overwhelmingly they took a hawkish stance on the Vietnam War. Their views had nothing at all to do with the politics of the underground press. It was no surprise that they mingled so easily with my old establishment friends. All of them belonged to the same social stratum, but my *Free Press* friends simply happened to be liberal in lifestyle values and adventurous in spirit. Each of them, perhaps on a whim, decided to use the underground press to find others like themselves. Eventually they found birds of the same feather.

In America, however, no one is capricious enough to spend money simply on a whim. These men really were searching for people. They wanted to meet somebody. In all their ads I heard the moans of the lonely. With precious few exceptions, all these ads asked for sex—but most asked for something more. The problems of their writers would have been easily resolved if they were just about a need for sex. The liberalization of sex in America has gone so far that I wonder if the profession of prostitution will survive. Worrying about sex in the simplest sense is disappearing. Desire is limitless, and there are plenty of predators brimming with sexual energy. Such men do not frighten me. They are always on the attack, but since they think themselves lucky if they make a hit, they are easy to deal with.

What frightens me is the moans of men starved for love. It is unpleasant to pull back one's hand suddenly after inadvertently touching the gaping wound of someone else's loneliness. There are so many lonely people in America. Amid the rapid liberalization of sex, the loneliness of those who cannot rescue themselves through sex is becoming more and more pathetic. This is what America is like today.

People starved for money are also starved for love and sex. This is true everywhere, but in America the loneliness of the elderly is even more acute.

"Seeking intelligent, healthy, moderately good-looking single girl under 30 with father complex. Will offer financial stability, travel, other various recreations," read one ad. The old man who posted it, a poet with his own publishing company, looked to me like a shriveled hawk. He had lost his wife some years before. He loved her so deeply that he still inserted passionate dedications to her in his books. That made it all the more difficult for him to endure the loneliness of living alone. He had traveled all over the world with his wife, and he still flew by himself to Paris or London to see the opera. He was so wealthy that he could return from London one day, only to fly there again the next because he had forgotten to see a certain play. But he found no pleasure in doing this alone. Without a partner to share his happiness, he said, there was nothing of value left for him in this world.

Given his extravagant lifestyle he could have attracted many young women, but snaring them so crudely did not satisfy him. What he desired above all was true love. He must have realized that at his age he no longer had any appeal as a man, so he came up with the idea of seeking women with a father complex. For him love was not an object of transaction.

Some wealthy men are satisfied with devotion bought by money, but most grow more difficult and more distrustful as they grow richer. That renders all their wealth practically useless. In the end the old man began seeking physically handicapped women, who, he thought, would be as lonely as he was and would truly need him. I do not know whether his plan succeeded or not.

Some men seem to have everything—wealth, honor, youth, charm, and family—yet are still haunted by loneliness. All the men who became my friends through the underground press were divorced and free, except for one married man who was intensely afraid of his wife.

"Seeking a very cautious friendship. Lonely 40-year-old married man. Sensitive, intelligent, nice-looking, financially stable. Want to share affection with married or single woman." This bland ad did not catch my attention, but since I had typed an extra letter I replied to it as an afterthought. By the time a reply arrived I had forgotten all about it. What the letter said, however, caught my eye. It was an exceedingly cautious letter containing no specifics. Nevertheless, it was clear that the writer was highly intelligent. After a long and laborious correspondence, with both of us hiding in the shadows of the postal service, we finally agreed to meet. I still remained ignorant of his name and profession. A major compromise like this was a first for me. Of course, I was supposed to be a Chinese woman named Min-ran Tao, so the deception was mutual.

The man who met me in a hotel lobby turned out to be compactly built but handsome, with the air of an elegant and keen-minded college professor. But as he kept looking around nervously I became irritated. "Everywhere I go I bump into acquaintances. I can't relax," he explained as we sat down at a corner table in the hotel restaurant.

Without even introducing himself, he began talking like a machine gun, eloquently discussing art and philosophy and history. He is a bit pedantic, I thought, but this was the kind of enriching conversation I had been starved for since coming to America. I became more talkative. As he talked and listened he had the habit of looking deep into one's eyes. Staring straight into my heart he seemed impervious to deception. As we finished our coffee, he fell silent for a while, then seemed to reach a resolution. "OK, I trust you," he said. "I want you to trust me as well. I will show you my office."

I wondered why he was taking me straight to his office after being so nervous about being seen by someone he knew. It turned out to be an elegant spacious study with a sitting room located on the top floor of a skyscraper.

"This is my office. There is nobody else here, and the walls are sound-proof so we can talk about anything," he said. "I work as a psychiatrist here, but I also teach at a university and work for the federal government and military. If you want to know more about me you can browse through my papers and books. You can judge for yourself if I am fit to be your close friend."

He had an impressive career. Since psychiatrists attract followers as if they were shamans, their profession enjoys unparalleled prestige in affluent America. Dr. C. was the crème de la crème who rose to prominence with remarkable speed and attracted numerous rich and famous patients—millionaires, movie stars, politicians. He himself was a member of the most privileged American elite. Why would a man like that be so lonely that he placed an ad in a notorious hippie newspaper to seek refuge in the friendship of a totally unknown woman like me?

In his daily life Dr. C. was a typical case of someone who achieved success at the expense of freedom. He had no time to himself. His day was divided into segments that lasted 57 or 59 minutes. Even when he returned home, he had to switch into the role model husband and father and had no time for private relaxation.

When one patient ended his therapeutic sessions, Dr. C. decided to allot the time to himself secretly instead of filling the slot with a patient on his waiting list. He had been searching for somebody totally unrelated to his world to be an accomplice in his little rebellion.

Every Saturday morning at 11, I became his client. Whenever I was about to board the elevator up to his office, a famous actress emerged from within. Her face looked quite horrendous up close. The fee she paid for an hour of whining about her sex life or whatever was enough to cover my weekly expenses. Out she came in her mink coat, and in I went. But with me it was the doctor who was going to pour his heart out. He had no chance to let his guard down as he coolly confronted a tsunami of private confessions all day. I did not believe myself qualified to be his interlocutor, but I did have enough knowledge and sensitivity to talk with him. I knew about loneliness, and I was, moreover, a foreign woman who would cause no future trouble and who was not interested in his money.

As I sat in his office, I casually overheard his phone conversations. As I sat with mouth agape, the maladies afflicting the so-called upper classes were laid out before me. A Supreme Court judge calls to say that his granddaughter is pregnant and asks for help. A university president seeks advice about his homosexual son. It seems that there were few families without problems, from drug and alcohol addiction to lack of affection between husband and wife. There is plenty of work for psychiatrists to do.

One day Dr. C. was so tired he could not even speak. The night before, his sleep had been interrupted by a call that one of his patients, a businessman, was sitting with a pistol in his hand about to commit suicide. All night he reasoned with the patient until at dawn he finally succeeded in disarming him and sedating him. He had no time to go back to sleep himself, and he came straight to work. As he told me all this he dozed off with his head on my lap. Looking down at his sleeping face, I felt as though I had glimpsed an immense black emptiness eating away at this affluent country, America. It made me painfully homesick. . . .

There is no end to stories of people like this. But what I can say about all those ads in the underground press, and what I found interesting about them, is that they were all direct and honest. Of course, sometimes they advertised attractiveness or intelligence that did not meet my expectations, but judgments about such attributes are subjective. When it came to concrete facts like age, race, profession, and education, not a single person had lied to me. I am the trusting type who tends to take people at their word, so sometimes I hesitated, fearing I would be laughed at for being so gullible, but in the end I concluded that doubting others was more troublesome than the potential problem of being deceived by them.

Americans . . . are generally so heedlessly frank that one is upset by their honesty. Being honest themselves, they are vehement in expecting the same kind of honesty from others. In America the authority of one eyewitness account carries more weight than a dozen items of material evidence would in Japan. If trust broke down in America, I think society would cease to function. If the checks that people write so casually on a daily basis were replaced by cash payments, economic circulation would come to a halt, and if suddenly people could no longer fill their gas tanks using credit cards, traffic would be at a standstill.

People say that crime does not pay. Americans might add with certain defiance that neither does lying. The no-holds-barred honesty of the underground newspaper ads takes this defiance to a pathological extreme. Although these ads may seem abnormal at first glance, they are important documents that expose the unadorned faces of those who can only be called true Americans.

The people who place these ads are truly lonely. America is like an awkward giant that bears his breast and screams, "I am lonely, I am lonely." I look back at such an America with puzzlement and affection.

YOSHIDA RUIKO, "HOT DAYS IN HARLEM" (1972)

After the photojournalist Yoshida Ruiko (1938–) graduated from Keiō University, she worked for a time as an announcer and then left for America on a Fulbright scholarship to study journalism at Columbia University. Her first contact with a black person was in Japan during her days as a radio announcer when she interviewed prominent jazz musicians visiting her country. They struck her as extremely dignified, and she wondered why they were subject to discrimination in America. Her first meeting with a black person on American soil occurred during a bus ride from Ohio to Washington, D.C. An impoverished and intoxicated black man asked if he could sit next to her. When the driver shouted at him to go to the rear, she told him to stay. He had been stationed in Japan and married a Japanese woman, he told her, but after living a year in Virginia she left him. Resigned to his inability as a black man to be a respectable breadwinner, he grew angry when Yoshida encouraged him to "fight against racial discrimination." The driver stopped the bus and dragged him to the rear. When they got off at Washington, the man repeatedly apologized. His "I am sorry" continued to haunt her. Yoshida spent nearly the entire turbulent 1960s living in and around Harlem. She recorded her experiences in both words and photographs. After returning to Japan in 1971, she presented her Harlem photographs at an exhibit titled "Black Is Beautiful," the subtitle of her book published the same year.

. . .

White people are not the only ones with prejudices against black people. Most yellow people in America, including Japanese, have discriminatory attitudes. Since yellow people tend to be in closer contact with blacks in their daily lives, their prejudice takes on a stronger reality.

A woman student from India, for example, told me, "In India, I sometimes wore Western clothes. But over here, I wear nothing but saris. If not, people mistake me for a Negro."

Yoshida Ruiko, "Hot Days in Harlem," source: Yoshida Ruiko, *Harlem no atsui hibi* (Tokyo: Kōdansha, 1972), 82–89.

A dentist from the Philippines said, "I don't mind being mistaken for a Vietnamese, a Jew, or a Japanese. As long as they don't think I'm a Negro."

A call girl from Taiwan, for her part, said, "Regardless of how much money he offers, I would never want to sleep with a Negro."

Many Japanese Americans are also anti-Negro. . . . I think this comes from their desire to distance themselves from Negroes, who continue to be maltreated as they [Japanese Americans] were in earlier times.

But it seems that Japanese Americans have more sympathy toward the blacks' situation than Japanese people from Japan do. My neighborhood grocery lady seemed to be expressing her heartfelt criticism of white supremacy when she said, "American white people are cold-hearted and violent."

In contrast to Japanese Americans who have experienced discrimination firsthand, Japanese who visit America for business or public purposes find themselves in a complex situation. Many of these Japanese are elite intellectuals. They are students of German philosophy or love French art and speak good English.

A [Japanese] trading company employee with a heavy tan . . . was visibly distressed when asked if he had come from Korea.

When I was in Japan, I seldom heard anything good said about Koreans. But the Koreans I met in America have big hearts and polite manners. Being a native of Hokkaido, I grew to love their continental temperament. I was moved by the simple elegance of a Korean woman who worked in the Korean restaurant. I felt the same way about Chinese people. I was impressed by their laid-back sense of humor.

By comparison, the Japanese living in New York are typically stressed out and constantly busy. They work till midnight. They go to restaurants in big groups, wearing the same gray suits and black ties. Spooked Americans often asked me, "Is it against Japanese custom for men to eat with women?" "Are the men all gay?" "Why are they all dressed the same?"

These Japanese intellectuals are college educated, and they have been taught that America's discrimination against blacks is an extension of slavery, a reprehensible practice that America is now striving to correct for the sake of democracy. They feel righteous rage when they hear stories of black children not being able to enter certain schools. . . . On the theoretical level, many intellectuals want to be on the side of the blacks.

But what happens when we step beyond theory? In practice, most Japanese visitors are prejudiced against blacks and try their best to avoid them.

For example, out of curiosity I once attended a party for Keiō University graduates in New York, like myself. Most of the alumni who attended were middle-aged men in corporate management posts. After the party, one of them offered me a ride home in his car, since he lived in an uptown hotel. It was a gray Oldsmobile.

"Can't own a car like this in Japan," he boasted, chatting about his family in Japan and pontificating on American women. Then he asked me where I lived.

"Harlem," I answered.

I can never forget the gentleman's reaction to my innocent response. His alcohol buzz seemed to evaporate instantly. His face grew pale, his hands shook, and he stopped talking.

"I live on 88th Street, so I'll take you to 110th. I've never been farther than that, so it's a bit scary to me," he finally said, looking at me apologetically with his timid eyes. I got out on 87th Street and took the subway home.

This sort of thing happens with young people too. A classmate once drove me home from Queens. After crossing the Triborough Bridge and entering Harlem, he told me to shut the windows and sit away from the door. Then he sped up. Having lived in Harlem for over a year, I thought this was strange. He explained to me that he always did this when driving through Harlem.

Fear is not the only factor keeping Japanese visitors away from Harlem. People are also concerned about their status and their business relations. One oil company employee explained, "I do business mostly with Anglo-Saxons, so I try my best to stay away from blacks."

It is true that American society turns a different gaze on yellow people with close ties to black people. One Japanese cameraman put it bluntly to me, "If you want to succeed in America, stay away from blacks." This, from a journalist who normally says progressive things. . . .

Some Japanese in America showed intense interest when they learned that I lived in Harlem. Some were journalists interested in the race problem. However, by far the most common question was, "I want to sleep with a Negro woman once. Do you know any good ones? Mind you, she must be a clean one."

And I got quite a few more of these than I expected: "Negro would be going too far for me. But one that's a bit lighter would be okay, like a Puerto Rican."

One evening I was having dinner with Michelle, an aspiring [black] actress, when a waitress approached and handed her a note. It is from that gentleman, she said, pointing across the room. "I want to talk to you. Call me at my hotel tonight," the note said. "That gentleman" was a 40-ish Japanese man in a white shirt, a towel around his neck and wielding a Japanese fan. He waved at us.

"Up to you," I said to Michelle. I did not hear about what happened afterward, and I did not want to.

Even worse was a young Japanese journalist who worked for a weekly magazine. He was disappointed that my husband was a blond white man. A sexy black man would have been perfect. This was not a nice thing for him to say, but I remained stoic. Then he said, "Please introduce me to a Japanese woman selling her body in Harlem. I want to tell readers in Japan about the misery that awaits Japanese women who marry black men."

I snapped. I told him to go look for himself and showed him the door.

Many Japanese women also show aversion toward black people. Faced with the choice of sitting in the subway next to a clean-cut black man and a drunken white man, many Japanese women would choose the white man. . . .

An elite Japanese housewife who boasts that her child attends a fine school with not even one black student is hideous. Copying white people's high fashion, she goes shopping on Fifth Avenue, feeling glamorous in her mink coat and diamonds. Clearly she is simply a nouveau riche with bad taste.

The women of New York's Japanese Club direct their quintessentially Japanese sticky malice toward me when I tell them I live in Harlem. When they learn I am a graduate of Keiō University and a Fulbright scholar, suddenly they become nice.

"Oh! My Tak is from such and such university!"

KŌSAKA MASATAKA,
"A PROPOSAL FOR ENCOURAGING AMERICA" (1980)

Kōsaka Masataka (1934–96), a professor of international politics at Kyoto University, was the son of a conservative professor of philosophy known for his ardent ideological support of the war against the United States. After graduation from Kyoto University, Kōsaka went to Amer-

Kōsaka Masataka, "A Proposal for Encouraging America," source: Kōsaka Masataka, "A Proposal for Encouraging America," *Japan Echo* 7, no. 1 (Spring 1980): 102–110.

ica in 1960 to study international politics at Harvard University. After returning to Japan he became famous for a 1963 essay, "A Realist's Perspective on Peace," criticizing overly idealistic arguments for Japan's unarmed neutrality offered by influential progressive intellectuals. In another widely read essay reassessing the legacy of the postwar prime minister Yoshida Shigeru, he portrayed Yoshida as a principled politician who established the philosophical underpinnings of postwar Japan's pragmatic conservatism. His positive assessment of Yoshida's cool-headed skepticism toward ideology may have been his way of criticizing not only left-wing postwar progressives but also the wartime collaboration of his father. In later years, he criticized Yoshida's policy of limited rearmament and his high-handed secretive style for stunting Japan's "independent spirit." His shifting assessment of Yoshida reflected the times in which he wrote. It seemed to him that there was an abnormal gap between Japan's rapid economic growth and its lack of political clout in international politics. In a best-selling book he advanced the view that Japan should play a role as a "maritime nation" based on foreign trade. This 1980 essay suggests that Japan's balance of power with the United States was changing to Japan's advantage.

. . .

I

America has fallen on hard times. Its politics are in disarray, its economy is blighted by stagflation, and its global influence has waned. Bad though this is for America, it cannot possibly bode well for Japan either, and we cannot let things drift along as they are. Nevertheless, America appears to have the potential to recover from this slump. When it does, although naturally the state of recovery will be decided by the American people themselves, the attitudes taken by Western Europe and Japan will also have a significant effect. Ultimately, the question of how Japan should relate to America is important in deciding Japan's place in the world.

II

Let us look first at the changes in America. The first thing that strikes the observer is the seriousness of the political and economic malaise, rooted as it is in what President Carter has termed the "crisis of confidence."

The gravity of the situation is borne out by the actions of the very man who coined the phrase. President Carter first used the term "crisis of confidence" in his energy address to the nation after he had returned from the Tokyo summit and collected his thoughts at Camp David. . . .

III

Needless to say, the American "crisis of confidence" originated in the failure in Vietnam. The shock was all the greater for Vietnam's having been the first defeat in America's history.

Simply describing it as a defeat does not do justice to the shock dealt by Vietnam. The important fact is that the Vietnam adventure was launched by "the best and the brightest" of a confident America.

The history of U.S. intervention in Vietnam goes back many years, but it was the Kennedy administration that embarked upon full-fledged military intervention. The error of this administration may be explained as one of excessive confidence in American might and mistaken American theory.

The Kennedy administration believed that America possessed great strength, and it planned to get the country moving again after the Eisenhower administration's standpattism. This confidence obviously grew when the Soviet Union backed down in the Cuban missile crisis.

The other error, the error of theory, can best be seen in the U.S. strategy of counterinsurgency and flexible response. The best minds of the Kennedy administration felt that the arena of competition between the U.S. and the USSR had shifted to the third world. It was assumed that all the third world nations wanted to modernize and that the Soviet-American competition would be decided in favor of the country that extended the better assistance and provided the better model. America was confident that it would win this competition. However, it saw the process of modernization as a process fraught with social upheaval. According to Walt Rostow, himself a theorist on the stages of economic growth, the stage prior to economic takeoff is a transitional stage in which the traditional society collapses and new loyalties appear. During this stage the developing country is susceptible to communism, and communism is a disease that it is America's duty to prevent.

More specifically, it was America's duty to stifle guerrilla wars, for guerrilla war was the communist strategy in the pre-takeoff stage. Thus America needed a counterinsurgency capability, which was all that was thought necessary to resolve the conflict. It was American strategic theory that the threat of aggression should be met not with the inflexible threat of massive retaliation but by readying the ability to fight guerrilla insurgencies and other limited conflicts, and that having superior strength at each stage would both make it possible to deter escalation by the other side and sap the enemy's will by retaining the option of escalation for the United States.

As David Halberstam has written, the U.S. failure in Vietnam was a failure by the best and the brightest. And it is precisely because it was a defeat of America's best and brightest that it was so devastating to America's national confidence,

The same thing happened in American domestic policy. American society, particularly American urban society, began to take on the aura of a wasteland in the late 1960s. Crime was rampant, and fear kept people off the streets at night. Of course, the dangers of the American city were exaggerated, and there were still many places where one could walk safely after dark, but there was an undeniable malaise throughout the land, reflected in the feeling that to go out alone was to court danger.

The American urban wasteland was not born of neglect. It was not the child of a lack of will or a lack of might. The American residential environment had changed greatly in the years following World War II, especially in the 1960s. To begin with, there was a boom in housing construction. Some 48 million housing units were built between 1950 and 1972, most of them in the suburbs but a considerable number in connection with the redevelopment of inner-city areas. In the 1960s, especially in the late 1960s, many new office buildings and public facilities were also built in downtown areas.

Indeed, this redevelopment may even be termed the American dream come true. And it was American might that made it possible. The development of the suburbs was consistent with the American ideal of choosing to live in a small community rather than a large city. It also reflected the American outlook on civilization, with the home seen as a bastion of individualism; once the home was secured, Americans sought to link the home and the place of work, as well as the home and other homes, functionally by means of a sophisticated transport system. Thus suburban development was begun as a desirable ideal.

As a result, major changes began to take place in the American residential environment with the 1960s, most of them lauded as changes for the better. Yet the fact is that these very changes created the American urban wasteland. This unexpected outcome can be attributed to the race problem. The reason the inner-city areas generally turned into slums was that the predominantly white middle class moved to the suburbs while waves of blacks and Hispanic people moved into the cities. . . .

In sum, it may be said that the devastation of America's cities was generated by America's dreams and strength running counter to expectations; it was an adverse side effect of the distinctively American dynamism. This is a characteristic that the urban problem shared with the Vietnam War. With these experiences at home and abroad, it is little wonder that America's confidence should have been so badly shaken.

IV

Nevertheless, this "crisis of confidence" may also be termed one stage in the process of America's maturation. There is, of course, a certain nostalgia for the America of old that believed in its own ideals, was faithful to them, and was naively confident of their success. However, universalism premised on the universal applicability of one's own ideals is bound to run aground on the shoals of international politics. And failure to recognize the limits of one's own power must surely beget disaster.

Thus it is a good thing that America has become aware of the limits of its power. Likewise, America is beginning to recognize the diverse values of diverse civilizations. This is clear first in dietary patterns and other aspects of life style. While America has long had diversity by virtue of its including a large number of ethnic groups, it is only recently that these ethnic groups have begun to adopt one another's dietary patterns.

Even more important has been the decline of the "melting pot" ideal. While this ideal was tolerant in its acceptance of ethnically diverse immigrants, it was intolerant in its assumption that their life styles could be melted down and homogenized. Today, the dominant idea is that America should comprise a single society with each ethnic group retaining its distinctive character, blacks living as blacks, Hispanics as Hispanics, and other groups retaining their ethnic identity in a broad social "mosaic."

This willingness to recognize diverse values is also linked to America's view of the world. . . .

Although by no means in the majority, such views are no longer laughed off. Americans are coming to recognize the worth of civilizations different from their own. At the same time, the American people have come to realize that good intentions, impeccable theory, and massive power do not necessarily guarantee good results. . . .

These are all signs of maturity. As a result, it is possible that America will get back on its feet again not by attempting to solve every problem with its own power alone but by recognizing diverse values and means and incorporating the views of other countries. Thereby it may regain its position of leadership among cooperating nations. . . .

VI

For Japan and Western Europe, and probably for the entire world, it is to be hoped that America will regain its position of leadership in maturity and not embark upon a narrowly self-centered unilateralism. Yet America needs support to enhance the possibility of mature leadership's winning out over nationalistic unilateralism.

Of course, a mere call for "support" is very abstract. There are a number of ways in which such support can be actually manifested. What I have in mind is that Japan, Western Europe, and America's other allies share the responsibility of managing the global political and economic systems in a degree commensurate with each nation's strength. This point has been made by countless others before me, but the idea that sharing responsibility will boost America has seldom been pointed out.

Yet who can deny that such responsible participation would have that effect? One of the reasons for America's fatigue is that, admittedly of its own free will, it has taken too much responsibility into its own hands. The psychological burden of this has been especially great. Sharing the responsibility would provide both material and spiritual support for America. . . .

Cooperating with America no longer need mean acknowledging American superiority. Once we recognize this, we can go on to recognize America's importance to Japan, and conflicts of interest with America can likewise be calmly reassessed, as can the limits of what can be done through Japan-U.S. cooperation. And as the next logical step, we may also come to comprehend the need for independent Japanese efforts.

Since the end of America's superiority in the early 1970s, Japan's policy makers have sought to respond to this new situation by restoring relations with China and otherwise pursuing "diplomatic diversification." However, in view of the tremendous importance of America in postwar Japanese foreign policy, it should be clear that there can be no fundamental change in Japanese foreign policy unless Japanese views of America are revised and the Japan-U.S. relationship is modified. The roundabout approach is fine, but basics must not be forgotten.

SHIMOMURA MITSUKO,
"GLORIOUS AMERICA, WHERE ARE YOU?" (1980)

After graduating from Keiō University with a degree in economics, Shimomura Mitsuko continued graduate study at New York University. In 1965 she decided to pursue a journalistic career as a way of promoting cross-cultural understanding. During her twenty-year career at the *Asahi shinbun*, she became the first woman sent abroad (New York) as a foreign correspondent, and she also became the first woman to become editor-in-chief of the *Asahi Journal*, a major weekly magazine. In 1987–88 she spent a year as a Nieman Fellow at Harvard University. The author of many books, she is known for her profile essays about renowned feminist role models such as Simone de Beauvoir, Margaret Thatcher, and Betty Friedan. After retiring from the *Asahi* in 1994, she continued to work as an independent writer and has been an energetic activist on gender, women's, and health issues. Her comments on the travails of daily life in America contrast substantially in 1980 with those of earlier generations.

. . .

When a Woman Is Dispatched Overseas

Before I knew it, a month had passed since my arrival in New York on assignment as a foreign correspondent. It had taken me quite some time to decide whether to accept this demanding long-term assignment. Everything it entailed was new to me: leaving my husband behind in Japan, being my newspaper's first female correspondent, and writing for both the newspaper and a magazine.

Why should I come all the way to New York at my age, live a lonely single life, and engage in strenuous work that would require me to travel back and forth across the country carrying a suitcase? No beauty adviser would recommend this sort of work to a woman of my age. Furthermore, it is not natural for a husband and wife to live apart for a period of several years. What is more, in my case it was the wife who was being transferred abroad on business. Some people are amused by the situation and call me a liberated woman; but things are not that simple. . . .

Shimomura Mitsuko, "Glorious America, Where Are You?" source: Shimomura Mitsuko, "Glorious America, Where Are You?" *Japan Echo* 8, no. 1 (Spring 1981): 119–122.

America's Fading Glory

Leaving aside such family matters, for me nothing could be more worthwhile than an assignment as a foreign correspondent, a job that enables me to observe the world in this age of global unrest from somewhere outside Japan.

Furthermore, from a journalistic point of view the United States is a most interesting country to observe even though, or perhaps because, it is said to be declining in influence and losing its position of international leadership. America, fortunately or unfortunately, and sometimes pitifully, has stuck its nose into the affairs of just about every country of the world on the pretext of kindness, and ends up bumping its head all over the place. Then with all the bumps on its head, which are of its own making, it throws a temper tantrum. However, because it is this kind of country, the United States is a treasure house for those in search of news and information on the various events and happenings taking place around the world. From the viewpoint of culture and living, the United States always leads the world in producing curious incidents, happenings beyond imagination, and new customs that run contrary to established ideas.

Above all, from a personal point of view New York occupies a warm place in my heart as the city where I spent part of my youth as a student. When I was living in New York back in the mid-1960s, the United States was still a glorious country to which Japan looked with admiration. It was a wealthy, happy nation shining with vitality like the America depicted in Hollywood movies. Viewed in retrospect, perhaps that was America at its peak just before its decline.

It was around that time that the United States started to bog down in the quagmire of the Vietnam War. On the domestic front the civil rights movement, which stemmed from discrimination against blacks, began to threaten the stability of the establishment. Then came the emergence of the new left and student unrest, economic collapse and turmoil brought about by the miserable defeat in Vietnam, Watergate, the relative decline in defense power, and the revolt of women in the form of the women's liberation movement. Thus glorious America was confronted by challenge after challenge, and its splendor steadily faded.

In the meantime Japan the hard-working developing nation transformed itself into Japan the giant. As it did so, we changed our measuring stick, which may be one reason that we no longer look on the United

States with the awe that we once did. The "poor student from Asia," who was once an object of pity and charity to the Americans, is now daring to write a critique of America. Still I do not do so out of any bitter feelings toward that country. "Watching the United States steadily lose its magnificence is like watching a former lover's beauty wither away. It makes me want to cover my eyes," *Asahi shinbun* editorial writer Matsuyama Yukio laments. I feel the same way.

"Wish I Had a Wife"

I arrived in New York by myself, looked for an apartment, found one and signed the lease, moved in, made arrangements for all the utilities, bought furniture, got a double-security lock for the door, and purchased pots, pans, other daily necessities, and a supply of food. However, none of these tasks went smoothly.

My first big problem was getting into my apartment. In a society where a written contract is considered so important that virtually nothing can be done without one, I signed a lease to rent an apartment and paid my rent but found myself unable to move in on the day specified in the lease. As a result I was forced to cancel on just a day's notice all the painstaking arrangements I had made with the electricity, gas, water, and telephone companies and the furniture store to have their representatives all come on the same day, the day I was supposed to move into the apartment. I pounded my desk and bellowed with rage, but of course this did nothing to improve the situation.

The cause of the problem was very simple. The realtor "forgot to give the lease to the landlord." In other words, the realtor was totally at fault. In such a case a Japanese would expect the realtor to apologize, negotiate with the landlord, and do everything possible to enable the tenant to move into the apartment on the date specified in the lease. However, the American realtor would rather have cut his throat than say he was sorry. I had to threaten him with the favorite American phrase "I'm going to talk to my lawyer!" (Of course, I have no such lawyer.) It was only then that the realtor started to do anything.

A week went by before I was finally able to move into the apartment. According to the lease, I should have been refunded the rent for the week that I did not occupy the apartment. However, the matter was ignored until I brought it up, and this I had to do formally in writing, since the spoken word would not constitute evidence. Moreover, the written request had to be legally faultless, and so I had to consult a lawyer. Only after taking these steps did the other party reluctantly admit the validity of my claim.

When the furniture was delivered, one piece was broken. I asked one of the men who brought the furniture to take it back, and he said, "My job is to bring furniture in, not to carry broken furniture out. That's somebody else's job." I had to call that "somebody else" every day for two weeks before he finally showed up.

When I put the key into the lock, which had cost me $100 and was supposed to be "top quality and unbreakable," I could not get it back out. Then when I complained, the locksmith had the nerve to tell me that I had not inserted the key correctly.

To get telephone service, I had to have someone from the phone company come and bore a hole in the wall and then do the rest myself. This entailed my going to a telephone store to buy the telephone and other attachments and then taking them home to install. I wanted an extension, so I bought two telephones, one of which I discovered was broken. Assuming that I would be able to exchange a faulty article, I tried to find out how to phone the manufacturer. I was told that the company's showroom could not be reached by phone and that the way to get the telephone exchanged was to go to the showroom myself. It is hard to believe that a telephone showroom would not have a phone, but it is true.

I finally reached the point where I no longer had the energy to get angry, but turned almost in desperation to making sarcastic jokes like "They probably sold everything, including their own telephones" and telling myself how fortunate I was to have ended up with only one broken phone instead of two.

"That's the way, that's the way. Here in this country you won't survive unless you take things easy. You'll get more wrinkles on your face if you keep on getting mad at every little thing," teased Ishi, a fellow correspondent in New York.

Ishi may be right, but how can I keep from getting angry at such things? I plan to keep my eyes open to find out why America, the land of efficiency, speed, and the pioneer spirit, has turned out the way it has.

One thing is certain. Going overseas and immediately having to handle such troublesome household affairs myself while working, for the first time I have come to envy men, who can devote all their time and energy to their work and leave household matters to their wives. Never before have I so earnestly wished that I too had an efficient wife.

SAEKI SHŌICHI, "REDISCOVERING
AMERICA'S DYNAMIC SOCIETY" (1987)

One of Saeki Shōichi's (1922–) favorite childhood books was *If We Fight,*
a novel about a future war between Japan and America, but he was so
impressed by reading *Moby Dick* that he decided to study American literature when he entered Tokyo Imperial University in 1941. After graduating he enrolled in the navy cadet school, but the war ended before he
saw any service. Shortly after the outbreak of the Korean War, Saeki went
to America to study at the University of Wisconsin in the first cohort of
GARIOA scholars [predecessors of the Fulbright scholars]. He was impressed by the overwhelming material affluence of American society, and
he admired the bold ahistoricism of American literary scholars, who com-
piled anthologies including selections from Plato to Edmund Wilson based
on their thematic relevance. He later became known for his own comparative literary analyses. Saeki was a vocal critic of Japan's "postwar
democracy." During the 1960 protests against the U.S.-Japan Security
Treaty, he excoriated the protestors for their emotional and incoherent
slogans. He was particularly annoyed at their facile overuse of *democracy* and provocatively proposed that the word be temporarily outlawed.
In 1966, returning home after teaching Japanese literature in America,
he published *Thinking about Japan,* a critique of the hypocritical nature
of Japan's postwar democracy. He also took issue with conventional wisdom about the revolutionary newness of Japan's postwar literature and
instead stressed the continuities spanning the 1945 divide. This perspective was shaped by his discussions of Japanese literature in the American classroom.

. . .

In 1987 I spent a semester teaching at the University of California's Berkeley campus. Although no longer the hub of student activism it was in the
sixties, it still overflows with vitality. During lunch hour the student plaza
is invariably crowded with people watching the events held there—rock
performances, choral singing, and so forth. On May Day students in Old
English costumes dance to flutes and hand out cakes to bystanders. The
atmosphere is open, easy, and relaxed. By the way, there are a tremendous number of dogs on this campus. Huge canines sprawl everywhere,

Saeki Shōichi, "Rediscovering America's Dynamic Society," source: Saeki Shōichi, "Rediscovering Dynamic America," *Japan Echo* 15, no. 1 (Spring 1988): 33–37.

and one has to take care not to stumble over them. In class I jokingly compared the situation to that under the "dog shogun," Tokugawa Tsunayoshi (1680–1709), when the people were commanded to make way for passing pooches. To this a student replied, "Professor Saeki, have you ever walked on the campus around five o'clock in the evening? There's a woman who shows up walking an enormous pig!"

Berkeley may not be a typical American campus, but the difference between it and any college campus in Japan is like night and day. It seems utterly unfettered, all its denizens free to do as they please. Call it frivolous if you will, but it has an order of its own, and few genuine disturbances occur. I would not hesitate to tell anyone who asked that American college campuses have far more vitality than their Japanese counterparts, and in general offer a more congenial environment.

A major reason is the atmosphere in the classrooms, the way students respond. At Berkeley I gave a course on Japanese literary theory using works translated into English. The lively, direct response of my American university students put to shame anything one could expect in Japan. Questions, comments, arguments, and counterarguments flew. In Japanese universities even considerable effort on the teacher's part usually fails to elicit any response or reaction. When the teacher solicits the students' opinions, they sit in stony silence, many of them casting their eyes downward lest they be called on.

This contrast between Japanese and American students has persisted despite Japan's socioeconomic maturation, despite its multifaceted Americanization, and despite the period of campus unrest that it shared with the United States. Superficially, the Japanese and American systems are almost identical. What, then, is the source of this deep-rooted difference?

Cultural Friction at the Source

Since returning to Japan, I have run across the term *Japan bashing* constantly. To be sure, the United States seems to be leveling an unending barrage of complaints against Japan on a wide range of issues. . . .

Indeed, American grumbling has escalated to the point where I am tempted to call it a case of "complaint inflation." Since the individual grievances deal with matters outside my field, I am not qualified to comment on their validity. What I wish to point out is that this sort of repeated confrontation is typical American behavior.

Make no mistake, demolishing a Toshiba radio cassette player with a hammer is embarrassingly childish behavior for any politician. But even this can be interpreted as a somewhat extreme manifestation of American-style directness. I would venture to add that it is probably preferable to allowing one's irritation and discontent to seethe within.

I am reminded of the classroom behavior of my Berkeley students. In America, college students bring all their gripes and grievances right out into the open and confront the instructor with them. It is almost expected for students to complain about the marks they receive on papers and tests. "I don't see why you gave me this grade," they insist. "Why did you give me a B? Show me where the problem is." And the teacher has to respond clearly to each of these queries and complaints.

Because it is unthinkable for a student to complain to a professor about test scores or grades in Japan, I was initially taken aback and even somewhat offended by this behavior. However, when I sat down and talked with the students, I found them neither emotional nor intractable. A few got a bit worked up, but once they had heard my explanation and their doubts were dispelled, they would generally say "O.K." with a relieved expression and depart cheerfully. Once they have received an explanation they can accept, the problem is solved. This direct approach, in other words, allows for a quick solution—provided, that is, that the instructor's explanation is frank and clear. It would probably never occur to most American students that their actions and reactions might provoke the professor to anger. I believe that the enviable vitality of the American classroom relates directly to this sort of thinking.

This attitude, this basic premise, is what Japanese classrooms most sorely lack. Japanese teachers are apt to bristle at any comment or question that challenges their authority. The students, for their part, doubtless think long and hard before speaking up. They worry that if they ask too simple a question they will be written off as dull-witted. They fear not only the professor's disapproval but also the disgusted looks of their classmates.

At Japanese universities this tendency holds even in seminars and small classes. These days you find a surprising number of students who do such a faultless job of preparing and presenting their reports that you are tempted to pat them on the head. Yet something is lacking. Their presentations are too conventional, too tidy. They research diligently and itemize all the different opinions and theories on a given theme or problem in an effort to compile a report with which no one can take issue. But they take too much care over each detail and end up with a presentation that lacks character. This seems to be the result of a powerful defense mechanism that urges them to avoid mistakes and thus prevent the teacher and classmates from finding fault or asking searching questions.

The disturbing thing is that exactly the same psychology is apparent in the Japanese government's responses to the opposition's questions in the National Diet. Instead of clearly presenting a policy or position, the targeted official replies with smooth, evasive formulas designed primarily to head off any further questioning. Conventional political wisdom prescribes the most unassailable, circumspect explanation possible. It would be nice if we could explain away such political double talk as typical of bureaucrats everywhere, but alas, in Japan the same phenomenon is evident even in university seminars.

The marked difference between the look and feel of classrooms in Japan and those in the United States comes to mind when I hear recent complaints of Japan bashing. Washington says whatever it pleases with brash assertiveness, while Tokyo responds with passive, defensive, evasive mumbling. That the behavior of college students should echo the rhythms of Japan-U.S. trade friction is perhaps less amusing than frightening. . . .

Asia in America

I have felt for some time that information about America in the Japanese media focuses excessively on Washington. Despite the relative importance of the Midwest, for example, not one Japanese newspaper has a Chicago correspondent. The result is a slanted view of American attitudes.

One thing I gained from living on the West Coast was a sense of the growing presence and influence of Asian immigrants, including South Koreans and Vietnamese. On the Berkeley campus Asian faces now constitute a highly visible minority. For one accustomed to the typical American university campus of earlier years, their numbers almost seem disproportionate. Yet this phenomenon does not appear to have triggered an adverse reaction or generated friction. In fact, if the student newspaper offers any indication, the student body is more concerned that the increase in students of Asian background inadequately reflects the number and qualifications of applicants. One item quoted university officials who, when challenged on the subject, denied that they were taking any measures to hold the ratio down and noted that they expected students of Asian ancestry eventually to account for about 30% of the student body.

When I was at Berkeley one of the nearby eateries had made a spectacular hit with the campus population. It was a Japanese restaurant called Musashi that specialized in *yakitori* (grilled skewered chicken) and sukiyaki lunches. For quite a while I avoided the place, intimidated by the long lines. When I finally did stop by during a school holiday, I was surprised to find that a *yakitori* lunch with a styrofoam cup of *miso* soup cost less than $3.00, a price that helped explain the restaurant's popularity. Two big California girls at the next table were using disposable chopsticks to wolf down the same *yakitori* lunch I had ordered and were chasing it with cola. These women probably gave little or no thought to the ethnic origins of the food they were eating; their choice was almost certainly based on the fact that it was cheap, filling, and not too fattening.

Along with the tremendously popular sushi bar, ordinary and inexpensive Japanese foods like these are steadily permeating the American market, a most welcome development from my viewpoint. A touch of exoticism no doubt lingers, but my impression was that everyday Japan is gradually filtering into American life and has largely ceased to be an object of curiosity. . . .

In the Wake of the Sixties

Be that as it may, we Japanese cannot help being concerned over the outlook for American society over the next 10 or 20 years. Today the U.S. economy is staggering under an enormous budget deficit, and the outlook for any rapid improvement in the situation is bleak. Economists prophesy disaster just over the horizon. Will the United States slide unchecked into a second Great Depression? The contemplation of this and other grim scenarios gives rise to theories of the "decline and fall of the American empire" and the "end of the American century." . . .

America has changed to an astonishing degree since the latter half of the 1960s, and it can never return to what it was. What happened to America during that period? While China was in the throes of the cultural revolution, America was undergoing a cultural revolution of its own. Certainly the Vietnam War acted as a powerful catalyst for change. Yet a foreign war that had no appreciable impact on domestic living conditions cannot fully account for such an extraordinary overhaul of morals and values.

It was only half a century ago that Americans imposed on themselves the Prohibition Amendment, which remained in effect for a dozen years. As late as 1950, most universities had strict rules against selling alcoholic beverages on campus; on arriving at the University of Wisconsin in 1950, I was amazed to hear that it was the only college in the entire country that allowed beer to be served in the student dining halls. However, in the wake of the marijuana boom of the 1960s, the nation swung to the opposite pole. All manner of drugs permeated society, creating a major social problem. Sexual mores, likewise, shifted from an almost absurd insistence on forbearance to a complete removal of taboos and restraints.

I would venture the opinion that this upheaval in American morals was basically a matter of religion. That is, it reflected the weakening of the society's Christian underpinnings. Of course, three centuries have passed since America was colonized by the Puritans, but the attitudes toward alcohol and sex that long held sway among Americans grew out of the religious strictures that the Puritans emphasized. Religion and morals provided the conceptual framework for American literature, from Hawthorne, Melville, and Emerson in the nineteenth century to Faulkner and Hemingway in the twentieth. Indeed, we of a non-Christian background often despaired of comprehending the extraordinary culture that grew up around that framework. But in the 1960s this massive, seemingly immovable foundation suddenly began to give way.

Since that time, Americans have been highly receptive to such Asian religions and philosophic systems as yoga, Zen, Lamaism, and Hari Krishna. Watching the thriving state of these spiritual imports, one can only conclude that they have moved in to fill the religious vacuum created by the decline of Christianity. Of course, these exotic faiths appeal mainly to the young intelligentsia. On a grass-roots level, the rise of Christian fundamentalism is probably even more worth watching. The foot-stomping "old-time religion" of the southern Bible belt has spread dramatically in the 1980s. Evangelism has invaded all the media, and fundamentalists have launched a broad-based campaign against "secular humanism." The American-style religious crusade is alive and well.

Struggling to Fill the Void

There is no escaping the impression that a vast chasm yawns within the soul of the American people, a gnawing hunger that, to the outsider, is almost grotesque. Certainly the fitness fever that made its first appearance at the beginning of the 1970s suggests the antics of a people desperate to fill some void. Might it not in fact be the random redirecting of a religious, moralistic impulse that suddenly finds itself without an object? The fervor of the recent antismoking movement, similarly, can be taken as an indication that the American proclivity for moralizing is alive and well.

The Japanese media all too easily convey the impression of an America helplessly watching its own decay with an irritation bordering on hysteria. Yet the frank, open-minded, and dispassionate attitudes of the younger generation, the bottomless crucible of a society that day after day, month after month absorbs countless new immigrants, and the presence of an extraordinary religious hunger and moralistic impulse are forces to be reckoned with.

America and Japan have shared a special destiny since Commodore Matthew Perry's "black ships" forced the opening of the country in the mid-nineteenth century. The two nations are bound in a close and virtually indissoluble partnership. For this reason each must do its utmost to understand the other's innermost workings. Precisely because Japan and the United States differ so markedly in so many ways, each provides the other with an important stimulus, as well as a valuable mirror. For Japan, America is still an enormous unknown quantity. We must not delude ourselves with instant analyses or facile judgments.

YOMOTA INUHIKO, "KOREANS IN NEW YORK" (1989)

As a high school student in the late 1960s, Yomota Inuhiko (1953–) joined in barricading his school as a protest against a renewal of the mutual security treaty with the United States. He was disappointed when the barricade came to a sudden and anti-climactic end. At Tokyo University he studied comparative literature, religion, and popular culture, then spent a year teaching Japanese and learning Korean at Seoul's Konkuk University. A book about his experiences in Korea was published with the title *Our "Other": Korea.* In 1987 he spent a research year at Columbia University, which was the basis for his book about life in New York. In the late 1980s Japan was flooded with information on New York's high culture, but Yomota chose to focus instead on Asians ("strangers") living in the city. His studied indifference to bilateral friction between Japan and the United States that so consumed other earlier commentators resulted not only from his confidence in Japan as an economic superpower but also from his conviction that the world was truly multipolar.

· · ·

Yomota Inuhiko, "Koreans in New York," source: Yomota Inuhiko, *Sutorenjā zan Nyū Yōku* (Tokyo: Asahi shinbunsha, 1989), 112–125.

About ten years ago, when Kim Soun, the doyen of Korean poets, was still alive and well, he told me about his experiences visiting New York in the 1950s while attending an international conference. . . .

"You know what really annoyed me," the old poet said in fluent Japanese, "was that I would be repeatedly accosted on the streets with 'Are you Japanese?' Every time I had to answer, 'I am Korean.' It was so humiliating. It drove home to me that, regardless of how hard we worked back home, our nation remained trapped in the third-class seats of Asia."

It is 1988—and how things have changed.

Just the other day, I was walking along Harlem's Martin Luther King Avenue (125th Street) when a large black man carrying a bag of beans from a garage suddenly accosted me with a friendly "Yoboseyo!" . . . It was clear he mistook me for a Korean. Where had he learned these words? From an employee of one of the Korean grocery shops recently expanding into Harlem? Or perhaps from a soldier from the Pemma (White Horse) Korean unit known for their bravery and cruelty in the Vietnam War? In any case, Harlem's black people undoubtedly see Koreans as more likable people and closer to them than the Japanese businessmen who congregate in the Midtown area.

I was startled by the sudden encounter but answered as if by reflex, "Anneyong haseyo!" (Hello!) The black man smiled happily and walked away with his bag of beans saying, "Bye-bye, brother."

Korean immigration into America has a long history. But it was during the 1970s, when the Korean government promoted emigration and the American government in turn showed a welcoming stance to the citizens of its Vietnam War ally, that the numbers took off. There are about 50,000 Japanese and 400,000 Chinese in New York. The Korean population is somewhere in between but rapidly approaching the latter number. . . . The stunning recent rise in Korean immigration is driven home by the fact that Zelda Stern's *The Complete Guide to Ethnic New York*, published in 1980, contains independent sections on Ukrainians and Puerto Ricans but none on Koreans. Together with Vietnamese refugees, Korean immigrants are a new addition to the American ethnic constitution. . . .

There are three striking characteristics of Korean restaurants [in New York].

First, the level of cooking is much higher than Korean restaurants in Tokyo. In Japan, Korean cuisine's rich variety of nonmeat dishes tends to be forgotten. Korean restaurants are seen simply as synonymous with *yakiniku* (BBQ) shops. The Korean restaurants on 32nd Street, by contrast, offer the variety of cuisine found in Korea. They have not been Americanized. The cooks have only recently immigrated into New York, and they cater primarily to Koreans.

The second trait seems to contradict the first: most of the restaurants also serve Japanese food. When you walk into a typical restaurant, there is a sushi bar located in the front. You may find a group of suit-clad Korean businessmen there, eating sushi and sipping Japanese sake. They are apparently feeling the freedom of enjoying Japanese food without concern for the critical gazes they would receive in Seoul. Further inside, you may find groups drinking Jinro *soju* and barbecuing *kalbi* beef side by side with families eating *naengmyeon* noodles. The menu is written in Korean, English, and Japanese. Japanese words that suddenly appear in places like this have an unsettling effect on me. Perhaps after immigrating to America, a position that frees them from their nation's official nationalism, Koreans for the first time seek to approach their nation's geographical neighbor with a cosmopolitan perspective—or perhaps they simply want to expand their customer base to include Japanese.

Third, a Protestant atmosphere floats about several of these restaurants. The Komtan House, open 24 hours every day, cites on its menu a passage from the New Testament in Korean translation and hangs on the wall a large reproduction of Millet's *The Angelus*. This reminded me that Christianity is a much more powerful presence in Korea than in Japan. Perhaps it is their Protestant ethic that supports the diligence of Koreans living in Manhattan.

Next I'd like to mention the grocery stores. . . .

These stores carry not only Korean food goods but also Japanese instant foods, kelp, and even wasabi paste. Reflecting the low percentage of single people in the Korean immigrant population, giant jars of kimchi line their shelves, organized by ingredient or by region. Vegetables and fish . . . not seen in other regular Manhattan stores are in abundant supply. . . . In one store a poster advertising a Korean film festival is posted on the wall, along with other miscellaneous informational memos, and a local Korean-language newspaper is for sale.

I gathered several leaflets stacked by the cash register. They included an advertisement for an English-language school, tourist information, and an announcement for a church gathering. The grocery store is not merely a place to buy food; it serves as a community nexus for the Koreans who gather there. A Japanese friend told me that in the 1960s, Japanese grocery stores played a similar function.

As I did my shopping, I was accosted twice by black women who asked me about the foods on display. Both were Caribbean women who recently discovered that strong Korean spices work well with their native cuisine. . . .

Koreans are the most recent actors in the long history of American immigration, but their character clearly distinguishes them from their predecessors.

First, they did not come from the impoverished lower classes of their home country. On the contrary, they belonged to the academically and economically privileged middle class. Next, Koreans were industrious and placed high value on education. [And finally] although they were ambivalent toward the military dictatorship ruling their country, they were not political refugees fleeing for their lives. The biggest common denominator of their motives seems to be simply a desire to escape their divided homeland with its narrow nationalism and crowded land, to fulfill their dreams, and to enjoy a better life in their new home through hard work.

The majority entering the country legally came with their families. It was not exceptional for an entire three-generation family to make the move. It was an unwritten rule that the illegal immigrants would be single males who would bring their wives and families over once they had successfully built their livelihoods. Fake marriages to obtain green cards were rampant, and not a few youthful hearts were broken by broken promises. . . . Despite such misfortunes, the Koreans endeavored to remain in America. . . . Diligence was their virtue. They brimmed with a strong sense of pride, unlike previous immigrant groups.

In the Korean language, America is referred to not as Beikoku ("rice country"), as it is in Japanese. Taking the *mi* character from the name "Amirika," they instead call it Miguk ("beautiful country"), as the Chinese do, though in China the characters are pronounced "Meiguo." If you see a sign that reads *Miin hehwa* ("pretty woman conversation"), it refers to an American conversation school. To South Koreans liberated from Japanese colonial rule in 1945, America represented democracy and Christianity. Reinforcing this positive image was the belief that the American landing in Inchon during the Korean War saved their country. America was indeed a "beautiful country" for them. Koreans, I think, more than any other nation in today's world, have been the purest believers in the American dream. Protestors may shout anti-Japanese slogans, but it is only recently that they have spoken out against America. When I lived in Korea for a year, I encountered a peculiar sense of national pride among some of my acquaintances. They saw their closeness to America as a way of looking down on Japan.

However, there seems to have been a recent shift in South Korean views of America. The student occupation of Seoul's U.S. Cultural Center in 1985 was a watershed event, the first time anti-Americanism was openly articulated. Political changes in the home country inevitably affect the loyalties of overseas Koreans. In May 1987, at the intersection of 32nd and Broadway, I saw three Korean international students passing out handbills and shouting with hoarse voices to Korean passersby. They were organizing a protest against the Kwangju massacre at the Korean consulate. "Who do you support?" I asked. One of them answered in English that he could no longer believe in any politician. Kim Yon Sam, Kim Dae Jun, and even America were no longer deserving of their trust, he said.

MORITA AKIO, "THE TROUBLE WITH THE AMERICAN ECONOMY" (1989)

Morita Akio (1921–99), the son of a sake brewer, graduated from the physics faculty at Osaka University, then joined the Imperial Japanese Navy as a technical officer. After the war ended, he and Ibuka Masaru, whom he had met in the navy, formed a company to manufacture electrical appliances in 1946. Their dream was someday to have their headquarters in a building with an elevator. When Morita first came to America in 1953, at the age of thirty-one, to secure permission from Bell Laboratories to use its transistor technology, he was overwhelmed by the scale and affluence of the country. It seemed to lack nothing. The company began selling transistor radios in America under a new brand name: Sony. It was chosen because it was easy to remember, and it sounded cheerful—like *sunny* or *sonny*. In 1962 Sony established a showroom on New York's Fifth Avenue, in Manhattan, where Morita and his family moved the following year, well before the wave of Japanese businessmen entered New York. He soon became the best-known Japanese businessman in America and many other parts of the world—and was certainly better known than any Japanese political figure. While Morita was also known in Japan for having an energetically entrepreneurial "American" temperament, he eventually became an outspoken critic of American business practices. His misgivings about the shift of the American economy from manufacturing to financial services were widely shared in Japan.

. . .

Morita Akio, "The Trouble with the American Economy," source: Morita Akio and Ishihara Shintarō, *"No" to ieru Nihon* (Tokyo: Kōbunsha, 1989), 22–34, 87–104.

"An America That Has Forgotten How to Produce Things"

As part of my work nowadays I give speeches in Europe and America. I have gone to international conferences and engaged in discussions with Americans and Europeans, but what worries me most is that they have forgotten how to make things.

In America, people can make a lot of money through the so-called money games and M&As (mergers and acquisitions). At present the yen/ dollar ratio changes rapidly, and the days of the stable ¥120/$1.00 ratio are over. People now take advantage of computers, satellites, and telephones spanning the globe to make huge instant profits simply by moving money this way or that.

Last summer there was a conference in Japan attended by 3,000 specialists dealing in currency transactions to discuss the future movement of money and finance. Since I have continually stated my view that the floating currency exchange system is shameful, I was asked to make a speech to them. It was like going in front of a group of stockbrokers to tell them that stock prices should be stable. It took guts to do so, but I insisted on telling them that moving money around and making money a market item should not be permitted.

Why is that so? Even though banks and stock traders may prosper, the bottom line is that money is needed because there are industries that produce things. In America, service industries are growing these days, and people are talking about a postindustrial society, but if you stop producing things you end up with America's present situation. America itself is not producing the goods it uses.

I have an American friend who always complains that Japan is unfair and shameful. Last summer he invited me over to his summer place to play golf. I rushed from my apartment to his golf club. When we arrived at the tee I took out my MacGregor golf club. My friend took out his. It was a Yonex. "Don't you always say I won't buy Japanese, I won't buy Japanese?" I complained. "I get more distance out of the ball with this one," he replied. "I guess I have to use it if I want more distance." Then the two of us began to play.

After our round, he invited me to his house. As his wife prepared dinner, he took me on a tour of the house. As we entered the garage, he told me that in upstate New York there is a lot of snow in the winter. "When it snows I go out and play with this," he said gleefully, showing me his Kawasaki snowmobile. "In the summer I go out on the lake," he continued, pointing to the motorboat parked adjacently. Right next to it was

いよいよ　なぐりこみ……

山田　紳

FIGURE 15. Growing tension over Japan's trade surpluses with America was frequently in the headlines during the 1970s and 1980s. From the early 1970s onward the American government put pressure on the Japanese government to reduce the surplus by revaluing the yen or imposing voluntary quotas on Japanese exports to the United States, but the surpluses continued to pile up, much to the frustration of the Americans. This 1985 cartoon portrays President Ronald Reagan threatening Japanese leaders with a club labeled "investigation of unfair trade practices," while the American Congress watches from behind. (*Asahi shinbun*, September 1985)

a small Japanese four-wheel-drive car. His garage was full of Japanese products.

When we went back to the house for dinner, of course, there was the Sony TV set, a Sony stereo, and other Japanese goods.

"You are always angry that Japan does not buy American goods. But you all buy Japanese things. What do you want us to buy from you?" I asked.

Today's America does not produce. Instead it plays at making profits by moving money.

"An America That Looks Only Ten Minutes Ahead Will Decline"

Awhile ago I gave a speech in Chicago on the theme "Ten Minutes vs. Ten Years." We Japanese work hard to develop products by looking ahead to see what will be needed ten years from now. When I asked an American money trader, "How far do you look ahead in making your transactions, one week?" His answer was, "No, no. Ten minutes." He moves the money on his computer by predicting what will happen in ten minutes. "In America you think on a ten-minute basis," I told him. "We are thinking ten years ahead. If you keep on doing your ten-minute thing, you will start having problems."

Peter Drucker recently warned that America needs to avoid becoming overreliant on a symbolic economy of numbers without substance, where only money moves. He writes that America needs to get back to a real economy, where the movement of money is based on production.

The problem is that in America institutional investors hold many shares as stock owners. Among these institutional investors are people called fund managers. They buy shares with huge amounts of money, then sell them if their profits rise. If stock prices go up just a few percentage points, they make huge profits. If there is poor management and profits fall, they sell the shares before their prices goes down. They focus only on how fast they can move their money and how efficiently they can make a profit.

It is said that the service industries will grow in America from now on, but since financial businesses are included in the service industries, neither American businessmen nor investors think about investing over the long run or about development over a ten-year period, as we Japanese do. The "hollowing out" of the economy suggests that America should return once again to producing, not just pursue service industries.

When defense spending decreases in America, research-and-development funds decrease too. Increased defense spending channels money to firms that carry out technological development. Thanks to these funds, such firms can develop fighter planes and so forth without worrying about profits. If the NASA or military budgets shrink, so do development expenditures.

If the government does not provide research-and-development funds, nobody else wants to think about long-term investments. The shortsighted "ten minutes" view of the economy prevails. Some large firms like IBM, Bell Telephone, AT&T, and DuPont do think ahead, but not everyone is doing that, so there is a gradual shift to a "symbolic economy." Many, moreover, are talking about the American service industry as a "third wave." If people are discouraged from producing things, the information industry will be equated with industry in the future. This is tantamount to "producing nothing." "Adding value" by applying knowledge to things and increasing their value is really what business is about. America is gradually losing sight of this fact. This is frightening.

In a talk the other day I asked why America, the world's number-one industrial nation, has no Department of Industry. Caldwell, the CEO of Ford Motor Company, was sitting next to me. "I agree," he said. "It's the Department of Transportation that oversees our industry." The Department of Transportation thinks about emissions and safety but not about the future of the automobile industry.

America is the only industrialized nation in the world that has no Department of Industry. That is very strange. Instead it has only a Department of Commerce and a USTR (United States Trade Representative), so the Americans complain about trade, but no one asks why Americans only buy things.

*"Let's Appreciate Japan's Profound Influence
on the World Economy"*

If things do not change, I think the American economy is headed for trouble. The new George H. [W.] Bush administration will probably implement various measures, but the fundamental problem is that the American people do not care about the federal deficit or the trade deficit.

Under Reaganomics, American incomes rose, American taxes went down, and Americans could buy things anywhere in the world. Since Americans think that Reagan brought prosperity, the Republicans won the election again. I wonder who is really worrying about the two deficits. President Bush says he will not raise taxes, but without raising taxes how can the country's finances be restored?

Take gasoline, for example. Gasoline consumption is rising drastically. Today in America the cost is less than $1.00 per gallon. The world average is about $4.00. Raising the gasoline tax just one cent would raise $1 billion of revenue; raising it ten cents would raise $10 billion; and raising it twenty-five cents would raise it an extraordinary amount. But the gasoline tax cannot be raised . . . because politicians are afraid of losing votes. . . .

American economic policy is not merely a matter of domestic concern. If America collapses, it will have enormous repercussions on the world at large. We should remember what happened on Black Monday of 1987. I am no pessimist. However, if the new Bush administration does not deal with the economic issues, I do believe it will lead to a world economic collapse. . . .

"America, the Land of Human Rights?"

Americans loudly denounce human rights abuses in South Africa and Afghanistan, but what about the rights of American workers? I always make a point of asking Americans about this. The American way of management is to expand aggressively by hiring workers and building factories when the economy is booming in order to raise profits. When a downturn occurs, the workers are promptly laid off in order to preserve the company's profits. But the laid-off workers are not the ones to blame for the economic downturn.

American managers do not worry much about layoffs. They believe that pursuing profit should be the company's goal and that workers should have savings to fall back on. But jobs have a meaning that goes beyond merely receiving a paycheck. Japanese workers work not only for their own profit but also for the sake of their group. This leads to high morale that derives from a sense of mission. American workers tend to only think of their paycheck, but with proper guidance they can also find a higher reason for working. When each individual worker feels a sense of belonging to the company, this invariably becomes an immense boon to the company. It is for this reason that I believe it is mistaken to promptly dispose of workers when they are no longer needed. . . .

When company profits rise in America, top management takes all the credit and reaps literally millions of dollars as their own bonuses. An American CEO I know once told me he could not use up his money. His company was making lots of money, and he himself was earning millions of dollars. "My children have left the house; my wife and I already have

FIGURE 16. This wordless 1990 cartoon summarizes the history of postwar U.S.-Japan relations as many Japanese saw it at the time, and it also predicts what many thought the future would bring with Japan becoming the largest economy in the world.

a county retreat, a yacht, and an airplane. There is no way the two of us can use this money." In Japan, we work hard all day to raise profits, but most of the money is taken away by taxes. The gap between Japan and America is too wide. . . . Even Mr. Matsushita, the richest man in Japan, flies commercial planes into Tokyo, but this would probably be unthinkable to American CEOs. . . .

Today Japanese top managers commute in company cars and use company funds to dine out. Such things did not happen when I was a child. . . . I think we must prevent society from criticizing these privileges. People work hard by looking up to these successful figures.

But in America these practices have gone too far. There is the system of rewarding managers called "the golden parachute." If somebody is a good performer, he is recruited left and right. He signs a new contract every time. Every time he switches companies he signs a new contract including incentive pay, stock options, and postretirement benefits. . . . If he turns out to be a failure and is fired by the board of directors, he still leaves with a generous severance payment because it was written into the contract. A contract is a contract. A veritable golden parachute.

Even if the company crashes, people with the golden parachutes have no worries. They still get their money, so they can retire to a pleasant place like Florida and live the good life. This situation is exerting a great strain on America. It is no wonder that the American economy will grow weak.

Notes

INTRODUCTION

1. Crevecoeur quoted in Henry Steele Commager, *America in Perspective: The United States through Foreign Eyes* (New York: Random House, 1947), 29.

2. Quoted ibid., 304.

3. Nagai Michio, "Nihon o seou tabi," in *Sekai no tabi: Hokubei tairiku,* vol. 6, ed. Ōya Sōichi et al. (Tokyo: Chūō kōronsha, 1962), 416.

4. Tsurumi Yūsuke, "America Kenkyūsōsho ni tsuite," in Taiheiyō kyōkai, ed., *Amerika kokuminsei no kenkyū* (Tokyo: Taiheiyō kyōkai shuppanbu, 1944), 6.

5. *Kokai Nikki: The Diary of the First Japanese Embassy to the United States of America* (Tokyo: Foreign Affairs Association of Japan, 1958), 91.

6. Quoted in Walter LaFeber, *The Clash: U.S.-Japan Relations through History* (New York: W. W. Norton, 1997), 38.

7. An interesting exception is a collection of essays by five such returned students: Taiheiyō kyōkai, *Amerika kokuminsei.*

8. Tsurumi Shunsuke, "Nihon chishikijin no Amerika-zō," *Chūō kōron* (July 1956): 173.

9. Quoted in Shimomura Mitsuko, "Glorious America, Where Are You?" *Japan Echo* (Spring 1981): 121.

10. Tanaka Akihiko, "Viewing Japan in an American Mirror," *Japan Echo* (December 1998): 6.

11. Uchimura Kanzō, *How I Became a Christian,* in *The Complete Works* (Tokyo: Kyobunkwan, 1971), 94.

12. Uchimura Kanzō, *Uchimura Kanzō chosakushū,* vol. 4 (Tokyo: Iwanami shoten, 1953–55), 642.

13. Susan Chira, "New Pride Changes Japan's View of U.S.," *New York Times,* June 30, 1988.

14. Nagai, "Nihon o seou tabi," 416.

CHAPTER 1. ILLUSION AND DISILLUSION

1. Quoted in Shunsuke Kamei, "The Sacred Land of Liberty: Image of America in Nineteenth Century Japan," in *Mutual Images: Essays in American-Japanese Relations,* ed. Akira Iriye (Cambridge, MA: Harvard University Press, 1975), 58.

2. Quoted ibid., 59.

3. Quoted ibid., 60.

4. Quoted in *The Japanese Discovery of America: A Brief History with Documents,* ed. Peter Duus (New York and Boston: Bedford Books, 1997), 198.

5. Uchimura Kanzō, "First Impressions of Christendom," in Uchimura Kanzō, *How I Became a Christian,* in *The Complete Works,* vol. 1, ed. Taijiro Yamamoto and Yoichi Moto (Tokyo: Kyobunkwan, 1971), 105.

6. Quoted in Walter LaFeber, *The Clash: U.S.-Japan Relations through History* (New York: W. W. Norton, 1997), 52.

7. Theodore Dwight Woolsey (1801–89), a law professor at Yale University, was the author of a widely read work on international law, *Introduction to the Study of International Law.*

8. On Sunday, January 22, 1905, Russian troops shot and killed peaceful demonstrators attempting to deliver a petition to the tsar.

CHAPTER 2. STUDENTS AND IMMIGRANTS

1. Quoted in Akira Iriye, *Pacific Estrangement: Japanese and American Expansionism, 1897–1911* (Cambridge, MA: Harvard University Press, 1972), 40–41.

2. Ibid., 132.

3. Quoted ibid., 86.

4. Quoted in Akira Iriye, "Japan as a Competitor, 1895–1917," in *Mutual Images: Essays in Japanese-American Relations,* ed. Akira Iriye (Cambridge, MA: Harvard University Press, 1975), 76–77.

5. *Chou* is the French word for "cabbage," but it is also used for "sweetheart." The ditty suggests that the president was not going to Paris solely for diplomacy.

CHAPTER 3. *MODAN* AMERICA

1. Quoted in Henry D. Smith, "From Wilsonian Democracy to Modan Life: Changing Japanese Conceptions of Americanism, 1916–1931," 18, unpublished paper prepared for the SSRC Bi-National Conference on Japanese-American Relations from World War I to the Manchurian Incident, January 5–9, 1976.

2. Quoted in Asada Sadao, "Nichi-Bei kankei no imēji," in *Nihon no shakai bunkashi,* vol. 7: *Sekai no naka Nihon.* ed. Miwa Kimitada (Tokyo: Kōdansha, 1974), 173.

3. Tsuru Shigeto, "Japanese Images of America," in Tsuru Shigeto, *Collected Works of Shigeto Tsuru*, vol. 13. (Tokyo: Kodansha, 1976), 359.

4. Quoted in Smith, "From Wilsonian Democracy to Modan Life," 25.

CHAPTER 4. THE AMERICAN ENEMY

1. Quoted in Ben-Ami Shillony, "Friend or Foe: The Ambivalent Images of the U.S. and China in Wartime Japan," in *The Ambivalence of Nationalism: Modern Japan between East and West*, ed. James W. White et al. (Lanham, MD: University Press of America, 1990), 189.

2. Hida Buntarō, "Nich-Bei mondai to hyōronka," *Kaizō* (March 1941): 218–219.

3. Quoted in Tsurumi Shunsuke, "Nihon chishikijin no Amerika-zō," *Chūō kōron* (July 1956): 171.

4. Quoted ibid., 172.

5. Watsuji Tetsurō, "Amerika no kokuminsei," in *Watsuji Tetsurō zenshū*, vol. 7 (Tokyo: Iwanami Shoten, 1961), 451–481.

6. Ibid., 481.

7. In 1934 Amau Eiji, a foreign ministry spokesman, told a press conference that Japan would maintain close ties to China and Manchukuo and rejected any interference by outside powers. The statement was sometimes referred to as the "Asian Monroe Doctrine," mentioned in the introduction to this chapter.

CHAPTER 5. THE AMERICAN OCCUPIERS

1. John Dower, *Embracing Defeat: Japan in the Wake of World War II* (New York: W. W. Norton, 1999), chapter 4.

2. Barak Kushner and Satō Masaharu, "Digesting Postwar Japanese Media," *Diplomatic History* 29, no. 1 (January 2005): 27–48.

3. For the remarkable spread of electrical products in postwar Japan, see Simon Partner, *Assembled in Japan: Electrical Goods and the Making of the Japanese Consumer* (Berkeley: University of California Press, 1999).

4. Oguma Eiji, *"Minshu" to "aikoku"* (Tokyo: Shinyōsha, 2003), 273–274.

5. All italicized words in the remainder of the document are in English in the original.

CHAPTER 6. AMERICA ASCENDANT

1. Michael Molasky, *The American Occupation of Japan and Okinawa* (London: Routledge, 1999).

2. John D. Rockefeller IV, "Students of Japan: An Intimate Glimpse," *New York Times Sunday Magazine*, June 5, 1960, 21–24.

3. Akio Morita, *Made in Japan: Akio Morita and SONY* (New York: E. P. Dutton, 1986), 65.

4. Yoshimi Shun'ya, *Shinbei to hanbei* (Tokyo: Iwanami shinsho, 2007).

5. The Japanese navy dispatched five midget submarines with two-man crews to torpedo American naval vessels during the air attack on Pearl Harbor. Es-

sentially they were sent on a suicide mission. Four of the submarines were sunk by the Americans, and a fifth ran aground. The only surviving crew member became the first Japanese POW captured in the war. News about the capture was suppressed in Japan—capture was seen as shameful—but the deaths of the other nine "military gods" were celebrated as heroic examples of the bravery that the country expected of its fighting men. Often their lives were the subject of stories and articles in boy's magazines. Only after the war was the truth revealed.

CHAPTER 7. AMERICA IN DECLINE

1. Thomas Havens, *Fire across the Sea: The Vietnam War and Japan, 1965–1971* (Princeton, NJ: Princeton University Press, 1987), 143.

2. Quoted in Walter LaFeber, *The Clash: U.S.-Japan Relations through History* (New York: W. W. Norton, 1997), 353.

3. Oda Mitsuo, *"Kōgai" no tanjō to shi* (Tokyo: Seikyūsha, 1997), 87.

4. Because Japan and the United States are on either side of the international date line, the attack on Pearl Harbor occurred on December 7 for Americans, December 8 for the Japanese.

5. [Honda's note] The "Deep South" includes the four states of Georgia, Alabama, Mississippi, and Louisiana. But the climate and the atmosphere in Florida, North and South Carolina, and East Texas are close to those in the Deep South.

6. [Honda's note] After the war, laws had been passed to protect the civil rights of Negroes, principally the right to vote, but the Civil Rights Law passed in July 1964 broke new ground by broadly banning discrimination in public facilities. However, many Negroes sacrificed themselves to bring implementation of the law.

7. [Honda's note] According to Griffin's *Black Like Me,* Negroes called this southern scowl a "look of hatred."

8. [Honda's note] A WASP is someone who is white, Anglo-Saxon, and Protestant. In the American racial hierarchy, they recognize themselves as the elite, but recently their position has eroded. Naturally the existence of an "Anglo-Saxon race" is merely a myth to establish the superiority of the Anglo-Saxons within the superiority of the white race.

9. General Nogi Maresuke, who broke the siege at Port Arthur during the Russo-Japanese War, committed suicide in 1912 when the Meiji emperor died. General Araki Sadao, a leader of the radical expansionist faction in the army during the 1930s, was convicted as a Class A war criminal after World War II but was released from prison on the grounds of poor health in 1954.

10. [Honda's note] An outdoor movie theater is a "drive-in theater" where you can watch movies sitting in your car under the open sky.

11. [Honda's note] The Confederate flag has thirteen white stars inside a blue cross on a red background. In 1861, the first year of the Civil War, it was designed as a "battle flag" by the War Department of the Confederacy. The Southern Stars and Bars design was chosen to avoid confusion with the Northern Stars and Stripes.

12. [Honda's note] Since white attacks on Negroes are so frightening, Negroes

in the Deep South are reluctant to speak with outsiders or to approach them. It is difficult even for Negro outsiders to penetrate local Negro society. Even though the outsiders are not persecuted by the whites, Negroes who have contacts with outsiders have been lynched. Recently, however, this situation has changed with the rise in Negro mass consciousness.

13. [Honda's note] In 1957 when nine Negro students attempted to attend Little Rock High School in Arkansas, 2,510 National Guardsmen were mobilized, but instead of letting them into the school safely they happily cooperated with a white mob in driving them off. Arkansas governor Faubus had declared, "We will use the National Guard to stop the Negroes from entering the school."

14. [Honda's note] The plight of the poor in the United States is treated in great detail in such books as Michael Harrington's *The Other America.*

15. [Honda's note] As cotton production has become increasingly mechanized, the demand for human manual labor has decreased. As a result, the Negro population has become urbanized, and there is a corresponding decrease in those living in rural areas. This trend has been going on slowly. The decline of the cotton industry and the growing demand for Negro workers in industrial areas in the North and the West are also factors [in explaining this trend].

TEXT
10/13 Sabon

DISPLAY
Sabon

COMPOSITOR
Integrated Composition Systems

PRINTER AND BINDER
Maple-Vail Book Manufacturing Group

US - Japan Security Treaty 1960

277